DEMATERIALIZED

THE MYSTERIOUS DISAPPEARANCE
OF MARCIA MOORE

DEMATERIALIZED

THE MYSTERIOUS DISAPPEARANCE
OF MARCIA MOORE

JOSEPH & MARINA DISOMMA

A POST HILL PRESS BOOK

ISBN: 978-1-63758-076-9
ISBN (eBook): 978-1-63758-077-6

Dematerialized:
The Mysterious Disappearance of Marcia Moore
© 2021 by Joseph & Marina DiSomma
All Rights Reserved

Cover art by Amie Chessmore
Marcia Moore Cover Photo courtesy of the Concord Free Public Library

Post Hill
PRESS

Post Hill Press, LLC
New York • Nashville
posthillpress.com

Published in the United States of America

1 2 3 4 5 6 7 8 9 10

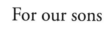

For our sons

TABLE OF CONTENTS

LIST OF NOTABLE CHARACTERS AND PLACES

In order of appearance:

John Moore—Marcia Moore's brother and custodian of Marcia's trust funds.

Robert L. Moore—Marcia Moore's father, co-founder of the Sheraton Hotel chain and architect of the Moore family fortune.

Robin Moore—accomplished author and older brother of Marcia.

Ketamine—an anesthetic that causes dissociative effects and psychedelic hallucinations in small doses.

Journeys into the Bright World—book documenting ketamine experimentation, co-authored by Marcia Moore and husband Howard Alltounian in 1978.

Howard "Sunny" Alltounian, M.D.—Marcia's fourth husband, an anesthesiologist who met Marcia in mid-1977, then married her in November of 1977.

Lieutenant Darrol Bemis—Snohomish County Sheriff's Office lieutenant who assumed control of Marcia Moore's case a couple days after her disappearance.

Snohomish County, WA—the county, approximately thirty miles north of Seattle, where Marcia and Howard resided when she disappeared. They lived in the town of Lynnwood (aka Alderwood Manor).

Ojai, CA—a town eighty miles northwest of Los Angeles, widely regarded as an epicenter of metaphysics.

Maria Comfort—astrologer friend of Marcia's from Sherman Oaks, CA.

Lani Morris—closest friend and protégé of Marcia's in Washington.

Stuart Roof [i]—one of Marcia Moore's two sons.

Ananta Foundation—Marcia Moore's nonprofit organization focused on metaphysics.

Sai Baba—East Indian spiritual guru who developed a following in the United States in the 1970s.

Marwayne Leipzig—astrologer, neighbor, and close friend to Howard and Marcia.

Dorothy B. Hughes—astrologer and owner of a local metaphysical bookstore where Marwayne taught her astrology course.

Tina Alltounian [i]—Howard Alltounian's ex-wife and mother to Howard's children, Kevin and Kimberly.

Kevin Alltounian [i]—Howard Alltounian's son.

Dr. Ed Severinghaus—psychiatrist and acquaintance of Howard and Marcia.

Cris Leipzig—daughter of Marwayne who lived a block away from Howard and Marcia's duplex.

Kareen Zebroff—Canadian author, yoga practitioner, TV personality, and friend of Marcia Moore.

Louisa Roof—Marcia and Simons Roof's firstborn.

Sergeant John Taylor—leader of the organized search for Marcia.

Elizabeth "Liz" Jenkins—psychic friend of Marwayne Leipzig, who tried to determine what happened to Marcia.

Eleanor Moore—Marcia Moore's mother.

Mary Olga—Robin Moore's wife and last known family contact by Marcia before her disappearance.

---

[i] Pseudonym

Kimberly Alltounian[ii]—Howard Alltounian's daughter.

Detective Don Seipel—detective who assisted Lieutenant Darrol Bemis.

Helena Blavatsky—esoteric philosopher and co-founder of the Theosophical Society. Several relatives of the Moore family were official members.

Alice Ann Bailey—esoteric philosopher, author, astrologer, and humanitarian. A personal friend of the Moore family who corresponded with Marcia as a young adult.

Ernest Henderson—Harvard classmate of Robert Moore and co-founder of the Sheraton Hotel chain.

Jane Newell—Marcia's influential, paternal grandmother who introduced her to Spiritualism, seances, and psychism.

Simons Roof—Marcia's first husband from 1947–1962, and father of all three of Marcia's children.

Christopher Roof—Marcia and Simons' third child. An author of children's books and nicknamed "Chrishna" by Marcia.

Louis Acker—a young astrologer who became Marcia's second husband from 1962–1965.

Sybil Leek—Occultist, self-proclaimed witch, and longtime friend of Marcia's.

Mark Douglas—third husband to Marcia from 1965–1977.

Meditation Mount—a nonprofit retreat in Ojai, CA, where people from diverse philosophical, religious, and cultural backgrounds can practice meditation.

Akeva—spiritual healer and boyfriend of Marcia's during her time in Ojai, CA, in the 1970s.

Lynn Powell—psychologist, writer, and boyfriend of Marcia's during her time in Ojai, CA, in the 1970s.

Robert Byron—astro-travel teacher and boyfriend of Marcia's during her time in Ojai, CA, in the 1970s.

Carol Phillips—astrologer friend of Marcia's from Seattle.

Jim Batchelor—a peculiar acquaintance of Marcia's.

[ii] Pseudonym

Rose Gallacher—a Canadian psychic used by the Victoria, British Columbia, police department to assist in solving cases.

Sheriff Bob Dodge—Lieutenant Bemis' superior in the Snohomish County Sheriff's Office.

Shelley Stark—a girlfriend Howard lived with for a couple of years after Marcia's remains were found.

AUTHORS' NOTE

Several quotes contained herein derive from police transcriptions, personal letters, and diary entries containing glaring spelling, grammar, and punctuation errors. In lieu of interrupting the reading experience by using "[sic]" to denote these errors, all quotes retain their original style.

INTRODUCTION

"I am going to pass my hand over your body, about a foot above it....
This will place a protective shield of light around you. At the same
time, you'll sink into a peaceful, deeply relaxed state. It will be the
most beautiful relaxation you've ever experienced,"[1] Marcia Moore told
a young woman under a hypnotic state, before a past-life regression.
The technique was popularized in the 18th century by Dr. Franz Anton
Mesmer, the namesake of "mesmerism."

According to Moore, it actually originated in ancient Egypt and was
practiced in Peru, Central Asia, even the lost city of Atlantis. The subject, or "sensor," would enter an altered state of consciousness, while
Marcia played the role of "facilitator."

To induce the deeper trance-like state necessary for total crossover,
she used a series of visualization techniques. One was to have the sensor
imagine ascending a mountainside, enjoying the clean air, wind, and
brilliant sky at its zenith. Another technique was to imagine walking
down a long staircase leading to an underground cavern, with a doorway
at the end. Each step represented a further descent into the subconscious.
If successful, the door would open to another realm or former existence.

The subject would often be asked to conjure a symbol such as an
astrological sign, hieroglyph, number, or even a sound. The meaning
could then be discussed as the sensor told the tale of their past life.

Marcia Moore's gift was using a delicate balance of freeform conversation and structured questioning to uncover meaningful insights for those seeking answers about unexplainable traits, troubles, or impulses. Even if the sensor hadn't truly tapped into a previous existence, the tale they spun might represent a latent fear or anxiety in their current life. Therefore, regression was still beneficial for causing a transmission from their subconscious to surface, so it could be examined and treated therapeutically.

As Moore gained experience regressing many who came to overcome neuroses they believed originated in past lives, her reputation blossomed throughout the metaphysical community. During the 1970s, she traveled the country on lecture circuits promoting the technique and began receiving several invitations to speak on the subject.

Shortly after New Year's 1979, Marcia received just such an invitation and was preparing for a long road trip on Monday, January 15, from her home near Seattle to Pasadena, where she'd give a prepared speech at a conference on past-life regression.

The week prior, she had chatted by phone with the festival organizer. She also informed her parents of travel plans for March, followed by speaking engagements lined up in April.

Tuesday, January 9, she began penning a letter to her brother John Moore but stopped midsentence. The partial note was later found in a wastebasket.

Wednesday, she spent the day making plans with her closest friend in Washington, who was also traveling to the convention.

Thursday night, she hosted the opening of her new center devoted to an East Indian spiritual guru.

Friday, she continued packing and finalizing arrangements.

Saturday, she called her brother's residence to discuss future writing projects. She then spoke by phone with her close friend to confirm their itinerary. Her bags were loaded into her compact car, and that afternoon she dropped off houseplants with her landlady.

Sunday night, less than twenty-four hours before hitting the road—she was gone.

* * *

I never intended to spend countless hours unraveling a mystifying disappearance, but from my very first exposure, Marcia Moore's story— her life, disappearance, and death—fascinated me.

Our story began in 2004. My wife, Marina, dragged me along to help her grandmother clear out her garage before moving from California to retire in Arizona. Taking only necessities, she gifted the remaining possessions to whichever family members wanted them. Rummaging through her treasured book collection, Marina fondly set aside some Pearl S. Buck novels. She passed on the rest, but a couple of other books caught her eye. The cover designs were clean and simple, white covers with intriguing titles in purple lettering: *Diet, Sex, and Yoga* and *An Astroanalysis of Jacqueline Onassis*. Her grandma had accumulated them through a shared book club in the 1980s, and this is how we inherited books authored by Marcia Moore.

I was busy thumbing through vintage Motown records, but was always a JFK buff, so the Jackie O book piqued my curiosity too. Astrology evoked memories of my childhood years in laidback and mountainous Thousand Oaks, California. As a hobby, my mother's neighbor friend would bring over large, busy astrological charts sent by mail order, and they'd gossip about certain astrological aspects of the children and husbands. As a boy, I hardly knew what they were talking about, but the charts were neat to look at. Everyone knew someone into astrology in the '70s and '80s, especially in Thousand Oaks. Some twenty years later in her grandmother's garage, Marina and I were having fun reminiscing about the colorful language of zodiac signs, houses, and planets.

On the dust jackets of the books, we learned some interesting biographical info about Marcia Moore, and would come to learn so much more. Marcia was the daughter of wealthy hotel magnate Robert L. Moore, co-founder of the Sheraton Hotel chain. She was also the sister of accomplished writer Robin Moore, author of bestselling novels *The Green Berets* and *The French Connection*, the latter adapted into the

1971 hit movie starring Gene Hackman. But it wasn't just these familial successes that make Moore's story unique.

Despite her upper-crust New England upbringing, Marcia openly rebelled against her social status. She abandoned the well-heeled life bestowed upon her, as her true passion became the study of yoga and the occult. Undoubtedly, she was also influenced by the area of Massachusetts where she was raised, renowned for its legacy of Transcendentalist philosophers.

In her youth, she roamed the very same woods that inspired Hawthorne, Frost, Emerson, and Thoreau, but Marcia's influences involved more than these local philosophical luminaries. Interestingly, we would come to discover that the Moore family tree is firmly rooted in certain movements that espouse belief in the supernatural, specifically Theosophy and Spiritualism. As a young girl, Marcia was introduced to séances through her paternal grandmother. It was easy to see how these influences shaped her worldview. She devoted her life to riding the new wave of esoteric trends, but tragically this relentless pursuit played a role in her demise.

Marcia Moore was lithe, petite, pretty, and so charismatic that she was often described as captivating. Shoulder-length raven hair with cropped bangs resembled the style of Cleopatra, whom Marcia believed she shared a past-life connection with. Large, luminous eyes amplified her gaze and augmented her most alluring quality: her silver tongue. Moore instinctively knew how to reach people and could quickly change her tone from passionate to assertive, from bold to breathless. She had an innate ability to eloquently sprinkle mystical prose in conversations and lectures that left listeners hanging on every word.

From 1955 to 1957, she lived in India studying yoga and reincarnation, fortifying her knowledge of mysticism. By the 1960s, Marcia's writing career was well established and her collection of published works on yoga, astrology, and reincarnation became part of the counterculture groundswell to advance the subjects to mainstream status.

By the 1970s, astrology in particular would become a popular fad, but we learned that such subjects were no mere craze in Marcia's circle.

She bristled at the notion of quick-fix astrology blurbs published in newspapers, rather than the ancient, intricate science she considered it to be.

The books were certainly interesting, but we moved on. During college, Marina had studied criminal justice and checked out practically the entire true crime section in our local library. I used to tease her that the FBI probably thought I was some kind of weirdo for the books she checked out using my library card, accounts so macabre yet engrossing that we couldn't put them down. We voraciously followed cases about Scott Peterson and Casey Anthony, while some stories, such as that of the Hillside Stranglers, were so sadistic and repulsive that I couldn't finish them.

Marina had devoured almost everything famous true crime author Ann Rule had published. All that was left was her short story volumes. That's when Marina happened upon the baffling disappearance of Marcia Moore, astonished to find she was the very same author of the books gifted by her grandmother. She scrambled to discover more about the incident beyond Ann Rule's short story. What we found were wild theories about her disappearance, ranging from plausible to outlandish, swirling around the case.

When Marcia vanished in 1979, Ann Rule was working as a reporter near the same area of northwest Washington. Following a stint as a Seattle policewoman, Rule had befriended fellow co-worker and infamous serial killer Ted Bundy while working for a suicide hotline center. She later recalled anecdotes where she and Bundy spoke intimately during downtime, locked up alone while manning the center well into the night. Rule even allowed Bundy to escort her to her car after shifts, unaware of course that he was devolving into a torturous psychopath. Her personal relationship with Bundy and subsequent chronicling of the case in *The Stranger Beside Me* made her a celebrated true crime author.

While covering Bundy's sensational 1979 murder trial in Florida, Rule caught wind of Marcia Moore's case. She was well-positioned to learn non-public info from contacts in the Seattle Police Department and published some vignettes. Turns out the short story Marina was reading decades later was originally an article published months after Moore's disappearance in mainstream newspapers like the *New York Daily Mail* and the provocative pulp magazine *True Detective* under Ann Rule's pen name, Andy Stack. Female true crime writers weren't taken seriously in those days.

It would be an understatement to say Marcia Moore's disappearance stuck with Marina. While most true crime stories conclude with some resolution, in this case any concrete explanation seemed to fade into the ether. Ann Rule herself wrote, "This is probably the strangest case I have ever written about. One day, there may be answers."[2]

My wife became obsessed with finding those answers. Her engrossment transcended mere curiosity. She could almost feel Marcia calling on us to look closer, that there was more to the story than the publicly held perception of her life—and death. Getting ready for work, I'd pass by Marina scribbling notes about the case, deep in thought and oblivious to my presence, while I fumbled through cabinets looking for my elusive favorite coffee mug.

Weekends used to entail trying a new recipe, catching a movie, or walking in the park. That soon changed into an awe-inspiring amount of research by Marina. We browsed used bookstores, looking for Moore's final published book, *Journeys into the Bright World*. We'd later hear that only about five hundred copies were distributed before Seattle area bookstores pulled them from shelves due to the controversial subject matter related to a psychedelic drug she researched.

Marcia experimented with ketamine hydrochloride, an anesthetic agent known in the party world as "Special K," or the "businessman's lunch,"[3] as its effects are short-lasting. Moore was never interested in a quick high. Rather, she took the psychotropic substance for what she hoped would be the next consciousness-expanding breakthrough, one that would also allow users to explore past lives in greater depth, and aid psychotherapy. Some mocked her for merely tripping out on a psychedelic, but Marcia, undeterred, became infatuated with returning to "the bright world," as she described it, through the ketamine portal.

In the 1960s, psychologist Timothy Leary garnered national attention for his study of LSD. Perhaps, Moore reasoned, she could achieve the same level of recognition with ketamine. It could open the door to grants and the publicity would be so intense, she fantasized, that she'd even have to move to escape the media spotlight. About six months prior to her disappearance, Moore phoned her editor and asked if he would hide her if need be. Around the same time, she remarked in a letter to her parents, "Thus far we have been holding publicity off at arm's length. When it really starts to hit we'll probably have to find a larger place farther out in the country."[4] This was the ticket, Marcia dreamed, the breakthrough that would allow her to finally, indelibly etch her name among famous mystics of the past.

Tragically, it wouldn't pan out that way.

In larger doses, ketamine, at the time sold under the brand names Ketalar and Ketavet, immobilizes and sedates patients for surgery without slowing heart rate or restricting breathing, making it a valuable anesthetic for children and animals more susceptible to death by anesthesia. In the minor doses Moore was taking of less than seventy-five milligrams intramuscularly, one can remain conscious, but some experience psychedelic hallucinations.

To Marcia Moore it was no mere hallucination but rather a key to access past, future, and alternate planes of existence. She came to revere the "Venusian substance" as a sentient entity. "The Goddess," as Marcia glowingly referred to ketamine, had a mind of its own. "Evidently, she has her own plan, program, and intent,"[5] Moore wrote in *Journeys into the Bright World*. "We could count on fair treatment from the goddess if only we played the game correctly."[6]

While learning to play the game, however, ketamine took a physical toll as she spent more and more time in the bright world. She lost weight and appeared pale. Although merely classified as a schedule III non-narcotic, and generally not chemically addictive, ketamine clearly had ahold of her. "It's as though the goddess were telling me 'Look, I call the shots,'" wrote Moore. "I'm going to stay with it until it's tamed. I won't tame it, really I know. But I have to keep trying until I've done this thing I have to do."[7]

While still enraptured, Marcia was cautioned about a dark side to the drug by Dr. John C. Lilly, a prominent neuroscientist and psychoanalyst who had experimented heavily with it in the 1960s. At first she rejected his criticism, extolling the virtues of ketamine without any perceivable side effects when used responsibly. In fact, she told him, "God willing I will ride this comet through to the end."[8]

Yet there were indications that she began having a change of heart. Shortly before Moore vanished, on a yellow notepad she scribbled a haunting warning she had received from Dr. Lilly: "ketamine, goddess or seductress?"[9]

In the months leading up to her disappearance, correspondence to friends and family revealed that she was moving on from ketamine, pivoting her career focus back to the study of reincarnation and past-life regression.

Just ten days before her disappearance, Marcia talked about her exploits, at which time she told a friend, "I did what I had to do, and now I don't have to do it anymore."[10] Additionally, in a letter to her father weeks before she vanished, she wrote: "Creatively I'm not doing an awful lot these days. Sort of waiting to see which way the wind blows and what opens up. In fact it's almost been a winter of hibernation. Possibly that is what was needed. Inwardly so much opened up so fast I'm still just assimilating. I seem to have gone so far beyond what can be expressed, or what the public is interested in knowing about. that it makes a kind of communications gap. On the whole, however, I guess the focus will remain on reincarnation and what its acceptance can mean for humanity."[11]

After finding *Journeys into the Bright World*, we attempted to glean even the minutest clues as to what might have happened. We discovered that Moore wrote it in a semi-diary format, with dates ending just months before she vanished. Beyond the psychedelic imagery of the documented ketamine sessions were disclosures about regular events in her life leading up to her disappearance. It was almost as if she had left behind a few breadcrumbs to get someone started on the trail.

As seasons passed, Marcia lingered in my wife's consciousness and perplexing aspects of the case projected in her mind, whether we were washing dishes together or watching a movie. She'd often ponder them aloud.

Could Marcia have overdosed? She was still experimenting with ketamine in the months leading up to her disappearance, but its chemical properties make it quite difficult to fatally overdose, especially when injected intramuscularly. After some initial experimentation, Marcia regimentally adhered to the small doses chronicled in her book.

A burglary gone wrong? But there were no signs of forced entry, no sign of struggle, no cash missing from the purse she left in plain sight.

Abduction? Even the FBI got involved and found no evidence of interstate or other kidnapping, nor ransom demands made to the Moore family.

Murder? She was from money and had only been with her new husband for a little over a year. Yet from the outside they appeared to be blissful newlyweds.

Suicide? The notion was put forth by her husband, and there were hints of a strained relationship with her family. Conversely, her frequent correspondence to parents and conversations with friends portrayed enthusiasm for the future and excitement about several projects she was developing. Although fascinated with reincarnation and life after death, Marcia resolutely objected to suicide as a fervent believer in karmic law.

These were simply the conventional theories. One of the stranger contentions, even suggested by her own brother Robin, was that she had been kidnapped by a coven of witches with whom Marcia had had past run-ins and perhaps beheaded in a satanic ritual sacrifice. Other random theories included a letter to police suggesting that it was a clear case of alien abduction.

Perhaps the most unusual theory, offered by psychics, fans, and even her husband Howard Alltounian, was *dematerialization*, a purported phenomenon in which someone who achieves a profound level of metaphysical wisdom can use supernatural powers to physically dissipate, only to rematerialize in some other place or time.

Conventional or bizarre, all of the theories conjectured then and now are hindered by a dearth of forensic evidence. Just over two years after she vanished, Marcia Moore's partial remains were found on March 20, 1981, in a tree-lined field behind a once-abandoned property, a couple of miles from her residence. Only the upper portion of her skull containing several gold crowns, and some smaller bones, were ever recovered.

Despite the commonly held belief that she simply flew too close to the sun with ketamine and died from exposure the night she disappeared, there would be no toxicology report to confirm.

Rumors of a quarter-sized hole created by a gunshot or blunt force trauma were not verified by the pathologist's report, which indicated nothing more than the scratches and bite marks of foraging animals. No shoes or hard objects were found around the skull. All of her personal effects remained at the home, even her wedding band. The glass and metal vials and syringes she exclusively used—she believed plastic syringes leeched toxic molecules—would have survived two years, but no paraphernalia was ever found nearby. For Marcia, the timing between ketamine injection and effect was about seventy seconds, limiting the distance she could've wandered away from them.

It was a daunting mystery, but we set out to uncover even the most trivial clues. Constructing a rough timeline using her last book and figuring out how it intersected with the sparse information available online was a start, but not enough to solve the puzzle, and the online information was so diffuse, speculative, and frequently incorrect that it required a healthy dose of skepticism. Even published news reports contained a few glaring inaccuracies. One stated that neighbors had last seen Moore on Sunday, January 14, 1979, when in fact it was the prior afternoon. This seemingly small detail left an additional twenty-four-hour window of time unaccounted for during the crucial first forty-eight hours of the case.

There just had to be more. After an exhaustive effort chronicling and cataloging, Marina began writing about it, but every time she approached the computer, looming ahead was the reality of no conclusive explanation for her disappearance. The realization set in that she could go no further without a deeper knowledge of the case.

While I worried about my wife's fixation, I had to admit that I was becoming hooked too. Dinners, driving, evening walks—all became opportune times to brainstorm, and the epiphany struck Marina that I knew almost as much about the case. Although an exceptional researcher, she was far too shy to establish the leads needed to advance the story. That's when she came up with one of her characteristically audacious plans.

One weekend she sprang the idea for me to call Darrol Bemis, a lieutenant who worked the case back in 1979. Needless to say, though more outgoing, I was apprehensive about calling a former law enforcement officer out of the clear blue. "Are you nuts?" I replied. Treasure hunting for materials about Marcia Moore was one thing; this was entirely different.

Despite the reservations, and after some pleading and prodding from Marina…I dialed. To our relief, Lieutenant Bemis was candid and forthcoming after realizing we had put in considerable research. Moore's inconclusive fate had haunted him his entire life, as the case had been a pivotal point in his career. He still lived in Snohomish County, Washington, and would occasionally drive past the places where it had all taken place over thirty years before.

This was the break we needed. Lt. Bemis provided the names of people who remembered the events. Shortly thereafter I flew to Washington to visit Lt. Bemis, speak to locals, and see the spot where Moore's remains had been discovered. Eventually we connected with several of Marcia's dear friends and family.

We began painstakingly gathering new materials that revealed Marcia's story: letters she had written, foundation bulletins she circulated to subscribers, an important diary a neighbor kept at the time, loved ones sharing stories about her. This evolved into a dense collection spanning the fifty years of Moore's life, a life as unusual and intriguing as her death. The forces that shaped her worldview, and the Moore family dynamics, became as inextricably relevant as the circumstances surrounding her disappearance. Perhaps most important to the case, crucial sources and documents revealed cracks in what turned out to be a carefully manicured façade presented to family, fans, law enforcement, and the press.

Finally, armed with these materials and interview transcripts, it's possible to write the complete story about what really happened to Marcia Moore. Beyond the compelling mystery of her disappearance, Marcia led a fascinating life.

This story is more than just the case of a missing heiress. This is the story of a bold woman, raised well-to-do just a stone's throw from Walden Pond, who took the road less traveled—and paid for it with her life.

SCHEDULED TRIP

The inclement weather on the night Marcia Moore was reported missing caused some Snohomish County shop owners to close up early in anticipation of less foot traffic, especially on a Sunday when many drivers avoided the hazardously slick, ice-covered roads.

In fact, it isn't often that the weather receives historical status, but the "cold wave of '78–'79" was just such an event. Beginning in December 1978, a frigid system walloped the Northeast and by January the vast majority of the United States was left paralyzed by the merciless front. Storms battered the Northeast Corridor with such ferocity that a new record of twenty-one inches was set in Boston for snowfall in a twenty-four-hour period. Eighty-mile-per-hour winds lashed Chicagoans, while woefully unprepared states south of the Mason-Dixon Line were left largely immobilized.

In certain cities, bans on travel were decreed in addition to school, store, road, and railway closures. Homeless shelters quickly exhausted capacity, while some travelers hopelessly trying to catch a canceled bus or train tragically froze to death. Before it was over, President Jimmy Carter would dispatch the Army Reserves to assist, as record lows were set in the lower forty-eight states and around the globe.

The Pacific Northwest got its share of the unusual polar vortex, which left downtown Seattle a ghost town at times. Small suburbs like

1

Lynnwood, Washington, Marcia Moore's new home, fared even worse. She could take solace, however, in the fact that she'd soon be back to her favorite locale, temperate Ojai, California. She even began using her Ojai letterhead again to inform friends and family alike that any correspondence should be addressed there for the foreseeable future.

The fifty-year-old author had only called the state of Washington home for a little over a year, beginning in October 1977, the month before she married her fourth husband, Howard "Sunny" Alltounian, M.D., an anesthesiologist nine years younger. At six feet tall, the hirsute man of Armenian descent towered over the petite five-foot-three Marcia. He once appeared in the John Wayne movie *McQ* that shot a scene at the hospital where he worked. "I got a stand-in part. I got one word. I played a doctor and I said 'critical,'"[12] Alltounian liked to say. "I went to a Roman Catholic school for 12 years, I was an altar boy for 7 years, I was head altar boy for 2, I took the entrance exam for Sacred Heart Seminary, I got the second highest grade and they didn't let me in because my mother and father had divorced. I wanted to be a priest. After I couldn't get into the seminary, I then went into medicine,"[13] he once described about himself.

Originally from Michigan, Howard loved the outdoorsy region of northwest Washington and the splendid fishing it offered. Snohomish County was very much his home, a region more rustic than any place Marcia had lived before. Using the trust fund set up long ago by Marcia's wealthy father, they rented the left half of a modest but quaint duplex apartment on Larch Way in the Seattle suburb of Lynnwood, encircled by forested residential developments, punctuated with charming lakes, brooks, and streams.

In the 1970s, a few giants like Boeing and Weyerhaeuser Lumber, along with their suppliers, distributors, and affiliates, employed a large swath of the working populace, while a contingent of mom-and-pop stores picked up some of the slack. This was over a decade (and thousands of stores) before Starbucks became a corporate behemoth, and two decades earlier than anyone knew what a ".com" like Amazon was.

Well into the second half of the twentieth century, some Washington residents still complained about the lack of paved roads, but most folks readily accepted this in return for the state's pristine beauty and recreational activities. In fact, the serene hunting scenes from the critically acclaimed 1978 movie *The Deer Hunter*, though set in the Allegheny Mountains of Pennsylvania, were actually filmed in the scenic Mount Baker area, north of Marcia's new home.

As an author of books on reincarnation, Marcia Moore was invited to speak at the International Cooperation Council's Rainbow Rose Festival, "a panorama of life and consciousness," to be held at the Pasadena Convention Center on January 20–27, 1979.

INTERNATIONAL
COOPERATION   ANNOUNCES
COUNCIL

THE RAINBOW
ROSE FESTIVAL

ICC'S 14th Annual World Celebration
Honoring the International Year of The Child

Sat., Jan. 20 thru Sat., Jan. 27, 1979

Pasadena Convention Center
Pasadena, Calif.

Share the Joy:
Speakers, Music, Dancing,
Art, Films, Children's
Workshops

INTERNATIONAL
COOPERATION
COUNCIL   A Panorama of Life and Consciousness

The festival Marcia was scheduled to speak at, but never made it to. "Marcia had that quality of breathlessness in her voice," one follower said.

Her plan was to drive part of the eleven-hundred-mile stretch, spend the night in San Francisco, then head the rest of the way down the central coast, according to her astrologer friend Maria Comfort, who Moore planned on staying with when she arrived in Southern California. Marcia had given considerable forethought to the day she would depart, writing to Maria that Jupiter was trining Mercury, creating a fortunate astrological aspect for taking the trip at that time.

At the convention, Moore would feature content from her 1976 book titled *Hypersentience*, a term she invented to describe the practice of unlocking past lives for therapeutic purposes using hypnosis.

Additionally, she'd plug her latest work, *Journeys into the Bright World*, and could always sample excerpts from unfinished books underway like *Time and Hypertime, Memories,* or *Alchemy of the Soul*—which would be to *Journeys* "as a phoenix is to a butterfly,"[14] Marcia touted.

As colleagues and friends in Moore's esoteric inner circle were converging for the convention, January of 1979 was also shaping up to be the perfect opportunity to reconnect in Ojai. Nestled in the foothills of Los Padres National Forest, eighty miles northwest of Los Angeles, the town of Ojai held cosmic significance. Marcia and her peers believed the land was a nexus of mystical forces existing along "ley" lines, supposedly a network of mystical energies that connect sacred sites across the globe like the Egyptian pyramids and Stonehenge, and was therefore a perfect spot for the flourishing New Age movement of the 1970s.

As the New Age movement advanced westward, Ojai had become a haven after renowned Theosophists Annie Besant and Helena Blavatsky left the Hollywood area to sow esoteric roots there in the first half of the twentieth century. There they advocated Theosophy's aim to reveal the prophetic, interwoven wisdom of all faiths through truth and science. Theosophists believe that masters of ancient wisdom have existed through the ages to spiritually guide mankind, even telepathically dictating arcane knowledge to those worthy of receiving it. Marcia's father Robert was a member of the Theosophical Society and Marcia yearned to be one of the next generation of pioneers to stand on their shoulders.

In 1972, Moore made Ojai home to her own nonprofit organization called the Ananta Foundation, "Ananta" being the Sanskrit term for limitless expansion. She dubbed it the "Ananta Ashram." Aspiring to help open a world college in Ojai focused on metaphysics, and after living in Washington a little over a year, she pushed hard to reestablish inroads. After what amounted to a sabbatical in Washington to complete *Journeys into the Bright World*, Marcia was eager to advance her career in the esoterically lively area of Ojai once again.

In the months leading up to her disappearance, she spent longer stretches in Ojai without her latest husband, Howard, intently focused on several projects she had in the works there. Collaborating with two esteemed colleagues, LaVedi Lafferty and well-known reincarnation skeptic turned believer Helen Wambach, Marcia hoped to launch a new magazine in the summer of 1979 devoted to reincarnation, the first of its kind.

Further demonstrating her commitment and marking an important development that would go completely unnoticed by detectives, Moore made a real estate investment, buying a stake in a property Lafferty operated her own Vortex Foundation out of, with its own hot springs up in the Matilija Canyon area.

Two months before she vanished, they held a housewarming party on November 12, 1978, in the modest Matilija Canyon house that would now serve as home to both their foundations.

After months of administrative reorganization within her foundation, Marcia was increasingly eager to return to Ojai. She had recently acquired tax exempt status for the Ananta Foundation, making donations, and more importantly withdrawals, from the foundation tax free. No minor detail, given the steep income tax rates of the late 1970s.

In a letter dated a week and a half before she vanished, Marcia wrote her father about the real estate purchase, and tax work recently carried out by her lawyer. "He had to make a special flight to Sacramento to do it (all in all it cost us an extra $1,500 which we have yet to pay him) but it was well worth while in terms of tax savings. After all, the foundation is legitimate and does accomplish a lot. At this point, however, much that we want to do is still a hope for the future. We do have the one hot spring outdoor pool in the canyon in pretty good working shape and people are being helped and healed there. We call it a 'healing center' but as you know one doesn't get much of a house for 19 thousand dollars in California and being so high it is also not very well heated."[15]

In the days leading up to mid-January, Marcia Moore was hammering out final details for the trip. "I spoke to her the day before, over the phone, we were talking about the Rose Festival down in California and making plans," Marcia's cheerful friend Lani Morris recalled. Like Moore, Lani was making the long drive from Washington down to Pasadena. "Marcia was very excited about the Rose Festival and she was excited to introduce me to a bunch of people she wanted me to meet down there,"[16] Lani said.

Marcia's closest friend in Washington, Lani, with her husband.

As the convention in Pasadena drew near, arrangements with friends had been ironed out and Marcia's bags packed with the magenta dress she often wore for special occasions, various Indian print tops, an assortment of velveteen pants, a purple nylon turtleneck, and a lavender cotton pantsuit she wore at public appearances.

Although she'd recently taken to a green motif, purple had long been Moore's signature color. "She would go to the thrift stores and buy up all the purple blouses and skirts she could find,"[17] Lani fondly remembered. Linens, dishes, and all their accompaniments were purple too. Moore even signed letters and autographed her books in purple ink. In fact, Marcia's love of everything purple occasionally perpetuated the myth that her radiant eyes were violet instead of their true color, hazel.

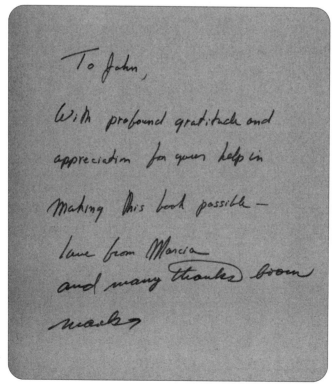

One of Marcia's books autographed in her signature purple ink.

The new stake in the hot springs property and the long-awaited tax exemption weren't the only reasons Marcia was keen on returning to California that January. Her twenty-eight-year-old son, Stuart, along with his wife, was driving from their home in Tucson to meet up with Marcia in Ojai before they set off on a two-month sojourn to India. Like his mother, Stuart had begun following an East Indian guru named Sathya Sai Baba, a frizzy-haired self-proclaimed reincarnation of Sai Baba of Shirdi, a spiritual master who lived from 1838 to 1918, widely revered as a saint in India.

Initially Marcia entertained the idea of accompanying them to take advantage of a group rate, but she couldn't recruit enough friends and family. Stuart remained committed to the Indian excursion after planning to meet up with Marcia near San Francisco. The couple set off from their Arizona home, arriving Wednesday, January 17, 1979, but would never see Marcia as planned.

Although things appeared to be falling into place for Marcia Moore, as if fleeing the debilitating cold wave symbolized new opportunities and clear skies ahead, she never left Washington on Monday the 15th, baffling family and friends converging to meet up with her.

MYSTERIOUS DISAPPEARANCE

Not a soul had seen or heard from Marcia on Sunday, except her husband, Howard Alltounian, who said she was resting comfortably in bed when he left at 8:30 p.m. for the movies. When he returned home (according to differing statements, sometime between midnight and 2:00 a.m.) Marcia had vanished.

Little would be reported in the papers about what transpired when Howard came home to find his wife missing, but in piecing together his comments to responding officers, private investigators, family, and friends, a picture began to emerge.

"So, at 1:00 o'clock in the morning, I went out with a flashlight. Now there was a full moon Saturday night, and you know the moon decreases a little bit each night after it is full," the husband told detectives. "This is Sunday and it is just a little bit smaller than full, so essentially it was full. I could see out there, you know, without my light. I could see the trails. And I have a big flashlight, so I looked for her for an hour. From one to two. I went right to the spots where I knew she would be usually. And she wasn't there. I got back here at 2:00 o'clock, and I went over to the house, [Marwayne's] house.

[Marwayne] and I are great friends, it's just two blocks from here. She unfortunately is in florida right now, but her son, Peter, was there."[18]

Actually, Marwayne Leipzig and her husband, Jim, were in Hawaii, not Florida, having left for a week's vacation with friends the morning before. Marwayne, who lived about a block away, began keeping a journal after Marcia disappeared. She made an entry about the farewell conversation she'd had with Howard. "The day I left for Honolulu, Saturday morning, Jan. 13, 1979, about 1/2 hour before we left the house, Howard phoned and said he just wanted to say that he was going to leave house keys with the neighbor for the period that I was in Hawaii," Marwayne wrote. "They wanted me to come down, take in their mail, and water houseplants, as I had done another time when they were away."[19]

Marwayne Leipzig pictured with her husband Jim.

Marwayne agreed to retrieve their house keys from the couple's land-lady when she returned from Hawaii, since she'd be back before they returned from California. Incidentally, the landlady would be the last person, other than Howard, to see Marcia—at 2:38 p.m. on Saturday, January 13, when Marcia stopped by to drop off her houseplants.

Marwayne Leipzig met Howard Alltounian in May 1977, just a month before he met Marcia Moore. At that time, he was the deputy chief of the anesthesia department at the United States Public Health Service Hospital in Seattle and was suffering through a divorce. "I had just given an anesthetic to a patient and I was taking the patient back to the recovery room," Howard would later tell private investigators. "As I'm taking this patient back and I'm depressed and I'm thinking what the hell's happening? Why is this happening to me? Why does it seem that every time I've just about had my act completely together the bottom drops out. There must be something that I don't know. There must be some body of knowledge that I'm not aware of. You know, and through the mud came this recall of the most reliable source of astrology."[20]

At that moment, Howard recalled the Dorothy B. Hughes book-store downtown, which he'd heard about on television a year ear-lier. He dropped in after work one day, chatted up the shop owner, and bought a book titled *Write Your Own Horoscope*. By the end of the weekend, he was convinced that astrology was the solution to his woes. "That next Monday I joined a beginning astrology class," Howard explained to investigators. "My first teacher was Marwayne Leipzig..."[21]

Marwayne Leipzig.

As those close to her characterized, Marwayne had a weakness for taking in every stray that came her way. The fifty-eight-year-old mother hen of sorts developed a soft spot for the hard-luck, if not clumsy, Howard, who was nearly two decades younger. Considered a reputable expert, Marwayne helped Howard astrologically navigate the fallout of his divorce from Tina, a woman he had already divorced and remarried before.

Howard considered the second divorce unfairly punitive and never got over it. He claimed Tina won by default. "He has always been incensed at the way the divorce was passed," Marwayne later reflected in her diary. "Seems his attorney failed to notify him of the court date."[22]

Often he'd vent that on the day the divorce was settled, Tina had come for a checkup at the hospital where he worked. She saw Howard there and was friendly but left directly to go to court—without mentioning that she was on her way to finalize the divorce.

He'd later tell detectives, "My wife went to court without my knowing about it, with her attorney, I had no legal representation, and railroaded a fantastic divorce settlement. I told you what she got everything. Plus $400 a month child support and $400 a month alimony. About a week or two later, after the fuckin' divorce, she calls me up and says oh, I just want to tell you something, you don't have to worry about it, the divorce is final, I'll send you the papers."[23]

The ink on the divorce was barely dry when Howard met Marcia Moore. "I heard her lecture, as I say. It was one month after my divorce. At that time, you know, my frame of mind was I never want to get married or anything to do with women, you know, just a natural reaction. I heard her speak, and I fell in love with her. I said, my god, this woman has her act completely together. And she was doing it. A Phi Beta Kappa, magna cum laude from Harvard."[24]

But Howard hadn't just serendipitously encountered Marcia at the lecture. He knew her brother was Robin Moore, famous author of *The French Connection*, as he'd seen Marcia on his favorite local morning TV show while recovering from a broken hand. "And while I was off, uh, God it was beautiful, I hadn't been out of the hospital, I hadn't had a vacation like that in ten years. It was in the spring. It was May, April, May, June, and every day my ex-wife and children would go off to school and I got in the habit of watching the *Seattle Today Show*. We got up, we all had breakfast, they went out the door and I'd watch the morning talk show."[25] Somebody brought Howard one of Marcia's books while he was recuperating, a friend said.

Marcia with her eldest brother Robin, telephoned the
day before she was said to have vanished.

She had made a few appearances on the show, advocating astrology
and past-life regression, and certainly piqued Howard's interest, given his
recent exploration of astrology, not to mention her beauty and prestige.
After seeing her on TV, he headed to a bookstore to find out as much
as possible.

As he'd later claim, a photo of Marcia on the dust jacket of one of
her books sucked him in like a tractor beam. An electric impulse leapt
off the page; he felt an instant connection. Now she was right there
in Washington, scheduled to speak in front of the Seattle Astrological
Society, and Howard wasn't going to miss it. He packed a tape recorder
and eagerly arrived early to secure a front row seat.

Through a mutual friend, Howard heard of a party to be held in
Marcia's honor after the lecture. Pleading for an introduction, he successfully crashed the party, trying to woo Marcia. The gambit worked,
and it certainly marked a fortunate turn of fate, given the post-divorce
predicament he'd found himself in. "When I met Marcia I had just gone
through a divorce, and my ex-wife, you know, got the house, the new car,

all our assets, and I was stuck with $7,000 in bills," Howard later griped to investigators. "I had nothing. She also, this is my ex-wife now, got $400.00 a month in child support, and $400.00 a month in alimony. She got like half my income, plus getting everything else, you know, that I owned."[26]

With Howard's ex retaining ownership of their house, he had been relegated to living in other people's homes, telling detectives, "Yeah, I was housesitting, you know, I was trying to make ends meet. [You] know with child support and alimony. And I was housesitting trying to get by. I lived, that summer I lived in seven places. I moved seven times.... I had, it's funny. I had seven boxes that would fit in my car, and it would take me an hour."[27]

Thanks to Marcia Moore, by the fall of 1977 Howard's vagabond circumstances markedly improved. After a brief courtship, they married, the small ceremony held the day after Thanksgiving at Marwayne's house, just a stone's throw from the modest duplex apartment the newlyweds would now call home in the quiet Seattle suburb of Lynnwood.

Marcia Moore on her wedding day, November 25, 1977.
Seen with Howard, his eleven-year-old daughter,
and friend Larry who served as best man.

Married for a fourth time.

Now, fourteen months later, Marcia was missing.

When Howard made his way to Marwayne's to search for Marcia in the early morning hours of Monday, January 15, 1979, he expected to find Marwayne's son Peter, but he wasn't home. Even so, because the Leipzig residence had become something of a neighborhood hangout, "the boat-builders and friends"[28] as Marwayne affectionately referred to them, Howard knew somebody would be there. Howard's teenage son, Kevin, and his friend Steve slept at Marwayne's that night. Kevin was crashing at Marwayne's because his soured relationship with his father had become so acrimonious that Howard refused to let his own son stay at the duplex.

For a time, Marwayne and Jim had allowed Kevin to stay at their place while he worked at becoming self-supporting, but the young man had since worn out his welcome. "When we took Kevin into the home because neither his mother or father would help him, and he had no job, Jim felt sorry for him, and we gave him a job and a home," Marwayne described. "That summer of 1978 was a difficult one with the boy, as he flaked off on the job, and Jim's partner wanted to fire him, which he finally did do. Howard and Marcia wanted the boy to go in the army, which he refused to do. It was all quite a strain on everybody."[29] By that summer, Howard was no longer employed, leaving most of the financial assistance for Howard's children—and his ex-wife—to fall to Marcia.

Kevin made himself doubly unwelcome, in addition to his irresponsibility and crashing with them rent-free, by pursuing Marwayne's granddaughter Dana. "Jim asked him to leave Dana alone, that she was too young. This was like asking the fox to stay out of the henhouse, and it became very obvious that they were much attracted to each other," Marwayne lamented in her diary. Dana was only fourteen and had little previous experience with boys. Kevin, an attractive young man, was going on nineteen and had plenty of experience drinking beer and smoking pot. Before long, Dana was staying out late, having trouble in school, and playing hooky. "Jim was disgusted with the boy for pursuing a 14-year old girl, and I was downright angry about it."[30]

But with Marwayne and her husband away in Hawaii, he seized the opportunity to crash at their place. "Kevin slept at our house the night Marcia disappeared, it turned out," Marwayne noted in her diary. "We had told him he must find another place to live, and he had done so, but as soon as we were gone, he slept here, which also made me angry.[31] …I asked Kevin how his dad seemed. He said he was so sleepy when he came, that he wasn't sure, but that he, Kevin, was not terribly alarmed as 'Marcia had done this before.'"[32]

In later talking to detectives, Howard's account was similar. "And I went to get Pete to get some help. And Pete was out. I woke up Steve, and I woke up my son, who was there Kevin, and told them Marcia is gone. I think she has walked into the woods, will you help me? I couldn't even wake 'em up. So I came home."[33]

While most of the town slept, Howard kept searching. "I drove to the cemetery and drove to the fountain where she always used to go and meditate," he later told detectives, although he got the name wrong by mentioning Evergreen Cemetery. It was actually Floral Hills Cemetery, two miles south from their duplex. Marcia occasionally went for walks there, where an impressive fountain served as a tranquil background for meditation. "That was the first place I went. And when I got down there, I got out of my car, and I almost fell on my bottom side because it was slippery. And then I got in the car and after checking around, I could hardly drive out of there because it was so icey. It was just glare ice. I just didn't think she would get too far. I thought we would find her in the back fense there."[34]

Detectives would also inspect the fountain. "It's a solid block of ice," a lieutenant noted. Additionally, Martha Lake, just a block and a half north of the duplex in the opposite direction, was searched by officers who found no broken ice, as Howard also confirmed, "But I tell you one thing, I did go to Martha Lake that night and look for her, and it was frozen over, and I was very happy to see that."[35]

If Marcia was somewhere in the woods as Howard suggested, time was running thin. Though a strict vegetarian who detested smoking and routinely practiced yoga, the ketamine use had also subdued her appetite, causing Marcia to dwindle to about ninety pounds. The cold wave suppressed the temperatures into the twenties that Sunday, creating a perilous situation for anyone exposed to the elements for any significant length of time. "That is so unusual, because first of all, we don't have this kind of cold weather in this area, usually in the winter time it is milder, it rains. We don't have freezing nights. Anda but that particular night, it was just solid glare ice,"[36] Howard stressed to detectives.

Before going to Marwayne's, Howard sought the advice of another friend named Dr. Ed Severinghaus, a local psychiatrist from Edmonds, although he wasn't treating Marcia or Howard for counseling. Their peculiar friendship largely revolved around their mutual admiration for the Indian guru Sathya Sai Baba. Although some considered him a charlatan, Sai Baba successfully gained a small following in the United States in the 1970s, riding the coattails of popular Indian gurus like Paramahansa Yogananda. Beyond interest in Sai Baba, Dr. Ed had also tried ketamine after Marcia and Howard suggested the idea of using it to aid psychotherapy.

Marwayne was also acquainted with Severinghaus but considered it quite a strange friendship with Howard and Marcia because of the Sai Baba devotion. She encountered Dr. Ed in what turned out to be the last time she'd ever see Marcia. In her journal, she flashbacked to the Thursday before the disappearance, when Marcia and Howard had held their first Sai Baba meeting at their new "Sai Center," a tiny cottage next to their apartment that they'd recently rented from the same landlord that owned the duplex.

Marcia once mentioned to Marwayne how nice it would be to have a place where guests from out of town could stay. She even inquired about renting a spare bedroom from Marwayne, but nothing became of it. Eventually, the little place next door was vacated by a young lady and Marcia rented it.

Howard labored through November 1978 cleaning the unit. Scraping and painting the inside entirely white, he hung louvered doors and put down an orange shag rug in tribute to Sai Baba's signature color. There was no furniture except a freestanding fireplace. Mats upholstered in cheery material lay about the floor amongst large, plush cushions. Guests were never to sleep in that room. Apparently, one of the ceremonial rules of establishing a Sai center was that it must not be used for more than that one purpose. A mantel held a pot of dried flowers, candles, and a picture of Sai Baba in a kind of semi-altar arrangement, with a hanging fern overhead. An orange-tinted lightbulb illuminated the main room. An office was outfitted for Howard's use, and there was another room relegated to a storage area, which he later intended to fix up for guests.

As Marwayne's departure for Hawaii neared on Saturday the 13th, she had only one day left to pack. Exhausted and still uninterested in Sai Baba, she only attended the Thursday night meeting out of courtesy to Marcia and Howard, it being their first. "I was early in arriving. I knocked at the front door of the little house, as all the lights were lit. No one was there," Marwayne recalled. "The door was locked, which I thought a bit strange. So I walked around to the back door, which was open (and is apparently kept open), and walked in, removed my shoes, went on into the Sai center, the 'living room' of the little house. The fire was lit. The rug was soft. I found a cushion for back support, and sat near a corner, by the fire, as it was cold and wet outside and I was cold, and quite tired."[37]

As Marwayne sat alone in the peculiar little prayer house, Howard walked in. "He was a bit surprised to find I was already there." About fifteen guests arrived. Men sat on one side, women the other, though in such small quarters they couldn't be too far apart. "Finally we began the singing or chants," Marwayne described. "In a little while Marcia came in, looking very lovely, and very fragile, I thought, pale and pretty." Marcia found a seat on a yellow cushion next to Marwayne and softly said hello. "She was barefooted, and as I attempted to follow the chants, I kept thinking about what pretty feet she had."[38]

Following the chants, Dr. Ed lifted his voice in a prayer-like address, "Oh, Sai Baba, who knows everything, and is always with us, we honor you, and we thank you for all your blessings. We lay at your feet all of our troubles,"[39] Marwayne journaled. Surveying all of the strange Sai Baba admiration, she felt a bit out of place.

Dr. Ed then spoke of his recent trip to India, reporting that he had been more or less snubbed by Sai Baba. Although trying repeatedly for private interviews, none of his attempts were successful. Nevertheless, the trip had been beneficial, he maintained, hedging that "one does not ask God for such a thing."[40]

Although a practicing astrologer, Marwayne was also Christian. Incredulous, she reflected, "I was rather shocked, and the 1st commandment came to my mind." As the meeting continued, Marwayne asked, "Do you believe that Sai Baba is God?"[41]

Dr. Ed thought a minute before answering. It was a puzzle he had been mulling over for a long time, he said. He could not say Sai Baba was God but believed he was a holy man, and yes, divine.

That left Marwayne disconcerted by the whole experience. Another guest was irked at her question and pointedly asked Marwayne why she had asked it, as if she had defied a cult-like devoutness to the guru.

Perhaps to break the tension, Marcia spoke up and suggested they talk about holding regular bhajans[iii] at their new Sai center of the north Seattle area.

A curt interjection followed. "Dr. Ed cut her off a little short, I thought, and said, 'that can be discussed later,'" Marwayne remembered. "I mention this, because Marcia was perfectly lucid, and seemed to me to be referring specifically to future affairs in hers and Howard's lives, when she asked that question."[42]

But as it turned out, that Thursday meeting would be Marcia's first and last in the new Sai Baba house. Marwayne's conversation with Marcia was minimal that Thursday. "That was the last time I ever saw her, sitting there on the floor of the Sai house, barefoot, looking very beautiful and sweet."[43]

Looking back, Marwayne wondered if she had missed any signs. "She seemed rather 'spacey' I thought, and I wondered if she was on ketamine." She knew Marcia had taken it in researching her book, but that had finished in October. "I was pretty sure she was not taking ketamine after that. However, she seemed so ethereal looking, and such a faraway look in her eyes, and I could not help but wonder." On the other hand, Marwayne also observed that evening, "she seemed perfectly lucid in all her remarks to me, as she prepared cups, poured tea, gave me instructions about honey, and passing of the tea etc."[44]

Four days later, Marcia was gone. Three thousand miles away on a Hawaiian vacation when she vanished, Marwayne had no idea what time Howard showed up at her house on Sunday night looking for Marcia, but learned that Dr. Ed was with him when he called police to report her as a missing person.

The account matched what Howard told detectives. "I called him up and he came over immediately. And I said, Ed, what should I do? I said, do you think I should call the police? And he said, yeah, I think we should call the police, he says, and then we'll go look for her. I called,

---

[iii] Indian term for prayer meeting.

you know, the police. They came over and got the report, and we went out and looked for her all night with flashlights. Not a trace."[45]

Howard eventually called police at 4:38 a.m. on Monday, January 15. In describing Marcia's state of mind, he revealed a surprising litany of troubling afflictions. "Distraught," "suffering from amnesia," "manic depressante," "mental disorder from use of ketamine," "threatened suicide this date…"[46] and in the past, were all part of the ominous details he told police, which were then noted on the missing person report.

Outside their home sat her car. Inside, her jewelry and purse containing keys, reading glasses, license, passport, checkbook, and plenty of spending money for the California trip were left untouched.

Howard also alerted the police that Marcia likely had no shoes or coat on, in spite of the subfreezing weather, and was possibly missing in the woods southeast of the duplex. To those who knew her, it presented a puzzling picture, as she wasn't known to stray from established footpaths and wander about in the woods.

Although it was not uncommon for Howard to do his own thing, like fishing or going into town, it was also perhaps an odd time to set out for a late movie or for Marcia to take a walk in the woods, since at dawn they were to embark on a twenty-hour drive to California.

Now, rather than the pair setting out for the trip, a police search was about to begin for Marcia Moore, just two weeks into the New Year, 1979.

"MISSING LYNNWOOD WOMAN"

By day break Monday, January 15, an official pursuit was underway for Marcia Moore, including an aerial search by helicopter over nearby Martha Lake, and the wooded areas surrounding her residence. A base camp was set up at a church on Larch Way just down the road from the duplex. As different units of the Snohomish County Sheriff's Office arrived, personnel were dispersed and began systematically combing the woods.

Steve and Howard's son Kevin, who wouldn't budge when Howard tried to wake them, had now joined the search, along with Marwayne's daughter Cris and son Peter. Cris immediately sensed something was off. How had Marcia managed a walk of any significance under such icy conditions with her ailing hip? She had been limping with such difficulty that she sometimes resorted to using two walking sticks. In fact, last summer Marcia would occasionally stroll over to the Leipzigs' to swim in their full-size pool to soothe her hip. Usually, by the time she made the one-block walk, she'd already be in pain.

Aiding in the Search—Horse Lover—Marwayne's daughter Cris.

Echoing similar observations about her hip, Marwayne had pressed Marcia to get it x-rayed, inferring that it may be severe arthritis. The advice fell on deaf ears, however. Marcia preferred to restore her hip through yoga, meditation, and healing waters, opting not to focus energy on what she didn't want to manifest. "But it appeared to me that it was getting worse and worse, and the last time I saw her walk away from my home, about 10 days before her disappearance, she seemed almost crippled with it, and could not put full weight of her body on that hip socket,"[47] discerned Marwayne.

Marcia once suspected that it may have even been a psychic attack by some malevolent witches she'd encountered in Vancouver. In *Journeys into the Bright World*, she described:

> At this point the ketamine was exerting its truth serum effect. I hadn't wanted to think about or admit that my mind was not strong enough to repel what appeared

to be a psychic attack. What had actually happened was that I had just arrived at Kareen Zebroff's house in British Columbia and was staying in the guesthouse. One night while in a state between sleeping and waking I had a dreamlike vision of two repulsive gray sluglike creatures coming at me, one from either side. It was impressed upon me that this was an emanation deliberately sent forth by the same satanists who had been so viciously harassing my friends over the telephone, and that probably they were using an effigy of my body in their rites. At that point my fatigue was so great I thought, "Oh I just don't care. I'm not going to fight it." Thereupon one of the protoplasmic masses seemed to penetrate my right side at the level of the hip joint. At that very instant the telephone rang once. This was not a hallucination; it actually did ring and wake me up. However, when I arose to answer it no one was on the line. But the spell was broken and I determined never to give in this way again. Looking at my watch I saw that it was three forty-five in the morning. Pondering this phenomenon I felt convinced that the ring of the phone had been an act of intervention designed to arouse me from my trancelike state.[48]

Marcia wouldn't give any further details, beyond that one woman was jealous and felt spurned at not being regressed by her.

Supernatural or not, determining the true cause of her debilitating hip pain was complicated by the ketamine use. In September 1978, Marcia's daughter, Louisa, visited with her briefly in Manchester-by-the-Sea, Massachusetts. "She was gray, haggard, skittish. Really seemed to want to avoid me/us. I was very disappointed because I'd hoped for a visit of at least a few days,"[49] Louisa remembered. "We expected her to stay a few days but after about one night she decided to take off for nearby Gloucester or Rockport.... We had 23 steps from the parking area to the main level of the house, and another 10 or so inside and she obviously was finding that difficult. She wouldn't talk about it much, but it was obvious. I thought she might have had arthritis or pulled a ligament from too much yoga."[50] Louisa noticed a wet area on her clothing and thought she might be injecting just below the hip, although hip problems also ran in the Moore family. There also appeared to be some bruising on her arms.

Now that Marcia was missing, investigators were forced to consider the poor condition of her hip and how far she could've walked. In case she was out in the woods, Howard Alltounian did all he could to help the bloodhound arranged through the State Department of Emergency Services locate his wife's scent. "Brought it right in the house," Howard told police. "Got 'em right in her bed, on her pillow, on her sheets. I took the dog in her closet. You know, he said, okay if I bring the dog in? And I says, certainly…. I brought that dog right in that bed, I brought her right in that closet with all her clothes."[51]

A capable bloodhound could pick up a person's trail up to forty-eight hours afterwards, though the severe cold could be a mitigating factor. The hound scampered off ahead of his twenty-foot leash, accompanied by Howard and officers. After searching behind the residence for a period, then in the front, the canine left the property heading south toward a new residential area, ultimately covering the woods for a few hours. "And that damn dog never picked up anything. I took him right to the trail where she starts,"[52] Howard would complain to a lieutenant. "And around noon, I really started to get worried. It just wasn't turning out the way I thought it was."[53]

Whatever way Howard expected it to turn out, as mid-day approached with no trace of his wife, he tried a more unconventional strategy, telephoning bookstore owner Dorothy B. Hughes. "Dorothy is a personal friend of both Marcia and myself. Not only is she a fine and competent astrologer but her sub-specialty is horary astrology, which is the art of answering questions by analyzing a chart drawn for the moment the question is asked,"[54] the husband explained.

Could the heavens yield any insight into Marcia's whereabouts? Alltounian hoped so, posing one question, "Where is Marcia?"[55] The astrologer got to work and called him back in twenty minutes. "And Dorothy drew up the chart and told me that Howard, she's confined and restrained. Check the hospital. So I checked the hospital. I called all the hospitals. Harborview and Stevens. There was nothing," he told detectives. "I called back, and I says, Dorothy, she is not in the hospitals. I think she is somewhere, you say she is confined and restrained, I think she is in the cemetery under a tree somewhere. Now does that fit in? And she says, yeah, that that fits. And I says, Dorothy, where in that cemetery is she located? She said southwest."[56]

Armed with this astrological affirmation of his hunch, Howard sought out Sergeant John Taylor, heading the search that Monday, and said, "I know this may sound hoaky, but you know my wife is a metaphysical author, has written several books on Astrology and consequently I have called an astrologer friend who says to look in the Southwest portion, which is the most heavily wooded.[57] .... We got to concentrate our efforts there."[58]

Sergeant Taylor indulged the unusual cosmic tip, dispatching additional people to the area. "He took me up in the helicopter and flew over that whole area. I couldn't see and I saw very quickly that you really can't see, at least I can't see too much from the helicopter. You can see the open areas in the woods, but you can't see the brush piles and the logs where I knew she would be,"[59] Howard said.

Back on land, one of the search teams discovered some articles of women's clothing approximately fifteen feet from the edge of a roadway, about two hundred feet from the grounds of nearby Floral Hills Cemetery. Despite concluding that the clothing had clearly been there for some time before Marcia disappeared, officers erred on the side of caution, marking off the area with a police perimeter, then contacted Howard to ascertain if the clothes could have belonged to her. "I asked Mr. Alltounian at this time if there was any chance that any of these items could have been part of his wife's clothing, and he said, negative, that there was not,"[60] Sergeant Taylor noted.

The only other potential lead came from a window washer who worked at the courthouse, who noticed a female fitting Marcia's description standing at a telephone booth at a Chevron station on Highway 2 in Snohomish, ten miles up the road. The woman, observed the witness, wore a blue ski jacket, not a bulky type for warmth but a dressy, sport type. Sergeant Taylor again consulted Howard. "He indicated his wife did have a blue ski jacket. We went to the closet and found that the blue ski jacket which she owned which was light blue in color, was in the closet."[61]

After that dead end, Howard drew attention to the hiking boots he had on, tan in color, with approximately a six-inch top and Vibram-type sole, indicating that Marcia also had a pair of that style boot. The sergeant set about the residence with Howard looking for like boots. Unable to locate any such footwear, Taylor provided updated information to advise searchers that Marcia could possibly be wearing this type of shoe.

The subject of the shoes would forever remain a mystery. "I don't remember her ever wearing boots,"[62] Marcia's friend Lani would later say. Lani would routinely take the ferry over from neighboring Vashon Island to visit, accompanying Marcia on walks and sleeping over at the duplex. They'd stargaze, do yoga under Marcia's apple tree, or go on pleasant walks. Whenever they ventured outdoors, Lani only knew Marcia to wear sturdy low-cut shoes, dark in color. Incidentally, that description sounded similar to the one Howard gave Sergeant Taylor on the first search day. "He indicated that she was possibly wearing a green turtle next sweater, bulky type, green cord pants and some type of low shoes, black in color with a short heel on them."[63] Those shoes, however, would be seen by Marwayne weeks later when searching the duplex with Howard. "Her loafers were still on the bedroom floor where she had kicked them off,"[64] she noted. It was uncertain what footwear she had on, if any.

The next few hours passed that Monday with no discovery of Marcia Moore. Multiple searches around the residence were conducted by air and ground personnel, and door to door contact was made with all available residents. Officers consulted Howard who offered no further locations. Eventually searchers emerged from the woods. "It was dark. The hunting and rescue thing was over. There was nothing we could do,"[65] the husband recapped to the lieutenant in an interview later that week.

Once again, Howard turned to the occult. "So Monday, okay now, Monday after we didn't find her in the southwest portion of the cemetery, I called up Seattle's best psychic, by the name of Elizabeth Jenkins." Liz Jenkins was a longtime friend of Marwayne's, and Howard grabbed her number from her place during the day. "So I called Elizabeth, you know, and she told me a lot of things today. She's alive, she's confined, she's restrained. Possibly that somebody picked her up in a car, and I says, no, I don't think so. The reason was, I think she walked in the woods, you know, where can I find her?"[66]

First Search Day—Wood Trails community down the street from the duplex. A housing development Howard pointed to during the search, which gave way to the woods.

In spite of his inkling, the psychic did not sense a connection to the woods but rather picked up on the number seven, suggesting Marcia would make contact at seven o'clock that very evening. Still, Howard persisted with his woods theory. While the search effort had already wrapped for the night, he phoned Sergeant Taylor pleading for the searchers to return. There was a possibility Marcia could be in the area, he said, specifically citing the intersection of Larch Way and Butternut Road. Ultimately a further search yielded negative results.

Meanwhile, the hour of 7:00 p.m. came and went. When Marcia failed to appear at that time, Howard called psychic Liz Jenkins again. "And she says, Howard, get a good nights sleep, you will hear from her at 7 in the morning."[67] With some help from a friend, the fatigued husband retired to Marcia's bedroom downstairs.

It would be night two for a missing Marcia.

ONE SEARCH DAY GONE

oward was sitting in his bathrobe when Dr. Ed came back to check
on him Tuesday morning. "Finally I got dressed,"[68] the husband
would tell the lieutenant. "So I woke up at five minutes to 8, and
there wasn't any Marcia." Psychic Liz Jenkins' 7:00 a.m. prediction came
and went. "She says, she'll walk in. Well, Marcia wasn't here."[69]

Eager to help, Marwayne's daughter Cris telephoned soon thereafter
and said, "I'm not working Howard, can I come over and help you look
for her today? And I says, sure, fine,"[70] Howard described.

Over the course of the search, Cris would assist wherever possible.
The young neighbor had been riding horseback since the age of twelve
and knew every trail in the area, like a gulley just south of the duplex the
neighborhood kids called "dead man's curve," or the lengthy, downhill
dirt road they nicknamed "thunder road."

After crossing North Road east of the duplex from Larch Way, thunder road turned into a steep, serpentine trail the local kids called "hidden
valley," which ended up at Bothell Everett Highway, but that was a couple of miles from the duplex. "Um, in fact you really had to know how
to ride to go up and down that thing. It was much too precarious to be
riding in the dark,"[71] Cris remembered.

That Tuesday, another piercingly frigid day loomed outside. Cris
saddled up her beloved black mare, Sophie Buck, offspring of a cele-

brated quarter horse named Frank Buck. While Howard covered the footpaths, Cris searched the trails yelling out for Marcia, though she'd later divulge, "I don't remember him searching that much. I did most of the searching." Just like Monday, there was no trace. "I rode my poor horse up and down those trails, I don't even know, at least twenty-five times.... And it was really cold, so icy my horse went down on her knees a couple of times coming back up the hill."[72]

Still on vacation, her mother, Marwayne, logged first learning the shocking news in her diary. "Tuesday Jan. 16...9:47 a.m., Honolulu. Phone call from Cris and Howard, reporting Marcia's disappearance to me."[73] What Howard told her about Marcia's state of mind was troubling. "Marwayne, she was suicidal. She always walked. She went for a walk after I left. I know, for certain, she is in the woods,"[74] he told her.

During the remainder of her vacation, Marwayne kept in frequent contact for updates. "I phoned Howard back that evening about 5 p.m. Hawaii time; Cris was still with him. They had searched all day Tuesday. Nothing.... Meanwhile I told Howard he must contact her family to let them know she had disappeared,"[75] Leipzig urged. But it would not be by way of Howard that Marcia's family would hear the shocking news.

"What bothered me was how I learned that she had disappeared,"[76] brother Robin Moore divulged to *News World* newspaper. The Moore family hadn't been notified until Tuesday when Robin received a call from a friend in Seattle who by chance heard of the incident on a local news broadcast.

The worrisome news befuddled Robin. Why, just the day before Marcia vanished, she had called his Westport, Connecticut home to discuss collaboration on future writing projects, specifically mentioning her upcoming trip to Southern California.

Robin immediately informed the rest of the Moore family. Marcia's younger brother John, an attorney living in Connecticut, flew to their parents' Massachusetts home to help bear the brunt of the devastating news. Their parents, Robert and Eleanor, had just returned from the Caribbean where they had wintered every year for thirty years.

They wanted information, but no one in Marcia's family had ever met Howard. "I should soon have some pictures of both of us to send you. You are sure to like him, and to approve,"[77] Marcia wrote about her new love interest back in October 1977. The Moore family had little chance to give their blessing. By the end of that October, Marcia had moved from California to Washington, and a month later she tied the knot in the absence of family or friends. Perhaps it was for the best, as long ago her family had learned that it was no use making any objection where her love life, or much else, was concerned. In the past they had tried to dissuade her from risky endeavors, but a headstrong Marcia heeded no forewarning. After three failed marriages, her family ultimately chalked it up to her long history of foolhardiness and naivety regarding relationships.

Marcia herself had spent less than two weeks with the anesthesiologist before getting engaged. Those "two glorious weeks" together took place in September 1977, when Howard invited Marcia to stay at a house on a wooded ravine in the Sand Point Peninsula. "Am having a fabulous time here in Seattle visiting Howard Alltounian," she wrote her parents about her new beau. "He has been house-sitting this month in a very beautiful home in the woods overlooking Lake Washington, so the surroundings are really delightful. And Howard treats me like twenty million dollars."[78]

In *Journeys into the Bright World*, she would justify the rash engagement by proclaiming that two marvelous ketamine trips they took together affirmed their love. For Howard, the ketamine trips transcended traditional love. He declared it a cosmic union. Perhaps he was borrowing from Marcia who professed, while under ketamine, that an organic sensation overcame her and much like wedding bells, every cell in her body reverberated Howard's name. Hauntingly, she also pondered where it would all lead.

Marcia and Howard from a series of engagement photos. One was
used as an author's photo for *Journeys into the Bright World.*

Although a few times Marcia mentioned visiting her parents in
Massachusetts so they could meet Howard, plans never materialized.
Now she was missing and they knew nothing of this fourth husband,
except what she had corresponded sparsely during the fourteen months
of their marriage.

Brother John Moore would get a crash course in making Howard's
acquaintance, as plans were made for him to fly out to Washington at once.

LAST KNOWN PHONE CALL TO THE FAMILY

The morning before she reportedly vanished, Saturday, January 13, Marcia called Robin at his Westport, Connecticut home. He was away, but his wife, Mary Olga, took the call and spoke with Marcia for about ten minutes. It marked the last time anyone from the family would speak with Marcia.

Left to right: Brother John, Marcia, Robin, and his wife Mary Olga.

It was perhaps ironic that for someone who spent her life pursuing ancient wisdom, the last person Marcia was known to have spoken to was someone the Moore family largely considered a trophy wife. Of Russian descent, Mary Olga was rumored to be the former mistress of wealthy elder New York socialite Huntington Hartford of the A&P supermarket fortune. Formerly a floor model for Bonwit Teller, she had attended a performing arts school. Her father was a car salesman and although she hadn't enjoyed the fancy upbringing of the Moore family, she was none-theless a bit of a princess.

Robin Moore gratuitously arranged a bit part for her in the film adaptation of his book, *The Happy Hooker*. Wearing a short wig, she sang and briefly played the part of a movie starlet. So that Mary Olga could lay claim to having a career, Robin was also willing to pay a substantial sum to include her in a choreographed show at the Rainbow Room, the landmark 1930s nightclub in Manhattan's Rockefeller Center. Years later, seventy-five-year-old Robin would leave his cancer-stricken wife for another woman, forcing Mary Olga to live off the jewelry she had squirreled away.

Marcia enjoyed a congenial relationship with her sister-in-law and, during the call, thoughtfully steered the conversation toward her book idea about beauty tips she thought would interest her. "She apolo-gized for not writing a long letter to Robin but she thought why not call instead. She said she hoped she wasn't disturbing me," Mary Olga recalled. "Then she got breathlessly excited when she proceeded to tell me about a new book idea."[79] Marcia actually referred to two books. One was half-finished, entitled *Memories*, about reincarnation, which she would send to Robin once completed, if he was interested.

The other work, Marcia raved, detailed Cleopatra's beauty secrets, featuring a regimen Marcia had been researching for several months. "She said she finally hit on the secret during a regression session," Mary Olga said. "Cleopatra's secret has something to do with exercising face muscles. The face, she said, is one big muscle so why not exercise it like any other part of the body." Her own face had filled out a bit through these exercises, taking away the sallow hollowness she used to have,

Marcia persuaded. "If women did this there would be no need for a face lift."[80]

As Marcia did not have time to write the book on Cleopatra's beauty secrets herself, she proposed that Robin could perhaps find a willing writer, and she'd produce it. "She kept repeating herself on this point. If Robin wasn't interested she would begin to peddle her idea in Los Angeles," Mary Olga learned. Should her brother want to return the call, she would be home all weekend, but there was no need to call if he received the information. "She said on Monday she and Howard would be going to Ojai, California."[81]

Robin Moore insisted his sister would not have disappeared without letting him know. "She was writing a book for my publishing company," and was very enthusiastic about it, he told a news outlet. The book would use horoscope projections to focus on the Kennedys. According to Marcia, Ted Kennedy should not run for president because his karmic involvement was such that he didn't deserve it, could not have it, and would be destroyed by it. "My wife said that Marcia was very enthusiastic, although she sounded repetitive and slightly confused about her theories,"[82] Robin said. There were instances where she trailed off in conversation, repeating something she had already made a point of, Mary Olga perceived. "She kept going back to her reincarnation book and if I'd remember to tell Robin about it."[83]

Upon hearing his sister was missing, Robin phoned her residence to get further details from Howard, even probing to determine his whereabouts Sunday evening. What movie had he seen? Robin inquired, "and after a pause Howard said Superman."[84] The movie title would become a discrepancy never resolved. Detectives also learned from Howard that he saw *Superman*, specifically noting 9:00 p.m. as the start time, and disclosed as much to reporters on Friday, January 20. But that information would later change…to a double feature of *The Pink Panther*.

Show times for *The Pink Panther*—the double feature Howard
said he saw on the night he came home to find Marcia missing,
alongside *Superman*, the movie he originally told police he'd seen.

THE CASE CHANGES HANDS

A fter two days passed with no sign of Marcia Moore, Lieutenant Darrol Bemis took over the case on Wednesday, January 17, 1979.

Lt. Darrol Bemis at his retirement party.

Earlier in his career, Lt. Bemis had been selected to attend the FBI Academy, one of the highest honors granted to a local policeman. "A balding veteran with the piercing eyes of a stubborn cop..."[85] is how one magazine would describe him. In his off-time, Bemis played goalie for a soccer team. He was married, with three children from a previous marriage.

As division chief in charge of detectives, Lt. Bemis didn't normally handle cases personally, but a series of unusual events forced his hand. For starters, a young officer had pleaded with the lieutenant to be reassigned off the case. Aside from the demands of having a newborn at home, the officer had become exasperated by Howard Alltounian's strange behavior. And that was just the beginning. Bemis soon realized that Marcia Moore was no ordinary missing Jane Doe.

The papers promptly dubbed her "heiress to the Sheraton Hotel fortune,"[86] likely to get out in front of and sensationalize another Patty Hearst-type news story. The Hearst abduction had played out globally to the ratings delight of the news media five years earlier.

"I'm just getting all kinds of calls on this case," Lt. Bemis would later vent to a *Seattle Times* reporter. "I mean, I had a New York paper call me today. They wanted to know about the kidnapping. I said, 'What kidnapping?' They wanted to know about the ransom note. I said, 'Hey, there's no ransom note!' The one thing I don't want to do is sensationalize this case. That's why I took it over personally."[87]

That day would mark one of the oddest of the lieutenant's career. As Howard described it, "John Moore, Marcia's younger brother, arrived late in the afternoon from Boston, rented a car and came out to the house and met with us after we conducted our search." The search was conducted by a small group Howard had assembled, including Marwayne's daughter Cris, and Lawrence Neal, his hunting and fishing buddy, who was best man at Howard and Marcia's wedding. "He is able to go through the woods like a deer or elk,"[88] Howard told police. "He is a woodsman, a logger. He grew up in the Oregon woods. His father had a jippo logging outfit. And he can go thru the thickest brush without any problem."[89]

Howard's impromptu search party drove to an area he had selected at 183rd Street and Bothell Everett Highway, about three miles southeast of the duplex by roadway. Sergeant Taylor arranged for them to use the bloodhound and his handler. Still fixated on the area, Howard got a temporary boost from a woman who lived nearby, who claimed to have seen Marcia exiting a gate sometime the previous summer. "And we spent the whole day in that area looking for her, and we covered it I think better than your rescue team could have done it. And nothing again,"[90] Howard later told Bemis.

After all his helpers left, Howard remained determined. "And I was here by myself. I says, god damn it, I'm going to find her. I've just got find her. I'm going to walk out of this house, I'm going to walk right to her. And I walked out of the house, and I ended up at the clothes, and you know the rest of it."[91]

Lt. Bemis certainly did know the rest of it. Decades later, it would remain a vivid memory. It was the day he would behold the bizarre scene of Howard sniffing women's undergarments. It all began shortly after 5:00 p.m. when Deputy Harold Sweeney, who was patrolling the area, encountered Howard. Sweeney was driving near the duplex when Howard darted into the middle of the road waving his arms in front of a truck, nearly getting run over by the patrol car and ending up on the hood. He had just scaled a barbed wire fence, gashing his hand so deeply it would later require stitches.

Unable to stop, a startled Sweeney continued until he could make a U-turn to assess the situation. He found Howard in the woods running and jumping, looking under logs, hollering, "I found her! I found her!" remembered Bemis. "The deputy thinks this guy's nuts or something."[92]

Sweeney directed Howard out of the woods. "Yeah he ordered me out with a flashlight. And of course I got upset,"[93] Howard admitted to Bemis.

The deputy learned that Howard had found some clothing he believed to be Marcia's. "So, the guy goes out in the woods with him, and here's a pile of clothes that have obviously been dumped there and have been there for ages,"[94] Bemis recalled. The ground was still frozen solid.

Howard handed Sweeney a business card, "And then, I says, will you please call John Taylor and get the rescue squad, you know. These are her clothes, you know. She's here. We can get her,"[95] Howard said.

The deputy radioed in and seven additional units were dispatched. Closely examining the scene, deputies determined that the clothing had been there well before Marcia was reported missing. Officers concluded they had no cause to use the German shepherd standing by in the canine unit. Capable of picking up fallout, small particles of skin that shed from a person twenty-four hours a day, the canine might've taken fresh scent, but this was already weeks old. The articles were stiff, weathered, and faded, according to Bemis. That area next to the cemetery was sometimes littered with trash. Hidden behind a well-groomed row of evergreen trees, people threw clothes, milk cartons, and beer cans, among other items. Cris was at the roadside and thought the clothes were obviously not something contemporary like Marcia would wear. They were in flamboyant colors, girlish patterns, and sizes more suited for a teen.

Meanwhile, Sergeant John Taylor arrived on scene a bit perplexed. The sheriff's office was already aware of the clothes from the first search day on Monday, when Howard confirmed that they did not belong to Marcia. Howard would later explain: "All John said at the time was, was she wearing a skirt? I said, no, she was wearing slacks and a sweater. I didn't know that there were several articles found, you know, and I would have a chance to maybe identify them."[96]

Lt. Bemis determined that the clothes be collected and booked into the property room, but Howard insisted that they be left in place so his daughter Kimberly and ex-wife Tina could make the hour's drive from North Bend and identify them. For some reason, Howard was convinced that his daughter would be better able to identify the clothing as Marcia's at the spot.

A standoff ensued between Howard and the detectives. Bemis said the clothing would be logged into the property room where Howard could inspect it, but the husband wanted nothing moved. Finally, Bemis assigned Detective Don Seipel to accompany Howard back home so he could telephone his daughter and friends. After placing some calls,

Howard returned to the scene with the deputy. Bemis reiterated that the articles would be taken to the property room.

"Mr. Alltounian then became quite verbal and crying that he had to have the clothes left in that place, because if they are his wife's, he's going to go out into the woods in the middle of the night and hunt for his ex-wife.... He then got on his knees and started begging, that we leave the clothes. We then advised him again that the property will be held as found property and possible evidence," the detective's report noted. "We stated that this property is to be held as evidence and possible foul play. He then asked what is foul play? We advised him at this time, what we considered as foul play and possibly that circumstances surrounding the disappearance of his wife."[97] Eventually Howard calmed down to the point where he and deputies could return to the duplex and look for similar clothes for comparison.

It marked the first time Bemis had the opportunity to inspect the shingled, blue-and-white-colored duplex, which looked like Alice in Wonderland's dress according to Howard's daughter. An old wooden shed sat at the back of the property beyond a grassy parking area. From the street view at the front, there were two doors, one to Marcia and Howard's unit on the left, their landlords' unit on the right. Often the owners would go off to Friday Harbor to visit their vacation home on San Juan Island, where they apparently were when Marcia vanished.

Inside the duplex, officers noted several packages addressed to Marcia from publishing companies sitting on the floor. The living room décor was mostly green. A couple of Indian tables and a decorative inlaid Indian screen added a touch of richness. The furniture was Danish teak. The kitchen was a warm yellow. On occasion, friends observed the jarring scene of the refrigerator pulled out from the wall, unplugged. A side effect of ketamine was amplified sensitivity to sound; when she was coming off a high, Marcia found even the hum of the fridge almost unbearable.

The rest of the unit, at basement level, consisted of an office, bathroom, and bedroom at the end of a hallway. In the office, the deputies saw an expensive IBM typewriter amongst other office equipment on a desk. They found no signs of disturbance or struggle. Everything was orderly, with numerous publications and pamphlets neatly laid about.

Howard said his wife had packed a bag for her trip to California, and he pulled that suitcase out of a closet. Rummaging through it, he didn't find anything matching the garments found near the road. From there they proceeded to the hallway where Howard searched through shelves. He located some pink pantyhose but could not determine if they were similar to what had been found.

Next stop was the bedroom, where flowery sheets and a matching quilt blanketed a queen-sized waterbed. Atop the headboard detectives noticed two wine glasses, apparently recently used, which Howard said he drank out of after Marcia went missing.

On the floor lay a bottle of grain alcohol and an empty brown glass bottle with a stopper, which appeared to have contained ether. Although ether has a long history of being inhaled in small amounts for a quick high, it was the volatile substance's other known use that piqued the lieutenant's interest. Long used as a surgical anesthetic, ether will quickly render someone deeply unconscious. Ironically, its potency and tendency to cause nausea, even death, led to the discovery of safer anesthetics like ketamine. That left ether mostly phased out for use in surgery by the 1970s.

When first questioned by detectives, Howard stated that the only drug Marcia was taking beyond her ketamine research was daily bladder medication, possibly for cystitis, a side effect of ketamine use. Many times in her books, Marcia strongly objected to taking medications. "I have always avoided drugs of all sorts and did not even keep aspirin in my medicine cabinet. Even now, although I am married to a physician, vitamin pills and some burn salve constitute my entire therapeutic repertoire. In our household anyone who gets sick can expect to be dosed with herb tea and encouraged to do yoga exercises. I have always opposed the taking of barbiturates, amphetamines, and all forms of uppers and downers, except in cases of real medical need. Resorting to such artificial aids is like borrowing money from a bank. Sooner or later whatever has been taken out has to be paid back with interest."[98]

Why would an open bottle of ether be casually lying around? Could it have been used to knock Marcia out? The questions would remain unanswered. The bottles were never taken as evidence.

In the bedroom, police found a small bulletin board with numerous phone numbers, and Marcia's purse on the floor. Curiously, Howard objected to its inspection. "At this time, Lt. Bemis started examining the purse and Mr. Alltounian became quite adamant and asked him to leave the personal property alone," Detective Seipel noted. "We then advised Mr. Alltounian that we are looking for clues, possible evidence in her disappearance. He became quite adamant again and insistant that we leave her personal property alone." Investigators resorted to asking him about his claim that Marcia had talked about suicide. "He stated yes, but he did not want to elaborate on it at this time."[99]

Without further insight into Marcia's disappearance, the group returned to the scene of the clothing on the roadside. Howard again insisted on taking possession of the clothes, but Bemis repeatedly explained why the clothing could not be given to him. This angered Howard, who even threatened to sue the county. Eventually they agreed to inspect the clothes at the station.

Detective Seipel encountered Howard on the fourth floor of the sheriff's office about twenty minutes after the items were booked into the property room. Accompanied by his ex-wife and their daughter, Howard proceeded to the property room where Lt. Bemis met them, and the clothing was laid on a table.

By now the pieces had thawed: one blue bra, a white bra, pink panties, purple hose, opaque hose, a brown print dress, an orange-and-white dress, and a dress in a blue, yellow, and pink print fabric. The only article that came close to matching Marcia's size was a white bra, labeled 36A. According to Howard, Marcia wore a 34B.

Officers stood by as Howard pawed through the items. While neither his daughter or ex-wife could positively identify any of the garments, he kept holding up the orange-and-white dress stating, "I think I seen this dress in the closet. I think I've seen this dress in the closet,"[100] constantly repeating himself after every sentence, the deputy noted.

Lt. Bemis surveyed the reaction of both witnesses, which seemed to alternate between uncertain, disinterested, and disbelief. For about ten seemingly endless minutes, officers looked on with raised eyebrows as Howard sniffed the clothing. "Mr. Alltounian kept on talking incoherent terms, concerning the disappearance of his wife and the smells of the panty hose and bras.... He kept saying that I know my wife's smell. I know what she's like. I am positive, he stated, that I think this could be her, but I'm not sure yet. He said if blood hounds could do it, I can.... Mr. Alltounian carried on and kept babbling to himself about his wife and her smells and that he possibly believes that with these articles and with the dogs again, that they can possibly trace down his wife in the woods."[101]

Lt. Bemis later recalled his astonishment when Howard then picked up a pair of panties, deeply inhaled, and proclaimed "Marcia! I'd know you anywhere!"[102] Bemis couldn't help but wonder if Howard wasn't high as a kite. At one point he tried to stuff a pair of pantyhose into his pocket but was stopped by a detective and told that the articles would need to remain in the property room, held as potential evidence, and if possible be processed through the crime lab. However, the deputy cautioned, the clothing had been frozen, wet, and probably lying out in the woods considerably longer than his wife had been missing. Even so, Howard wanted more time to sniff the items. Ultimately, he was advised to contact the homicide office first thing the next morning.

"Mr. Alltounian was very difficult to work with in the aspects that he did not volunteer information freely. Things had to be asked of him in regard to his wife, what she could be wearing, was there any relatives in the area, was there any chance that she might have left with somebody else. Everything had to be asked of him before finding out. And then unless you asked the specific thing, he wouldn't elaborate any more than the exact thing that you asked him,"[103] one officer's report had concluded of the day.

Conversely, Howard later offered his own depiction. "From the outset, I tried to work hand-in-hand with the police. However, their attitude seemed to be to keep me at arms length and generally to ignore what I would tell them."[104]

Three search days had now passed with no discovery of Marcia Moore. The next morning Lt. Bemis would drive back out to the duplex and review the bleak—and increasingly strange—situation on record.

MANY QUESTIONS, FEW ANSWERS

On Thursday, January 18, Lt. Bemis recorded a group interview with Howard. Bemis was accompanied by Doris Twitchell, a kindly sixty-five-year-old detective assigned to help.

Also present were Cris Leipzig and Marcia's younger brother, John, the first of the Moore family to ever meet Howard. "They did not seem to like each other very well…" Cris later told her mother. "I had some conversations with Cris separately from conversations with Howard while, I was in Honolulu," Marwayne journaled. "Cris felt that Howard had not told all he knew, although she had nothing to base it on. She said John also felt the same way." John told Cris that Howard was so much like Marcia's former husband that it was uncanny. "She sure could pick 'em,"[105] John scoffed to Cris, who got along well with Marcia's brother.

Meanwhile, an ominous and crucial development occurred after John Moore's arrival Wednesday. Howard gave John a concise but troubling note, purportedly typed by Marcia the morning she disappeared. The note requested that all of the money in one of her trusts go to Howard, because she was in failing health and about to die. It was unclear why he waited three days to give it to John, instead of police on the day he reported Marcia missing. Adding to the confusion, the letter was not dated the day she was said to have disappeared on Sunday, January 14, but the Tuesday before, on the 9th.

The lieutenant tried to get to the bottom of it in the group interview.

"Now Howard Alltounian, could we go back through this situation again and what happened during the night of her disappearance and what led up to this?"[106] Bemis began.

"Sure,"[107] Howard replied.

"Okay do you want to tell me basically what happened Sunday?"[108] Bemis reiterated.

"Sunday morning when I woke up she just finishing typing this letter and signed it,"[109] Howard said.

"Mr. Alltounian you have just handed me a letter 09 January 1979. This is addressed to 'Dear John'. Who is this John?"[110] Bemis asked.

"John is…"[111] Howard began.

"This is John Moore?"[112] Bemis interjected.

"Moore, right,"[113] Howard confirmed, with John sitting nearby.

"And he would be the brother of Marcia? Okay,"[114] Bemis replied.

For the record, Bemis read aloud to the group the typewritten note, which was signed simply "Marcia" in purple ink, above her typed first name:

This is a sad letter to have to write so I'll try to make it brief. I am in severe pain and do not know how much longer I have to live. When I go I am most anxious to have the funds in my personal trust account go to Howard who has been so good to me and seen me through so many difficult times. Please do this for me.

Marcia[115]

Marcia Moore was the beneficiary of two trust funds. One held a substantial balance of approximately $300,000 and was completely irrevocable, to be bequeathed and distributed only to her children in the event of her death. "Marcia gets a monthly income from that, something in the order of $1,000 or $1,200 at a time,"[116] her brother John would explain to Lt. Bemis in a private interview the next day. The "personal" smaller trust referred to in the typed note held a principal value of about $80,000, from which Marcia received $400 a month.

Shortly after their marriage, Howard had taken an interest in Marcia's trusts. He called The Old Colony Trust Company in Boston, asking about the funds, policy details, and how the money was being invested. "That concerned me a little bit," John later told Bemis. "I had never met Howard, and I thought it was a little untoward for a new husband to immediately call the bank to get information about Marcia's trust without going thru her brother, who, he must have known was one of the trustees.[117] … He did this without my knowledge which was unusual since I was a co-trustee of the two trusts."[118]

In addition to contacting the bank, there had also been what John considered an unpleasant exchange six months before Marcia vanished. She had written to their father Robert, expressing her and Howard's displeasure with the way the trust funds were being invested, suggesting that all management responsibilities be turned over to Howard. "Marcia said, well, he is very interested now in getting into money matters. That he has been very unsophisticated about money, that he has spent all his life in medical things, and he wanted to learn about money management. So he has been trying to find out how people handle money,"[119] John told Bemis.

Irked by the insinuation of mismanagement, Robert Moore dismissed his daughter's complaint in a stinging reply back then. "Do you realize that under the bank's management that the trust is now earning and paying you more than at the time when it was created? I consider that a very creditable performance."[120]His pointed response included his own misgivings regarding her new husband's sudden interest in the trusts' performance. "I was much interested in hearing that Howard has resigned his job. I am sorry that he had reached a point where he could no longer 'take it.' It is interesting that he is now looking into a career in 'Money Management'. I would suppose that the first step would be in a comprehensive course in accounting followed by a study of such elements as depth analysis of operating reports and balance sheets with, in many cases, special reference to a company's use of depreciation allowances and tax implications. That last, of course, is vital in any business venture and the trouble there is that the government is apt to change the rules substantially every year or two. It takes a lot of study and much experience, usually over a long period to become a good money manager."[121]

Clearly wary of his daughter's sudden decision to turn over financial control to this new man in her life after three failed marriages, Robert concluded: "In retrospect I am now very glad that I had sense enough to make these trusts irrevocable and unamendable in view of all the changes that have taken place and may again in the future, they have so far well served their basic purpose. I could write much more about all this but just now only just want to try to lay at rest some of your many misjudgements and misapprehensions."[122]

Despite the undertone of disapproval, her father relented about control of the smaller trust. "I am not familiar with the provisions of the second smaller trust. You can take this up with John. I was under the impression that you had set this up for the benefit of your children."[123]

In their private interview, John Moore told Bemis what happened next. "And Marcia when she got the reply said, well, that settles it, that's okay, fine, I'm sorry I wrote these letters. She seemed to be calmed down and quiet about it. And no problem." When her brother next saw Marcia, in September 1978 at the family's summer home, there were no lingering money matters. "She had no quarrel or problem with the way finances were being handled and we really didn't discuss very much about the money situation, except she apologized, said she was sorry that she had sent these other letters."[124]

A month later, John wrote about liquidating the smaller trust. "I didn't want to make a big issue out of it at all, as I was pretty much ready to write that all off anyway, just to keep peace in the family and peace of mind, etc. So I said if you really wanted to use these funds, let me know,"[125] John told Bemis.

Marcia thanked John for his note, and in her reply indicated, "Needless to say we would not cash in any stock in such a way as to result in unnecessary taxes. But I think that probably we will want to invest this amount in our foundation work and that it would be a financially sensible and worthwhile thing to do."[126] John was under the impression that Howard would be in touch, but there was no follow-up from either of them.

With Marcia now missing, Lt. Bemis and John Moore were left to interpret this troubling typewritten note about the trust. If Marcia wrote it on Sunday morning, January 14, why was it dated Tuesday, January 9? And why had Howard been indecisive in contacting authorities Sunday night if her condition was rapidly deteriorating as early as Tuesday, five days before she vanished? From the beginning of the investigation, detectives had inquired about Marcia's state of mind, and Bemis had been in contact with Howard several times before John's arrival. In all those conversations, Howard never mentioned the note, not when he phoned the dispatcher nor to any investigating officer.

Not even Marwayne, still in Hawaii, was made aware of the note despite Howard's insistence that Marcia "was suicidal that morning, and had asked him if there was anything she could take that would make it look like a heart attack,"[127] a comment he never shared with detectives. The note, initially withheld from police, was only given to Marcia's brother when he arrived Wednesday.

In the private interview with John Moore, Lt. Bemis tried to get more answers by asking for background information about Marcia Moore. "She had always been interested in metaphysics and in arcane and esoteric studies when she was growing up. So she had always looked forward to going to India,"[128] John informed Bemis. "At seven, she had been struck by mention of the word reincarnation, and couldn't turn it out of her mind." By fourteen, Marcia had read Paul Brunton's *A Search in Secret India*, and "dreamed of the day she would settle in the Himalayas—the Abode of the snow,"[129] she once described of herself to an author.

As Lt. Bemis' interview with Marcia's brother continued, it became increasingly clear that he couldn't just understand her past by reading a blurb from one of her books. From living abroad in India, to studying everything from astrology to yoga to extraterrestrials, Marcia Moore wasn't merely a devout student of the occult; she was fairly well connected. The heiress befriended prominent astrologer Zipporah Dobyns and did astrological charts for actor and singer Burl Ives, whom she'd met in Montecito. She made presentations at a big festival where John Denver was a performer. Her family knew the Hiltons, who had consulted with her father on hotel business. Her parents visited Errol Flynn at his Jamaican estate every winter. Bobby Kennedy was a classmate of her brother Robin.

Marcia was said to have known Marilyn Monroe, who was known to have an interest in yoga. They were both Gemini and like the actress, Marcia was proud of her initials—both ladies often signing simply "MM." "Metamorphosis. That's my initials. M.M. stands for metamorphosis,"[130] Marcia once explained. Unfortunately, like Marilyn, Marcia's fate would unfold under a cloud of suspicion of drug use. In Marcia's case, not barbiturates or prescription drugs, but a powerful substance used to tranquilize horses and anesthetize people for surgery.

Lt. Bemis invested considerable time trying to make sense of that first week after Marcia's disappearance. With each passing hour, the prospects of finding Marcia alive diminished. But in some ways, he'd just scratched the surface.

"I've ended up spending all of my free time reading the books she has written so I can understand the terminology these psychics use,"[131] Bemis later told a magazine. "I had to read books at night, you know? All of 'em, you know, trying to figure out what the hell they're talking about even.[132] … Some of them are pretty far out."[133]

There were already several perplexing aspects of the case. Howard was certainly a strange character, erratic and at times evasive. Yet Marcia spoke glowingly about their love in letters and even in *Journeys into the Bright World.*

Moreover, the very first chapter was titled "You Have to Die to Be Reborn." Was it a message? Did Marcia Moore want to die? Four years earlier in *Hypersentience*, she had written: "As far back as I can remember, my mind has been inordinately preoccupied with the subject of death.

There was never any fear of it but the itch of curiosity was so great that as a small child I often toyed with the thought of jumping in front of a truck in order to find out what would happen next."[134] Compounding the situation was the matter of her health—and the ominous note.

Still, despite the more pressing questions of the investigation, one question couldn't escape Bemis' mind. How did this sophisticated Brahmin woman, well established in esoteric circles, end up in a tiny apartment in a secluded rural town in northwest Washington?

Marcia Moore, as Lt. Bemis would learn, led a fascinatingly unconventional life.

ESOTERIC ROOTS

Marcia's father, clean cut and well-mannered Robert Lowell Moore, certainly looked the part of a blue-blooded Bostonian aristocrat, but his family tree held a great secret, a secret rooted in the harmonizing of traditional religion and the occult.

The Moore family settled in what is now the Middlesex County area of Massachusetts in the 1600s, after emigrating from England. The family moved to Cambridge from Littleton, Massachusetts in 1810, following a failed attempt at running a country store. Their new house on Brattle Street was large enough to take on a few boarders, one of whom was transcendentalist Amos Bronson Alcott, father of *Little Women* author Louisa May Alcott.

They eventually joined the burgeoning Unitarian Church, a liberal Christian denomination that rejects the notion of the Holy Trinity in favor of belief in one God and Jesus as a prophet, but then a controversial new movement would become intertwined with Unitarianism and the Moore family. Three hundred fifty miles west of Cambridge, an unusual incident in the mid-nineteenth century would usher in the Spiritualist movement.

On March 31, 1848, two young sisters, Kate and Maggie Fox, were purportedly startled by inexplicable and persistent knockings heard inside their modest Hydesville, New York cottage. The girls claimed that the rapping wasn't the random clanking of bad pipes or animals making a home inside the walls, but some sort of supernatural entity that deliberately responded to their own hand clapping and questions.

Not long after their unnerved parents called a neighbor to observe the phenomenon, hundreds of friends and curiosity seekers alike descended upon the cottage in the days that followed. It seems hard to believe that a singular ghost story of this kind could mark the genesis of a religion, but consensus holds that the Hydesville Rappings marked the beginning of Spiritualism.

Seemingly overnight, mediums began surfacing, and shortly thereafter the Fox sisters even performed in a traveling act to demonstrate the episode to an American public hungry for theatrical entertainment. In the decades that followed, séances became a popular form of attempted communication with spirits, sometimes accessorized with the sensationalized Ouija boards and crystal balls.

Unfortunately for the credibility of Spiritualism, séances attracted charlatans looking to cash in on the trend. Some self-proclaimed mediums were exposed as using cheap parlor tricks to conjure fake spirits. Famous escape artist Harry Houdini even undertook a personal cause of exposing fraudsters and the entire Spiritualist movement, as he considered it predatory on the vulnerable who had lost loved ones.

Yet the Spiritualist movement endured and another catalyst sustained its momentum well into the twentieth century: war. The enormous number of American and European casualties resulting from the Civil War and WWI created scores of average citizens eager to communicate with the dearly departed, who now felt that the means to do so was accessible to the masses.

It's difficult to contextualize just how popular séances were in the second half of the nineteenth and early twentieth centuries, but several prominent figures espoused Spiritualism, including Sir Arthur Conan Doyle, Victor Hugo, and some prominent political figures. Following the death of her eleven-year-old son Willie, Mary Todd Lincoln held séances in the White House primarily in an attempt to contact her beloved son.

An interesting aspect of Marcia Moore's journey is how the Spiritualist movement would shape her life and the direct contact her ancestors enjoyed with the movement's founders. A handful of key advocates legitimized the Spiritualist movement, including Andrew Jackson Davis, Henry Steel Olcott, Helena Blavatsky, Helena Roerich, and Alice Bailey, and they in turn would become personally intertwined with the Moore family.

Andrew Jackson Davis, regarded by many as the "father of modern Spiritualism," became a close friend of Robert Moore's grandfather Augustus Moore and his great grandfather, also named Augustus. In addition to Amos Bronson Alcott, Davis boarded for a time at the family home on Brattle Street.

Davis claimed a hypnotism session changed his life by allowing him to discover his own abilities as a clairvoyant. He abandoned the fire and brimstone of his strict Calvinist faith and would go on to lecture and write numerous books, inspiring thousands interested in Spiritualism and the occult, greatly influencing the Moore family lineage.

A man named Colonel Henry Steel Olcott met and was inspired by Andrew Jackson Davis' displays of mesmerism. In 1849, Olcott converted to Spiritualism and would become a founding member of the New York Conference of Spiritualists in 1853. In the two decades that followed, interrupted by a stint as a colonel in the Civil War, Olcott continued his advocacy of Spiritualism. However, concern was still mounting that the charlatanism that had infiltrated the Spiritualist movement was a significant impediment to its legitimacy. Davis urged Olcott to become a reformer of the movement.

The opportunity to do so would present itself in 1874 while Olcott was investigating claims of paranormal materializations at the famous Eddy Farm in Vermont after reading an article in a well-known Spiritualist publication circulated out of Boston called *Banner of Light*. Another up-and-coming Spiritualist, Helena Blavatsky, traveled there in particular to meet Olcott and by all accounts, he became impressed with her intellect and vigor.

To some, Helena Blavatsky was a transformative philosopher who outlined a doctrine coalescing the wisdom and synchronicity of all faiths. To others, she was a capricious, at times petulant, opportunist who craved fame and sought to undermine the Western Judeo-Christian religious establishment.

Miserable and prone to fits and tantrums during her aristocratic upbringing, she fled Russia weeks after marrying in her teenage years, and wild theories about her travels in the years that followed are subject to debate.

Blavatsky claimed that throughout childhood she experienced visions of a Hindu man named Master Morya, whom she would later describe as a "Master of Wisdom." After leaving Russia, she supposedly encountered this mysterious figure in the flesh at Hyde Park, London in 1851. There he bestowed upon her the duty of founding the Theosophical Society, with the aim of establishing a place where the tenets of all faiths can be explored.

Whether the encounter was truth or fiction, Blavatsky and Olcott succeeded, not only in reforming the Spiritualist movement but also in advancing it into the twentieth century and infusing it with Eastern philosophies. In fact, by 1880, Blavatsky and Olcott had both converted to Buddhism. Five years after establishing the Theosophical Society in New York in 1875, they left America behind and relocated the headquarters to Adyar, India, where Marcia Moore would travel in the late 1950s to study yoga, Hindi, and Sanskrit.

The Theosophical Society began refocusing their philosophy away from Spiritualism, toward masters and spiritual guides, and on the principles Blavatsky outlined in her esoteric magnum opus, *The Secret Doctrine*.

Spiritualism, meanwhile, maintained more of its concentration on paranormal and psychic studies, all the while attempting to increase legitimacy. In the 1880s, the American and British Societies for Psychical Research began the first scientific investigation of paranormal phenomena. Three decades after the Hydesville Rappings, the humble beginnings of the Spiritualist movement had now evolved into an international phenomenon, at times rebuking the established major religions of the world.

Furthering the break from the rigidity of Puritanism, Protestantism, and Catholicism was the concurrent movement of new philosophers from the Concord area of Massachusetts where Marcia was raised. Most notably Ralph Waldo Emerson, Nathaniel Hawthorne, Amos Bronson Alcott, and Henry David Thoreau ushered in the Transcendentalist movement.

As the Unitarian Church's open and tolerant disposition progressed in the American Northeast during this time, it became the ideal faith to coexist with the Spiritualist, Theosophist, and Transcendentalist movements in the Boston area. These exploratory philosophies, plus the daisy chain of mystical ambassadors associated with the Moore family, would cast a long shadow over the life of Marcia Moore.

While her father mostly confined himself to philosophical contemplation with a focus on Theosophy, the pursuit of arcane knowledge became a burning passion for Marcia, magnified in her formative years by her own willfulness and intense ambition—something Robert would unsuccessfully try to temper.

"THE HEIRESS"

Marcia Sheldon Moore—"Sheldon" a commonly
used name from her mother's side.

Marcia Sheldon Moore arrived in the world at 9:10 on the morning of May 22, 1928, in Cambridge, Massachusetts—with every advantage in life one could ask for.

She was raised in a three-story colonial mansion set on a two-acre estate in the historic town of Concord. Complete with servants' quarters, Japanese garden, grape arbor, raspberry patch, and apple orchard, it had six bedrooms, twelve rooms in all, plus a two-story studio with a glass-enclosed sun porch, twin summer houses, and a croquet field.

Entrance Side of Residence

Studio and West Side of Residence

Handsome 2-Acre Country Estate • Concord Massachusetts

Croquet Lawn and Grounds

From its pioneer beginning in 1635, Concord has become an outstanding community of lovely homes and country estates. Here in this beautifully planned 12-room Colonial residence is found every essential to create a charming, dignified and smoothly running home. The tastefully landscaped grounds, in one of this historic town's fine residential sections, are designed to give desired protection as well as visual loveliness, yet are within ¾'s of a mile of the railroad station, affording convenient commuting to Boston or Cambridge. Connected to the house by a covered passage with brick floor is a 2-story Studio with balcony on one end, with its own gas heating unit and thermostat. The Studio also has a separate front entrance. Just

arbor, cultivated raspberry patch, and asparagus bed. Enclosed Japanese garden with many rare importations.

RESIDENCE: *12 Rooms* (6 master bedrooms, 4 baths; 2 servants' bedrooms, 1 bath). Distinguished frame Colonial residence, shingle exterior on stone foundation with composition shingled roof (new 2 years ago). Small-pane windows, hardwood floors, brass and copper plumbing, Rockwool insulation. Oil vacuum steam heating system with new Delco burner and attached water heater. Two 275 gal. oil tanks. Town water, gas and sewerage. New electric wiring, and telephone with 4 extensions.

FIRST FLOOR: Center Hall running through. *Living Room* with fireplace—opens on glass-

Moore family mansion.

Patriarch Robert Moore had made his fortune as an entrepreneur, starting in 1914 while enrolled at Harvard. One evening at a stag dance with students from Harvard's all-female equivalent, Radcliffe College, he met fellow student and future business partner Ernest Henderson, grandson of Baron von Bunsen, inventor of the Bunsen burner. The reserved Robert immediately hit it off with personable Ernest. The young men spoke about future financial endeavors, marking the beginnings of a formidable business relationship.

With little discretionary money between them, they purchased broken-down automobiles, still a relatively new technology. The bright, ambitious young men, imbued with a tireless can-do attitude, refurbished the cars and profitably sold them right from their dormitory lawn as a hobby.

Their carefree college days were interrupted, however, by a geopolitical vortex. World War I broke out, and scores of young American men succumbed to patriotic duty like a fever. Less than three years into college, both Robert and Ernest enlisted.

Robert left Harvard at midyear as a sophomore to join the Norton-Harjes Ambulance Corps. Later he trained at the MIT ground school, then sailed for Europe with the first group of aviators sent to France. Moore was transferred to the gunnery school at Cazaux, where he stayed until 1918 as a pursuit pilot.

After spending some time in England at the Hythe gunnery school, he returned to France to act as an aerial gunnery instructor, then was sent to the front with the French Army's Groupe de Bombardement 9. During aerial combat, he was wounded by an enemy formation of pursuit planes 4,800 meters over German lines. In the opening round of fire, Moore's observer was killed, his body slumping on his controls, wedging them. Moore lost control of the aircraft, plummeting in pursuit by two enemy fighters, which poured incessant fire into his plane. He succeeded in regaining control and descended in regular spirals. The enemy persisted, perforating the hull and wounding Moore on the arm and right side.

Thanks to presence of mind, he succeeded in landing his aircraft, riddled with bullets and critically damaged. Seriously wounded, he was immediately dispatched to the nearest hospital and evacuated to Paris. After his recovery, he was put in charge of the Aero-Gunnery School at Clermont-Ferrand.

Fortunately, by then, much of the horrific carnage had already taken place. In November of 1918, the Great War was over. Grateful to be alive, Robert and Ernest returned to the United States. They devised business strategies based on what they had seen in Europe. Their principal observation was the significant volatility in foreign exchange rates resulting from the war. In the early twentieth century, it was still common for banks to quote different exchange rates for foreign currencies. Financial intermediaries could profit from arbitraging the variations in rates before the markets reached equilibrium, especially across continents. Along with Ernest's brother, the duo seized the opportunity and opened a modest shop called Henderson Brothers-Bankers-Foreign Exchange.[135] A few large conversion arbitrages provided the shrewd young entrepreneurs with the nest egg to pursue more promising ideas.

One country's currency in particular had moved predominately in one direction. In the aftermath of WWI, the German mark was decimated by the debt and sanctions imposed on a defeated Germany under the Treaty of Versailles. Robert and Ernest observed this firsthand as the war came to a close and perceptively monitored its regression in the following decade. They soon realized that importing goods of all types in hyper-inflated marks, then selling them at a reasonable price in increasingly stronger dollars in the U.S. could be lucrative.

Soon the young men were importing everything from razor blades to paper-fiber suits for medical purposes, and selling them at a tidy profit. They even inquired about importing German police dogs, and although they didn't formally place an order, about fifty canines soon arrived at a port in Boston! Fortunately, the dogs were eventually sold to the public and Robert and the Henderson brothers resumed their thriving import business.

A couple years later, competition in the importing industry became increasingly fierce. Realizing they couldn't count on the lucrative disparity in currencies forever, they turned their attention to yet another strategy. By the end of the 1920s, the radio had become an entertainment phenomenon and technological advances soon made them available to homes across the world. In the early twentieth century, many homes in the Unites States still did not have electric power, but in addition to advancements in airplane and automobile technology, the electric grid expanded into even the most rural areas. No invention was better positioned to take advantage of this than the radio.

Ernest's experience as a radio operator during the war, their combined experience refurbishing cars, and established contacts with parts suppliers left them perfectly suited to capitalize on the radio boom. They started buying surplus vacuum tubes and reselling them via mail order. Business soared. At one point, World Radio Corporation in Boston bought such a large quantity, the company decided that simply turning itself over to Moore and Henderson was preferable to paying the bill. The local papers boasted about the Harvard boys who turned $1,000 into a corporation controlling $30 million in assets. What the press neglected to mention was that World Radio Corporation was leveraged to the hilt.

Nevertheless, the most admirable quality of their business relationship is how dynamic and nimble they were. The frugal team managed to pay down the debt and even raise some surplus cash. They constantly adapted their business structure, responding to new trends and taking advantage of resources that closed the gap between themselves and larger corporations, like mail order and radio/print advertisements.

Hard work, thrift, and gumption paved the way for them to seamlessly transition from foreign exchange, to importation, to hardgoods assembly and resale. In 1926, they expanded to wholesale purchasing fine walnut cabinets, tubes, and other components, then assembling complete radio sets for mail-order customers. Many customers preferred their radio sets to those of larger manufacturers due to the quality, durability, and lower prices.

The fruits of their collective labor allowed Robert and Ernest to turn some personal attention to starting families, and their steadfast approach to preserving capital would prepare them for a severe shock to the global economy in just a few years' time. For while the duo was capitalizing on the radio boom comparable to today's smartphones, the U.S. stock market was experiencing a frenzy of its own.

Prior to the 1920s, the extension of credit from banks to ordinary citizens was largely forbidden and also culturally shunned. In the "Roaring Twenties," however, boundaries were being crashed through in all walks of American society culturally, technologically, and financially. By the end of the '20s, traders on Wall Street became infatuated with a seemingly indomitable rise of the stock market. But unlike the previous century, buying stocks was no longer confined to bankers and the societal elite. The mania spread like wildfire to ordinary citizens and soon the proverbial butcher, baker, and candlestick maker were getting in on the act before tremors in the markets surfaced near the decade's end.

On Black Tuesday, October 29, 1929, the roof caved in. The Dow Jones Industrial Average fell 23 percent in two days. In addition to suffering losses on credit extended to investors, banks also suffered losses on their own bets, wiping out many customer deposits. The carnage would continue over the next couple years, with the stock market plunging 89 percent from the 1929 peak until finally bottoming out in 1932, portending the Great Depression.

While the 1929 crash would wipe out billions in assets and impoverish millions, ironically this decade of turmoil created the opportunity that would catapult the Moore family into the societal stratosphere in Massachusetts. The catastrophic aftermath afforded Robert and Ernest a golden opportunity to set their sights on larger game by capitalizing on seizures in the credit markets.

The Moore family—Left to right: William, Eleanor, John, Robin, Robert, and Marcia.

The partners deployed the hard-fought liquidity of World Radio Corporation to purchase controlling stakes in other investment companies drastically weakened in the Depression. In 1931, Robert and Ernest created their own investment company, snapping up defaulted securities and impaired common stocks of companies that still retained a sliver of hope of recovery. Owning stakes in corporations across multiple industries instantaneously provided Robert and Ernest direct investment in many American corporations starved for vanishing liquidity.

In the early 1930s, scores of banks simply shut their doors as a consequence of bank runs reminiscent of the famous scene in *It's a Wonderful Life*. By 1933, approximately eleven thousand banks, or a staggering 40 percent of the banks in operation across the nation, went bankrupt. Many farmers went belly-up overnight as crop prices plunged in half along with other commodities across the world financial markets.

Robert and Ernest seized the moment, and although they didn't initially target the hotel industry, they shrewdly realized that real estate would recover faster than most asset classes and present a once-in-a-lifetime opportunity for those who had preserved capital in the wake of so many who had lost everything.

In 1933, they bid on the Continental, a modest but beautifully built brick hotel in the historic town of Cambridge. Although financially moribund and encumbered with liens, the aftermath of the bank holiday declared by Franklin Delano Roosevelt allowed Robert and Ernest to acquire the hotel for less than one third of its original cost from a desperate bank. Once again, the pair deployed their frugal approach toward operations, and the hotel swiftly recovered into the black.

In 1937, they acquired a significant stake in undervalued shares of Standard Investing Company. Unfortunately, a second wave of the Depression hit the financial markets, and adding fuel to the fire was a quickly approaching debt obligation. A significant portion of the company's assets were sold to settle the debt. Despite the fire sale, Robert and Ernest retained a few attractive pieces, including ownership of their second hotel, the Stonehaven Hotel in Springfield, Massachusetts. Once again, with frugality and sound management imposed, the hotel flourished.

Ernest's confidence and thrifty personality complimented Robert's unassuming yet forthright nature and shrewd business acumen as they transitioned to the hotel industry. Robert accepted the role of secretary and treasurer, eventually becoming chairman of the board. With a taste of early operational success, they began to dream of expansion.

A subsequent family-owned acquisition named the Sheraton Hotel was saddled with an enormous electric sign that proved too costly to remove. Their solution was to simply rename all of their hotel properties. This innocuous decision marked the origin of the Sheraton Hotel chain, now part of a multi-national, multibillion-dollar corporation.

By the mid-1940s, Sheraton Corporation had made hotel acquisitions throughout the Northeast and was on a roll. In 1945, Sheraton was the first hotel chain to be listed on the New York Stock Exchange and was perfectly positioned for post-WWII America. Returning soldiers, jubilant citizens, and newfound postwar affluence deluged the hotel industry with eager vacationers.

By Marcia's twelfth birthday, Robert and his partner had acquired a handful of hotels in the Boston area, notably the illustrious Copley Plaza which, as Ernest Henderson would describe, put them in the "major league."[136]

Robert Moore's steady success afforded his family the opportunity to relocate from Cambridge to Weston, then on to stately Concord. There, in 1935, they began construction of the Moore estate, intermingled with picturesque, maple tree–lined streets, dotted with colonial homes. Nearby are Harvard, MIT, and some of the most advanced medical centers in the world.

Concord lays claim to the first battle of the American Revolution, but the surrounding region is also a pinnacle of technology and academia. It proudly and seamlessly blends cutting-edge facilities and provincial charm, though it is sometimes parochial towards outsiders. Residency in Concord is a symbol of aspiration for the privileged few who can afford it, and Robert's achievements left Marcia and her siblings destined to a life of affluence in the upper crust. Money being no obstacle, Marcia attended Meadowbrook in Weston, then Concord Academy, a private high school that presently costs upwards of $50,000 per year.

The family would also acquire a summer home on the small island of Cuttyhunk, Massachusetts, the last of a chain of the Elizabeth Islands, west of the cobalt blue waters of Martha's Vineyard.

The Moore's summer home at Cuttyhunk.

Marcia's parents fell in love with the tiny island and purchased the Cuttyhunk Club from Cornelius "Connie" Wood of the American Woolen fortune. Set on nine acres, the sprawling house had once been a getaway fishing club frequented by Presidents Teddy Roosevelt, Grover Cleveland, and William Taft. The Moores moved in the following summer and bought the "Barnacle" boat barn with another couple acres, including "the knoll" overlooking Vineyard Sound.

"The Club of President Makers," 1902.
The Moore family vacation home was previously an elite fishing club. Several distinguished members pictured including Theodore Roosevelt, William H. Taft, millionaire William Woodhull, John D. Archbold, heir of Standard Oil, and his son John F. Archbold.

Robert Moore was now amassing the kind of wealth that would insulate his children from ever experiencing financial hardship. Although Marcia was stifled at times by her parents to conform to traditional womanhood, the worry over money that might prevent a young woman from devoting her life to esoteric studies had been quelled by the shrewd business ventures made by her father—rising like a phoenix out of the ashes of America's greatest hardship.

Marcia and family at Cuttyhunk.

"A STRANGE CHILD"

Young Marcia.

To her mother Eleanor, Marcia had always been a strange child. Eleanor even forewarned her first husband, Simons, just before they wed, catching the young groom off guard.

There were quite a few glimpses of her daring, willful side both physically and intellectually. Like the time Marcia entered a Christian Science Reading Room in Concord and conspicuously dropped a bunch of occult books all over the floor. She was once asked to leave because her books weren't "CS material," generating whispers and aspersions about the shocking young lady.

Another time Marcia dove in despite warning and swam about a nautical mile from Nashawena Island back to Cuttyhunk against perilously rough Atlantic currents, against her parents' forbiddance—a reckless lark talked about in the family for some time. "It's probably safe to say she was attention-seeking at times,"[137] remarked a family member. Marcia had a daredevil aspect to her personality.

Marcia with friend Sally in 1941.

With books on her shelves that might have been taboo in other households, like *Men Who Have Walked with God*, by Sheldon Warren Cheney, or works by Carl Jung whom Marcia fascinatingly discovered kept trained astrologers on staff, Marcia became exceedingly riveted by topics that might have been off limits to other kids in the still predominately Protestant and Catholic Boston area, especially at such an early age.

Young Marcia consumed books about famous clairvoyant Edgar Cayce, who some consider the true founder of the New Age movement. She became engrossed with Madame Roerich, who wrote the Agni Yoga series said to be dictated by the Master Morya, and the teachings of a mysterious Tibetan Master named Djwal Khul, later communicated to prominent esoteric writer Alice Bailey.

As a teen, she encountered the "Great Invocation," which she'd from then on describe as her personal mantra. The metaphysical world prayer about light, love, and harmony, asking the Masters of Wisdom to seal out evil, was purportedly telepathically dictated to Bailey by Djwal Kuhl in 1945, to be shared with the world.

Marcia hadn't just stumbled upon esoteric studies; it was passed down and reinforced through her bloodlines. During Marcia's upbringing, and part of family lore, was that her grandmother Jane, then in her seventies, travelled to Duke University in the 1930s to participate in Joseph Banks Rhine's famous ESP experiments. The experiments involved testing of potentially psychic participants' ability to perceive symbols on hidden cards. Rhine actually coined the term "Extrasensory Perception" and published a book by that title in 1934.

Although Robert's mother was quite persuasive and influential, the reserved Robert downplayed Jane and Marcia's fervent belief in the supernatural and the power they believed could be wielded with the practice of astrology, mediumship, and even witchcraft.

While Marcia's father, Robert, did not follow in the supernatural footsteps of his mother or the ecclesiastical footsteps of his grandfather or brother, he remained a parishioner at the First Unitarian Church in Cambridge and continued his studies of other spiritual philosophies. Despite his buttoned-up appearance, Robert's deep-seated faith and philosophical attitude toward all religions would remain an outward part of his personality and become a perpetual topic of conversation in the frequent correspondence between Marcia and her parents.

Robert also established formal relationships with the Theosophical Society and Alice Bailey's Arcane School. Founded in 1923, it offered an esoteric correspondence course located on Wall Street. Mr. Moore made sizable donations to the Lucis Trust, established by Alice and her husband Foster Bailey. Despite some current-day conspiracy theories that the organization espoused Luciferianism or was associated with satanic rituals, its purpose was to advance arcane knowledge and promote charitable works.

Like Helena Blavatsky, Alice Ann Bailey escaped both an unhappy aristocratic upbringing and marriage in England in the early twentieth century to pursue her true calling: esoteric writing and charitable service. When Bailey was just a teen, she claimed to have been visited metaphysically by a man she described as one of the Masters of Wisdom, Koot Hoomi, an experience that would change her life and usher her down the spiritual path.

Bailey became influenced by Helena Blavatsky's writings, joining the Theosophical Society in 1918. However, a few years after becoming a member, she'd part ways due to disenchantment with infighting, sectarianism, and stricter rules about who could be admitted.

After breaking ties, Alice Bailey continued to author several books she claimed were telepathically dictated by Djwal Khul. Above all, Bailey devoted her life to writing about the synchronicity of human spirituality to the solar system, the power of meditation, and the importance of humble self-sacrifice. In her unfinished autobiography, she wrote, "Looking back, I can imagine nothing more appalling than the perpetuation of the Victorian era, for instance, with its ugliness, its smugness, and the excessive comfort of the upper classes (so-called) and the frightful condition under which the labouring classes struggled."[138]

Robert Moore became a bit torn as he also remained a member of the Theosophical Society. In letters to the Baileys, he lamented the infighting between the very people who were supposed to be focused on tolerance of diverse beliefs. Marcia's father had become a personal acquaintance of the Baileys, even serving as somewhat of an instructor for the Arcane School by reviewing student papers, in addition to indexing chapters of Bailey's books.

While Robert did not express much interest in Bailey's astrological concepts, his young daughter did fervently, perhaps in an attempt to set herself apart and establish her own identity. Like Marcia, Bailey was a Gemini, and in the autobiography, she wrote: "This always means a conflict between the opposites—poverty and riches, the heights of happiness and the depths of sorrow, the pull between the soul and personality or between the higher self and the lower nature. ... I have never lived for any length of time in one place, for the Gemini person is always on the move."[139] Marcia likely identified with Bailey's depiction based on her own feelings of duality, restlessness, and reluctant acceptance of a life of affluence.

Marcia became a personal acquaintance of Alice Bailey and in 1949, at age twenty-one, wrote asking her advice about whether becoming vegetarian would make her a more devout student of ancient wisdom. Bailey rejected the notion but emphasized that practicing vegetarianism would be beneficial at the time of "initiation," and for the purpose of psychic work on the astral plane.

In an excerpt from Bailey's reply, she advised Marcia: "You can be deeply spiritual and a real healer—if that is where you feel your service lies—and eat exactly what you like. It is not the physical discipline that you and I so much need; that is for people in the early stages of the Probationary Path and, believe me, Marcia, you have left that behind. You are working on the Path of Discipleship."[140]

The timing of these influences in Marcia's early life was profound. It was undoubtedly influential and confidence-building for a preeminent mystic like Alice Bailey to acknowledge her as working on the path toward discipleship.

Moore's mentor also wrote, "I want to make it easier for such disciples in the future, and to 'debunk' the nonsense put out by many esoteric (so-called) schools of thought. The claim of discipleship is ever permissible; it gives nothing away and only carries weight if backed by a life of service."[141] Bailey even paraphrased her response to Marcia's letter in her autobiography on the topic of vegetarianism. She urged Marcia to "walk the walk" beyond mere study.

Sadly, just two months after her response to Marcia, Alice Bailey died in New York City. Her death undeniably impacted Marcia, who likely felt the import and responsibility of esoteric activism suddenly thrust upon her. Given her aspirations, Marcia perhaps felt that she could be next in line of these strong female occult ambassadors, now sanctified by Bailey herself.

Over the next three decades, Marcia Moore immersed herself in myriad esoteric disciplines, dabbling in yoga, astrology, lost worlds, extraterrestrials, and reincarnation, among others, always yearning that one of them would allow her to break through. An insatiable desire to help others through metaphysics left her with a deep well of esoteric knowledge, but sadly, never the approval and adulation she craved from her parents.

FAMILY DYNAMICS

From the outset, Marcia Moore's mother favored her eldest son, Robin, and youngest son, John, over Marcia and her other brother, Bill. No matter how incompetent or foolishly Robin or John behaved, Eleanor tolerated no criticism of them.

Eleanor had fairly conservative midwestern attitudes owing to her Baptist grandparents. A strict fundamentalist, her grandmother taught the power of condemnation. As a result, Marcia's mother was formidable and no pushover. From a young age, Marcia learned to "weasel word," strategically slipping out from her mother's disapproval. Family members observed the dynamics of the difficult relationship between them: some love, some competition for Robert's intellectual companionship, and perhaps Eleanor's insecurities about her inferior education compared to her daughter's.

A graduate of Roycemore School in Evanston, Illinois, Eleanor was certainly shrewd but achieved little more than a finishing school education beyond the twelfth grade. Married at eighteen, she was pregnant by nineteen and saw no need or urgency to match wits, given Robert's education and philosophical knowledge.

Conversely Marcia was a voracious reader, gifted at divining the most insightful, intriguing, even salacious elements from a book. Marcia's tastes were abstruse and sophisticated from an early age.

Eleanor read avidly but mostly to entertain and advance topics of conversation around the dinner table. This may explain why Mrs. Moore cared little to join in her husband and daughter's philosophical discussions.

The children learned to wait until their mother left the table before exploring free-ranging conversation. If Eleanor didn't like the way a conversation was going, she interjected with light and cheery dinner table conversation topics, like the reproductive cycles of monarch butterflies. Robert left most dinner conversation to his wife and from the outset of their relationship, Robert and Eleanor were in lockstep.

Robert and Eleanor Moore, with Marcia in the background.

Marcia's parents met on the Fourth of July in 1923, aboard the transatlantic ocean liner SS *George Washington*. Robert was traveling to Europe on business when he met seventeen-year-old Eleanor Turner. Ellie, as friends called her, was off to Paris for the summer to study art. At least, that was the pretense. Back then, wealthy bachelors often made such voyages in the hopes of finding a suitable wife and accordingly, many mothers exploited these excursions to put their daughters' best foot forward in hopes of finding a suitor.

After port, they met up to explore the famous catacombs beneath the streets of Paris, a massive ossuary containing the bones of thousands of Parisians, some even decoratively displayed. Eleanor found it dark and spooky, but despite the macabre setting, they fell in love.

By this time, Robert Moore was seven prosperous years removed from his collegiate career at Harvard. Just four months after her eighteenth birthday, twenty-eight-year-old Robert had whisked his young bride from the modest surroundings of her conservative Chicago suburb to the fine residential town of Cambridge, Massachusetts, where she found herself in another world, married to a social climber.

It wasn't all wine and roses of course. Over the years, Eleanor believed that the horrors of WWI had affected Robert deeply, making him more aloof or emotionally detached than he otherwise might have been. Robert wasn't cold, but he wasn't demonstrative either. Years later, Eleanor would remark that she'd been terribly hurt by Robert not being present on Halloween night 1925, for the birth of their first son, Robert Jr., or "Robin" as they affectionately called him.

Believing a respectable husband should support his wife, the "manly" thing to do, Robert Moore held the position that a woman shouldn't work. The chauvinistic culture surrounding Harvard at the time merely reinforced his beliefs. The outlook was also agreeable to his traditionally raised bride. Each held a need for status and social acceptance, as Eleanor retained some childhood scars of inferiority.

It stuck with Eleanor in her formative years that when the family entertained visitors, her mother would instruct her to walk them the long way around town. Ellie was to avoid crossing the railroad tracks, their home being on "the wrong side of the tracks."[142]

Front row: Siblings Robin, Marcia, John, and William.
Middle row: Paternal grandfather and grandmother,
parents Eleanor and Robert.
Back row: Paternal uncle and aunt.

Young Marcia would grow up somewhat detached from her three brothers. The Moore estate was so spacious that she could live on the third floor separately from the boys, who were on the second. The four children "only seemed to have loyalty, and maybe affection, towards their parents; not to each other or to their children,"[143] a relative would reflect.

The Moore Children—Left to right: William,
Robin holding John, and Marcia.

Somewhat overlooked by the family, the third eldest child, William or "Bill," was mostly a nonworking geologist with a bachelor's degree from Harvard and a master's in geology from Boston University. Eventually he settled in Reno, Nevada, where he spent the rest of his life with his own family, carving out a small fortune from a chemical breakthrough in kitty litter processing. Although emotionally stilted and aloof, he had a savant-like gift for card counting, resulting in a ban from certain casinos. He also ultimately left his heirs in dire straits by squandering his share of the Moore family fortune.

Serving as confidant and dutiful son to Robert and Eleanor, their youngest, John, never wandered far physically and temperamentally from his parents. Essentially tied to his mother's apron strings, John didn't marry until age forty-five and spent most of his life on the East Coast in close proximity to his parents.

Conversely, Marcia's eldest brother, Robin, was a provocateur from a young age. Eleanor found him unmanageable. When he went off to private school in first grade, he got kicked out for trying to burn down his desk. For a time, he was sent to live with an aunt, uncle, and two cousins on the Maine coast, a wholesome, religious, musical relation with a family string quartet. The infusion of structure had little impact. Brash, opportunistic, and controversial, Robin Moore was patriotic, however, and therefore more endearing to Eleanor than the outspoken, more liberal Marcia.

Although appreciative of the beauty in Christian tradition, like a Protestant hymn called "Abide with Me (Eventide)," Marcia rejected what she considered the myopic and restrictive Christian doctrine prevalent in the first half of the twentieth century, quickly putting her at loggerheads with her mother.

Both staunch, red-blooded Republicans, Robert and Eleanor were pro-nuclear power and objected to the spreading anti-war protest marches dividing the nation in the 1960s. Eleanor would express more frustration over Marcia teaching yoga, becoming a vegetarian, and practicing astrology than about her brother Robin shooting a Viet Cong soldier point blank in cold blood while embedded with the Green Berets.

Although proud and patriotic, Marcia's father also suffered some insecurity about background and social acceptability, owing to a period his father, James Moore, spent in prison when Robert was an infant. James was a naïve and trusting soul, honest but easily used. He worked at a Boston bank where some higher-ups embezzled money and set him up to take the rap.

Marcia with her grandfather, James Lowell Moore, 1928.
Robin Moore in the background.

Robert's mother, Jane Newell, married later in life at forty, and was well educated for the times, having attended Vassar College in Poughkeepsie. With James incarcerated, she was fortunate enough to find work as a kindergarten teacher to support Robert and his brother, although it influenced young Robert's critical outlook on parental responsibilities. From then on, he objected to women working outside the home.

Although Robert stifled any career ambitions for his wife, she loved him and their lifestyle. Eleanor maintained an interest in painting, ceramics, pottery, writing, and gardening. A gifted artist, she wrote and illustrated many books including her last titled *Frontal Island* about Aruba.

"Water Baby" by Eleanor Moore, and "Girl with Lamb," by Marcia Moore. Ceramics inspired by Marcia's daughter Louisa.

Eleanor Moore's other aim in life, a duty she believed in wholeheartedly, was to be an upstanding member of society. Together Marcia's parents made for a formidable couple in Concord. They donated large sums to First Parish Church of Concord, the Concord Free Public Library, and Emerson Hospital where they were honored with a plaque.

During the town's 1965 Patriot's Day celebration, the Moores were the recipients of Concord's "Most Honored Citizens" award for befriending and assisting students from many countries and sponsoring the Concord "Declaration of Goodwill," which Eleanor helped initiate. On display at Concord Library, the declaration stated that anyone was welcome to move to Concord, regardless of race, color, creed, or religion. In reality, it was a tad smarmy. After all, how many outsiders and minorities of the time could afford Concord? The open arms also had limits. As the family knew all too well, Eleanor was known to have an itchy trigger finger for the scissors whenever she saw shaggy-haired hippie types.

Still, Eleanor was a caring soul who esteemed a sense of community. Her memberships included the Woman's Club of Concord, League of Women Voters, Ladies' Tuesday Club, Concord Antiquarian Society, and the Emerson Hospital Auxiliary. She was also co-founder of the Thoreau Lyceum in Concord, a museum and repository of Henry David Thoreau memorabilia. This all garnered her a lot of goodwill among the locals. A generous benefactor for Cuttyhunk as well, she provided an art studio to the island and served as a trustee and on the board of directors at Cuttyhunk United Methodist Church.

Marcia's mother Eleanor, with a neighbor at Cuttyhunk.

This mounting collection of achievements and social recognition held little interest for Marcia. From an early age, Miss Moore considered such a pedestrian, mundane existence anathema to her destiny. "One thing also I do know is that I'm not going to fritter my time away over coffee parties and cocktail parties and general social life…playing golf at the country club (delightful as that is) and pursuing the general round of social life with its clubs and committees and pleasant diversions,"[144] she once wrote her parents, conveying both defiance and a touch of criticism.

Miss Moore.

Although her parents were in complete unison on family matters, an unexpected dynamic emerged between Marcia and her father, which filled a need for both. While Eleanor never gave much thought to the supernatural, in the household there was one child, Marcia, in whom Robert found an outlet for discussing his esoteric interests. Almost immediately the discussions became a conduit for Marcia to impress her father and seek his approval, not to mention a way for her to stand out. Despite the special bond, Robert became increasingly concerned with his daughter's fervent interest in the occult and would periodically attempt to temper it, albeit unsuccessfully.

An extraverted and precocious child, Marcia was a fine student who displayed an early aptitude as a writer and deep thinker. By her high school years, an intense passion for esotericism was firmly entrenched in her soul. However, unlike Robert's reserved and studious nature, Marcia did not shy away from controversial thoughts or actions, at times even seeking them out.

While others at the Concord Academy might have been busy rehearsing an English madrigal in the all-girls' choir, in 1946, Marcia Moore became literary editor of *The Chameleon*, a school publication. Eschewing the trite poems and editorials objecting to consumerism submitted by the other girls, Marcia boldly published a provocative, imagined dialogue between Adolf Hitler and Judas Iscariot titled *A Conversation Piece*. Clearly hers was not the mindset of a typical eighteen-year-old girl preoccupied with socials and boy gossip. Rather, it was an early glimpse at Marcia's unbridled disposition and markedly unrestrained personality.

Always the writer, Marcia Moore, age ten. From a long line of authors.

Her outspokenness was not without consequence. It sowed early seeds of discord with her parents, especially Eleanor, who felt that her daughter was becoming increasingly insolent in the face of the well-heeled path laid out before her. After all, affluence had already been packaged and bowed. Her mother couldn't come to grips with Marcia's refusal to simply reach out and embrace it, let alone engage in anything remotely controversial.

Marcia Moore pictured before a nose job.

As her formative years unfurled, Robert and Eleanor were unsympathetic to any of Marcia's career ideas. They wanted her to settle down, become a good wife and mother, maybe do some volunteer work. Although in her teens, Marcia volunteered at a state school for the mentally disabled, it wasn't quite enough for the family to brag about and failed to impress Eleanor.

After completing only her freshman year at Radcliffe College, Marcia dropped out and married a handsome southerner by the name of Simons Roof. Succumbing to her parents' wishes temporarily satiated them, but time would prove that Marcia was too young—and far too ambitious.

FIRST HUSBAND—1950S

Simons Lucas Roof, or "Sim" as friends called him, left his South Carolina home to serve his country, and at twenty-three became the youngest U.S. Navy lieutenant commander in charge of a mine-sweeper in the South Pacific during WWII.

As the war ended, Roof was sent to the Boston Naval Hospital for malaria. An affinity for Boston set in, and he accepted a position as a superintendent of employee and public relations at the Boston Naval Shipyard. There he met Robin Moore, who like his father Robert, enlisted in the Air Force and served as a pilot.

Anecdotally, Sim would provide a glimpse into the social scene. After the war, Bostonian socialites would host wonderful weekend house parties. It was a memorable time for Sim, who years later recalled with amusement how he'd labored down to breakfast after a festive evening and was greeted by the stylish hostess with a martini at just ten o'clock one cheery morning. There was plenty of drinking and cigarettes in those days.

Robin and Simons hit it off from the outset. Marcia's gregarious older brother used to hold court at Boston's Sheraton Plaza, now the Fairmont Copley Plaza, where he was accustomed to running up exorbitant tabs hosting food, drinks, and rooms for his pals and former Harvard class-mates, including Robert F. Kennedy.

The young men informally referred to themselves as the "Copley Club" and members had some pretty wild nights, like one after heavy partying when Robin got cut off by the hotel bar. The group he was entertaining, including Simons, was three sheets to the wind. Even though they had apartments on Beacon Hill, within walking distance if one were reasonably sober, they ended up sleeping it off in a nearby park. Cognizant of "boys being boys," mother Eleanor would sometimes discreetly pay the bills so Robert wouldn't find out.

In 1946, Robin introduced Simons to his mesmerizing sister Marcia, just eighteen. By this point, Robin was quite popular and merely through the frequency of introducing people had become somewhat of an unintended matchmaker. Robin held a long list of impressive acquaintances that would only grow following his successful books, *The Green Berets* and *The French Connection*. He once joked that he could reach anyone in the world in four phone calls, except the leader of Red China. Obviously an exaggeration, but the young provocateur did know everyone who was anyone and introduced lots of people who ended up marrying, including Simons' sister to a future vice president for Ford Motor Company.

It wasn't difficult for Marcia to find Simons irresistible at first blush. Eight years her senior, Sim had done such odd jobs as modeling for advertising agencies. In the Navy, he'd been profiled as a "pin-up" boy, an eligible, handsome, "well-bred," young gentlemen—tying for first place in a military beauty contest. In addition to his movie-star smile, Sim was funny and genteel. Even if he played it up for effect at times, he wielded southern charm with a great speaking voice and was a gifted storyteller. During their courtship, Marcia and Simons became part of the jet set, featured in the society section of newspapers like the *Sunday Post* and the *Boston Herald*.

Miss Marcia Moore of Concord, and her fiance, Simons Lucas Roof of Charleston, S. C., who have chosen July 12 for their wedding day, slip off for an evening of dancing at the Sheraton.

Engaged—Marcia and Simons captured in the "Society" pages of such papers as the *Sunday Post* and *Boston Sunday Herald*.

Of all Marcia's marriages, it would be the only one her parents would approve of in the three decades that followed. Along with exceptional social skills, Sim's familial standing was suitable. Born in the foothills of the Blue Ridge Mountains of Lincolnton, North Carolina, young Mr. Roof was raised in Charleston, then moved to Rock Hill where he attended high school. He carried a good education and distinguished war record and was a suitable equal to Miss Moore. If Marcia could say she descended from Roger Williams, the founder of Rhode Island, Simons could offer three South Carolina governors, four plantation owners, a farmer with sizable land holdings, aristocrats, ministers, and writers, and detail the genealogy back generations on his side. Sim's mother came from an aristocratic Charleston family and was raised to desire good breeding.

After receiving his high school diploma at sixteen, Sim graduated with honors in comparative literature from the University of North Carolina in 1941, with a heavy concentration in philosophy and religion. The following year, he entered graduate school to study English and taught freshmen at the University of Florida. At the end of the school year, two courses short of a master's degree, he enrolled in the University of Notre Dame midshipmen's school, from which he was commissioned as an ensign in the navy.

Top to bottom: Marcia's first husband Simons Roof,
and her brother Robin Moore.

For Marcia, crossing paths with Simons would mark the beginning
of her emerging belief in fated relationships and predestined occurrences,
a conviction that would reverberate for better or worse throughout her
life. Both Marcia and Simons shared a keen interest in religion, philosophy, and esoteric studies. When it was time for her coming-out party,
Simons was her special date at the large formal gathering held at her
Concord estate, replete with an orchestra, dining, and dancing.

Marcia Moore featured in the Society section of the *Boston Herald*.

Mr. and Mrs. Robert Lowell Moore

request the pleasure of your company

at a small dance

in honor of their daughter

Miss Marcia Sheldon Moore

on Friday evening, the second of May

at ten o'clock

42 Elm Street
Concord

Please reply

Debutante Ball—Marcia and father Robert at her coming out party.

Eighteen-year-old Marcia at her debut with beau Simons Roof.

Marcia and Simons.

Just twenty days after her introduction to society, Marcia and Simons announced their engagement, an event readily blessed by her parents. Months later, they married on July 12, 1947, enjoying a fairy-tale wedding reception punctuated with a helicopter send-off right from the grounds of the Moore's Concord estate. Marcia was just nineteen.

Wedding Event—in the life and times section, *Boston Society*.

Grand Entrance—helicopter landing from the church to reception.

Oil Painting—Marcia's wedding day portrait.

Mr. and Mrs. Simons Roof.

Around 1950, the newlyweds built a house with Simons' G.I. loan, on two acres of land in Concord gifted by Marcia's parents. No need for a street number in those days, the little slab ranch was only about a thousand square feet, but later an addition was built to make it a split level.

First Home—"Land's End" on what would become
Simon Willard Road. Marcia later renamed it to "Star's
End," which her family thought pretentious.

On the surface, Mr. and Mrs. Simons Roof appeared to be a picture-perfect affluent postwar American family. Their firstborn, Louisa, arrived in 1948, followed by two sons, Christopher in 1951, and Stuart in 1953. Robert and Eleanor were pleased that their daughter had established roots and begun a family.

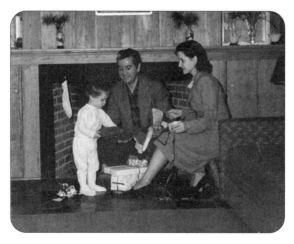

Picture perfect family.

Marcia with daughter Louisa.

Marcia, paying off what she called her "kiddie karma."

While marrying was a way for her to become her own mistress and escape her mother's dominion, beneath the still waters, powerful currents of restlessness were stirring in Marcia, who just six years removed from high school found herself settled down with three children.

During the first half of the 1950s, Marcia played the role her mother Eleanor envisioned, devoting most of her energy toward a traditional life with Simons in Concord, but soon thereafter would discover that her intense mystical ambitions would not be so easily suppressed.

Marcia looking stylish with her son.
"I simply can't begin to tell you how thrilled I am with the gorgeous fur wrap, and how deeply touched by all the care and thought you showed in selecting it. Every once in a while I have a piece of clothing that really seems to belong to me, something that expresses in a special way the way I feel I am." —Marcia Moore in a thank you letter to friends, August 24, 1954.

INDIA BECKONS

The seduction of making a name for both Marcia and Simons as esoteric philosophers proved irresistible. Soon Marcia's letters were laced with comments attempting to cajole her parents to share their metaphysical aspirations. "It certainly beats getting stuck in a mundane job in the suburbs and sweating it out over the problems of raising a bunch of children in this inflation-ridden society,"[145] she once remarked, repeating the sentiment throughout her life.

Like Marcia, Simons yearned to transition from his own "mundane job" in public relations and become an esteemed writer who could introduce a fresh perspective on the fusion of philosophy, psychology, and religion, by expounding on the Eastern elements introduced by the Theosophical Society.

Both Marcia and Simons were avid Theosophists early in their marriage, with Simons later serving as president of the Boston Theosophical Society in 1960. He was deeply interested in the relationship of meditative states to other altered states of consciousness and spent seven years studying esotericism and meditation, writing in a college essay, "I seem always to have been aware, even as a child, of a sense of life-mission. This was initiated and nourished by sporadic mystical experiences, beginning in my pre-kindergarten years; and have been sustained and expanded for many years through meditative and related experiences."[146]

The young couple was also inspired by the popular 1946 film adaptation of W. Somerset Maugham's book *The Razor's Edge*, about an American pilot profoundly impacted by the scars of war, who foregoes a return to traditional American society by traveling to the Himalayas in search of a deeper meaning in life. Likewise, excited about the prospects and adventure of an unconventional path, Simons and Marcia formulated a plan to leave their comfortable Concord life behind and venture to exotic India, so he could research and write his first novel covering his studies of Hinduism and Buddhism, titled *Journeys on the Razor-Edged Path*.

Having also studied creative and journalistic writing, Simons did have an early taste of success getting published in numerous local magazines and college publications. Roof wrote fiction and nonfiction articles, serving four years as a nature columnist with the *Charlotte Observer* and writing poetry in the *Saturday Review of Literature*, *Evergreen Review*, *Guideposts*, *Poetry* magazine, and the *Evening Reader*. Beginning in the 1940s, he also published articles in *The Beacon* magazine, a Theosophical Society publication out of Illinois.

One day in 1955, seemingly out of the blue, Simons quit his job, setting the plan to move to India in motion—and on a collision course with Marcia's parents. To them it was extremely foolish and rash. After all, Simons had no job awaiting him overseas, and there was no guarantee that his book would even amount to much or be a surefire sell. Their son-in-law was jettisoning a secure job Robert had delivered on a silver platter as director of advertising and public relations for Sheraton Corporation of America.

Robert and Eleanor cautioned that the children would be exposed to poverty and diseases, and possibly fall behind in school with limited access to formal education and medical facilities. Eleanor even fretted about the possibility of floods in India or exotic foods that wouldn't agree with them. For all she knew, there would be poisonous snakes like in Rudyard Kipling's "Rikki-Tikki-Tavi." At two, four, and six years old, the children were simply too young in their eyes.

Amplifying her parents' concern, the couple made vague comments about staying in Ceylon at some point, suggesting they may eventually return homeward via Japan and Hawaii down the line, but provided no specifics of how long they would live abroad. For the ambitious young couple, it wasn't sufficient to merely spend a few weeks overseas; they wanted to immerse themselves in Indian culture. Simons felt it crucial to attain deeper knowledge than what was readily available through spiritual books.

It turns out there was another reason for taking the trip. "The marriage had gone on the rocks before we went to India; that held it together longer; but I unwisely stalled several more years,"[147] Simons would later reveal in personal writings.

SEEKING ENLIGHTENMENT

Despite her parents' consternation, in May of 1955, Marcia and Simons embarked for India by way of England with their three children, the youngest just two years old.

Robert's reservation about the move was limited given his own lifelong advocacy of rigorous spiritual contemplation and study. Eleanor, on the other hand, was more vociferous. She grew increasingly frustrated by Marcia's grandiose dreams, seemingly untethered to the realities of life and raising a family, intensified by the fact that she had the nerve to do it on Robert's dime. Although Simons collected a modest Navy pension, the couple predominantly covered their expenses with Marcia's stipend from Robert, leaving them entirely beholden to her parents.

Initially, Marcia and Simons revealed that their stay in India would likely last only a few months, but this became difficult for her parents to pin down. Their ultimate destination was Santiniketan, a small but culturally rich town in the Indian state of West Bengal, about ninety miles north of Calcutta. Unfortunately, emigration hinged on confirmation of visas formally approved by the Indian government, a matter they heedlessly left unsettled given the consequence of delay or denial.

As they would learn, waiting for India's bureaucratic wheels to turn was often a frustrating, time-consuming process. Simons urgently asked for definitive news about their visas until the last moment but received no confirmation. As a result, they were forced to depart for Karachi and travel en route to the Himalayas, dependent upon one-year Pakistani visas previously secured.

Already getting off on the wrong foot, the development troubled Robert, who regularly kept abreast of international news and political instability. Marcia's parents became increasingly concerned for their small children, owing to the fact that they had been rerouted to a nation less welcoming to Westerners. Additionally, the "Red Menace" of communism, considered an existential threat to the United States in the 1950s, had infiltrated a significant portion of eastern Pakistan.

The visa delays required them to remain in England a few more weeks, affording the young family the privilege to explore England in depth, including all the famous tourist spots like Big Ben and Parliament, the changing of the guards at Buckingham Palace, Piccadilly Circus, Hyde Park, and Arundel Castle. Leisure time consisted of walks along the Thames, through Oxford, Cambridge, Hampton Court, and the Royal Horticulture Gardens at Wisley.

In an obvious attempt to demonstrate his writing prowess and placate her parents that his abrupt departure from an established advertising career at Sheraton was not in vain, Simons wrote a colorful depiction of English life:

> The lack of bright color in women's clothing, and English gentlemen, always set off by a derby and a slim umbrella, who seem perpetually dressed in mourning clothes and on the way to a funeral. Gardens everywhere: window-boxes even in the downtown London shopping district; tiny gardens of wallflowers, tulips, and 'rock-garden blossoms' even in the poorest districts, sometimes in foot-square patches of soil; romantic-looking gardens around all of the lovelier homes, with a walled-in garden usually at the back; and spectacular public gardens in and near every city, town, and many villages. In the countryside, quaint little villages with thatch-topped

and tile-topped houses, old inns and pubs, and narrow streets. The vast sweep of green rolling hills and flocks of cattle and sheep. Over everything—towns, countryside, and people—an air of moderation and quiet dignity— and 40,000,000 people, who regardless of what they are doing, drop everything at four o'clock in the afternoon and relax with a spot of tea.[148]

The Roofs also enjoyed a stay at the Beach Hotel in Littlehampton, Sussex, a quaint lodge-style hotel set within walled-in gardens and situated across from a vast greensward leading to a broad, sandy shore. It marked some of their most pleasant time as family.

Often Simons took the children for adventurous walks, sang songs along the way, frolicked at the beach, or visited a nearby amusement park. "In our serene seaside interlude it seemed no time at all before we were loading fifteen pieces of baggage and ourselves into a black beetle of a car and wending our way past ancient gray walls and 'Robin Hood' woods on our journey to London, Liverpool and points East, bearing with us the happiest of memories and…all the mystery of the Orient ahead…"[149] Marcia wrote her parents.

On the train to Liverpool—children Christopher, Stuart, and Louisa.

At June's end, 1955, the family set sail from Liverpool to Karachi, Pakistan, aboard the RMS *Caledonia*. Cognizant of her parents' wariness, Marcia made sure to emphasize the positives of life abroad, relaying an account of ship life as altogether delightful. "We have about three hundred passengers and countless Indians to wait on them, and attend to every need with unobtrusive efficiency. They all wear dazzling white uniforms and the officers have just switched to their white tropical shorts. Fans are everywhere and each room is kept supplied with ice water, everything looks fresh painted, spotless and shining. It is really a beautiful ship and built for comfort. We are quite an international outfit—the crew are mostly Indians, officers and women are Scotch and the passengers about equally British and Indian and Pakistani with a small sprinkling of other nationalities."[150]

Despite the first-class accommodations, letters revealed a glimpse that Marcia was not oblivious to strife and poverty in the world around her, as she commented on the unfortunate circumstances of sixty ship workers. All Roman Catholics from the Portuguese colony of Goa, a small coastal enclave on the west Indian coast, they saw their families but once a year. It struck her that, like them, most were young, married, and with small children, unable to return home while hostility continued between India and Portugal. They were even restricted from sending money to their families.

Additionally, Marcia wrote about the omnipresent repression of women encountered overseas. "The Indian women look very exotic in their gorgeous saris and the Pakistanis in silken pajamas and flowing garments but they don't seem to have much fun. Mostly they huddle together in one of the sitting rooms and talk to each other. The rest of us swim and play games and enjoy the view from the deck."[151]

Expanding their horizons, the confines of the ship afforded them the opportunity to encounter diverse and interesting people they certainly wouldn't meet back in Concord, including Hindus, Muslims, Sikhs, and even a Parsee or Zoroastrian fire worshipper.

The Roofs became intrigued by depictions of their next port of call, Port Said, at the entrance to the Suez Canal in northeast Egypt, which they were told was one of the wickedest cities in the world. Later, Marcia hoped to do a bit of shopping in Aden, where a charming Indian girl offered to help her pick out a sari. The illusion of their leisurely voyage was abruptly shattered, however.

Upon approach of Port Said, a low-set city glittering across the water, the peculiar smell of an unwashed multitude assaulted their senses. They docked at sunset near a Woolworth's and noticed a neon Johnnie Walker sign, but it was deceptive, for this was an entirely Eastern city. "We disembarked briefly that evening and were immediately surrounded by a voracious crowd of scroungy peddlers, many wearing what appeared to be long night-shirts and all trying to sell us 'peectures' chcap jcwclry and bags as though their last breath depended on it,"[152] Marcia wrote in a 1955 letter. Mixed among the knock-offs and poorly fabricated items were Swiss jeweled watches, evidently stolen or smuggled, and sold for a few dollars among suitcases made of decent leather but poorly stitched. They stuck to window shopping, though one "golly-golly man"[153] managed to separate them from some loose change.

Marcia had a bad habit of flippantly revealing worrisome aspects of their surroundings, unmindful of her parents' mounting concern, even when sympathizing with the oppressed. "Port Said attracts the scum of the earth and of course the Farouk regime ground the people down even more," she observed, recalling the corrupt monarch who had been overthrown three years earlier. "Although we stayed mostly in the new nd better part of town we still got a good dose of the fabled oriental squalor. Have seldom seen so many little children everywhere. Some about Chris and Stuart's ages were picking for rags in the dump and others wandered about barefoot and filthy among the goats in the streets. The women were the worst sight of all, many swaddled in heavy black veils all over, in spite of the heat and wandering about like spectres."[154]

Exacerbating the alarm suddenly thrust upon Eleanor, the visa problems forced a three-week stay in Karachi, Pakistan. In addition to the abject poverty, susceptibility to disease, and ill-prepared visa status, the family was now in a foreign land beset by diverse, often conflicting, religious and political factions. "Karachi has grown ten times since the war so you can imagine some of its problems," Marcia wrote. "You can't walk down any st. without seeing people sprawled all over sleeping—whole families live on the sidewalks for mile upon mile with only rags or card-board over their heads and neighbors a few feet away."[155]

Attempting to reassure her parents, Marcia reported that friends in high places were aiding them, such as the Swamis of Ramakrishna Mission and a close confidant of Jawaharlal Nehru, India's prime minister. Their second application for entrance to India evidently languished in some clerk's drawer, but the third was processed, Marcia believed, thanks to their new influential friends. Acquaintances from the ship graciously helped them arrange cholera inoculations, a comment that likely simultaneously worried and relieved her parents. Fortunately for the young family, the gears of the Indian bureaucratic machine finally began to dislodge.

A postcard from Marcia to her parents, from their hotel in New Delhi.

The fall of 1955 found the Roofs ensconced in a spacious suite at Hotel Imperial, New Delhi, spread over fifty acres of sprawling land with well-maintained lawns. The hotel manager assigned them the manager's suite, where they had an entire wing to themselves. All of this for the five of them came out to slightly more than eleven dollars a day. "We are living like royalty and becoming thoroughly spoiled so you can see why we are content to remain here a while at least," Marcia wrote her parents. "The only sour note is the grinding poverty of the people.... The beauty of the arts and crafts is in almost incredible contrast to the abysmal ugliness and filth of the villages and ramshackle city tenements. On postcards they look quaint and picturesque—much, I imagine as a visitor from Mars might find a Haarlem slum 'quaint.'"[156]

They relocated to Oberoi Maidens Hotel, widely considered the best hotel in Delhi, accentuated by tall leafy trees and gardens, and a swimming pool where the family spent lots of time cooling off. One unforgettable morning, they looked out of their third-story suite to a view of clothes strewn all over the rooftops. Monkeys had gotten into one or more of the rooms during the night, they'd learn from the manager, who advised they be careful and close their windows before bedtime. It was thrilling to think that monkeys were living in the trees all around them in a city!

After a three-month stay in Delhi, the family resettled to Nedou's Hotel in Srinagar, Kashmir, well known for beautiful gardens and abundant lakes but also a protracted religious and cultural tug-of-war between Hindus, Buddhists, and Muslims that continues to this day. Additionally, continued fear of communism was pervasive back in the States in 1955. India made overtures toward siding with the Soviet Union after condemning a few public comments about India from the Eisenhower administration.

That fall, a few thousand unarmed Indian activists led a non-violent liberation march in Goa, which had been under Portuguese control for over four centuries. Portuguese police opened fire, killing more than twenty people, inciting an Indian nation hungry for complete independence post-British withdrawal. Shortly thereafter, U.S. Secretary of State John Foster Dulles referred to Goa as a "province" of Portugal rather than a colony, a comment construed as insensitive and inflammatory given India's long history of colonization and subjugation by foreign invaders.

In addition to continued spiritual discourse, Robert would send Marcia newspaper clippings and copies of *Newsweek* to discuss these current events, with the ulterior motive of reminding them that they were far removed from the comfort and security of America, particularly

Concord. This backfired as Marcia sometimes sided with India or criticized U.S. foreign policy, leaving Eleanor to accuse her of being gullible and swallowing the "commie line."

Additionally, Marcia's disparaging comments about overbearing Christian missionaries aggravated Robert and more so Eleanor, who was raised a patriotic Baptist. Robert would occasionally put Marcia in her place, reminding her of all that American democracy and capitalism had afforded her. He even criticized that they were indulging in a life of leisure abroad with paid servants, in contrast to the earnest esoteric study and social work she promised when justifying their journey.

Marcia would typically acquiesce regarding the political discord but responded indignantly to the suggestion of idleness. "Your fear that our exotic life in India is spoiling us for life in Concord, Mass. is a misconception too silly even to refute. I only hope that life in Concord and Cuttyhunk is not spoiling you for an eventual trip round the world with a long stop in India to visit us! Its all a matter of how you look at it. A dhobi[iv] was a luxury but so is a washing machine and the dhobi costs us less than repair bills on the machine not counting soap, water and electricity," Marcia argued. "And I can assure you that if you are conscious of the poverty here we who are in the midst of it are not oblivious. But it has become the fashion for Americans to come to India and revel in describing the dirt and poverty so if I must go to an extreme it will be the opposite one."[157]

[iv] A washing servant.

"Exotic Life"—Marcia with her daughter Louisa, 1956.

Meanwhile, on the status of the book, Simons reported, "I know you are curious too about the publication possibilities for the book. I think I mentioned that the literary agency (one of the largest in New York) calls it 'very publishable'. My last letter from them says that a large publishing company now has its editors reading the book; the company has had the book about four weeks. Still no word. Naturally, we'll let you know what happens; in the meantime, just keep praying, please! The agency tells me that 'it's now just a matter of time' in finding a responsive publisher; and we hope the agency is right!"[158]

While for Simons' sake everything was riding on his book being published, Marcia was the one actually getting a travel piece into print. Robert had asked her to write a few letters about her exploits in India that he could furnish to his friends at the *Concord Journal*. Using the opportunity to experiment and flaunt her writing ability, the following was published in a September issue: "But the most refined—the ultimate—in gourmet connoisseurship of the lotus is to drift through a dreamy afternoon in a shikara along winding waterways until the mountains are haloed by the sunset glow with a diffused inner fire. The lakes are then transfigured into a realm of strange perceptions and a mauve glamour of rippling light reflects from a sky below the waters. Then the aura of enchantment cast over the vale breaks into a scintillating spectrum of rhapsodic tones that yearn like the surging chromaticisms of the music of Tristram and Ysolde and melt into an ecstasy in which duty and morality dissolve in a bliss of rapturous imaginings."[159]

Infusing mythology with concepts such as transformation, synthesis, and existentialism, she clearly attempts to evoke a dreamy, otherworldly, mystical quality in her writing. "Still, for the one who has the strength to sublimate this sensuously elusive allure of the past, the vanishing of clearcut outlines and the soul's surrender to a dimly sensed glory can become like the prenatal stage of an expanded existence. It is as though within the protective mold of conventionality, a vital inner self stirs and wakens to grow toward a new vision of light even as the crawling caterpillar must soften to a liquid jelly before it can re-form to burst from the chrysalis as the butterfly which flies in the face of the sun."[160]

From Chrysalis to Butterfly
"Transformation"—a constant theme in
Marcia Moore's said philosophy.

It marked an early glimpse of Marcia's future writing talent, which would crystallize upon return to the States years later. While perhaps merely laden with ethereal adjectives and lacking profundity, years later it would prove to be a successful style to attract a certain readership interested in metaphysics.

Robert passed along Marcia's work to Indian newspaper correspondent Eddie Bernays, the "father of modern public relations," who responded, "I enjoyed reading Mrs. Roof's letters from India. She shouldn't be wasting her time chasing mystic moonbeams. She should be writing travel books. Personally I think she writes even better than John Gunther."[161]

Subconsciously it may have become a mounting point of resentment between Marcia and Simons. After all, he had abdicated a promising advertising career against the wishes of his new in-laws who were paying their way. Now he felt his wife was upstaging him instead of supporting his writing at every turn, rubbing salt in the wound.

Marcia abruptly dispelled the suggestion from her parents that she consider writing professionally, saying, "No, I most definitely am not writing a book but I do try to put time in on the esoteric work. That sounds very impractical and it is impossible to describe but you will see it bear fruit someday."[162]

MOUNTING PROBLEMS
IN INDIA

The Roof family finally reached their intended home, relocating to Santiniketan in November 1955. Marcia immediately became enchanted with their new location, about ninety miles from Calcutta, home of Indian poet Rabindranath Tagore's international university.

She delved into esoteric astrology, gushing, "Dearest Daddy…sometime I want to do your chart. Do you know at what time you were born? I think it must have been early in the evening because you almost certainly have Cancer as a rising sign—same as mine. Its motto is 'I will build a lighted house and therein dwell.'…Well right now the Hindi and social welfare work are taking full time but I shall get to this eventually."[163]

In the summer, Marcia enthusiastically informed her parents that Simons' book concept had drawn interest from publisher Simon & Schuster. Now it was just a matter of reworking his manuscript. Meanwhile, Marcia attended lectures at Sriniketan University on rural economics, psychology, and craft making. She studied Hindi, Bengali, Kashmiri, and Sanskrit by means of a tutor three days a week, closing letters with "Namaskar!" which is to say, "I salute the divinity within you."[164]

A silk Marcia had made to order in India for her parents.

She fell in love with Indian culture and the deeply ingrained, ancient meditative practices that are part of everyday life. While most travelers from America's elite ventured only to tourist spots or stopped short of anything they considered uncivilized, Marcia embraced seeing how the other half lived, albeit from the comfort of comparatively posh surroundings.

Her parents considered it all foolish, and every slip in Marcia's letters became fertile ground for criticism. "Somehow I just can't take housekeeping very seriously here—it all seems like playing house," Marcia wrote. "There is a little servant girl who sweeps and scrubs the entire house each day, scrubs the pots and pans and looks after the children.

She is absolutely the most gorgeous looking creature I have ever seen in my life with a figure any Hollywood star would envy, clean as can be, and it would be well worth the 20¢ a day we pay her (considered very good wages) just to keep her around as a decoration."[165]

Referring to the young servant girl as a bauble irked her parents. In another display of the friction between them, Eleanor replied derisively about the perceived lack of attention Marcia was paying to her children, and with disapproval of her exploitation of the cast of servants she was employing as a result of India's poverty, using Robert's money. Marcia replied defiantly but deferentially. "Naturally I know you don't really think we are stupid and yet I feel a certain frustration in trying to convey our basic attitudes.… If you could see the marvellous figure and posture our little 'slave girl' has you would probably go right out and have a well dug so you could haul water too. I have never seen a more beautiful face and form and she is clean and neat as anyone could ask."[166]

On the left: The most beautiful girl Marcia said she had ever seen.

Beyond the hired help, Marcia's increasing obsession with mysticism was met with a constant overhang of Eleanor's disapproval. Drawing from a personal account of some acquaintances in their social circles, Robert attempted to intervene and smooth things out, cautioning, "Did you know that their mother, Frances' sister is right here in Boston but is a member of an esoteric group and says her group meetings and study work are much more vital to her than her children and more important for her attention on a day like Christmas? A fanaticism of this sort seems to be an ever present danger in many cases, yet I firmly believe that Spiritual advancement and effective school study work requires a background of a certain amount of normality in life."[167] Robert tried to assure his daughter that there wasn't any reason why she and Simons couldn't be themselves and engage in esoteric studies back home. But Marcia knew that she couldn't legitimately understand yoga and esoterism until she walked in the footsteps of renowned mystics who came before her, like Alice Bailey.

In a lengthy letter revealing deep insight into Marcia's restless feelings, she wrote: "Our children will not grow up neurotic from neglect… and you can count on that. Now let me make a few 'points' and I would like to know what you think about them. As far as living in the 'real' world goes, or even that of group activity which is the Aquarian ideal, is that the same as participating in a great deal of outer activity. Personally I get more of a group sense of creative accomplishment from one minute of meditating with my spiritual group that I could from a year of work for the League of Women Voters or even—the Unitarian Church!"[168]

Marcia had made up her mind about her ambitions amounting to more than a mere hobby, refusing to turn a blind eye to the wretched poverty while benefiting from their culture:

> But there is another world of which I have seen a good bit the last couple of years though not its full extent by any means. This is the world of the poor—of women who look fifty when they are twenty five, children with legs bent like soft candles, and oozing sores, twelve year old children blind from weaving rugs in poor light—I know I sound over dramatic but these things do happen. Now which of these worlds is "realer" I honestly don't know (I'm beginning to hate that word) but since a

choice must be made then I choose the latter. You must at least admit that it is considerably larger!

Perhaps, however, that will not be. Probably I shall return to Concord and get caught up in our big beautiful American way of life and forget all about it. After all our taxes are helping those people and can't I be just as useful doing Friendly Aid work? I will forget that I have spent eight hours a day on language studies (mostly at night after the children are sleeping) and all the bright dreams of doing something "big" for others. No, I won't forget but it will all look slightly ridiculous as I walk along the Milldam and stop to chat and make my purchases. And I'll give a sigh of relief that at last I've gotten over that adolescent dream. But there may be an occasional bad moment when I see and hear of those who are doing the great things I might have done. And of course there will be those years when the children are grown and it is too late to begin again—and it will be too late for what I have in mind.[169]

KALIMPONG

The spring of 1956 saw the Roof family resettling to Kalimpong. Their new abode named "Ahava" included a nice garden with strawberry beds in front and papaya trees in the backyard. Inscribed on the doors were uplifting words like "Power" and "Redemption." It was cozy, very "hill station," colonial in atmosphere. "The house is one of these elegant delapidated affairs with bad pipes and lovely woodwork. We have been a bit extravagant investing in some gorgeous linins...brass and bright bedspreads etc. which will make it all very impressive and take attention away from the cracks in the walls and lack of rugs etc. And of course the view is beyond description.[170]... This guest house is just like a little piece of England picked up and set down in the midst of this gorgeous pagan wilderness," Marcia described in letters to her parents, in hopes of winning them over. "If you should decide to visit us this is the ideal place.... You would not feel at all that this is India—is entirely Tibetan in atmosphere."[171]

They then took up residence at a house named "Cargill," on the grounds of Dr. Graham's Homes, a Scottish Presbyterian missionary school established by Reverend Dr. John Anderson Graham at the turn of the twentieth century. It provided a small measure of relief to Marcia's parents that they had relocated to a more modern facility that included a school for Westerners at an important stage for the children.

"Here we are in Kalimpong and all is well—in fact better than we had even dared hope," Marcia reported. "These are by far the most spectacular mountains we have seen anywhere. Kanchenjunga looms up outside the window of our room here and three or four ridges down we can just see Darjeeling. I simply can't begin to describe the absolute beauty of this place."[172] The Teesta River was visible far below.

The surrounding skyline, awe-inspiringly framed by the snow-covered peaks of the Himalayas, was highlighted by Mount Kanchenjunga, the third highest mountain in the world. The surrounding inhabitants consider the sacred mountain to be a deity, and legend has it that there is a valley of immortality hidden within its peaks. They were just twenty-eight miles from the Tibetan border, she and Simons liked to boast.

Up in the clouds—Kanchenjunga, Himalayas.

The estate included a chicken coup and well-tended garden with lots of cosmos, marigolds, and gardenia. "This morning I saw some chickens running around in the kitchen so I guess we'll have chicken for dinner,"[173] she wrote her parents. With an ex-British Army cook and helpers, the Roof family enjoyed English-style cream soups, roast chicken, and pound cake, plus four o'clock tea. There was also a gardener and a sixteen-year-old Anglo-Indian ayah who made their stay pleasant, allowing Marcia to play memsahib.[v] "These Indian servants are practically mind readers in the way they anticipate every desire!"[174] she reported.

The Roof household's cook during their stay in Kalimpong, 1957.

It wasn't always smooth sailing. Occasionally Simons would have to break up fights between cook and gardener, who apparently didn't

---

[v]   Commonly defined as a white upper-class woman living abroad in India.

like the chickens scratching around the flower beds. They got along so poorly that they'd sometimes chase each other around the yard with knives or machetes.

To the chagrin of her folks yet again, letters hinted at prolonging their stay. "The thought of going back to Concord really impresses upon me how spoiled I've become with servants, flowers everywhere, mountains and so many congenial friends here. But one never knows what the future holds and perhaps someday Simons will get an Indian assignment,"[175] Marcia wrote.

By virtue of being American and at the right place at the right time, suddenly they were the center of attention, visiting with a lot of interesting people. Simons wielded a great voice and told remarkable stories. They were both socially skilled and made acquaintances of Rabindranath Tagore's children and Gandhi's children. They befriended the companion to Gandhiji, founder of India's freedom movement. Marcia and Simons enjoyed tea with the former maharaja and maharani of Jammu and Kashmir. They knew famous photographer Margaret Bourke-White, who was in India doing social welfare work, and visited the only woman governor in India at her beautiful palace, where they watched her trained dogs perform a variety of tricks.

They also interacted with such interesting dignitaries as Prince Peter of Greece and Denmark. "He is a psychologist studying Polyandry in Tibet. His wife is a demonoligist and calls herself a witch," Marcia wrote of her intriguing new connections. "People here are quite frankly terrified of her as she deals in the lowest most obscene and horrible forms of black magic. Fortunately we didn't meet her as her magic is now rebounding and she is sick all the time.[176]... They had also an interesting collection of anti-Western propaganda and in one paper he was described as being 'a nest of spies'...At least two or three people have told us they were likely spies."[177]

"Friends in high places"—Marcia pictured with the Princess of Kashmir.

At one point, Marcia was even personally blessed by the Dalai Lama, just twenty-one years old at the time. A Buddhist monk procession, accompanied by the Dalai Lama and his retinue of forty, clad in orange brocade and fur-lined caps, passed through Kalimpong. The whole scene was spectacular, with thousands of Tibetans, Bhutanese, Sikkimese, and hill people from all over spinning prayer wheels, blowing trumpets, beating drums, chanting, and praying.

At a procession for the Dalai Lama, Marcia Moore
photographed with a French monk.

"Needless to say there was also deep emotion as the crowds filed
by to be individually blessed, even to the extent that a child was tram-
pled to death in the general confusion," Marcia described. "A Tibetan
man had been run over by a car and was bleeding all over the road and
almost dead.… So we tried to have him put in another car but the driver
wouldn't take him as he was afraid the blood would stain the upholstery.
I thrust some rupees into our driver's hand and told him to pick him up
and take him to the hospital but he would not go near the scene. Finally
a jeep did pick him up after considerable persuasion. And all the people
involved were wearing the red ribbon showing they had just received the
Dalai Lama's personal benediction! Ah, Mother India!"[178]

Life in India was turning out to be an ideal situation from Marcia's
vantage point. While Simons stewed over the book, and with Robert and
Eleanor kept at arm's length, she freely dabbled in university and yoga
classes, as long she reminded her parents that the kids were happy with
everything under control.

Marcia was even asked to address a class on various topics regarding American life and relished the opportunity, mostly to set the record straight that American women are not all idle memsahibs—and perhaps enlighten the predominantly male class of the notion that granting women freedom will not result in a complete breakdown of society. Of course, the students were unaware that Marcia had been accused of just such idleness by her parents. "I don't particularly relish the idea of giving lectures but consider it a service opportunity and therefore a duty,"[179] Marcia told them.

This all allowed her to cut her teeth for lecturing on astrology and past-life regression years later in Boston and across the United States. Most importantly, Marcia began stacking up experiences that would provide the bona fides to write and speak about the occult back in America, paving the way for her career in the coming decades. "When I lived in India…" she'd often say to eager listeners throughout her life.

In addition to touristy sites like the Taj Mahal or side trips to Ladakh, two places in India held special significance in occult circles. One, in the Kullu Valley near Kashmir, was the former residence of Theosophist Helena Roerich, where she wrote the Agni Yoga series purportedly dictated by Master Morya. The second, a beautiful Buddhist monastery nestled along a mountainside, was supposedly the dwelling of the mysterious figure known as Djwal Kuhl, also known as "The Tibetan." Kuhl was considered by the Theosophical Society as one of the few sacred Masters of Wisdom, and Alice Bailey claimed that he telepathically dictated much of the material that would comprise her published esoteric writings. They'd also visit the Theosophical Society headquarters in Adyar near Chennai, formerly Madras.

Letters began revealing important insight into Marcia's continued spiritual metamorphosis, clearly influenced by the same prominent esoteric figures like Helena Roerich and Helena Blavatsky, that Robert and her grandmother Jane had introduced her to at a young age.

As 1955 came to a close, Marcia cast aside any lingering pretense in a personal letter to Robert, with an outspoken belief in reincarnation. "Someday—perhaps when I understand it better myself—I shall tell you all that happened in Kashmir. Or perhaps circumstances will reveal it. It was for me like a kind of recapitulation, a remembrance of things past with a vision of what these might mean in the future. It is, of course, pretty obvious that most of us have had Indian incarnations—but this one I think has special implications, in terms of this present life."[180]

Much to her parents' dismay, the probability of a return to traditional life in Concord was becoming increasingly remote.

TIPPING POINT

The summer of 1956 became a critical juncture for Simons as his writing prospects began to sour. In May, Marcia had informed her parents, "Still no word from Simons' publisher—well anything can happen and it is a touchy subject. But the waiting is getting to be rather a strain."[181]

Meanwhile, Marcia's brother Robin began achieving comparatively more publishing success back home, beginning a bit of a sibling rivalry. Robin, who worked in the public relations department at Sheraton, was also elected to Sheraton's board of directors, demonstrating that it was possible to prudently maintain an executive career while moonlighting as a writer. Marcia praised him: "We are so delighted to hear that Robin's book will go into print. Please congratulate him for us. It is wonderful news."[182]

Secretly, however, she'd inform a friend, "Glad you haven't read Pitchman. Please don't!!"[183] The story was about a womanizing TV ad exec who unscrupulously tries to get ahead in the TV biz. Robin often wrote about the provocative and seedy side of life. Her parents caught wind of the criticism, forcing Marcia to explain, "Needless to say I don't believe that vulgarization and sacrifice of integrity holds the key to success but one can certainly build up a case for that point of view."[184]

The feedback marked another source of disharmony between her and her parents. "One thing, however, did rather distress me and that is that you found my reaction to the book of Robin's 'shocked and explosive,'" Marcia wrote. "There wasn't a great deal I felt I could say as it is not a way of life that is particularly well known to me (though I may have seen more of it than you would think) and so I went on to indicate ways in which I felt the theme was of world wide application, i.e. the trend toward vulgarization of art forms for the masses. But that was no criticism of the book!"[185]

Even Simons tried to explain to Robin, "My reaction to the story, which you'll expect from an old fashioned moralist who likes to see the 'good men' get the best of 'the bad', is now that you've shown how a nice guy can become an s.o.b., you'll try the other side of the picture and show how an s.o.b. can become a nice guy!"[186]

They didn't have much of a leg to stand on, however, considering the status of Simons' book. The silence from the publisher caused stress and tension that mounted with each passing month. In June, Marcia finally reported the devastating blow to Simons' dream: "We finally had word about the book from Simon and Schuster—bad news I regret to say. They wanted Simons to make the book more intimate and personal in tone which he tried to do for three months in Kashmir, and finally discarded the entire three months of work. The end result was that he stepped the tone of the book up rather than down and the publishers feel that it does not have enough popular appeal. But he can not write what he does not feel and so I guess we will just have to go on waiting a while longer until he finds a sympathetic company. I have complete faith in its ultimate success but it is pretty hard for Simons now."[187]

In response, likely on behalf of Robert, Robin offered a renewed advertising position to Simons at Sheraton, given his dwindling writing prospects. Unrealistically, Simons responded conveying their future plans to stay in India.

Marcia assured her parents that Simons was enthusiastically on to his next novel, a comedy this time: "Simons is working quite cheerfully on the next opus.[188]...You will be glad to know that the next book is a novel and very very funny—I think it will surely sell. A complete change from the last one."[189] A week later she reported that "Simons is very happily at work on two books at once and both, I think are very fine and probably will appeal to publishers as well as people."[190]

The news did little to assuage Robert and Eleanor's conclusion that he had taken his shot and failed. Despite their daughter and son-in-law's objection, they felt it was time for the young family to come home.

Eventually, complications cropped up that even Marcia could no longer forestall. Louisa required eye surgery. Marcia tried to appease her mother by claiming the medical issues weren't urgent and could be delayed until the following season. Yet Marcia also revealed, "We are keeping Chris home from school for a third round of the flu has broken out and about seventy children are in the hospital with it…"[191]

Robert and Eleanor proposed that at the very least they send the children back. In addition to health issues, Eleanor was concerned that the children might not be on track for reentering school in the U.S. However, Marcia had advised, "We would like to have one more summer in the mountains and then by slow stages work our way back through southern India, Ceylon, Japan and Hawaii arriving perhaps in the spring time a year from this coming spring."[192]

By this time, Eleanor's aggravation was boiling over following the revelation that they'd extended their visas another year. Then Marcia revealed the bombshell that Louisa had contracted jaundice. "I was just on the way up to the hospital with Louisa whose eyes were looking suspiciously yellow after a week of low fever. Turned out my apprehension was justified and she has jaundice which has been going around the school in a mild form. She has had it a week or two but in such a way that we had not realized anything was wrong except a boil on the foot."[193]

Quest for enlightenment aside, Marcia was finally forced to admit that there was limited access to essential services for the children, and reluctantly wrote about more definitive plans.

Holding onto her idealized life in India to the bitter end, Marcia audaciously arranged for eight-year-old Louisa to fly back to the states alone to address her medical problems. "Our main arguments against it were expense and also the fear that if the whole family returned we might not get back to India again."[194]

18 BOSTON DAILY RECORD, WEDNESDAY, JULY 3, 1957

Here From India

Louisa with a Pan American stewardess, arriving home unaccompanied, as captured in the *Boston Daily Record.*

A chance to be "famous" went a long way toward stirring up Louisa's enthusiasm. "She is quite thrilled with the idea of the trip because it is an Adventure beyond even those the heroines of her Little Maid books are having. We will put her on the plane in Calcutta and she can go through to Boston with no difficulty. She is infinitely more sophisticated and self-reliant than I was at that age and will be quite all right.[195]... The plane goes right through with one change in London and only one or two hour stops along the way."[196]

As it turned out, on June 29, 1956, Miss Louisa Lowell Roof would become the youngest person to make a transatlantic flight unaccompanied. The event made a few newspapers, including some warm-hearted pictures.

Two months later, the rest of the family finally left India behind. As Marcia wistfully described of their departure, "even though it was only 6:15 A.M. the head of the school…and his family came to see us off and also teachers and children. Many of the children lined up along the road to wave as we went by—a sentimental parting."[197]

Reluctant to return home, they made an extended stay in Italy, where they visited associates of Alice Bailey's original group, Olga Bata, and psychiatrist Roberto Assagioli, founder of the "psychosynthesis" movement.

Meanwhile, Simons was finally coming to grips with the possibility that he might not fulfill his dream as an accomplished writer in the fields of psychology and theology. Consequently, he had devised a new plan to enroll in Harvard Divinity School, deducing that it would boost his authorship prestige to highlight such an affiliation. Given that the Moore family carried a lineage of Harvard alums, he pressed Robert to put in a good word with the admissions department, offering that it would satisfy Marcia's folks' desire for them to return to the family bosom in Concord.

However, Marcia interjected conditions for their eventual return with an air of defiance, refusing to conform back into socialite life. "I recall we had some serious conflicts over this matter so am beginning early to warn you in hopes that the going will be a bit smoother when we take up the threads of life in America again. Neither Simons nor I are getting any younger and we feel we simply can't afford to spend time and money cocktailing.… If all this is understood before we return then perhaps you will not be so disappointed in us. Incidentally I have given up drinking altogether though otherwise have acquired no new habits except a fondness for curry. It is not so much for the moral idea as because I simply can't bear to spend what amounts to two weeks salary for someone here for an evening's cocktail's."[198]

Robert and Eleanor wrote back admonishing her for portraying them as partygoers. Marcia would reply apologizing once again. "I simply can't bear to have to live with the persistant nagging feeling that you are disappointed in us because we do not and can not conform to the social standard of the community,"[199] Marcia lamented.

The feelings of inadequacy and disapproval would cast a pall over their marriage and continue to weigh on Marcia for the rest of her life.

Back in the States.

Former days of socializing left behind.

BLAME IT ON THE
BOSSA NOVA

Upon return from India, a crestfallen Simons retreated from his aspirations, reluctantly kowtowing in acceptance of a director of advertising position at Avis Rent-a-Car, then working as a commercial writer for companies like A-Car and Honeywell Computers.

The weight of Simons' dashed lifelong dream crushed his spirit. Despite having told Marcia's parents he had lost all taste for liquor, he quickly descended into chain smoking and alcoholism. Late night coping sessions of drinking and smoking would impact Simons' job. Marcia resorted to covering for his absences by telling his boss that he'd contracted yet another cold.

While Simons self-destructed, in 1960, Marcia was blossoming, forming friendships with occultists in the Boston area. Serving as executive secretary, she helped launch Astro-Dynamics Research, a would-be foundation that never made it off the ground. Its mission statement in part was: "To establish the validity and reliability of scientific astrological techniques for measuring Man's relationship to the Universe, and for understanding the Cosmic laws by which he is governed."[200]

Marcia and her cohorts would never scientifically prove their rather lofty goals, but that was beside the point. Moore was now finally and fully engaged in her crusade to carve her name in esoteric circles. In a 1961 letter to friends, she posed the question, "Does this letter look official? It is supposed to be on our new stationery.... Anyway I thought that with a fancy name and fancy paper like this the government might think we were exploring outer space or building rockets or something and give us a few million dollars as a grant! Enough for now. But it is fun to play with these grandiose ideas while fetching groceries and making the dinner."[201]

Marcia's partner on the project was Bob Pelletier, highly regarded in Boston's astrological circles. The association would become another log on the fire between Marcia and Simons. Bob being gay drove Simons absolutely nuts. Despite his open arms when it came to diverse religious beliefs, he still retained conservative Southern views about women and spousal roles, not to mention homosexuality. Sim thought Bob was a terrible influence and actually perverted. Marcia stuck to her guns, insisting on forming some sort of arrangement with Bob, such as an astrology business or studio, with her as the financial backer. Simons grew increasingly vitriolic and got her parents involved, candidly expressing his feelings. Marcia eventually caved but moved on to another bold idea.

Irritating Eleanor, who had accused her daughter of neglect, Marcia enrolled in a yoga camp in Montreal, having to leave the children at home for a couple of months. She discovered a natural gift and returned quite accomplished in yoga, able to perfectly perform all the exercises. Marcia could now boast that she had been personally instructed by the popular Swami Vishnudevananda and had made connections with such notables as author Yogi Vithaldas. Additionally, she'd establish a working partnership with Dr. R.S. Mishra in which she provided food to yoga students traveling from his ashram in New York to her location on weekends.

Yoga Camp—Summer of 1960. Marcia Moore stayed at the
year-round retreat in Val-Morin, Montreal, to study yoga.

"I am now at the yoga camp in Canada. It is the healthiest life you
can imagine. We do exercises, breathe, take long walks and chant,
meditate and live on a strict vegetarian diet, not even eggs. It is
really fun and I am meeting all kinds of people from actresses to
engineers and just plain housewives like me. It is lovely here and
I like it better all the time. Weather is just perfect now and I also
enjoy getting to know the people. About half of them are French.
Time passes quickly once one is used to the routine. You would be
surprised to see how much better I am getting at yoga. The swami
is wonderful and when he meditates the air is filled with incense."

Photos from the retreat in Val-Morin, Montreal,
where Marcia Moore studied yoga.

Calls Shots in Bay State Yoga School

Groans Out

Serenity Above All — "Look serene, even in the most excruciating position," Marcia Moore tells her students as they do an excruciating leg stretch. It's one of many Yoga exercises she teaches.

Teacher Shows How — Yoga teacher Marcia Moore shows bearded astrologer Roger Parris of New York how to do the "Cobra." Parris attends non-profit classes Marcia conducts for friends at her Concord home. (Photos by Jack Sheahan)

out for deep breathing, and my strength would come surging back.

From the warm-up exercises, Marcia suddenly catapulted us into the head-stand, toughest of all Yoga positions.

When it came my turn to try, I clumsily heaved my hind quarters and feet into the air—and promptly turned

a somersault. Enviously, I peeked at my neighbor, Marian Sarekian of Watertown, Marcia's star pupil. Her feet were pointing at the sky and her ballerina's body was straight as a birch tree.

And then I remembered that she had told me that Yoga had helped her conquer a heart murmur.

Marcia came to my aid. She grabbed my ankles and balanced me on my head. Sweat blinded me, I felt dizzy, and undiscovered muscles in my back shrieked for relief. I toppled when she let go of my feet.

"Guess you need more conditioning," Marcia commented.

I had better luck with the shoulder stand. After a couple of failures, I finally did a creditable one. My example was Frank C. Vogel of Newton Upper Falls, an erect, tanned man of 66 who looks 50. Frank, a retired bank employee who claims he hasn't seen a doctor in 15 years, thanks to Yoga—made the shoulder-stand look effortless.

"Keep it up," Marcia encouraged me. "It's good for your thyroid."

After that brisk workout, I felt both pleasantly tired and curiously refreshed. My muscles tingled, my blood raced. I was starved and made a sizable dent in the vegetarian buffet Marcia served. (She just nibbled, she leads her strenuous life on only 800 calories a day).

And when I left Marcia's "ashram"—dwelling place in the forest—at sunset, I felt that I had at least caught a glimpse of the promise Yoga holds out to its devotees.

Master Yogi—"Woman Calls Shots" headline In the *Boston Sunday Globe,* featuring a yoga class held every weekend by Marcia, in the forested grove behind her home.

By this time, Marcia's public speaking ability had also blossomed. She shrewdly played up her legitimacy, having spent two years in exotic India. As far as her captivated listeners and readers knew, she had profoundly unlocked the ancient mysteries of the Orient. When she wed Simons, she had only finished freshman year at Radcliffe. After a ten-year hiatus to marry and have three children, she returned to finish her degree in social relations.

Simons scoffed at the ambition and his disaffection with Marcia worsened in lockstep with his descent into acute alcoholism. The two fought constantly. They tried not to argue in front of the children. But often, while lying in bed, the children could hear their parents bicker in hushed, but heated, angry tones.

While drinking, Simons would commandeer the living room with his bongo drums and record collection. Smoking like a demon, he'd play *Unforgettable* by Nat King Cole or bossa nova records over and over, making the whole family miserable. On top of the disdain for his resentment and broken will, Marcia loathed the cigarette smoke that saturated the carpets, walls, and furniture of their Concord home.

Somehow Simons failed to make the connection between his behavior and his son's health. Stuart developed such severe asthma he occasionally had to be taken to the hospital during the middle of the night. The constant haze of tobacco smoke around Simons' study was a major turn-off for Marcia. Oxygen was vital to her now. Harnessing the pranic power of Hatha yoga,[vi] she proclaimed that she could primarily live off it, only nibbling on food.

Simons had gripes of his own. He bristled at the string of cars often parked along the dead end in front of their house and at the strange cast of characters who came and went for Hatha yoga classes. The next-door neighbor didn't like it either, particularly since her husband found Marcia attractive enough to make Simons jealous. Good-looking, young Harvard students would come to Concord to be taught by Marcia, routinely dressed in her white cropped tank top and capri shorts. The flattery was abundant; a male friend once told her she was "from Venus."

During the 1961 holiday season, Robert Moore noticed palpable tension. He could no longer hold his tongue. "I have been deeply concerned lately, particularly since Christmas that things do not seem to be going well with you, Sim, and the children. I add the children because if things go badly with you and Sim it is automatically bad with the children and I think it begins to show already on Louisa.… A note of personal foreboding kept creeping in spite of myself, perhaps it was just

---

[vi] Defined by Marcia Moore as a yoga system of manifold discipline, designed to develop the body through a five-point program of exercise, breathing, diet, relaxation, and positive thinking.

imagination, but I thought you seemed somewhat distraut, very strained, rather disinterested and even as if you wished it were not happening or were elsewhere."[202]

The children had noticed. Although Simons wasn't boisterous, and the fights were carried on mutedly, they sensed the bad vibes: bitterness, anger, hostility, especially resentment.

Simons' mother, who had enough chops to sing on the radio and a popular television show, had sacrificed a promising career to marry his father and raise four children. He expected that Marcia should likewise devote her energies as a housewife, look up to him, and accept his superiority as a writer. Marcia's ambition made this an impossibility; no one was more important than her dreams.

A pattern that Marcia followed in her relationships may have helped conceal a great deal of deception surrounding her disappearance. She never revealed even a glimpse of any problems until they collapsed. After implosion, the claws came out. That occurred as 1961 began, when Marcia finally revealed to her parents what was happening behind the scenes. "Re. our personal affairs. Yes things surely have reached the crisis stage and I for one have had it. For almost five years Simons has been accusing me of every kind of failing—including infidelity in front of the children. As far as they know the word "bitch" is synonomous with the word 'Mother'. They have been subjected to discussions of homosexuality with no holds barred. They have been told that their mother doesn't love them, neglects them and wants to abandon them altogether. Do you wonder they are disturbed?"[203]

Marcia had made up her mind. All she had left to do was inform her parents. "But anyway this last weekend was really the ultimate. And I decided that I was sick of being called unfaithful in front of the kids as he repeatedly did. They were all almost hysterical after he had finished with them."[204]

The infidelity mentioned related to what Marcia characterized as a lifelong friendship formed in India with a Theosophist and astrologer named Peter Hoffman, who was about Simons' age. Like Marcia, Peter was also the child of a prominent establishment figure. Hoffman's father worked closely with President Dwight Eisenhower as chairman of the Ford Foundation. Marcia denied the affair and reported to her parents: "Yes, I know you are aware that things are bad but believe me you have no idea even now just how bad or how long. He began this before we went to India so no individual is involved. Personally I think he is out of his mind and the acute alcoholism is only a symptom of a deeper mental derangement. No doubt he has told you that I have misconducted myself with this person in India. He is in a frenzy of jealousy because he found a letter (he searches all my papers, closet etc. systematically and destroys what doesn't please him) which mentioned in a postscript the situation. It was a large three page typed letter about a piece of mine they were thinking of publishing and the postscript was the only personal thing in it. The reason was not that I am in the habit of confiding my problems but that Peter was so <u>shocked</u> by his treatment of me in Adyar and some things that happened later that he couldn't help knowing. Also he was my teacher of astrology and saw the charts. But I <u>never, never, never</u>, mention astrology to Simons. It is he who claims that I predetermine actions because of it. It only shows that he knows nothing of it."[205]

While the children were away at summer camps in Maine and New Hampshire, Marcia and Simons separated. As with the end to all her other relationships, Marcia had another troublesome, passive-aggressive habit. Instead of breaking up outright, she would separate under the pretense of possibly staying together, leaving her life littered with loose ends. "Well I don't want to upset you with more of this. I wrote the lawyer and have an appointment with him Monday. Simons is terribly concerned that if any publicity comes about it will hurt his reputation as a great spiritual guide. But as far as the children and I are concerned he couldn't care less. Actually I see only one solution, considering his feelings. And that is for him to take a job somewhere else and just go away for a while. That wouldn't have to be legal and at least it would give everyone a breathing spell,"[206] Marcia apprised her father.

At the time, divorces in Massachusetts were expensive, time-consuming, socially shunned, and attainable on only limited grounds. So in the spring of 1962, Marcia spent six weeks in St. Thomas, the Virgin

Islands, boarding with an elderly Danish lady while filing for divorce. Robert and Eleanor were always kind to Simons and for the most part took his side, allowing him to stay with them regularly so he could see the children on weekends. With the marriage over, Simons tried to pick up the pieces and eventually found a lesser-known publisher, Thomas Y. Crowell, for *Journeys on the Razor-Edged Path*.

He'd also remarry and return to school, but ultimately admit himself into an institution for treatment of alcoholism. As Simons would reflect years later in a personal memoir, he had married his mother's ideal for himself. "We shared, it seemed at first, mutual spiritual interest. But the cleavage between our principles and values deepened and our interests took us in conflicting directions."[207]

Even years after their marriage crumbled, however, Simons still held Marcia in some allure, remarking, "She had an ethereal quality, mystical, beautiful, a little mysterious, a little elusive maybe."[208]

Marcia ready for her new life without Simons.

SECOND HUSBAND

Marcia Moore broke free in 1962, living with a series of potential love interests who stayed at the small ranch-style house she and Simons had built. Wary of the offbeat, eccentric reputation she already had around Concord, her parents usually stayed away from Marcia's home. Despite living just over the hill, her father almost never visited.

The artsy folks she befriended held great affection for her, but most acquaintances yielded to Concord's conservative atmosphere that reacted with pearl-clutching disapproval. Marcia socialized with an elite bohemian fringe of the Harvard social scene, which included several ostracized gay men. Eleanor found herself consumed with damage control over her daughter in her social circle.

The Moores grew very concerned about Marcia's lifestyle and disregard for the institution of marriage, especially for sake of the grandchildren, her reputation, and their own. An accomplished, respectable man may have found her too flaky and eccentric, they reasoned. They had a point, as some strange characters filled the void.

First came an Egyptologist named Newton who hung around making cow eyes at Marcia, winning her heart after lamenting that he'd never enjoyed a homemade pie before, which she of course made for him. In her children's eyes, he had loser written all over him.

Later she put up a houseguest named Lou, a Floridian who was into mediumship. Most of the strays she took in wouldn't have even offered, but he was generous enough to take everyone out to lunch once *and* pay for it.

Marcia then met an affable beatnik-type from California named Lenny, accompanied by a sidekick with a pretty shady background; both moved in with her and the children. It was mainly a physical attraction on Marcia's part, making up for lost time since she'd married so young. Although Lenny was married to a folksinger, he "appeared" to be separated. Bringing his expertise to this new relationship, Marcia and Lenny started a coffeehouse called the Moondial, out of an old synagogue on Berkeley Street in Boston's South End, with Marcia providing the funding of course. It involved extensive, costly renovations, including some payola to city officials. When it finally opened, Odetta, an up-and-coming folksinger and civil rights activist who would perform at the 1963 March on Washington, opened the place to a small crowd. Eventually the place went bust. Marcia, and by extension her father, lost a considerable sum of money. Predictably, that also marked the end of the relationship, and Lenny eventually rambled on.

A young man named Bill from Falls Church, Virginia, soon moved in. Bill was an opera buff, which Marcia figured would endear him to her daughter, who was into opera and held a lifelong interest in music, achieving a bachelor of music from Boston University. The pandering had little effect as neither her daughter nor sons liked him. Bill spent a few months sitting around in leotards with Marcia practicing yoga, watching the kids coming and going, and never saying a word. After a few months, another parasitic relationship petered out.

The next man Marcia moved in with would become her second husband. Through astrological circles in Cambridge, Marcia had met a well-built, six-foot-tall, redheaded college student who wore dark-rimmed glasses. His name was Louis Acker. He had been exposed to astrology by his mother and knew a great deal more than Marcia. Acker was a student at Windham College in Vermont who transferred to Boston University and moved in with Moore and her three children, the eldest just eight years younger than him.

Robert and Eleanor Moore were beside themselves with Marcia letting him move in, especially after learning that they affirmed the engagement based predominately on their compatible astrological charts. Even on Louis' end, there were many heated exchanges between him and his mother ending in arguments like, "Well Mother, I'm twenty-one and I'm an adult and I think I can do what I want now!"[209] The Moores and Ackers genuinely liked each other; they just didn't think thirty-three-year-old Marcia and twenty-one-year-old Louis should marry. And why would Louis want to take on three not especially young children, they wondered. Before getting involved with Marcia, Louis hadn't even dated much; but the pair became hot and heavy, practicing astrology and yoga together.

As would become an unfortunate lifelong habit, at first Marcia contended she could never remarry. Then she said she wouldn't remarry until at least next fall. Shortly thereafter, however, she married Louis, only six weeks after her divorce from Simons was finalized. The small, casual ceremony was held in the Japanese garden of her parent's Concord estate. Thirteen-year-old Louisa couldn't handle the whole affair and spent the day with her best friend's family at a picnic in a neighboring town.

Marcia and Louis taking their vows in the
Japanese arbor of her parents' estate.

Just married.

The Moore-Acker lawn soon became an ashram or "Marshram" as Marcia and Louis jokingly referred to it, with an interesting assortment of astrologers, mystics, and novices flocking to learn yoga.

THREE LECTURES ON ASTROLOGY
with Spontaneous Personal Readings

LOUIS S. ACKER
Research Coordinator, Astro-Dynamics
Member of American Federation of Astrologers

Mr. Acker has cast and delineated hundreds of horoscopes, and given personal counselling and guidance to individuals in all walks of life.

EXCLUSIVE MANAGEMENT

flora frame... *Club Program Bureau*
154 NEWBURY STREET • BOSTON 16, MASSACHUSETTS • COmmonwealth 6-6318

YOGA FOR YOU...
Lecture and Demonstration of Exercises

MARCIA MOORE
Author · Lecturer · Teacher

Marcia Moore's approach to this time-proven system of physical, mental, and spiritual self-development combines the ancient wisdom of the East with modern Western psychology. A Radcliffe graduate Phi Beta Kappa, she has travelled extensively throughout India studying its languages, culture, and philosophy. She now instructs individuals and groups in yoga under the general guidance of her teacher, Swami Vishnudevananda of India.

EXCLUSIVE MANAGEMENT

flora frame... *Club Program Bureau*
154 NEWBURY STREET • BOSTON 16, MASSACHUSETTS • COmmonwealth 6-6318

Second husband—Marcia and Louis promoting astrology in the 1960s.

Although Marcia took her children to traditional music lessons and attended some of their recitals, it was a quirky adolescence for the kids. At summer Camp Ogontz in Lisbon, New Hampshire, Louisa watched other youths open care packages of binoculars or canteens, while she unwrapped a Ouija board. At home, the children were exposed to tarot cards and séances in their living room.

The eccentric visitors continued unabated. Sybil Leek, dubbed "Britain's most famous witch," stayed at Marcia's pad for a few weeks in the early 1960s, writing about it in one of her most successful books, *Diary of a Witch*. Leek, an internationally known psychic and acquaintance of notorious black magician Aleister Crowley, dabbled in several occult practices, authoring such books as *Moon Signs* and *Star Speak*. She even appeared on television talk shows like *Tonight* with both Jack Paar and Johnny Carson.

Shortly thereafter, Marcia caught a huge break that greatly amplified her exposure in the Boston area and to some degree nationally. An accomplished writer by the name of Jess Stearn, who authored such books as *The Door to the Future* and the bestseller *Edgar Cayce: The Sleeping*

Prophet, published *Yoga, Youth, and Reincarnation* about his three-month stretch completing Marcia's yoga course at her home in Massachusetts.

Following sporadic communication and Marcia's assistance with astrology research, Stearn met Marcia in New York where she was lecturing on yoga, clad in her lavender leotard. Since their first encounter, he was quite taken by Marcia's appearance, stunned that she was old enough to have three children, one that was fifteen.

While *Yoga, Youth, and Reincarnation* documented Stearn's physical experimentation, it also served as a testimonial to the "life-altering" power of yoga and meditation. Most importantly, the book included a photomontage of Marcia displaying several difficult yoga positions, showcasing her lithe figure while influentially capturing her sweetish look and magnetism. A rendering of Marcia doing yoga appeared on the cover. Here was a pretty, youthful, well-to-do Bostonian woman displaying an enthusiastic immersion in yoga and openly espousing esotericism, making it socially acceptable. It gave her instant recognition with the burgeoning interest in mysticism.

Marcia Moore was at the right place at the right time. The first half of the 1960s birthed the counterculture movement as a result of cultural upheaval sprouting in multiple walks of American life. In 1962, the Cuban Missile Crisis abruptly made the specter of nuclear war a reality. The following year, President John F. Kennedy, a charismatic symbol of youth, peace, and prosperity, was tragically assassinated. Shortly after, the United States fully committed to the war in Vietnam that many objected to, especially the drafted youth who felt they had no say in the matter.

As the fabric of traditional American society began fraying, counterculture revolutionaries in art and music amplified the dissident feelings of the youth. The Beatles began infusing Eastern elements into their music. On the opposite coast, Haight-Ashbury in San Francisco became a home base for the hippie movement, culminating in the "Summer of Love" in 1967, setting the stage for Woodstock as the decade came to a close.

During these years, Marcia couldn't help but notice the nationwide buzz psychologist Timothy Leary had garnered with his championing of consciousness experimentation, fueled by psychedelic drugs popular at the time. Moore marveled at his pied-piper ability to get kids of diverse backgrounds across America to "turn on, tune in, and drop out," with the help of LSD. Although Marcia objected to the use of harder drugs like LSD and acid, she befriended Leary, who taught at Harvard and spent time in the Cambridge area before moving to Berkeley. The observation of his influence clearly had an impact on her future endeavors with ketamine.

With traditional American boundaries falling by the wayside, fascination and participation in the occult took root. The stigma of mystical practices like yoga and astrology, which had been ingrained into the still predominately Protestant and Catholic society, began to dissolve with the help of trailblazers like Marcia, who was perfectly positioned to ride the trend. It was around this time that Marcia Moore changed the pronunciation of her name. Although family and old friends continued to call her "Mar-sha," with her new bohemian, vegetarian lifestyle, she instructed people to call her the more exotic-sounding "Mar-cee-a."

The back of a photograph spelling Marcia's name the way her parents intended it to be pronounced, "Marsha."

Jess Stearn's book also provided a glimpse of Louis Acker's quirky personality, such as his unusual workout of moving boulders across the lawn, or oddly staring into the sky, claiming he could meditatively focus his mental energy into a beam that could disintegrate clouds. The offbeat eccentric would stand around campus causing others to wonder what he was looking at.

Louis had other intriguing abilities Marcia would go on to teach future companions, including her fourth husband, Howard Alltounian, like standing on his head for extended periods, and one that should have been of particular interest to investigators after Marcia disappeared. "I fooled the polygraph machine completely," Louis reported to Marcia in front of Jess Stearn. "This is just an extreme example of what yogi-like concentration can do for the individual," Marcia boasted. "Through exercising with control, and practicing deep breathing, Louis has built up such detachment that he can isolate virtually any area of his body and make it respond at will."[210]

The exposure from the book paved the way for Marcia and Louis professionally, but after three years of marriage, their age difference caught up with them. "She used to put Louis down, talk to him like a child, other people saw that,"[211] one family member said. The divorce came by mutual consent. Louis went on to publish some well-regarded books on astrology with Frances Sakoian. Despite another failed marriage, it wasn't a total loss. Marcia soaked up all she could before moving on, in this case greatly refining her knowledge of astrology.

Just weeks after divorcing Louis, Marcia Moore would remarry again. Unfortunately, her third husband would be nowhere near as easy to contend with as a youthful eccentric.

THIRD TIME'S FAR FROM CHARMED

MARCIA MOORE AND **MARK DOUGLAS**

Pictured with her third husband in a stock photo for a book.

During the fall of 1965, Marcia's soon-to-be third husband, Mark Douglas, moved into her Concord home. As with most of her relationships, Marcia claimed to have spent a past-lifetime with Mark Douglas. She believed Mark's past-life alter-ego was called "Mabus," a name curiously referred to as the third anti-Christ according to Nostradamus.

Just like her next husband, Mark Douglas would first see Marcia on a television talk show. And just like Howard Alltounian, Mark sought out the place where she was scheduled to speak. Douglas drove down from his home in Maine to join a Sunday afternoon class, conducted behind her home. Like others who encountered Marcia for the first time, Mark would have the memorable experience of watching her riskily perform a handstand atop a table.

Recognizing that most of her patrons were students from Harvard or MIT, freeloaders, or wanderers who didn't have much money, Marcia didn't charge for lessons. "She didn't ask for money, must have thought it was beneath her or maybe didn't know how to place value on her services,"[212] one family member reflected. Perhaps that's why Marcia became so enchanted with Mark Douglas. The day he showed up in her backyard, he was the only one who put a sizable tip—ten dollars—in her little blue wooden donation box.

That very day, within hours of meeting Marcia, Mark moved in and stayed until she married him. Marking his territory, he brought in an ugly brown sofa and old beige carpeting to replace the worn green rug in her living room. The children, by this time disenchanted by the procession of male colleagues or potential suitors who'd followed their father Simons, didn't like it. But they had never been consulted before—and weren't this time either.

If Louis had been a half step down from Concord's upper class, Mark was a distinct social class beneath Marcia. His style was embarrassingly lowbrow, shown by his shabby furniture and green janitor pants. McDonald's was a favorite of Mark's, a place totally foreign to Marcia. He had served in combat in Korea and become some kind of officer with seniority, but never having earned more than a high school diploma, lacked social skills. *How to Win Friends & Influence People* was his bible, but he wasn't reading it to overcome shyness or inspire. His motivation was manipulating people.

Perhaps because he had been raised in a funeral home, Mark Douglas was socially awkward. "The thing that sets him off the most is having company," Marcia would explain to her parents. "The whole time he was growing up his mother never entertained anyone, not even relations. So he has practically no capacity to deal with people on that basis and goes into a neurotic panic over it."[213]

Once aiming to charm Marcia's mother, Mark remarked how much Eleanor resembled Marilyn Monroe. Mrs. Moore knew all too well she looked nothing like the Hollywood star by the wildest stretch of anyone's imagination. By then in her sixties, Eleanor had never been glamorous. She didn't wear much makeup, save for a bit of lipstick with powder or rouge on formal occasions. His attempt at flattery was ham-handed, leaving it glaringly obvious he was trying too hard. When Eleanor didn't respond, he clumsily repeated the compliment to make sure it registered. She thought it sounded creepy, if not sociopathic.

Born in 1927, Mark Douglas was closer to Marcia's own age of forty years. This time it wasn't age that concerned Marcia's family. Dorothy Douglas, Mark's ex-wife, had telephoned to forewarn Marcia's parents. She knew him by his middle name, Frank, and claimed that he was a terrible person who beat her and owed $8,000 in back child support for their son and daughter, in addition to monthly alimony. A troublesome holiday season ensued. On Christmas Eve, Mark was arrested at Marcia's house and charged with nonsupport of his two children.

The Moore family grew exceedingly disturbed about Mark living with their grandchildren, and privately ordered a background check on him. Marcia's brother John, by this time the appointed custodian of the family trusts, and closest confidant of Robert and Eleanor for family business, spearheaded the investigation. The findings yielded even more alarm.

Mark's questionable past was marred by shady associations and business dealings, possibly even organized crime. If ever Marcia should have heeded her family's cautionary counsel, it was then. Rumor had it that Douglas owed the mob $80,000, a massive sum in 1965. Robert and Eleanor were so alarmed, they worried for a time that Douglas might even kidnap Louisa for ransom, and cautioned their granddaughter to be alert while at boarding school.

A judge ordered Mark to pay Dorothy the balance of $3,875 before being granted release from jail on the civil contempt order. Unfortunately, a headstrong Marcia made excuses for him. "He doesn't smoke, drink, wear expensive clothes or engage in any kind of recreation that would give him the incentive to grab hold of my (or anyone else's) money,"[214] she asserted.

On the Sunday following his arrest, Marcia married Douglas. "Mark and I are leaving for Jamaica and by the time we return to this scene will be married—a legally square fair knot. Two lawyers are seeing to it. He is most anxious to be a good father to the children so since it is a 'fait accompli' there seems little point in prejudicing them against him," Marcia defiantly wrote her parents. "Mark is planning to take care of his affairs in New Hampshire as soon as we return and has all the machinery set in motion toward this end. So—if we can only be left to manage our own affairs things should work out for the best. I do hope you will realize that we are grown and must be allowed to live our own lives as you have lived yours. Everything is going to work out for the best."[215]

Soon after they married, a justice of the peace affair with none of her family present, Marcia gushed that Mark was such a wonderful, loving man and stepfather to the children. Yet it became painfully obvious that her parents disliked him from the outset, and subsequent visits were strained. Letters dropped off. By the mid-1960s, Marcia was spending less time summering with her family at Cuttyhunk.

Robert and Eleanor's intuition turned out to be prescient. Mark was a conman of no means, a hustler who wanted to amass money by hook or crook. He figured he'd hit the jackpot with Marcia. He was right, and wasted little time before pushing her around to get what he wanted.

The small-time opportunist quickly realized that what his new wife craved most was to publish books on metaphysics, and he could exploit that. "It wasn't a matter of if something was going to happen, it was a matter of when," one family member would later remark. Blinded by ambition, Marcia was somewhat oblivious to ulterior motives. This left her vulnerable throughout her life. All Mark had to tell her was "Honey, I'll make you a star."[216] The stage was set. A showcase for Marcia was his meal ticket.

Douglas saw the potential of capitalizing on the recognition Moore had recently accrued from Jess Stearn's book *Yoga, Youth, and Reincarnation*, and there was some steak beneath the sizzle. Marcia was intelligent, charismatic, articulate, considered adept at astrology, and undeniably talented at yoga. She held affiliations with interesting people in occult circles. Mark saw prospective book money; she already had an established writing style and was comfortable appearing on television. Shrewdly, he insisted that his name be added to all of the books and connived that royalties be remitted to him.

While he was no expert, Mark did have some interest in the paranormal and occult as early as his time in Korea. He contributed a bit to the substance of the books but had few fresh ideas and did none of the writing. To his credit, Douglas found the editors, typesetters, and printers and saw to the business end of self-publishing. In a promotional capacity, he could lay on the charm, but unsettlingly got off on the thrill of convincing people he was highly educated, if not an expert. Presenting themselves as a happy, successful couple, Mark would fill up their station wagon with vegetarian food and Alice Bailey books that they'd distribute at virtually no profit, alongside their "co-authored" books.

With Marcia's backing, he leased a shingle-roofed office building in charming York Harbor, Maine, which served as the headquarters for Arcane Books, his newly formed publishing company. On the first floor, Mark set up a metaphysical shop and health food vitamin store where Marcia could sell her books. Upstairs was a spacious three-bedroom apartment, where it was rumored that Mark would bring mistresses. According to friends, their open marriage was hardly a secret.

Meanwhile, Douglas had a number of other ideas in mind, for Marcia to fund with her money of course. From a trailer park venture to a bowling alley, he kept trying his hand at different businesses but couldn't make a go of them.

The kids would frequently overhear Marcia say, "Mark can't get along with people because of his bad temper."[217] Luckily for him, Marcia put up with it all. Counted among his short-lived business ventures, Douglas established a steak house in Maine. In contradiction to her well-crafted vegetarian lifestyle, Mark drove Marcia and her children for a meal to see the newly opened Steer Inn, in which he had just become partner, but not for long.

Almost everything turned out to be a financial disaster and his deal-ings tended to be murky. For some reason he wanted Louisa to keep his large Buick sedan on campus at Weston in Cambridge, though she wasn't allowed to use it. Mark just wanted it somewhere else, away from the house. Then one day when Louisa was at Arcane Books, an IRS agent came in looking for Mark. Louisa could hear the agent's frustration. "You know why I'm here!"[218] Mark scuttled out the back door.

By now their irresponsibility with money was impacting Marcia's trust funds. As the New Year of 1966 began, her brother John was obli-gated to write a letter concerning her finances. In addition to Mark and Marcia's elusiveness in paying real estate taxes, she had requested discre-tionary disbursements exceeding the money they had already advanced her for January. "In answer to your question about the Trust, the purpose of the trust is to help in the support of you and the children. The two trustees, Dad and myself, have discretion to pay out income and principal to meet your needs. The manner and amount of payments is left up to the discretion of the trustees," John advised his sister. "We intend to continue to pay out all the Trust income to you and the children, so there will be no change. The only thing that we are doing is to pay the bills directly instead of giving you a lump sum each month to pay the bills yourself. At the moment the balance of the Trust is zero until we receive the div-idend check in February. Daddy recently had to advance $1,500 of his own funds into the Trust to make the monthly payments that we have been making. We therefore will not have anything more than the $800 a month for the foreseeable future, and will probably have to borrow addi-tional funds to meet the children's school bills,"[219] John cautioned.

Throughout the 1950s, Sheraton had flourished. In the 1960s, con-glomerate mergers were all the rage. In the 1968, multinational conglomerate International Telephone and Telegraph Corporation (ITT) began gobbling up numerous companies.[220] Among them was the Sheraton Hotel chain for about $200 million, leaving Robert Moore with a windfall of millions in cash and ITT stock.[221] Robert prudently created trusts for his four children. With Mark pulling the strings, they imprudently continued exceeding the monthly disbursements.

These developments were sorely dismaying for the Moore family. After all the safeguards Robert had tried to erect for his daughter's security, this scoundrel was now usurping her fortune. Soon they were asking for loans. "We hope you have been having a good summer at Cuttyhunk and are extremely grateful for all you and Mother have done for the children," she wrote her father in the fall of 1966, hoping to borrow over $4,000 to cover the cost of self-publishing five thousand copies of their new book. "Naturally we would expect to pay interest and would pay off the loan out of sales just as soon as possible," Marcia implored. "The fact that Jess Stearn's book sold over forty thousand copies shows there is a market for this kind of thing."[222]

Dubiously, her father retorted, "I have been thinking a lot more about your book publishing venture and I have great reservations about the desirability of printing five thousand copies right away. Books do not sell themselves. It takes a strong publishing organization with a sales force, contacts in the trade, with the book stores, the reviewers, the know-how of promotion and a name of standing to make a book go. Also some expensive advertising. And there are many other expenses, packaging, mailing correspondence, etc. etc.… It was only this sort of effort and advertising that made Jess Stern's book sell as it did."[223]

By this time, Marcia had sold her house in Concord for more than $60,000, a considerable sum for the time, and foolishly turned over the proceeds to Mark. He used it to initiate a lease on a fourteen-room mansion called Greystone Manor, set on six acres on the southern coast of Maine.

Marcia held affection for the Maine coast, having spent pockets of her childhood at her grandmother Jane's home in Cape Elizabeth, where she was introduced to Spiritualism and psychism. To Marcia it was another sign of fate; Mark finds this mansion that she felt truly destined for. As she astutely perceived while growing up in her parents' Concord estate, people could be swayed by the power of an impressive structure.

Marcia visiting her grandmother Jeannie's home in Maine.

Despite being somewhat run down and vastly more space than they needed, the mansion impressed visitors with its glorious ocean views. It would later become a Junior League Decorators' Show House, as well as the set of a movie titled *Bed & Breakfast*. Its protagonist, played by Roger Moore of James Bond fame, washes up on the mansion's beachfront and falls in love with the lady who lives there, played by Talia Shire of *Rocky* and the *Godfather* movies.

"Greystone"—cliffside mansion in Maine where Marcia
lived with her third husband Mark Douglas.

With Greystone, Marcia would win points with a lot of prominent occultists. Attending conferences and befriending coastal area astrologers, she'd invite credible amateurs to the house to learn and exchange ideas. A budding reputation followed, as she dabbled in performing astrological readings. Later the idea occurred to Mark to practice hypnotic regression in the living room.

Perhaps fittingly for the mystique of the place, some of Marcia's guests would report supernatural experiences at the mansion. One summer, her daughter was in a third-floor bedroom, bejeweled with lurid red, blue, and green lights of the psychedelic era. Louisa switched off the red light to turn in, while the hall light was kept on and the door opened a crack. Lying in the double bed, she felt as if someone was in the room, sleeping on their stomach beside her. The presence slowly turned over and she suddenly felt a weight on her chest, suffocating her. Startled, she recited the Lord's Prayer and the weight slowly lifted and dissipated. When she turned on the light, she noticed a peacock feather from a vase and a stuffed animal from the shelf had been knocked over. For the rest of the night, she kept a radio and the light on. In the morning she told her mother that she refused to stay in that room, and moved to a second-floor bedroom closer to everyone else.

Others who slept at Greystone reported feeling disturbing presences too, like a young bookstore employee who responded by hanging up a wooden cross. They heard footsteps just outside their room, creaking, and what sounded like multiple people whispering. Jumping out of bed to catch the supposed intruder, they would find nobody there. In certain rooms at the back of the house, guests felt an especially eerie feeling around the servants' quarters and nanny's room.

Although Mark became quite handy with plumbing and had a well drilled, the mansion was inadequately insulated and bitterly cold, so he and Marcia couldn't spend much time at Greystone in the winters. Much of the time draping herself in an electric blanket, she and Mark cloistered themselves in two rooms that could just be adequately heated to a survivable temperature. Even though Louisa hated dorm life, it was a relief to return to her heated room at Boston University after breaks.

When the mansion was uninhabitable, the couple house-sat or stayed with Mark's parents in the Methuen, Massachusetts funeral home where he'd been raised. Always one to spin her circumstances, Marcia bragged about how neat it was to sleep in the embalming room.

The miserable Maine winters and purported hauntings were the least of their troubles. The whole affair turned out to be another one of Mark's scams. In 1966, he had clandestinely worked out some kind of lease-to-own deal for Greystone, but hadn't paid the rent in two years. Meanwhile, seemingly oblivious, Marcia was under the impression they owned the place. Once she ignorantly remarked to her children in a voice of wonder, "Can you believe that the Concord house sold for $60,000, and that's exactly the same amount it cost us to buy this house?!"[224] Believing what their mother said, the children were stunned when the real owner showed up with a moving truck, nearly coming to blows with Mark as she tried to reclaim her oversized custom drapes.

A Mrs. Pearl Ziebarth Higley did manage to retain some of her furniture, but resorted to writing a desperate letter to Marcia's father: "Dear Mr. Moore: I met a friend of yours, who told me what a good and fair person you were. It was like a prayer from heaven. In June 1966 your daughter, Marcia Douglas Moore, and I came to an agreement for her to buy my house in Cape Neddick, Maine. They failed to pay the taxes and at one time I did not hear from her for two years although I tried to contact her a number of times. When I finally did contact her I asked that she vacate the house but she has never answered my request. About a year ago they evidently borrowed some money and gave it to me. It was a check from Mark Douglas's father. Dear Mr. Moore, I need the money to educate my children and other obligations. Do you think you could prevail upon Marcia to vacate the house?"[225]

Robert Moore was at his summer home when he undertook the awkward task of replying: "Dear Mrs. Higley, I hasten to acknowledge your letter of June 27 which, has just reached me here. I have no knowledge of the details of the purchase of your house in York which, I understand was negotiated by Marcia's husband, Mr Douglas. I have never talked with him about the transaction. I was told recently that they had already paid $65,000 for it but that title was not yet complete which was a bit ununderstandable to me. I do not see how I can help in this affair since I do not know anything about it. Marcia seems to leave everything to her husband and perhaps does not herself know about all the details. My only present suggestion would be that you have your attorneys try to contact her personally to see what can be worked out in this situation."[226]

Meanwhile, relations with her parents soured so much so that Marcia griped directly to her father. "I wonder if you are aware of the fact that in seven years you have never made even a single positive comment about our work of our books,"[227] Marcia wrote.

"The only comment I remember is when Jess Stearn's book came out you said 'Thank God the family name wasn't mentioned.' After that icy silence. When we go to your house we hear all about your trips, gourds, paintings, and various interests and really <u>enjoy</u> hearing the news. But I can't for the life of me remember when you have asked us how our work was going or shown even the least inkling of interest in our lives or work. You used to—but that was a long time ago.

Anyway, none of that bothers me too much because at least I know that our work is good and is helping others. But there is one thing that does bother me and at long last I feel that I really must speak of it.

That is your attitude toward Mark. It is very obvious that you will not stay in the same room with him and feel awkward in his company. Yet he has not hurt you in any way, and has made a new and wonderful life for me and the children. He is the hardest working, most conscientious and loving person I have ever known and really hasn't done anything to merit this treatment. He does more for the children than you will ever know and thinks constantly of their welfare. And he has given me more real happiness than I have ever known in my life. In many ways these last two years have been idyllic."[228]

So divided had the family become that it was no longer possible to spend holidays or festive occasions together. "The thing that makes it so strange is the way you and Mother lavish all your care and attention on Simons who never had anything but contempt for the family," Marcia complained. "When we were divorced, for example, you appeared to believe the lies he told about my being unfaithful—which incidentally I was not—yet you never came to me and said 'Now what is the truth of this matter?' The same thing happened with Mark. His exwife said a lot of mean things, but you were never willing to say to him, 'Well what is the real story.'"[229]

The scams, shady associations, and deceit became exacerbated by other ominous developments. One summer evening when Louisa stayed at Greystone, she sauntered down the hall to ask her mother a question. As Louisa approached their bedroom, she heard muffled groans and whimpers. The door was closed, but she knew Mark was beating her.

She surmised from the sound that he was hitting her midsection, where no one would detect the bruises. An angry Louisa banged on the door, wanting to rescue her. Then Marcia screamed, "Leave her alone! Don't touch her!"[230] Louisa felt threatened and was prepared to run, but she was so angry she didn't care at first. It was clear Marcia thought he might harm her. Finally, Louisa backed off and didn't say anything else. Years later she would hear from one of Marcia's friends that Mark had made threats to harm both Louisa's and Marcia's parents.

The children increasingly noticed something evasive about their mother. Marcia developed a skittish, sometimes haggard quality and avoided eye contact. Over time she'd become less presentable. It struck family and friends that she had seemingly lost her fashion sense. In reality, her controlling husband was buying her clothes and even cutting her hair.

Mark would go through all the mail and routinely disconnect the phone, making it difficult for her parents and children to reach her. Years later Marcia revealed that Mark purposely kept her isolated to focus on the writing, quipping that she felt like a "word merchant." "Marcia also told me, that one time they had friends visiting…and she was out on the lawn talking to them, and Marc came out and physically drug her back into the house to 'work'. He insisted she keep writing, no matter what. Marcia told me that,"[231] a friend remembered.

Then in the fall of 1966, to Louisa's horror, her mother showed up at her Boston apartment with a black eye. Marcia didn't have to admit to her problems anymore; they were becoming visible to everyone. It wasn't the first time she'd suffered black eyes from Mark. Louisa was ready to call the cops, but, in typical fashion, Marcia made excuses. "He does have a ferocious and uncontrollable temper and this is what has caused most of the trouble. When he is himself he is fine and considerate and everything goes well. But a lot of the time he works himself to the point of exhaustion and then looses his grip. Afterward he is contrite and apologetic and really feels bad about it."[232]

Robert Moore never physically abused Eleanor, so it's unclear why such an outspoken, apparently confident woman like Marcia accepted it. Perhaps the confidence was a front. Friends thought Marcia was an appeaser, wanting to placate people, play the peacemaker. There were other reasons. Marcia also confided to friends that she was afraid to leave Mark because of threats against her parents and daughter. Living with the abuse became necessary to protect them.

One night, Marcia literally walked out on Mark. She had watched carefully and made note of where he kept the key for the safe in their bedroom. It was dark; she was alone in the house. Grabbing all the bonds she could carry, she fled the mansion and kept walking until she reached the Trailways bus stop. She caught a bus to Boston, then a train to her parent's house in Concord. The bonds she managed to salvage were a Pyrrhic victory, a minor portion of her assets. Within a few months, Mark sold off over $120,000 worth of her stock, and with Marcia seemingly unaware, managed to have her sign over Greystone, the apartment, and the store to a trust he'd created solely for himself.

Early in their marriage, Marcia unwisely granted Mark power of attorney. Douglas usurped the bowling alley Marcia financed, an extremely valuable piece of property where a large shopping center and apartment complex had since sprung up, increasing the value. He'd even managed to get a hold of her Radcliffe thesis, hoping to publish it for profit, which Marcia had written on the subject of airplane crashes and the related astrological aspects.

After her escape, Marcia was eager to flee the East Coast, far away from the stifling, condemnatory familial and marital forces orbiting her life. As long ago as her time in India, her parents had mailed her clippings about California. She replied at the time, "I felt as though we had hit the jack-pot today when the mail arrived with bundles of magazines and all the material which you sent from California.... I hadn't realized just how beautiful the mountains out West are...."[233]

The idea of moving to Ojai, California, appealed to her because of its well-known history as a haven for Theosophists, and because her father had donated about $2 million to a center for spiritual meditation there, called Meditation Mount.

Years before, Robert Moore had found inspiration in a rewrite of an Alice Bailey pamphlet titled *Religion in the New Age*, deciding to invest in "a place dedicated to beauty and to people where all creeds and races go and mingle freely without separativeness—where they can see and learn of the Buddha, the ancient Greek Gods, the Christ and his disciples, and the whole panorama of man's upward struggle towards his God in all lands and races and in all modes of expression."[234]

Shortly after arriving in Ojai, Marcia informed her father from Meditation Mount, "Main thing is that I want you to know that I am truly grateful to you for making this place possible and for making it possible for me to be here. I will do my best to carry on the dream—which is also a very beautiful reality."[235]

Soon however, Marcia Moore would discover that she was not so welcome.

1970S OJAI

"**O**nce Marcia left Mark...she was remarkably rootless and wandering,"[236] a family member would later characterize, though she managed to maintain a professional relationship with him. Roaming between various residences, love interests, and friends, everywhere Marcia explored became a way to expand her network of gurus.

Like one morning when she attended a lecture by prominent occultist Manly P. Hall in Los Angeles and gushed about how extremely well organized and appointed his research center was. "Shall probably be doing some work in the library there,"[237] she wrote her parents, though it would never come to pass.

In another instance, after visiting Berkeley, Moore began writing that she'd likely secure a teaching job in the vicinity or even enroll as a student herself. Again, the venture simply petered out, forcing Marcia to relent: "The people to whom I talked really wanted me and they sent for the recommendation etc. But at the end it was quashed on a higher level. Not surprising really.[238]... Now that so much is opening up here in Ojai I feel less drawn to Berkeley."[239]

Nowhere was Marcia's desire to be involved more evident than it was at Meditation Mount, the institution to which her father had substantially donated. "I never expected to become so attached to the people here in Ojai, the group at the Mount, or to have so many new avenues of self-expression open up," Marcia said. "In any event, I have a strong desire to remain here for a while longer, and feel that I can be useful in various ways. And of course I am having a lovely time myself! So it is providential that it didn't work out to go to Berkeley,"[240] was how she spun it to her parents.

Beyond offering to teach Mount members yoga exercises, Marcia willingly took her turn at menial tasks like watering the garden, receiving visitors, or making granola and vegetarian dishes for the food line. On a typical day, she'd set up her typewriter in the Mount's auditorium, and by midmorning, revel at the sun streaming in. "I know that it seems like an extravagance to be here but if you could see all that has to be done you would understand. Also, it is so beautiful. At the moment I am sitting at a big door-size table looking out over a row of pure white lillies, down past the green fields and orchards, and then up at the mountains which are lit by the sunset."[241]

Unfortunately, she also began inserting herself into matters where she was not necessarily wanted. Like the time she wanted to bring together the leaders of all the spiritual groups in Ojai. "The ideal thing would be if we could use the auditorium at Meditation Mount for this, but I know that the people there like to keep it just for full Moon meetings,"[242] she wrote her parents.

Marcia's administrative suggestions were met with resistance by Florence, the chief administrator, and her assistant, Frances, who helped run the Mount. Additionally, Marcia began making promotional recommendations that mortified her parents. "I believe that eventually the real work of the Mount will have a lot to being broadcast to the world via TV. Perhaps even as early as 1975 or 6…. I think that the problem is that it is hard for people bogged down in present problems to envision the sweep and grandeur of the message which is destined to go out from Meditation Mount…. It has been a great source of pleasure and satisfaction to me personally to know that I can be helpful in the work at the Mount, and that all this has happened so spontaneously with no pushing or forcing."[243]

Administrators at Meditation Mount, Robert
Moore's beloved philanthropic endeavor.

To her parents, however, pushy is precisely how her advances were received. Meditation Mount was her father's cherished philanthropic endeavor. Like most other causes he and Eleanor generously contributed to, he was content to be a devoted, yet silent, partner in the spirit of Rockefeller, Carnegie, and Mellon. Robert's creative contribution was

170

limited mostly to a booklet he wrote and published at his own expense titled *A Personal Search*, detailing his pensive outlook on religion, karma, reincarnation, and how mankind can achieve ultimate altruism. He had no inclination to meddle in the administrative affairs of the Mount, designed to function mostly as a sanctuary for all to engage in peaceful meditation.

Conversely, Marcia saw great potential in making Meditation Mount more renowned, even internationally recognized, if she could just convince the administrators. "By and large everything seems peaceful here without too many undercurrents or any real discontent on anyone's part. The only thing that doesn't seem just right is the autocratic set-up of the administrative structure which puts all the power in one person's hands—fortunately an altogether benevolent dictator…. As I see it…a large part of the problem lies in the exclusion of staff members from the Board of Directors…. It seems strange that the affairs of this organization should be guided by a group of people who, with the exception of Florence, do not live in Ojai and are not closely in touch with what is going on here."[244]

Robert Moore tried to push back in his gentle, diplomatic manner. "It might be well to remember that the Mount was built and its work dedicated to the extension of the GMC[vii] and MGNA[viii] and in the furthering of the Tibetan's teachings…. I know that visitors are always welcome there, and encouraged but have some doubts if they would want to have outside groups come in as groups for other teachings. You may recall that their by-laws specifically rule out healing teachings for instance and to bring in groups for promoting most of the subjects you mention, acupuncture, etc etc etc would, I think, meet with resistance and to me quite properly so. They are set up 'to do their own thing' without dilution,"[245] her father cautioned.

Gentleness quickly ran its course when Marcia wrote about Mark Douglas, of all people, staying a stretch in Ojai to work on a book. That forced Robert's hand. He immediately forewarned the Mount staff. "As

---

[vii] Group for Meditative Creativity
[viii] Meditation Groups for the New Age

to the arrival of Mark at Ojai, ostensibly to work with Marcia on her book, there is little that I can put in a letter…. For Meditation Mount I only want to ensure protection from any dark forces that might seek to infiltrate. There could be real danger to the work and to the group in allowing a seemingly harmless entity with subtly ingratiating ways, proffering only to help to insinuate itself into our work and group…be on guard."[246]

The Moores traveled to Ojai every year to attend the annual spring meetings. Planning to be in town for a board meeting, they certainly did not want to encounter Mark. Marcia was notified and responded incredulously. "Why you are afraid that he would, or could, move in on Meditation Mount baffled me utterly…. But to demand that he forego the vacation (albeit a work vacation) on which we have both counted seems to me unesoteric to say the least."[247]

Marcia's parents, Robert and Eleanor Moore.

With her aspirations for the Mount increasingly dashed, Marcia Moore took up a new crusade to establish her own reputation in the valley. For some time, she had been enchanted by a house which sat upon the opposite ridge called High Winds. Up until then, she stayed with friends, rented their houses, or house-sat. At one point she stayed in a small Roshi[ix] house, and another time lived at a cottage in the Theosophical Society retirement community.

Nearby she found a lady who served inexpensive vegetarian dinners out of her home, or she'd go have one-dollar lunches at Krotona Institute of Theosophy, founded by prominent theosophist Annie Besant in the early twentieth century. Ultimately, Marcia longed to build her own metaphysical college in the vicinity. High Winds was the perfect spot, just a few miles from Meditation Mount.

"Commune"—Marcia Moore pictured at "High Winds."

When some tenants moved out at High Winds, Marcia pounced on a one-year lease, moving in with a woman named Margery Chenery, a

---

[ix]   Japanese for Zen master or teacher.

thirty-year-old single mother she had recently befriended. Considerably younger than Marcia, Margery had three young children.

In typical fashion, her parents were unconvinced that things would go smoothly. Over time, finances didn't seem to add up for her new roommate. As she had done numerous times for other "charity cases," as she had referred to them, Marcia once again turned to asking her parents for money, but they refused.

Every new acquaintance was a potential source of bringing her ambitions for the High Winds property to fruition. Daughter Louisa remembered an embarrassing anecdote of Marcia telling a wealthy property owner she was considering buying the million-dollar house, thinking she could turn on the charm: "This man came over. He owned property in another part of town. Marcia was interested in meeting him. Somehow, she got word that she'd like to see him at High Winds and he was clearly puzzled as to why she wanted to meet him. He was about ten years younger than she was, and Marcia tried to flirt with him. It didn't seem to register to her that her behavior was embarrassing. For one thing she had food on her face. She was trying to draw him in with her magnetism, way overestimating her own sexuality and looks. Trying to charm him. Trying to come across like she was thirty. But already she had a wan, haggard, bony look. Not as attractive as she was when she was younger. And he had no idea who she was, that she had been subject of a book. She was fishing in the wrong place. He wasn't impressed. She thought with the house she was renting, she could project this aura of wealth and fame and image. Nothing came of it, and Ojai was pretty small."[248]

Marcia was always caught between opposing forces: her dreams and her parents. She was willing to put in tremendous work and hustle to set her metaphysical projects in motion but was always under the thumb of the Moore family fortune. She earned a decent income from her accomplished crop of books but not enough to finance her grander vision, constantly leaving her on Robert and Eleanor's leash.

Despite this, these few years in Ojai marked one of the most enriching periods of Marcia's life. Freed from the shackles of failed marriages and at least physically removed from her parents' disapproval, she developed caring, lifelong friendships with the most kindred of spirits.

Moore's true gift was shepherding novices, some with a passing fancy, others sincerely seeking help they weren't finding in traditional religion or medicine. She gratifyingly expanded their horizons through yoga, astrology, and past-life regression.

As always, Marcia was a generous and considerate friend, peer, and practitioner. Routinely she regressed people for free and charged little to nothing for yoga, spending considerable time teaching and mentoring people interested in New Age topics and parapsychology. "There are a number of people in the valley who want me to start a yoga class and I told them that if they could find a place in a school, church, or someone's home I would be glad to oblige," she wrote her parents. "Thought I'd charge a dollar and donate the proceeds to the group."[249] Later, she'd say, "It isn't that I'm all that great a philanthropist but again with times so bad for so many people even the least little bit of help can make the difference between life and death."[250]

Additionally, Marcia would prepare large vegetarian meals and serve them in the spacious dining room at High Winds, which had become a sort of commune. Her richly furnished camper, with a rounded top, teak interior, bright rugs, and cooking amenities, doubled as a guest room. "There is a man coming around who wants to make a movie about us,"[251] she'd tell her parents.

An eccentric cast of characters flocked to Marcia, but her open arms sometimes paved the way for leeches and scoundrels. She consulted with all sorts of mavens who studied diverse metaphysical fields, including some who may have had associations to cults. One companion described her as a walking encyclopedia, soaking up knowledge from books and the colorful collective of specialists who passed through her life.

Those days saw Marcia consumed in a whirlwind of activity. "Tomorrow I am going to the opening of a new astrology center in Santa Barbara,"[252] she wrote her parents. One week she'd be off to a hypnotist convention, the next to San Francisco for a gathering of three thousand astrologers, while the next she'd report, "I am going with some friends to a Japanese sukiyaki dinner in LA. Have been meeting a number of Japanese people who are plugging the Tenrikio…cult which specializes in healing."[253] Then it was off again, "leaving for L.A. where I am giving a lecture tonight and a small talk tomorrow for the festival of light."[254] She attended major New Age conferences, like Gnosticon, which offered lectures on everything from "mundane astrology" to "sex magick/witchcraft."

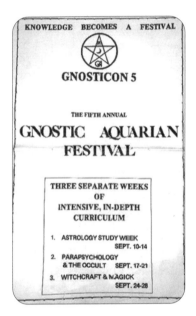

A brochure from one of the festivals Marcia lectured at.

Solstices and full moons saw Marcia participating in festivals at local parks where she'd do Hatha yoga on the lawn amongst other practitioners who offered astrology, tarot, I Ching, Sufi dancing, T'ai chi ch'üan, and even juggling, with spontaneous music heralding "an atmosphere of love and harmony." The hit musical *Hair* captured the whimsical, experimental spirit of the time. Marcia was even rumored to have brought the phrase "Age of Aquarius" into the American lexicon.

Earnestly delving into a plethora of belief systems and occult disciplines, eventually she knew enough to adeptly converse after learning from experts who had dedicated their lives to one particular area.

"During the course of thirty-five years of metaphysical investigations I have studied many different maps of consciousness. I have delved into the profundities of the twelve zodiacal signs, the ten Cabalistic sephiroth, the nine Catholic orders of angels, the eightfold wheel of the Buddhists, the seven rays of the theosophists, the six-pointed Solomon's seal of the Hebrews, the five elements of the Chinese, the four essences of the Greeks, the sacred trinity of the Christians, and the polarized duality of the Gnostics,"[255] Marcia touted.

Soon Moore was conducting traveling "hypersensing" workshops to explore the recovery of past or even future lives. Held at the homes of various enthusiasts dabbling in esoteric studies, each participant was instructed to bring ten dollars, a vegetarian potluck item, and a blanket or small pillow. Additionally, Moore intended to present similar programs featuring yoga, telepathy, and other New Age methods of consciousness expansion. She finally began fulfilling her childhood dream.

Amplifying her burgeoning reputation in Ojai, Marcia had created an impressive body of published works during her writing years with Mark: *Reincarnation, Key to Immortality*; *Astrology Today*; *Yoga, Science of the Self*; and *An Astroanalysis of Jacqueline Onassis*. There was also *Diet, Sex, and Yoga* which displayed over one hundred black-and-white photographs of a svelte Marcia in cat-eye-like eyeliner, with a sharp, chopped Cleopatra-like hairstyle, demonstrating flexible poses in formfitting leotards and tights.

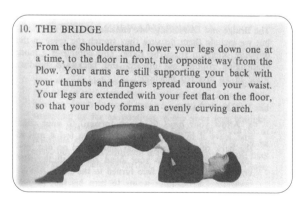

10. THE BRIDGE

From the Shoulderstand, lower your legs down one at a time, to the floor in front, the opposite way from the Plow. Your arms are still supporting your back with your thumbs and fingers spread around your waist. Your legs are extended with your feet flat on the floor, so that your body forms an evenly curving arch.

Yoga pose by Marcia Moore from her book *Diet, Sex, and Yoga*.

"The Cobra"

The most accomplished, which she would refer to as her magnum opus, was the thick, encyclopedic *Astrology the Divine Science*, with a foreword written by a well-known astrologist, Dane Rudhyar. "There is no other adequate history of astrology and much of the other material is very new and original,"[256] Marcia boasted. It would later be translated into Spanish and released in such places as Argentina. According to Marcia, the comprehensive introduction to astrology was once used by USC as a college text.

Various books by Marcia Moore.

Having broken free from Mark's clutches, Marcia started penning her solo project, *Hypersentience*. As with her final book, *Journeys into the Bright World*, she fantasized that she may even have to go incognito due to publicity that may arise. "I see it as an extremely valuable new form of therapy,"[257] she wrote her folks. "Eventually I may have to change my phone number, but in the meanwhile it is pleasant to be available to some of the people who are always trying to get in touch with me."[258]

"Many apparently irrational attitudes, phobias, fetishes, and compulsions can be explained in terms of previous life experiences." —Marcia Moore from her book *Hypersentience*.

Regardless of plentiful ventures, Marcia Moore never stopped working towards her dream of purchasing High Winds for the seat of her esoteric world college. "The Aquarian University of Man,"[259] whose abbreviation sounded like the Hindu meditation syllable "Aum" or "Om," Marcia promoted. Beyond yoga, astrology, and reincarnation, she planned to offer classes on acupuncture, Aikido, Cabala, vegetarian cooking, massage, palmistry, parapsychology, pottery, pyramidology, tarot, and thanatology.

No matter how kooky the idea to raise the money, she threw every-thing at the wall to see what would stick, once offering to moonlight as a silver coin saleswoman on commission to raise the funds, but they never panned out.

Undeterred, Marcia had a lawyer draw up rather elaborate agree-ments for the purchase of High Winds, telling Florence that she knew a man who boasted of unlimited funds from "the mafia or Cosa Nostra."[260] Florence tipped off Marcia's parents, and even Marcia's lawyer became so concerned that he telephoned her father. Robert and Eleanor were relieved to discover that since High Winds and its two hundred fifty acres had become so embroiled in a rather public five-year-long legal dis-pute, it became too complicated for her to pursue further. It was aggra-vating for her parents that she should resort to such financial gymnastics. Marcia should've had the wherewithal to buy any house desired, but her calamitous separation from Mark greatly strained her finances.

In anticipation of someday owning High Winds, Marcia began calling the place Ananta Ashram, center of a small esoteric group in its infancy as an organization. "Having a center makes it easier to get con-tributions and grants,"[261] she said. The camper Mark had allowed her to temporarily keep, which Marcia nicknamed "The White Whale,"[262] lent to the appearance of legitimacy with its license plate "ASHRAM."[263] Zipping around the windy canyon country, she'd dart between lectures and workshops.

Unfortunately, after living at High Winds about six months, the arrangement with her roommate predictably imploded. In addition to Margery's financial shortcomings, there were personality clashes. In fact, it had created a rather tumultuous shake-up at the ashram. Although Margery had endeared herself to the group, it was Moore who had paid to establish the foundation. Therefore, it was Margery who'd have to leave.

In the fallout, Margery became retributive and perhaps jealous, as disparaging comments were circulated about Marcia in the Ojai com-munity. The sour parting of ways tarnished her reputation at the Mount, which reached the ear of her parents. In defense Marcia wrote, "Please take these rumors with a grain of salt because in this case at least they simply aren't true. People are always so quick to believe the worst. For a long time I felt hurt that Florence, after knowing me almost thirty years, and after all I had done there at the Mount, would believe Margery Chenery's absurd fabrications and never even give me a chance to speak for myself."[264]

Marcia Moore found herself on the move once again.

SEARCHING FOR COMPANIONSHIP

Hopes dashed for High Winds, Marcia retreated to a small house in Ojai with a boyfriend who called himself Akeva. In his sixties, the affable Leo man was tall and, while not handsome in the classical sense, carried a lot of magnetism and good humor. At one time he had been a manufacturer's representative with a solid income, but he now lived off Social Security.

Previously he had lived in Los Angeles with his wife and children, but a traumatic incident caused him to abandon that life. One day his twelve-year-old son answered a ring at the doorbell to an adolescent neighbor friend wielding a new gun. Believing the gun was unloaded, the neighbor pointed it at Akeva's son as a lark and pulled the trigger. The first pull was a harmless click. The second discharged a bullet through his son's mouth, killing him instantly. The horrific tragedy took its toll on Akeva's marriage; his wife subsequently left and remarried.

Akeva dropped out of everything and everyone. Driving out to the desert, he lived in his car, only to slowly reassemble his life after moving to Ojai. There he discovered Theosophy and worked at a bookstore where Marcia crossed his path in trying to persuade him to stock her books. Although previously unsuccessful, with Akeva now managing the store, Marcia got her wish. The two became fast friends and eventually lived together as lovers.

Marcia with "Akeva" in Ojai.

To some degree it was an enjoyable time for both after years of psychological hardship and failed relationships. Two wounded birds flocking together, touring the country on a spiritual quest to help those in need. Together they'd hit the road in the White Whale, conducting hypersensing workshops for people who wished to recollect details of their former, or even future, incarnations. "Although hypersentience may evoke memories of previous incarnations, it is not exclusively preoccupied with the past," Marcia once wrote. "The individual who sets out to explore the uncharted realms of his own psyche, and of the mind of the universe, endeavors to enter a dimension of wholeness which contains the archetypal plan of the kind of human being he may become."[265]

It was a carefree and exploratory time; the people they regressed believed they had discovered interesting, sometimes even silly sagas about their past-lives. Moore encountered one woman who was convinced that she'd been condemned as a witch, burned to death during the Inquisition. "A few subjects have traced their origins to a musical note, or to a realm of pure vibratory impulses,"[266] Marcia said. One participant imagined he'd been a bootlegger, gunned down by mobsters in the 1920s. Another traced a previous existence to India, where she'd been a member of the "cobra cult."

"Yesterday I had a session with a poor woman who for several years has had no teeth at all because she gags every time the dentist trys to work on her. Was able to discover that the reason was because during a stay in a mental institution for a nervous breakdown she had been force fed through the nose.... Akeva and I both worked on her and I am certain that she will soon be able to have the dental work accomplished,"[267] Marcia wrote.

According to Moore, she and Akeva had crossed paths in a past-life too. "A couple of thousand years ago in China we were very happily married with a big bustling Chinese household," she told her parents. "It amazes me when I look back and think of the progress he has made in the last couple of years. When I first saw him I thought he was just an overgrown hippie and would barely talk to him. Now he has become a man of such power and spirituality that his reputation is rapidly spreading."[268]

Creatively, Marcia began self-publishing *Hypersentience Bulletins*, which were circulated to subscribers for a modest fee. In addition to keeping her growing fanbase abreast of her upcoming engagements, they afforded Marcia the opportunity to narrate colorful past-life regression sessions and discuss interesting astrological charts of notable people or events.

Marcia on the covers of her foundation bulletins.

When Akeva decided to go to Japan to study Tenrikyo, their relationship reverted to platonic. Marcia then took up with a man named Lynn Powell. Related to Arthur Edward Powell, who authored such occult classics as *The Astral Body*, *The Etheric Double*, and *The Mental Body*, Lynn wrote screenplays. He maintained an answering service but no residence in California. Travelling constantly, he lived a high-class hippie existence from his van and avoided income taxes. Rumored to be a triple Ph.D. and Anglican priest from England, Lynn would perform an unction, and sometimes even last rites, to Marcia's New Age cohorts.

After spending an intimate summer together, the relationship between Marcia and Lynn fell apart. Marcia then took up with another man she'd end up financially supporting. Byron, whose real name was Robert, was an intriguing, attractive man with a wiry frame, sandy hair and mustache. In San Diego, he'd taught astral travel and claimed to be the reincarnation of the nineteenth-century British poet, Lord Byron. "Have been spending many many hours with the reincarnated Byron and find that his story corroborates what we were getting in every detail. He is the only direct male descendent of the original Byron and suffers from the same disease," Moore enthusiastically told her parents. "They always say that souls incarnate in groups and thus we seem to be bringing together various members of that original constellation of writers. Considering the number of people I have regressed it is hardly surprising that I should at last be getting some 'biggies.'"[269]

Part of that original constellation included her friend Barbara Devlin, who claimed to be the reincarnation of *Frankenstein* author Mary Shelley. Devlin attempted to substantiate Byron's reincarnation claim in her book, *I Am Mary Shelley*. Among other similarities, the poet Lord Byron had a club foot, and Marcia's new companion shared the same affliction.

Things became serious enough with Byron that Marcia thought about marrying him, hinting to her parents, "I see Byron just about every day and we will be together at High Winds. I suppose you could say that he is my present romantic interest—and quite a lot more. Mark arrives the day after Christmas and this time we should take care of all the final final arrangements on the book plus a divorce."[270] Yet despite professing deep feelings, Byron ultimately abandoned her.

Marcia's friend Kareen Zebroff was there to soften the blow. Kareen, a famous Canadian author and television personality who hosted a series on yoga, had first met Marcia when she got on a rickety table and performed her patented headstand to prove total balance as a yogi. Afraid she'd fall over, Kareen reached out to steady the table, and that was the start of another dear friendship.

Marcia had been traveling on a lecture circuit for several months straight when Byron stood her up. They had planned a romantic sabbatical at Kareen's house in Canada. Byron was supposed to meet her there but never showed, leaving Marcia crestfallen.

After their relationship soured, Marcia then criticized Byron, depicting him dismissively in one of her bulletins: "I once worked closely with a man who was formerly a famous but arrogant and cruel romantic poet. He is now occasionally employed as a Hollywood ghost writer but shows little of his onetime talent, partly because of a disease which has sapped both his body and mind."[271]

Almost as if it were an ominous sign to leave, another tragedy befell Marcia—she suffered a horrific rape in Ojai. The '76 Chevy Vega that ex-husband Mark finally traded her for the camper broke down. She had wanted to get out from under the hefty motorhome payments for some time and into something less gas-guzzling. Marcia took it to a town mechanic. On the way back, she apparently accepted a ride from someone who saw her walking. Purportedly, this man may have been buzzing around her esoteric entourage and offered a ride. He drove into a secluded wooded area, dragged her out of the car, then violently beat and raped her for hours.

The scenic mountains, trees, and open canyon country that endeared Marcia to Ojai turned into a nightmare, as it served as a remote enough spot for no one to hear her screams. She mustered just enough strength to fight him off and escape. Marcia's lifelong commitment to remain physically fit quite possibly saved her life, as she outran the perpetrator. He was eventually caught, booked, and sentenced to a state mental hospital.

Whether ashamed or not wanting to relive it, Marcia never even told her own family. Scorned by her parents for the better part of her life, she couldn't bring herself to inform them that another venture had ended terribly. As she was prone to do, Marcia internalized the trauma and moved on. The Moore family eventually discovered the rape when private investigators, hired by the Moore family after Marcia's disappearance, looked into her time in Ojai for clues. Even Ojai, the sanctuary far away from parents and ex-husbands, resulted in misery.

In 1977, she'd get away from it all yet again. Trying to put the rejection and heartbreaking incidents behind her, Marcia continued drifting onward through a four-month lecture tour. Ultimately, she'd travel north and become even more excited about a project she dreamed would finally catapult her name into the stratosphere of metaphysical recognition.

In what turned out to be a fateful trip, she'd meet her fourth and last husband, Howard "Sunny" Alltounian.

"TWIN FLAME"

In her final book, *Journeys into the Bright World*, Marcia Moore gives a glowing account of meeting her fourth husband, Howard Alltounian. She wrote that he first stumbled upon a photograph on the back of one of her books while browsing a Seattle bookstore. Apparently so taken by it, he felt some sort of magnetism radiating off the page, thinking what an ideal wife she'd make.

In reality, it seems Howard first glimpsed Marcia on a local television program. Moore had been a guest on *Seattle Today*, a morning show hosted by charismatic blonde Shirley Hudson and her amusing cohost, Cliff—two talky Geminis who kept it light and sometimes quite funny. They'd give household tips, muddle through recipes while spilling things and laughing, and give out tickets to restaurants or prizes for best home remedy. Marcia had been invited on to speak about karma and past-life regression. As fate would have it, Howard would later appear on the show to discuss Marcia's disappearance.

The morning program had become a favorite of Howard's while he was recovering from a fall. "One morning, on the way to the hospital, I was a few minutes late and I was running for the elevator and I fell and broke my hand," he described. "Because of my poor circulation it didn't heal. They pinned it again. I was out about two, two and a half months. And while I was off, uh, God it was beautiful, I hadn't been out of the hospital, I hadn't had a vacation like that in ten years. It was in the spring…. I got in the habit of watching the Seattle Today Show."[272]

When the Seattle Astrological Society booked Marcia as a guest lecturer, Howard remembered her and showed up early to nab a front row seat, equipped with a tape recorder to capture every word. To emphasize how surely fated the encounter was, Marcia highlighted that she wasn't originally scheduled to stop in Seattle. It was a last-minute decision to add more dates by her astrologer friend and unofficial manager, Mac McLaughlin. He arranged it through his friend Carol Phillips, president of a local astrological association. Carol set up the lecture showcasing Marcia at a Seattle museum, followed by some workshops at her home.

Ironically fate did seem to be involved, but not in the way Marcia could have known. Turns out Howard knew Carol, and at one time was interested in her. He showered her young daughter with gifts and arranged for Carol to get free medical treatment at the Seattle Public Health Hospital, where he worked. Having become acquainted with Marcia's friend, he suddenly had an inroad.

Howard managed to be at every event Marcia attended that weekend. After the Friday night lecture, he appeared at a Sunday workshop, followed by a group dinner. A friend of Carol's threw a party in Moore's honor to cap off the weekend. It appeared Howard attended the party by chance, but "Carol told me that he pressured her into taking him to the party, and that she gave in and took him although she did not want to,"[273] Howard's friend Marwayne Leipzig later revealed.

As the guests departed the party that evening, Howard asked Marcia to take a walk, and they got to talking about drugs. "I asked her if she had smoked any pot and she said yes she had, but she didn't think too much of it," Howard described. "And she said the only drug that she thought was interesting was ketamine. And I said, ketamine, that's an anesthetic agent. You know, I had used it as an anesthetic."[274]

It was also a mind-expanding substance, a psychedelic like LSD, Marcia replied. When Moore discovered Howard was an anesthesiologist familiar with ketamine, her eyes lit up and it cemented her belief that they were destined to meet. Suddenly they were on a fast track to getting to know each other intimately. An idea for a new book would strike her shortly thereafter—she'd write about ketamine.

During their walk, Howard seized the opportunity to kiss Marcia, who later described to her parents, "Much to my astonishment he said that he was in love with me and wanted to marry me. Anyway, I didn't take it very seriously, even though he is a most attractive man."[275]

Marwayne Leipzig would find herself playing a pivotal role in his pursuit of Marcia. After their encounter in Seattle, Moore's next stop was a ten-day engagement in Canada conducting workshops at the Mystic Arts bookstore in Surrey, British Columbia. Howard repeatedly called there but couldn't get through. "Finally, on the last night before she was to leave, I stayed up all night, writing these letters, in a last ditch effort to communicate with her before her departure, knowing very well that once she left the area, most probably I would never see her again," he wrote anecdotally. "After completing the two letters, I called the postal service, and they would not guarantee that the letters would be delivered the next day. At the time, I was Deputy Chief of the Anesthesia Department at the United States Public Health Service Hospital. The Chief was away and we were short-handed because of summer vacations. There was only one soul on the planet that would help at this crucial time, my good earth angel, Marwayne! I called her at 4 o'clock in the morning to ask her if she would drive up and hand deliver the letters."[276]

"Earth Angel" Marwayne Leipzig in a photo she used for professional purposes, astrology career, letterhead, and the like.

As she was prone to do, Marwayne took pity on the lovesick Howard, agreeing to drive the 150 miles into Canada at daybreak. "I did not know Marcia before they met, by the way. I first met her when I hand-delivered letters to her in Vancouver, from Howard…another one of his emergencies, requiring help."[277] By that afternoon in July 1977, she arrived with two envelopes addressed to Marcia Moore.

The first, which Howard made a point to note had been written at 3:32 a.m., stated: "Dear Marcia, <u>Check one or more of the following:</u> 1. Road manager 2. Pick strawberries while you make yogurt. 3. Co-host on t.v. 4. Feet warmer…this incarnation only (smile). 5. Procurer of money for the Foundation. 6. Help keep clean that tacky little house that we rent. 7. Personal physician. 8. Learn to stand on my head. 9. Listen to a Gemini, ad infinitum 10. Co-spiritual leader in "Hypersentience Movement". 11. One and one are two, and two is love, and you're the one I love, Howard."[278]

In the second letter, Alltounian pleaded, "Dear Marcia, It is a pure psychic-destiny phenomonen that has attracted me to you. You <u>must</u> see me before you leave! Love, Sincerely, Howard P.S. If you don't, I'm going to call Sybil Leek (smile)."[279]

Upon receiving the love notes, Marcia fatefully agreed to stop by Seattle to see Howard on her way back to California. "I was housesitting for a friend, and I got two of those big kerosene torches and put them at either side of the entrance so she could see where I was at. We were soul mates,"[280] Howard depicted. Moore arrived at 2:00 a.m. to an ostentatious display of romance. He lavished her with champagne, flowers, music, and an opal-diamond talisman he purchased, representing her sign Gemini with the planet Saturn. "I knew that we would meet only briefly before you left the area and would not be together again for some time. The thought occurred to me to buy you a token piece of jewelry to remember me by. I wandered into a jewelry store and saw the talisman exactly as I had visualized it during the regression session. It was a case of pure precognition,"[281] he'd tell Marcia.

"After greeting me warmly he handed me an elegantly wrapped package and exclaimed, 'Marcia, I know my destiny is either with you or through you,'" Moore wrote in *Journeys into the Bright World*. "Opening the box I saw that he had presented me with a most beautiful and unusual pendant. 'Wear it always,' he said. 'I think it has healing powers.' I asked him to fasten the chain around my neck and since then have seldom taken it off."[282]

After spending several hours together, Marcia had to leave Seattle. Following a stop in Ojai, she traveled to Maine to finish some books with ex-husband Mark Douglas at the mansion they once called home. "Dear Mother and Dad, It feels strange to be once again ensconced at Graystone and pounding the typewriter. The two books Mark and I are producing will the the greatest literary masterpieces ever to hit the astrological market—otherwise I wouldn't be here. All the same, it is quiet and beautiful and a good respite from four months on the road."[283] Howard frenetically corresponded with calls, letters, mailgrams, and packages, scrawling, "My Dearest and Most Precious, Brilliant and Beautiful Hypersentience Princess."[284]

Last her parents heard, Marcia was on the brink of marrying Byron. Now that things were blossoming with Howard, she took up the task of informing them that was off, but she had a new man in her life.

Howard invited Marcia to spend an interlude with him in September 1977. Besides the weekend they'd spent together previously, it marked their only time together before tying the knot. "Altogether, Howard and I had spent ten days together. Nevertheless, we went ahead with plans to be married at Marwayne's home in Lynwood, Washington,"[285] Moore wrote in *Journeys into the Bright World*. Howard had secured a house in the Sand Point Peninsula. "Am having a fabulous time here in Seattle visiting Howard Alltounian. He has been house-sitting this month in a very beautiful home in the woods overlooking Lake Washington, so the surroundings are really delightful. And Howard treats me like twenty million dollars,"[286] Marcia gushed. By the end of September, she would even add him to the Ananta Foundation's board of directors.

Marcia affectionately referred to the surrounding woods there as Sherwood Forest, contending that they were reconnecting to an actual past-life where they'd dwelled among forest people. "In Sherwood Forest he fashioned the weapons for the outlaw band. Now, as the spearhead of the ketamine research program, and one of the few who are legally permitted to give injections, he is still wielding a sharp pointed instrument for the sake of human liberation,"[287] Marcia wrote of Howard's role.

For a smitten Marcia, those days were a dizzying courtship of long walks, intimate talks, and her new favorite pastime—using ketamine together. "Our first joint ketamine session took place in a spacious upstairs room of the house in 'Sherwood Forest.' As Howard made the preparations I took the phone off the hook and lay against the bed pillows, wondering where in the universe I would go this time," Moore described. "In retrospect it seems as though becoming engaged to someone with whom I had spent little more than a week was a daring step to take, though at the time it all seemed logical, sensible, and inevitable. Certainly our confidence in the rightness of the decision was spurred by the fact that during my ten days in the Seattle area Howard and I took two spectacular mind trips together."[288] In kind, Howard proclaimed, "It was the first time that I had ever taken ketamine with her, and had a cosmic marriage…"[289]

Although they had already begun talking marriage, Marcia hadn't yet filled in her parents. In September 1977, she began paving the way. "Sunday the 18th I leave for Seattle. It is for personal, not professional, reasons that I am making the trip. I will have plenty of time there and will sit down and write you a proper letter and send some pictures."[290]

In keeping with her penchant for scorching former lovers, it was now no holds barred in casting out Byron. "Strangely enough Byron and I are now better friends than before, now that his supremely Byronic— Leonian ego is no longer threatened by my fame/notoriety…."[291] In a way I felt badly about this because Byron had asked me to move in with him, and I had very seriously considered the possibility. But I was also very turned off by Byron's self-destructive ways—terrible eating habits, smoking four or more packs of cigarettes a day, etc. He is now so emaciated that he weighs less than I do. However, I am not being a rat deserting a sinking ship. Byron had every opportunity to opt for health and self-regeneration but the death wish is just too strong, even though there is a part of him that wants very much to live. It was strictly his choice to cultivate the chaotic lifestyle that is so rapidly hastening his demise. Barbie and I have done everything possible to try to help, but at this point it has to be up to him. Anyway, he looked terrible when I left, and was so weak he could barely walk, I really wondered whether I would ever again see him alive. But back to Howard. By contrast, he is a vegetarian—six feet tall health food enthusiast, is now doing an hour a day of yoga, and is very deep into astrology, hypersentience, and the whole spectrum of contemporary metaphysics."[292]

Marcia almost sounded like a schoolgirl. "When I first met him he didn't have the beard but when I told him I liked beards he immediately grew one.[293] ...It would be impossible for any man to be kinder or more romantic than Howard. He makes me feel like a princess all the time."[294] Although they'd just met, Marcia also reported, "He is now on the board of directors of Ananta Foundation and says he hopes to be of special help in the fund-raising department."[295]

Now that things were consummating with Howard, she'd finally finalize her divorce with Mark, forgoing whatever favorable settlement there was to be had in order to remarry. Curiously, Marcia also began laying the groundwork to her parents that Howard might quit his job, so they could focus their energies on her new book about ketamine, which carried the added legitimacy that he was an anesthesiologist. "The pay is good and problems minimal. Nevertheless he is becoming bored with administering anesthesia and hopes soon to move on to more challenging fields of medicine.[296]... As soon as possible he would like to resign from his job as deputy chief of the department of anesthesiology at the Seattle Public Health Hospital and go full time into holistic medicine, but that probably won't happen for some time.... He is having an engagement ring made for me and is still talking marriage. I guess it will happen—maybe in June—but neither of us wish to rush things. He is eager to get his financial situation cleared up first. So that's where things are now, and I must say I am very very happy."[297]

Despite the accumulated misery that resulted from Marcia rushing into her previous marriages, waiting until June 1978 suddenly became too far away. "Things here have been moving so fast I can hardly believe it," she wrote in the fall of '77. "Howard called twice today. The first time was to say that he had found what he considered to be an ideal living spot about a forty-minute commute from his hospital. He also suggested that we get married early in November, so we could have right in and start out as husband and wife. Needless to say, I assented.[298] … The enclosed pictures are actually quite a lot like him since he is just about always smiling. Very much like his middle name which is 'Sunny.'"[299]

Howard's clever signature. The letter "E" inside a drawing of the sun, to represent his legal middle name Sunny, a nickname Marcia liked.

Notice was hardly given to the Moore family. In a letter dated November 17, her parents learned that the wedding was just eight days away. "Everything here is going fantastically well. This afternoon I am meeting Howard at the hospital so we can go and confer with the Unity minister who is marrying us on the 25th at the home of our friend Marwayne Leipzig,"[300] Marcia excitedly reported.

"The Farm" (the Leipzig's residence).
About a block away from Marcia and Howard's duplex.

Marwayne threw them an engagement party, but she'd later confess to John Moore, "I guess you know I have had mixed feelings about Howard and Marcia ever since they met each other!"[301] Unbeknownst to Marcia, Marwayne had requested marriage compatibility charts from some astrologers. One of them knew Moore, having spoken at the same lecture in the '60s. "I had a feeling there was more froth than substance to her,"[302] the astrologer wrote.

Another astrologer gave ominous warnings about Marcia: "Don't let her pick your brains. She will rob you of your leadership.... Be careful.... The thing that bothers me most about this chart is that moon...

her emotions…you know I spoke to you about the vampire in olden times…. Well, Pluto conjunct moon, I think has a vampirish effect. That is, it can rob the emotions of their true expressions…what is the skeleton in her closet? What is the dirt she is sweeping under her rug?"[303]

Presciently, the astrologer also noted, "She likes people that feed her mind…that can give her ideas and she can develop them. Under other circumstances, she might be a plagiarist, but I don't think she is…The 'thing she adores' is leadership, fame and to lead the parade…this gal has an ambition which hits her up…burns her up…gives a great deal of zeal and enthusiasm, but not too much stick-to-it-iveness…"[304]

Regarding their marriage, the astrologer prognosticated, "She is willing to sacrifice her gain or popularity or what have you for a romance, love affair or marriage for a while. And I think when she is emotionally depleted by a new relationship that she feels 'well, what the heck. I have been through this before'…'I don't need a man'."[305]

Death was also examined: "When the last call comes, I think it will be sudden and clean and she probably wants to be cremated."[306]

In closing, the astrologer remarked, "But I'll tell you, I am glad she is your <u>friend</u> because this woman can be a power, and I think you get along very well with her, but then you get along with almost everyone."[307] Whatever reservations Marwayne had, she kept them close to the vest. In fact, Marcia would agree to dedicate *Journeys into the Bright World* to "our good angel, Marwayne Leipzig."[308]

In an effort to win over her parents, Marcia relished the opportunity to say that she was marrying a doctor, hoping to restore the notion that she was capable of settling down with an accomplished, respectable man. "I spent the morning of my departure from Seattle watching operations. Fascinating! Howard has given me two scrub suits, a doctor's white coat, and taught me to take blood pressure." Jumping the gun, Marcia began addressing her letters, "Mrs. Howard Alltounian,"[309] weeks ahead of their marriage.

There was, however, no mention of ketamine until months later, and then all Marcia would hint was "Am also on the edge of a new thrust of activity which will go as far beyond the hypersentience as hypersentience goes beyond yoga. Like everything else I do it will, or may, be controversial for a while."[310]

Shortly after, she'd write, "For my own part, I am working in an easy way on a new book on altered states of consciousness. It will be a completely new departure and even though I am not pushing it the ms. is proceeding rapidly. It will be quite controversial and probably will sell very well."[311]

The concept would evolve into her final book, *Journeys into the Bright World*.

Final published book.

KETAMINE, GODDESS OR SEDUCTRESS?

Marcia and Howard began using ketamine together from the very start of their relationship. She found her groove after experimenting with several substances like LSD, which she'd tried on two occasions.

One time her daughter came up to Maine for a visit, bringing along a boyfriend. Marcia treated them to dinner, then shockingly asked if he could obtain some LSD for her. Apparently through his job at a bar, she figured he'd have contacts he could score from.

While alone, Marcia took the small white capsule of LSD but didn't have the benign consciousness expansion she'd hoped for. "Demonic flames danced behind my eyes and there appeared no doubt but that insanity was pressing in," she wrote. "An hour later there seemed little chance of surviving the night. Surely I was dying! What would happen when my lifeless corpse was discovered?"[312]

On another occasion, when she visited a friend at his beach house on the north shore overlooking Wingaersheek Beach in Gloucester, Moore ingested morning glory seeds. Some users lauded the seeds' ability to fuse normally discreet human senses like sight and sound in a profound way. For Marcia, they failed to generate a great effect and actually caused nausea due to the large quantities needed to induce hallucination.

A couple of other times, she experimented with mescaline, which offered some mystical insights but ravaged the body. Marijuana also failed to impress. It wasn't until ketamine that Marcia Moore found something to write home about.

Back in 1974, an acquaintance had mentioned ketamine researcher Dr. John C. Lilly's book *The Center of the Cyclone*, but it wasn't until April 1976 that Marcia had the opportunity to try it while on tour with her self-proclaimed psychic colleague, Isabel Buell. Tall and regal with black, silvery hair and beautiful dark eyes, Isabel was said to be even prettier than Marcia by those who knew them. "There was such a welcoming sense of lightness and laughter in them. It was intoxicating,"[313] a friend described. They each wore their own signature colored jewelry, in Marcia's case purple, in Isabel's pink, while both wore a small "God's eye" around their necks. Together they visited Marcia's friend Jane at her upscale home in Big Sur, enjoying the seaside ride up picturesque Pacific Coast Highway 1 on the way.

Apparently, Jane had taken ketamine at least two hundred times herself, highly recommending it, as she knew Marcia was seeking a gentler way to expand her mind. Continuing a lifelong quest to attain Samadhi, or "god-realization" as the mystics understand it, and keenly interested in the ability to reach the other side, Marcia thought ketamine sounded enticing indeed. She cast aside any reservations. "After all, someone had to eat the first oyster, undergo the first appendectomy and land on the moon, despite the hazards involved," Marcia would write. "To join the elite vanguard would not only be a challenge, it would be a privilege and an honor."[314]

It was an altogether beautiful day for her first ketamine trip. Earlier Jane, Isabel, and Marcia visited the renowned Esalen Institute, where they soaked in mineral baths and enjoyed a sunset ushering in the stars against the backdrop of the ocean. Highlighted by a glow of candles and the scent of incense, Marcia likened the experience to bath rituals used in Ancient Greece and the mythical lost city of Atlantis.

The ladies returned supple and relaxed to Jane's house, where she made them a sumptuous vegetarian meal as they indulged in glasses of wine. Later, Jane introduced them to her mysterious friend known only as Rama, a slender young man with long hair, who lived in the hills and occasionally made trips to Mexico to obtain ketamine.

While Isabel passed on trying it, Marcia plunged right in. After ensuring Marcia was relaxed, Rama began administering a dose into her arm. Jane set the ambience with a record of Hindu chants. Within two minutes the substance began to take effect—and what an effect it was. "I noticed that the fluid was as clear as water and took only a couple of seconds to leave the syringe. In less than two minutes, far sooner than expected, the rush began.... It started with a slight giddiness and a noise like the chirping of crickets. The cricket chorus rapidly swelled to a smooth purring roar similar to that produced by the motor of a well-tuned racing car. This was not one solid sound but rather a propeller-like staccato whirr which seemed to come from an external source," Marcia described. "The sensation was reminiscent of the times I had inhaled nitrous oxide at the dentist's office. But that had been like standing at a door. This time I was going in. It also felt like going home. My voice thickened; speech was impossible, and then I was spinning round and round like tumbleweed and the sense of familiarity was becoming greater and greater...."[315]

Marcia felt comfortable and elated while streaks of colored light danced across the ceiling in geometric patterns. Any personal concerns were being grinded away, as if through a millwheel. Even her sense of self seemed to dissipate. "There was nothing, absolutely nothing that could be done except to submit and let it be,"[316] Marcia wrote.

The recollection struck that she still possessed a living body, and she contemplated how she could possibly return all the way back into her physical husk. Her ongoing speaking engagements on hypersentience popped into her mind, but although the term rang a bell, she could now only grasp at remembering the meaning. "Oh dear, I have completely blown my mind," Marcia thought. "Now my friends will have to deal with a zombie."[317]

Intense love for Jane overcame her, accompanied by a familiar feeling, as if they'd experienced a similar existence before:

> It seemed so terribly important that she should be there, and that we should be sharing this sacred interval together. I fancied that we were fellow priestesses in ancient Egypt, that I had been lying in a stone sarcophagus in a death-like trance, and that she was my hierophant who would usher me back to the world of the living. Images of colonnaded temples, sphinxes, pyramids, and winged figures floated behind her. I loved her enormously and felt that we had been through something like this before in one of the mystery schools of legendary eras. Surely we would remain soul sisters forever. "You are my initiator," I whispered, certain that she would understand.
>
> For some reason I also wanted to convey to her that I thought that ketamine was a gift from Venus. Not just that it was a Venusian substance in the astrological sense but that I felt as though it had actually been brought, or manifested, from another, higher planet as a gift of grace to help relieve the present human plight. But the idea was too complex and I gave up trying to speak of it.[318]

That initial experience left her feeling like a new person. "Stepping outside was like witnessing the dawn of creation. Every leaf and flower was polished to a brilliant sheen, the sea sparkled and the air was dewy fresh.... Seemingly, some element of my former personality had died, but some other part that was far more vital had been reborn."[319]

Marcia Moore had indeed been reborn yet again. Remarried for the third time, having cast away the wreckage of failings at Meditation Mount, High Winds, with Byron, and all the other grandiose plans, she began anew with Howard in Washington as 1977 came to a close.

Over the next year Marcia diligently set her ketamine project in motion, to be capped by a new book detailing her experimentation, in the hopes of revealing the sheer power of ketamine to unchain the mind from the temporal and physical boundaries of the world around us.

Initially things went smoothly. The FDA permitted Marcia and Howard to proceed with clinical studies on humans based on her claimed qualifications as a psychotherapist, to be assisted by her anesthesiologist husband as a coinvestigator. Taping her sessions and transcribing them in *Journeys into the Bright World*, Moore attempted to put readers directly in her shoes, as if they had experienced it themselves. Ketamine's power was unique, altering normal dimensions of distance, space, and even time.

Marcia Moore wasn't just tripping in the privacy of her own home; she was accessing whole other realms. The "bright world," which she likened to an ancient Hindu concept called the "*anima mundi*" or "soul of the world"[320] had different dominions within. She invented the term "cosmatrix"[x] to describe the stratification of encountered realms. The pinnacle layer was of formless, pure essence, the next layer consisted of archetypes, and the last was one of majesty.

Different doses could get her to different levels, as Moore tried to calibrate and harness it. "Twenty-five milligrams would open the door to an easily remembered esthetic archetypal realm of of purely sensuous enjoyment, whereas fifty would still wring out tears of frustration at my continuing inability to make the connections between the 'here' and the 'there.'"[321]

To Marcia, the anesthetic agent wasn't just catalyzing physiological changes in oxygen or bloodstream; an actual entity came through—a goddess. The goddess had her own agenda, and would convey messages according to her own vision, not Marcia's, which surprised her. It was as if confirmation to her that the goddess was real. Presumably, the goddess would reveal more important secrets only when she was ready. "They're not going to give me the biggie yet," Marcia wrote. "The next present will be after the New Year. This one was all pretty pretty pretty packaging.

---

[x]   Short for "cosmic matrix."

Tinsel and paper and fluff and light and love and massage and Merry Christmas. It was all Santa Claus and no Christ."[322]

The goddess also permitted taking ketamine recreationally. "I felt as though somebody loved me. I think my high self wants me to know that.... I don't even have to use it for the book. In fact I think I won't. They don't even want me to have to bother with typing it. This is just a little red tinselly bow saying 'Merry Christmas we love you. We're going to be with you for a little while. You and Howard can do your thing together...and then you can come back to us. Have fun.'"[323]

Moore came to understand that she was subservient. The goddess was a mystical sage, and Moore felt it would be an honor to serve as her priestess. This nurturing, sentient essence was eager to bestow the precious gift of ketamine to an increasingly fractious humanity.

But to an extent Marcia was becoming obsessed. At first she was afraid to re-emerge from a ketamine trip without Howard assisting, but soon she was taking trips alone. She took to calling, not her apartment, but the bright world "home," where she was eager to return with the swiftness of a dose. Soon Marcia was hoping, waiting to blast off to the bright world alone. One weekend in February, after Howard left for a fishing trip, Marcia rushed helter-skelter to unplug the phone before injecting a thirty-five milligram dose.

The goddess convinced Moore that she had discovered the fast track to enlightenment. No need for the intense discipline of yoga, or rigorous study of the intricate and celestial alignments of astrology. Even those with no arcane knowledge could be edified. Now that Marcia wielded ketamine, kowtowing to other supposed "master" mystics was a thing of the past. Ketamine instantly supplanted countless hours of meditation. Arcane wisdom was now just an injection away. The notion would later be met with staunch derision by some in the metaphysical community for espousing such chemical shortcuts.

Marcia traveled so deep while under ketamine that worrisome commentary began surfacing in her writings. "When I'm really under I don't care if I never function again,"[324] she curiously wrote after one trip. "This is the deepest I've ever been. I wish I didn't have to come back,[325]...I don't want to come back,"[326] she ominously described after another.

And there was an incredible frustration of not being able to connect the two worlds. Increasingly she became consumed with trying to fuse the magical realm of ketamine with our material world but couldn't manage to do it.

Otherworldly insights were deluging her mind, and although Marcia couldn't always make sense of them, she couldn't shake them from her thoughts. She was on the cusp of grasping how to enter another stream of consciousness that sits above the earth. She postulated that the key was to metaphorically associate it with design of the Great Pyramid of Giza. Our material domain was like the platform that ultimately ascends and converges to one triangular point that culminates in the bright world.

Not all trips were profound; some were lighter in nature. One trip transported her to a tinsel-town movie set reminiscent of the popular television show *Gidget*. A beefy twenty-something Howard frolicked on the beach with an exquisitely svelte, teenage Marcia in all the radiance of her golden youth.

Several times her anesthesiologist husband commented that her repeated use was causing a diminished reaction. It surprised Howard that in one session, the ketamine wore off after fifteen minutes. But instead of responsibly cautioning her to tap the brakes, he suggested upping the dosage. Marcia denied the tolerance, deflecting that it was merely a psychological response. Besides, ketamine wasn't habit forming, Moore reasoned. It was a healthy practice, as addictive as meditation, yoga, or the way joggers get hooked on a "runner's high." Technically she was right. Although reactions vary, the medical literature on ketamine indicated little in the way of chemical dependence. Even after she vanished, Howard would describe to police at length its classification as a non-narcotic.

Gauging the effects, Marcia calibrated her own desired dosage, just enough to induce the hypnotic state allowing total crossover, not to exceed seventy-five milligrams intramuscularly. Anything over that was deemed too potent.

Moore hoped their research would be useable to the FDA. Among other things, ketamine could be helpful for weight control and treatment of anxiety, she touted. Once, when Marcia found herself in a tense state over the administrative duties of her foundation and stressed about an upcoming dinner party, Howard administered a twelve-milligram booster beforehand. According to Marcia, ketamine helped her pull herself together and enriched the occasion.

At the same time, there seemed to be odd contradictions in her logic. While a look underneath her clothing would have revealed some injection marks that troubled friends and family, Marcia seemed to see superiority in abstaining from alcohol or even seeking relief from aspirin for a mild headache. After a fifteen-milligram predinner dose she wrote, "Whereas a predinner cocktail would have dulled the senses this easeful upliftment intensified this every detail of that memorable meal. Yellow corn, green lima beans and red peppers in a casserole sparkled mysteriously in the candlelight. The salad of green and purple cabbage and orange carrots ringed with scolloped cucumbers on a bed of lettuce could have been nature's crown jewels. I had no more desire to consume these beauteous vegetables than to munch on emeralds and rubies, yet my soul was sumptuously fed."[327]

However, Dr. Lilly warned her that ketamine would amplify what was already latent in a user, a hard lesson Marcia learned when she encountered her first bad trip. "There I was skittering down the lower side of the mandala unable to halt the descent. 'Oh this can't be,' I protested incredulously. 'I've never yet had a downer. It just doesn't happen,'" she lamented. "But what I was seeing now was the garbage bin of this milieu where the only known expletives seem to be 'shit' and 'fuck' and where grossest substances are used to produce whacked out crude, lewd and smutty 'highs.'"[328] In another trip she felt extremely frail and delicate like fine bone porcelain, as if she could easily splinter into thousands of pieces.

Perhaps she was overdoing it. Marcia's own usage and the lasting impression of Dr. Lilly's warning forced her to admit that ketamine could carry side effects. Introspection was now needed to determine what underlying negative forces had come to the surface. Yet Marcia even began rationalizing the goddess's dark side. Disciplinary punishment was an unfortunate necessity. It was she, who like a rebellious toddler, had pushed the limits and thrown the tantrum. Now the goddess had had enough, responsibly putting her in her place, defining the boundaries and restoring maternal authority.

Meanwhile, back in the real world, the FDA grew increasingly skeptical about the validity of the project, specifically whether it was being properly documented and conducted in even a semi-controlled environment. The FDA hadn't granted permission for her to simply affirm her own personal adoration of ketamine. Following a stern letter warning them of a possible shutdown, Marcia immediately switched gears to placate them, opening the experimentations up to other subjects. "As we began to work with individuals and launched our Friday night 'group samadhi' sessions my private journeys also began to take more account of other beings,"[329] she announced.

The FDA's findings determined that they were failing to record and maintain proper case studies. As a result, the second half of *Journeys into the Bright World* shows a shift in style, somewhat mish-mashed and crammed, with superfluous information that didn't make for as interesting or organized a read.

Conveniently, Marcia used Howard's medical license number to buy as much ketamine as she liked via mail order, spending hundreds seemingly to accumulate a stockpile. The honeymoon phase of their marriage was still in effect and during the first half of 1978, Howard was still employed, leaving them plenty of money to fuel the research.

Like the duality of her zodiac sign Gemini, however, the second half of 1978 would unfold into a completely different story. Howard quit his job in June yet contributed little to alleviating the pressure of finishing *Journeys into the Bright World*. In fact, by the fall of 1978, the FDA issued a cease-and-desist order after they failed to provide adequate documentation that they were administering the ketamine in a controlled clinical setting. "The FDA instructed us to halt proceedings until new information could be gathered. We have conscientiously complied with all their requests but remain enmeshed in the coils of this inscrutable government agency,"[330] Marcia grumbled.

Moore would soon find that it wasn't so easy to find test subjects either. Some of her friends gave in to trying ketamine but objected a second time. Her friend Maria Comfort agreed only after learning that a twenty-five-milligram dose wasn't enough to knock a person out, but she didn't attain bliss like Marcia. Instead, ketamine made her hallucinate and vulnerable to suggestion. Marcia said, "Turn all the walls purple, and suddenly all the walls were purple."[331] When somebody else said a tiger was coming out of the chandelier, a tiger leaped toward her. Luckily, Maria had no fear of tigers or she might have had a heart attack, she'd later remark. Not being in control of her own mind scared her, and Maria refused ketamine when Marcia asked again.

Other participants held their own opinions. Marcia invited Marwayne's son Peter and his young friends over for a ketamine injection. They all remarked that it was "just another drug trip," or "Marcia's just tripping," Marwayne's daughter Cris remembered. The boys mockingly laughed and said "they had 'done lots of research' in their time, but that they 'weren't smart enough to write it all down.'"[332]

Halfway through writing *Journeys into the Bright World*, Marcia was still living a double life to an extent. Correspondence to her parents and fans conveyed nothing of her ketamine use, just teasers laying the groundwork to someday break the news. "It will describe the results of a unique research project which takes advantage of the synergistic effect of his fifteen years as a practicing anesthesiologist and my thirty-five years of metaphysical studies. We have been calling this new departure project 'B'—the big 'B' standing both for *book* and for *bombshell*. Probably we should warn you in advance that it is sure to be controversial,"[333] she hinted.

Moore was right to be apprehensive about telling her folks. It eventually sent shockwaves throughout the family. Marcia even asked her daughter and her husband to try it. They were alarmed that she was promoting something that required needles, as were Robert and Eleanor. She urged her son Christopher to try it. Instead, he pleaded with her to stop.

News even reached Meditation Mount back in Ojai, causing administrator Frances to write, "Dear Bob and Eleanor: I suppose I have been having second thoughts about sending you a copy of Marcia's letter, but it seems to me that I agreed to keep you informed of her 'approaches' to the Mount. If this is just turning the knife in the wound, and you would rather not have details in the future, do let me know, and I can just say that I've had a letter."[334]

Marcia's mother immediately launched into damage control mode. "It is extremely distressing to us that Marcia has intruded into the life of the Mount with her controversial (to say the very least) work, attitudes, and misapprehensions.... We believe the Mount should stand free, completely, from Marcia's work establishing 'new strengthened links with Ojai.' The Ketamine Therapy could cause legal and mental situations with which the Mount should have NO LINKS."[335]

Robert affirmed the sentiment. "Dear Frances, I quite agree with Eleanor's evaluation of this situation.... We have not yet heard directly from Marcia about her intention to spend some time in Ojai this fall and until we do we cannot easily convey to her our strong impression that she should not try to 'cooperate' in her current work and ideas with the very specialized work at the Mount."[336]

With the FDA hindering the legitimacy of the project, there was a knock-on effect on Marcia's daily life. Hidden behind a blissful façade in letters to her parents and fans, conflict and complications in the marriage began surfacing. The dwindling funds as a result of Howard quitting his job only fanned the flames. Soon Howard was spending more and more time with his ex-wife at their old house in North Bend. In kind, Marcia began taking more solo trips out of state, particularly to Ojai.

For a woman who so passionately believed in omens, synchronicity, and predestiny, by mid-December 1978 an unprecedented polar storm began waylaying northwest Washington, symbolic of the storm hitting yet another shaky situation Marcia made for herself. In a letter to her father, she wrote, "Creatively I'm not doing an awful lot these days. Sort of waiting to see which way the wind blows and what opens up. In fact it's almost been a winter of hibernation. Possibly that is what was needed. Inwardly so much opened up so fast I'm still just assimilating. I seem to have gone so far beyond what can be expressed, or what the public is interested in knowing about. that it makes a kind of communications gap. On the whole, however, I guess the focus will remain on reincarnation and what its acceptance can mean for humanity."[337]

As the New Year of 1979 began, it was almost as if the historic cold front was holding her captive from fleeing back to Ojai. "Dear Dad, Forgive me for not sending a proper card for your birthday this year," she wrote on January 3. "I suddenly realized that that time has come and do want to say that I am thinking of you and sending you all love. But I can't get to the store because Howard is in North Bend looking after his ailing ex-wife (I insisted he stay and help out) and in the cold my car won't start."[338]

Less than two weeks later, Marcia Moore would vanish without a trace.

MISSING

MARCIA MOORE
Astrologer, Author, Lecturer

On January 14, Marcia Moore disappeared from her Seattle, Washington home. If seen please contact - Detective Daryl D. Blemis, Snohomish County Court House, Everett, Washington 98201

A search flyer (misspelled Lt. Darrol Bemis).

BACK ON THE CASE

L t. Darrol Bemis had an awful lot to digest on Friday, January 19, 1979, five days after Marcia Moore was reported missing, but in some ways he had just scratched the surface. He'd spent late nights reading *Journeys into the Bright World* and anything else he could get his hands on.

He was battling a growing Hydra of a case after personally taking it over from his detectives. One dragon head was the peculiar husband, another head the budding contingent of psychics, another the mixed messages from the Moore family, yet another the ketamine angle, and finally there was the press. Even with all of that to contend with, Lt. Bemis couldn't have prepared himself for that first weekend, as Howard Alltounian kicked off a parade of new theories, beyond his initial claims of suicide and amnesia.

After consulting various astrologers, mediums, numerologists, tarot card and Ouija board readers, Howard called author Jess Stearn, Marcia's old friend who'd written a book about his experience practicing yoga with her in Massachusetts back in the 1960s. Stearn referred Howard to a Florida psychic who sensed a connection to one of Marcia's ex-husbands, and also perceived the name Campbell.

Howard immediately made the association to Marcia's incorrigible ex-husband, Mark Douglas, and informed Bemis of the new lead. He pointed to a quarrel between Marcia and Mark last December about republishing two of the books they cowrote, *Astrology the Divine Science* and *Astrology in Action*, which he claimed Douglas refused to allow. The most commercially successful books of their careers, Marcia hoped to further capitalize on them by penetrating new markets in paperback.

Howard told a dramatic anecdote in the group interview with police on Thursday, January 18: "And she says, I just got to get out of this body, which would be the description that Marcia would use, use to kill herself. And I says, why? And she says, I just don't have the strength to go on. She says, my spirit is broken. I can't get Mark to publish those two books. Two books that she had worked eight years on."[339]

That melodrama was puzzling, as contrary to Howard's account, there appeared to be cooperation between Marcia and Mark. *Astrology the Divine Science* arrived in the mail before she vanished, sent by Mark with no covers marked "workbook," to be rewritten. Marcia had even written her folks about having Mark touch base regarding the European rights. Additionally, John Moore reviewed a recent letter to Marcia from Mark. "A perfectly friendly letter, chatty letter, talking about books they might do together, and books that he had read, and he wondered if she had had a chance to see, and what her opinion was,"[340] he informed Bemis.

Still, Howard persisted that Mark drove cross-country in his motorhome and may have purposely or accidently killed Marcia during a heated argument over the books, somehow managing to capitalize on the five-hour window when Howard was at the movies that frigid Sunday evening. According to his theory, Mark then drove to Oregon, parked in a public garage, flew back to New England, and established an alibi.

Improbable as it sounded, this notion actually clicked momentarily with a real lead. Some neighbors reported seeing a fancy motorhome parked in the neighborhood around the time Marcia went missing, that Sunday afternoon or shortly before. But investigators eventually tracked down the motorhome belonging to a couple who provided photos matching the one seen by neighbors.

Complicating Howard's theory further, Mark was just released from a hospital. He was bedridden from January 8 through 17, recuperating from a heart attack, as Bemis and John ascertained when they called to confirm his whereabouts on the night of January 14. All Mark could offer was that Marcia seemed "profoundly unhappy"[341] when he spoke to her recently around Christmas. He denied Howard's contention that it had anything to do with republishing their books.

By the time Howard conceded the improbability of Mark's involvement, he had quickly moved on to another suspect, pointing the finger squarely at Jim Batchelor, an acquaintance of Marcia's who lived about twenty miles away in Snohomish. Marwayne later described Batchelor as a strong-looking man of medium height with broad shoulders and sandy hair, around forty-five years old, but looked thirty-five or younger.

"Howard says Batchelor is an extremely violent type of person, and could be capable of almost anything," John Moore relayed to Bemis. "The first time I heard about him was this morning about 4:00 o'clock… Howard came down to the bedroom and chatted about half an hour,"[342] said John, who stayed at the duplex during the search.

Duplex apartment in Lynnwood, Washington. It was painted blue and white at the time. Somewhat of a fish out of water, Marcia's new town was the type of place one might hear locals say "anda" instead of and, "hiya" rather than hi, or "verra" for very.

Jim Batchelor could very well have made a viable suspect, having followed Marcia to two states. "He said that Jim Batchelor first heard about Marcia by reading one of her books," John said about Howard's account. "And then he took off on his motorcycle from Indiana and roared into Ojai where Marcia was set up at that point.... And he said he was a big man, an ex-policeman and violent type of guy. And very much involved in esoteric matters."[343]

Lt. Bemis contacted Batchelor, who told him an odd backstory about meeting Marcia. Batchelor claimed to have had a vision in which he perceived Marcia's first and last name, well before he knew anything about her. Then one day while walking past a storefront in Indiana, he was awestruck when he saw Marcia's name on a sign, matching his vision, promoting her hypersentience and past-life regression workshop. From that moment Batchelor believed their fates were somehow intertwined.

Batchelor had unsuccessfully tried hypnosis before, so he offered Marcia one hundred dollars to regress him, but she too was unsuccessful. After that encounter, he learned Marcia lived in Ojai and decided to relocate there himself. Although his wife objected and filed for divorce, Batchelor moved from Indiana to California. There he met a new girlfriend, Wendy, who agreed to relocate with him from California to Washington. The couple settled at an old CCC[xi] camp in Snohomish that had been converted into a chicken hatchery.

Apparently, Batchelor did enjoy some rapport with Marcia. "Shortly after the last time I saw her in California, I was aware that she was going to marry or had married Mr. Alltounian, and were going to be moving north," Batchelor later told Bemis. "And I guess I had heard where they were moving, but I didn't really pay much attention to it. It was just out of that area and out of my scope of concern. I felt however at the time, and I had had visions that Marcia Moore and myself had a work to do, somehow, that was connected to the type of work the Edgar [Cayce] had done."[344] Under a tacit business agreement, and with his experience as

---

[xi] Civilian Conservation Corps

a carpenter, Batchelor claimed, he would help Marcia construct a new foundation in north Washington.

It's unclear whether Marcia had a close relationship with Batchelor, or if he was just another in the cast of characters with whom she made unfulfilled plans. The first time Howard met Batchelor was during a trip to Ojai, where he encountered him sitting on Akeva's porch. Then, some days later, Batchelor attended a party where Howard overheard him say that he and Marcia were going to buy a piece of land near Medford, Oregon, to start a healing center. "Who is this fellow," Howard asked at the time. "I don't have any particular, I don't know, and I don't particularly want to be close to him,"[345] Marcia responded, according to Howard.

They didn't hear anything further from Batchelor until one day in September 1978 when he called their Lynnwood apartment. Howard answered and asked if Marcia wanted to take the call, but she reportedly said no. "And so Howard put him off,"[346] John Moore later told Bemis. Batchelor called back a few times, but each time Howard answered, and he never got through. When he didn't hear back from Marcia, he wondered if Howard ever passed on the messages. But Batchelor claimed it was Marcia who'd originally contacted him about a reading. "He stated absolutely that it was she who had initiated the calls,"[347] Marwayne later learned.

Howard warned Lt. Bemis, John, and Marwayne about Batchelor, now suspecting him of complicity in Marcia's disappearance. Around 1:30 a.m. on Friday, January 19, Howard called Lt. Bemis with his new lead, asserting that Batchelor was known to Marcia's old friend Akeva as a "prophet of doom," and was "a person that they should try to avoid."[348]

The next evening, Howard asked a couple of friends to accompany him to Batchelor's residence, convinced that he was hiding Marcia, dead or alive, on his property. Batchelor had little forewarning. His only clue was that Howard telephoned to ask if he'd seen Marcia. Batchelor said no, he was sorry to hear she had left or disappeared, and hoped everything turned out okay. It was a surprise then when Howard showed up with the two other fellows. "I just thought I would bring you a copy of our book, that you would like to have one, and it is all autographed,"[349]

Howard said when he arrived. Batchelor was glad his two sons, both wrestlers, were home, wondering if Howard and his gang intended to rough him up.

One of the friends who accompanied Howard on the mission was a business associate named Heinz. The other was Bob Bevis, one of the fellows who sometimes stayed over at Marwayne's house. Howard asked the two to come along, he said, because he didn't trust himself alone with Jim Batchelor and did not want to be arrested for assault.

Things started cordially enough. Batchelor invited them in for coffee, but his girlfriend Wendy took an immediate dislike to Howard, wondering if he was loaded on some drug. Batchelor had his suspicions too. "I immediately determined that Howard was there for reasons other than what he had indicated and told him that he was not being straight with me and for him to, if he wanted to talk to me, to please be truthful and honest. He respected that by just merely saying, yes, but then changed the subject and went on to some other communication that was non-sensical or inconsequential concerning Marcia and her disappearance,"[350] he later said in a police statement.

Batchelor indulged Howard's stall tactics, causing Wendy to later tell him, "At that moment, you sealed our relationship. You knew I did not want him in the house, yet you brought him in."[351] The couple had been having problems, even before Howard showed up. Privately they agreed that Batchelor would not be involved with anyone connected to parapsychology, anyone like Howard. Several times during their conversation, Batchelor mentioned this promise to Howard. By then it was too late.

Batchelor assured Howard that he had nothing to do with Marcia's disappearance, and agreed to a search of his property. Wendy left the room for a moment and returned to find Batchelor holding Howard's hand, telling him how sincerely sorry he was that Marcia was missing, but that he had nothing to do with it. Incensed at Jim for letting them in in the first place, Wendy continued to seethe, holding their chicken dinner for three hours while Howard stalled for time drinking coffee. Eventually even Howard's friends said they had to leave, but not before

Howard finally confronted Batchelor about his suspicion, catching Batchelor off guard and throwing Wendy into a huff.

Wendy then stepped in to get firm where Jim would not. "I repeatedly requested that 'Howard and Heinz' leave and when they refused I informed them that I would call the police department and have them removed."[352] She called the Snohomish County Sheriff's Office. Lt. Bemis called back and asked to speak directly to Howard, who pleaded with him to send deputies for an immediate search. He was certain that he sensed Marcia's presence nearby. As proof, he claimed, a psychic had perceived the approximate location of the old CCC camp where Batchelor lived. Trying to cinch his argument, he reiterated that he'd heard secondhand that Jim Batchelor once referred to himself as a "prophet of doom." Howard refused to leave until deputies arrived.

Batchelor later described the incident: "Howard made the statement, 'she is here. I have seen her. I see her. I know she is here.' And this startled, not startled me but startled my son and Heins who looked up at me with a great question and pitiful expression, and I looked at Howard who immediately became very emotional and upset, making demands and requests that Lt. Bemis come and search the place, because she was here."[353] At one point, even Heinz said, "She is not here Howard," to which Howard replied, "You are not my friend if you say that, you are betraying me."[354]

As Bob, the other fellow Howard brought along, remembered the incident, he felt Howard had embellished quite a bit, putting on a histrionic show of determination to find his missing wife. Wendy's police statement captured the moment: "'Howard' fell to his knees, clutched 'Jim's' hands—I beg you, please help me find my wife, I will not prosecute you. I love her, we are soul-mates, all I want is her—all she wants is me. She is here and sick. I know she is in one of those buildings—I can feel it."[355] When sheriff's deputies arrived, they handcuffed Howard. He was taken to Everett General Hospital for a psych evaluation. Batchelor took pity on him and agreed to accompany him, "so that I would not be out of his sight until he was confident that Marcia was not at my residence, or that I had nothing to do with her disappearance,"[356] he said.

Doctors informed Lt. Bemis that while Howard exhibited some psychotic conditions, he was not declared a danger to himself or others, and was released late that evening. However, Howard insisted that Batchelor not be let out of his sight until the camp was searched. Instead of the two of them being released to their residences, the evening took another bizarre turn. Surprisingly, Bemis put both men up in the same motel room until sunrise.

In later recounting the incident to Marwayne, Batchelor said neither one slept that night. At one point, emotionally and physically drained, Batchelor shucked his trousers to get some sleep, but Howard became unhinged when he saw his jockey shorts, claiming they were his. He accused him of having an affair with Marcia. Each suspicious of the other, neither one slept a wink. They left the television on and stared "eyeball to eyeball"[357] the entire night.

The next day they accompanied while Lt. Bemis, along with search and rescue, scoured the CCC camp, including about twenty-four buildings and a stream on ten wooded acres. Bemis let a wound-up Howard exhaust his energy tramping all over. "We went through and I personally went under every building. No Marcia,"[358] Howard relented. Forced to admit his suspicions and psychic leads were off, he still maintained to Bemis that Batchelor was his prime suspect.

Months later, Marwayne would receive a surprise phone call from Batchelor, who got her number from Howard after asking if he knew a good astrologer. Marwayne agreed to do his chart, so he went to her house a couple of times for astrology readings. Batchelor had a pleasant voice and nice smile, but there was a blankness to his eyes, Marwayne thought. Despite Bemis ruling him out as a suspect, Marwayne learned some interesting details about Batchelor's past. He had contracted viral conjunctivitis and was in danger of losing his vision. He also had emotional issues. Batchelor said he'd been exposed to sexual activity with a sister and a neighbor as a toddler. He had other childhood scars. Once, he crawled under a barn in search of his brother, who'd set fire to it. Another time, an older brother and neighborhood kid tied him to a bull and spun him out of a barn.

Howard eventually dropped the Batchelor accusation but soon latched onto another suspect. "I'll bet it is Lynn Powell," Marcia's old boyfriend, he declared. Marwayne noted the new fixation in her diary. "Then he became so caught up with this idea as to be almost obsessed, and in the next 24 hours he was obsessed with this theory."[359]

Howard said he got the idea in revisiting a horary chart Marwayne completed around the time of the disappearance. He theorized that Powell, whom he characterized as a drifter who occasionally sponged off Marcia's money, may have driven to Washington from California. Like his accusation against Mark Douglas, he said Powell may have kidnapped or killed her while Howard was at the movies.

According to Howard, Marcia's brother John once suspected Powell, in part because Marcia's mother once heard Powell and Marcia arguing, and Powell was reportedly pretty nasty. As more evidence, Howard said an astrologer friend of Marcia's had long ago warned her to part with Powell because his Pluto was on Marcia's ascendant, meaning that he was incredibly dangerous to her. But by that rationale, Howard would be a suspect too, Marwayne realized. Howard's Pluto was also on Marcia's ascendant.

And so, as Marwayne noted, the big chase after another suspect was again "on."[360] Skeptical of Howard's latest accusation, Lt. Bemis nevertheless sent out an attempt-to-locate bulletin for Lynn Powell, around his old stomping grounds in Santa Monica. The lead came up dry. Powell hadn't even been to California for months. He was traced back to Austin, Texas, where his parents lived, and had been there the whole time. "A new low," Marwayne observed in her diary. "Howard's spirits were very low, when the Lynn Powell possible suspect did not pan out."[361]

Despite this, Howard informed media, "I can tell you that there is a prime suspect. The police have been informed. There is an all-points bulletin on him. The picture fits; they're looking for him. I think we'll have her back by the weekend."[362] But there was never a prime suspect, Bemis corrected to the press.

Meanwhile, John Moore told Bemis that "Howard is going full blast on the telephone and putting up a terrific front if he is guilty.... If there is no news of Marcia by this weekend it might be time for you to take off the gloves and confront Howard with some of the inconsistancies in his statements."[363]

Having indulged Howard with yet another wild goose chase, an exasperated Lt. Bemis asked Howard to take a polygraph exam. "At first I resented this man because he suspected me," Howard later wrote. "In fact, the entire first week I was interrogated, and harassed subliminally in true 'Colombo' fashion. The house was searched time and time again, and finally Lt. Bemis said, 'Howard, there is only one way to remove yourself as a prime suspect, and that is if you would be willing to take a polygraph test.? As the sound of the word 'graph' was still resonating in the atmosphere, I said 'absolutely'."[364]

POLYGRAPH

On January 22, 1979, Howard stopped by Marwayne's nicely dressed in a new pair of tan tweed pants and a cream turtleneck knit shirt paired with a stylish blue, coat-style sweater. "He told me these were new clothes which he had purchased to go to the conference (so it might appear that Howard did indeed look forward to that conference),"[365] Marwayne wrote.

He was on his way to meet Bemis at 3:00 p.m. for the polygraph. A week removed from Marcia's disappearance, Howard now found himself hooked up to a lie detector. Polygraph examiner John Cooper asked Howard to recap the night of January 14, to compare to his earlier statements, then asked a series of direct questions, four of which appeared in his report.

1. Have you told me the complete truth about Marcia's disappearance?
2. Did you kill Marcia?
3. Are you deliberately lying to me today to justify Marcia's disappearance?
4. Are you attempting to withhold any information about Marcia's disappearance?

Howard answered affirmatively to the first question and negatively to the rest. Officially, the examiner considered Howard's statements truthful and consistent with his physiological responses. Unofficially, Cooper told Bemis that he thought Howard may be lying but couldn't prove it with the polygraph results.

The topic Howard was officially shaky on was how much ketamine he and Marcia had been using. Nevertheless, Cooper disclosed off the record that even the answers consistent with truthfulness struck him as unusual, confiding to Bemis that the needle behaved unusually still. "It was absolutely straight. I mean just deadpan, every question asked, nothing," Bemis recalled. "Marcia taught all of her husbands how to beat the polygraph,"[366] he maintained.

Suspecting that Howard had been on one or more drugs since the moment the investigation started, Bemis ultimately decided not to drug test Howard before he was hooked up to the polygraph. Nor did he question him about substances like valium and marijuana, which he knew Howard used, that could affect the results.

Howard summarized the experience: "I met with Lt. Bemis in his office and chatted with him for an hour and a half. At 4:30 I took the polygraph and of course passed it with flying colors. Afterward, Lt. Bemis took me in to meet the Chief of Police, and his first words were, 'Well, we have to start all over again.'"[367]

Early that morning, Marwayne had finally returned from her Hawaiian vacation trying to get caught up on the torrent of troubling events. After the polygraph, Alltounian visited Marwayne's house. She journaled that "he did not seem at all relieved that he had passed and I would say acted as if he expected to pass it. Later he told me that the only thing he had not told them was that he had suggested the writing of the 'suicide' note to her brother John."[368]

Later that day, Howard asked for Marwayne's help in going through Marcia's clothes, to see if they could figure what she had on the night she disappeared. It was the first time she had an opportunity to inspect the duplex since Marcia vanished. Rummaging through closets and drawers was a surreal feeling for Marwayne, who couldn't believe all that had transpired since she left for Hawaii a week ago. "Her fairly new dark green light-weight slacks were there, atrociously shortened, as she was a poor sewer.… I had lengthened a pair she had shortened TOO SHORT, and she was, indeed, no expert with the needle. I laughed in fondness at the overcasting on the bottom of those green slacks when I saw them."[369]

Before leaving for the movies the night Marcia vanished, Howard said he was certain she was clad in a green turtleneck and matching corduroy pants. He also claimed she owned a pair of hiking boots that were missing, although this contradicted the attempt-to-locate bulletin stating possibly "no shoes," and Bemis' police report recapping the night of January 14. In the report, Howard stated that she was likely wearing "some type of low shoes, black in color with a short heel on them."[370] As Marwayne now surveyed the bedroom, she noticed those dark, low-cut shoes, in a position that appeared as though they had been casually kicked off beside the bed. The green turtleneck he was certain she wore turned up in the closet, leaving Howard unsure of what she may have been wearing. Her purse containing a driver's license, house and car keys, checkbook, and cash were also in the bedroom. After looking through phone numbers and all her desk papers, there were no clues readily apparent.

In the kitchen, Howard pulled Marcia's passport down from atop the fridge, along with the typewritten note he'd given to brother John Moore. It was the first time Marwayne had a chance to inspect the ominous note, purportedly typewritten by Marcia, conveying her impending death. The note had been given exclusively to John, before a copy was provided to Lt. Bemis. In addition to the content of the note, requesting that her smaller trust proceeds be turned over to Howard in the event of her death, Marwayne noticed that it was dated January 9 and had two or three careful erasures. "It was signed in her purple ink, which she always used, in her funny printed signature, 'Marcia'. There seemed to me to be no doubt that the signature was hers,"[371] Marwayne noted.

While John Moore was in town, he'd gone through the wastebaskets and found a few syringes, which he turned over to police. Marwayne looked through the wastebasket herself and noticed several sheets of yellow paper with Marcia's handwriting on them, possibly rough drafts of ideas she was working on. One mentioned "ketamine, goddess or seductress?"[372] There was also a piece of paper that police took, with the sentences "OK—so I am a high class ketamine junkie who has to write to support an expensive parapsychological addition. Why not make the confession."[373] The comments appeared to be a preface Marcia was writing for her next book, sarcastically referring to the public perception of her ketamine experimentation. Without anything else to go on, they called it a day.

The next day, acting on Bemis' suggestion as well as Dorothy Hughes' horary chart interpretation that Marcia was "confided and restrained,"[374] Marwayne helped Howard distribute pictures at rest homes, sanitariums, and halfway houses as well as to the Bothell Police Department.

Earlier that day, Howard had sought Marwayne's comfort. "He sat down on the bed, and fell into my arms, and wept copiously, saying over and over 'Marcia, where are you. I love you Marcia, I can't live without you. If you have committed suicide, I will too. I must be with you', and much of it was incoherent as he wept and the tears flowed. I just held him in my arms and rocked him, as if he were a little child, and patted him."[375]

That night Marwayne called on close friend and psychic, Liz Jenkins, to see if she could be of any assistance. Liz invited them over and requested they bring articles of clothing for use psychically. They brought the green turtleneck and a rumpled, cream-colored silk kimono with blue and lavender flowers Marcia casually wore around the home.

Clutching the articles, Liz's impression was one of fear. "'I am so afraid', she said, 'so afraid,'" elaborating that Marcia was possibly still alive, which gave Howard hope. "Liz told him the lower portion of his house was terrible vibrations, to sleep upstairs, in fact to leave that house as soon as feasible,"[376] Marwayne jotted in her diary.

Privately to Marwayne, however, she later revealed the premonition that Howard and Marcia possibly had fought so intensely that she leaped from their car, hurt herself, and was picked up by someone.

After returning home, Howard reverted to an inconsolable state, again threatening to commit suicide. Marwayne admonished and reminded him of the impact on his ex-wife and two children. "I love Marcia more than any of them," she journaled of his reply. "'I can't live without her. I just want to be with her. If she is dead, then I want to be dead…. It is all my fault. I never should have left her that night. I shall never forgive myself. Oh why did I leave her that night? I should never have left her. She was suicidal that morning. I shouldn't have left her', and he would weep bitter tears and remonstrate with himself."[377] He lamented to Marwayne that in the event that she was dead, he believed she would reincarnate and come back to him, and that he would wait forever, for the rest of his life, if necessary.

Further demonstrating his heartache, he had converted the Sai Baba side house adjacent to the duplex into somewhat of a shrine to Marcia, with candles surrounding several framed pictures of Marcia and of them as a couple. In the event that she returned, two large, hand-painted posters hung nearby reading: "MY DEAREST & MOST PRECIOUS, BRILLIANT & BEAUTIFUL HYPERSENTIENCE PRINCESS" and "WELCOME HOME SOULMATE."[378]

Altar set up by Howard in the "Sai House"—shown to news agencies covering the disappearance, featuring "Fire Lady" painting owned by Marcia, alongside photos, and posters drawn by Howard using his pet names for her.

Later that summer, the *National Enquirer* would publish an article titled "Missing Psychic has Become Invisible & 'Is Somewhere Out in the Cosmos,'" that captured the scene. Although it discussed some details of the case, it mostly exploited the supernatural hook and focused on Howard's heartache. Both Lt. Bemis and John Moore are briefly quoted about the case hitting a dead end, before Howard supplied his own far-out theory. "It all points to dematerialization," the tabloid quoted. As support, Howard cited the case of a Salt Lake City woman who purportedly dematerialized from her home, only to reappear at her attorney's office in two weeks' time. Commenting that he expected her to return in August, Howard emphasized that to prove his devotion in the meantime, he had "taken a vow of celibacy and keeps a lighted candle for his wife's expected re-materialization."[379]

Elaborating on their marriage, the article closed with a dramatic quote: "Marcia and I were inseparable. I loved her with all my heart. Our marriage was idyllic. Everything we did, we did together. Only that weekend we had been planning to go to the Rose Festival in Pasadena. We had even planned a trip to India in February. Marcia will come back…. And until she does, I'm going to sit here and wait for her."[380]

Although Marwayne didn't doubt his sincerity when he broke down crying in her arms, she recalled contrary sentiment from the couple, noting in her journal: "My own observation was that Marcia and Howard were not very close, during the last few months, when I saw them…each time I saw Marcia, I saw pain and sorrow in her eyes. I do not think they were close anymore."[381]

Reflecting back even further, she suddenly remembered what had happened just before their wedding fourteen months ago. "He had wooed her, courted her, pursued her, with flowers, poetry, love letters, momentos of their times together, so in love with Marcia that he had to have her. Now that she was here, and the wedding license had been applied for, and they were in my living room, visiting with us, he seemed very quiet and rather distant. The next day I said to him, 'What is wrong, Howard? Do you feel differently?' He replied, 'Does it show that much?'

227

'My God,' I said, 'What happened?' Does Marcia know that you feel this way?' 'No, oh, no', he replied, 'Marwayne, what should I do?'"[382]

Back then she advised him to be straight with Marcia if his feelings had changed, rather than enter into a marriage with dishonesty, but Howard demurred and said he couldn't do that to her. By phone the next day, she again asked if he had told Marcia about the change of heart. "'No', he said, 'I haven't. Marwayne I just can't do that to her. She loves me too much.'"[383]

TURNING TO THE OCCULT

The new leads put forth by Howard, psychics, astrologers, and random tipsters continued to pile up at the feet of Lt. Bemis, as did the requisite volume of police reports, statements, and manpower exerted on the case. "When the stories went out on the wire service, the sheriff's office telephone switchboard lit up like a Christmas tree and stayed that way for weeks,"[384] a reporter for the *Startling Detective* wrote. Sometimes Lt. Bemis would get up to fifteen calls a night at home.

Already the story was garnering a fair amount of national attention thanks to Marcia's opportunistic older brother, Robin Moore. As a part-time columnist for a New York-based paper, he helped publish an article capitalizing on the sensational aspects of the investigation, saying that Marcia "led a strange existence. She was friendly with a great many unusual and strange people in the fields of witchcraft, reincarnation and yoga."[385]

Lt. Bemis advised the Moore family that putting up a reward might bring even more cranks into the pot. Howard affirmed that "kooks" were already beginning to come out of the woodwork. One note mailed to the husband suggested, "Dear Howard, I feel sorry for you. I have done a horary chart and Marcia has gone to India."[386]

Another person called and said, "After reading about Marcia in the newspaper, I had a vision of Marcia out in the moonlight with an abductor, struggling to get away,"[387] and thought she was dead.

One letter informed Lt. Bemis, as a public service, that they were certain they had seen Robin Moore's name and picture in a porn advertisement recently, just to keep him abreast of the filth corrupting the youth of society. Another noted that Robin had advocated for the legalization of marijuana and cocaine.

From Pennsylvania to Wisconsin to Washington, maps were sent in, offering their imaginings of where Marcia might be found. One tip from Montana noted that Marcia looked like prominent psychic Barbara Easton, suggesting some sort of hoax in which Barbara may really be Marcia, hiding behind colored contact lenses.

Another tipster from Kentucky zanily wrote [all misspellings original]: "I read of your amazing case in a magazine…This is my view: It will go against goverment bull shit. But a person going thru: mind blowing experments could have joined: thoes flying saucers; its not to far fetched…. Thoes flying saucers give our goverment a head ache denying they exist. Thoes people helping; with there houcks poucks knew what happend…. But like our people seeing saucers a trip to the looney bin shortens the memorys. To our goverment relief."[388]

Others' tips were maddeningly non-specific. Marcia Moore possessed features resembling lots of women, generating many reported lookalikes. From sightings at a convenience store, to a café, to a shopping mall in Federal Way, there were numerous people who believed they saw Marcia in person.

On the other hand, elements of certain tips would come hauntingly close. "Just how an Astrologer could consider herself competent and still marry a man who's stars are so inimical to hers,is a mystery…" the tipster wrote. "I would suggest using a helicopter and a infrared camera, cut down on expense by staying close to roads that lead out from her homesite, and sticking to high places and roundtop hills, the highest places in the land, next straggling barns, lumberyards and especially near where fire is or has been …."[389]

A common theory was Marcia being buried at the cemetery, after multiple news articles highlighted her unusual habit of taking walks there. One of the many tipsters would write, "My gut feeling is that Marcia's Moore's body can be found sharing a grave in Floral Hill Cemetery—put there by her husband the night she disappeared. By checking the graves that were open that night—prepared for next day burials—if this can be done—should make it easy to find her body."[390]

"I have run in 5,000 different directions at the whim of astrologers, clairvoyants, friends' tips and whatever. I couldn't even begin to count the number of psychics who have contacted me,"[391] Bemis told the *Seattle Times*. Despite the already daunting task of sifting through it all, Bemis added fuel to the fire with a few decisions that would have far-reaching implications for the course of the investigation. On the heels of unsolicited psychics and astrologers adding their two cents, as well as Howard's own supernatural theories, Bemis compounded the issue by also turning to the occult for help.

It marked a controversial gambit for Bemis, and for the increasingly overwhelmed Snohomish County Sheriff's Office. Three years prior, in adjacent King County, a police captain by the name of Herb Swindler had been unceremoniously transferred out of the Seattle Police Crimes Against Persons Unit and off the infamous Ted Bundy investigation. "There were rumors that Herb's preoccupation with psychics and astrologers, in all the occult possibilities in the mass killings, had begun to annoy the brass,"[392] Ann Rule wrote in *The Stranger Beside Me*. Lt. Bemis was now sticking his neck out in much the same vein.

On Tuesday evening, January 23, the Snohomish County Sheriff's Office officially brought in its own psychic known only as Harold, at Bemis' behest. Using a technique known as psychometry, the holding of someone's personal possessions to perceive psychic impressions, Harold had convinced Bemis of his psychic acumen. He accurately predicted the color of a jeweled pendant Howard gave Marcia, in addition to the first name of the Florida psychic Howard contacted and the direction of the CCC camp where the bizarre Batchelor incident unfolded, and stood in

Bemis' office facing the exact direction of the hospital where the psych evaluation was given.

Marcia wearing the pendant Howard gave her. According to Marwayne, it was found in a bathroom drawer, while her wedding ring was found on the floor behind the bed.

At around 8:00 p.m., Howard signed a permission-to-search form, consenting to Harold's use of his psychometric technique inside the duplex. Little discovery of import came of the exercise; apparently the waterbed interfered with his abilities. Like psychic Liz Jenkins, however, Harold sensed terrible vibrations from the downstairs bedroom, also picking up on the names Joan, Campbell, and a northern location. Although the name Campbell had also been perceived by the Florida psychic, Harold couldn't elaborate further. Putting together all the information gathered, he predicted to Bemis that Marcia could possibly be found just southwest of Banff, Canada, but none of his predictions were proven useful.

Meanwhile, Lani, Marcia's close friend and unofficial protégé, returned from the Rose Festival in Pasadena, stopping by Marwayne's to discuss her devastation that Marcia never arrived to meet up with her as well as the circumstances surrounding the disappearance. Lani revealed that, despite Howard's contention to authorities, there was serious friction in their marriage leading up to the day she went missing. "Lani said to me that 'if Marcia wanted to leave Howard, she would know how to accomplish it,'"[393] Marwayne journaled. "Lani told me that Marcia had told her about Howard, 'The only things Howard loves are Kimberly and fishing.'...Once she heard Howard say to Marcia, 'You just can't wait to go out and get in that car and go to Ojai, can you?' in a critical way. She knew that they were not very close. Once Marcia told Lani forcefully, almost angrily, that she could not stand the mundane, the cooking every day etc., that she was made for something more than that or, again, words to that effect...as we talked, she expressed to me a considerable amount about Marcia's disenchantment with the marriage, as related previously, and we were in agreement that Marcia had not been very happy for quite a long time."[394] Lani considered the possibility, however, that Marcia went for a walk and became disoriented owing to her poor sense of direction. She thought Marcia might have suffered from a mild form of dyslexia and possibly had trouble reading street names.

Lani's first and last name came up in the case file a few times, including in a handwritten note by Marcia retrieved by authorities from the duplex. Howard also commented, during a taped and transcribed session, that Lani was a close friend who had visited Marcia the Wednesday before she vanished. Despite this, no one from the Snohomish County Sheriff's Office ever tracked down or interviewed her. Not wanting to draw the attention of law enforcement, Lani never came forward voluntarily, owing to the fact that she once tried ketamine and was illegally making side money from a marijuana farm on their Vashon Island property to put her children through school.

Through a contact at a university, Lani obtained a strand of medical grade marijuana and had a chance to go into business for herself. "You learn to do it," Moore had encouraged. Lani's husband was never going to support her, as it was his Pisces nature to just float along through life, Marcia counseled Lani. "She was bound and determined that I was protected," Lani recalled. Incidentally, after Howard expressed interest in her side venture, Marcia surprised Lani by saying, "Don't confide in Howard, you can't trust him."[395]

Having stayed in the Pasadena area for the duration of the convention, Lani was completely oblivious to Howard's portrayal to police of Marcia's troubled state of mind just before she vanished.

During that week, Mac McLaughlin, Marcia's gentle friend and unofficial manager of Marcia for her lecture and workshop circuits in Canada, caught wind of Marcia's disappearance. An anguished Mac was at one point on Howard's long list of suspects, subsequently ruled out by Lt. Bemis. Mac tried to help in his own way, making contact with the police department in Victoria, British Columbia.

They recommended the services of yet another psychic by the name of Rose Gallacher. "Sergeant Mills informs me that you intend to use the psychic powers of Mrs. Rose Gallacher in a missing persons investigation," Chief Constable J.F. Gregory wrote to Bemis. He endorsed Gallacher, stating that she had assisted in a 1978 double homicide investigation and, according to the two sergeants who worked the case, "Mrs. Gallacher's services were invaluable."[396] They credited her with providing information that led to a conviction and life sentence for the perpetrator. Her self-proclaimed pedigree was a third-generation psychic from her maternal lineage in Scotland, with a portfolio of police investigation and private work to back it up. Rose agreed to travel, at her own expense, to Snohomish County to assist with the case.

On January 28, Bemis arrived at Howard's residence with Rose Gallacher. During the drive, she'd convinced Bemis of her psychic ability by describing certain medical difficulties the lieutenant's wife was experiencing at the time. Howard readily invited them into the duplex and allowed Rose to survey the rooms, feeling objects for psychometry along the way.

Touching a glass syringe Marcia used to inject ketamine, she sensed multiple drugs used in the home. Howard claimed that aside from ketamine, the only drug ever used was occasionally a small dose of valium for sleep and some bladder medication.

After proceeding through the bedroom, they left the duplex for the adjacent Sai Baba house. Again, Rose insisted that Marcia used or had been given an injection containing a mixture of drugs, as noted in the taped session: "The vibration I did pick up here, was another drug, okay? Now whether it is just innocently the valium, but I don't think so. I felt it was something a little stronger than valium."[397]

Unfamiliar with ketamine, she asked Howard about its potency. "Well, ketamine is the safest anesthetic known to man," he explained. "It is so safe that it is used at both ends of the fragile scale of anesthesia.... It's used for open heart surgery, and poor risk infants, you know, for induction.... And the reason is, all anesthetic agents are simple nervous system depressants. Ketamine is a central nervous system stimulant. So it raises blood pressure and it raises pulse. Consequently you have somebody who is in shock, I give him ketamine, will stimulant their blood pressure and pulse, and so it is very safe. It has been known to have given people ten times its maximum safe dose, and they have lived. It would have been impossible for her, you know, to do herself in with ketamine, intramuscular."[398]

Rose asked if Marcia was addicted. "Well, it's not addicting," he responded. "See ketamine is not a grade A narcotic. Narcotics are addicting. You can develop a psychological dependency to anything, you know with abuse. So, she was psychologically dependent on it. But she wasn't addicted."[399]

After asking Howard if he was still using ketamine, he conceded that he had used it the night before, in an attempt to locate Marcia on the "astral plane." The admission angered Bemis, who then confronted Howard that he lied about turning over all the ketamine in the duplex, a considerable quantity of twenty-six vials confiscated the night he brought psychic Harold over for psychometry. Scrambling for an explanation, Howard explained, "And the reason I kept that one bottle is because I wanted to get out of my body and reach her, and tell her I love her and to come back."[400] Elaborating, he claimed that in a candle-lit ketamine session accompanied by Barbra Streisand's classical album a couple nights ago, he saw a vision of Marcia sitting radiantly in a lotus position, with Sai Baba grinning nearby. Howard took it as a good omen.

Segueing to his former occupation, Rose sensed that Howard's departure as interim chief anesthesiologist at the Seattle Public Health Hospital the previous summer was due to scandal, contradicting his claim that he left the hospital voluntarily, and at Marcia's urging, so they could focus on writing *Journeys into the Bright World*. Flatly denying the insinuation, he countered with his sixteen untarnished years of experience—but admitted there was friction with a doctor who at first was his subordinate but later made his boss, concluding that he had been passed over due to office politics.

Interrupting Howard, Rose pivoted to something personal she suddenly psychically perceived. They stopped the recording to allow Howard to discreetly discuss the fact that he had been sexually molested by his stepfather, then moved on to the topic of Howard's and Marcia's previous marriages. "Howard, your wife, your previous marriage, why do I feel? I felt tenticles coming around you in that marriage. Does that make sense? Was she kind of squeezing the life out of you? Financially or emotionally?" Rose asked. "Well, both,"[401] Howard answered.

After further discussion of other drugs Marcia may have been taking, Rose coaxed Howard into remaining behind in the Sai Baba house to meditate while she spoke privately to Lt. Bemis, who noted her conclusion on the recording: "At this time I have been advised by Rose Gallacher that she sees that Howard had killed Marcia and has done her in. Can you explain why you feel this?" Bemis asked. "Yeah. The man is hedging," Rose answered. "The man is in another world. Look how he lied to you.... I do believe in all sincerity that it is accidental, and he cannot reach her unless he takes his katemine."[402]

While they were alone, she performed psychometry on the silk kimono Marwayne and Howard previously allowed psychic Liz Jenkins to feel for psychic impression. "I have just been advised by Rose Gallacher upon her performing psychometry on a kimono type robe in the house that Howard has struck Marcia on several occasions in the past. We find in this kimono a small stain of blood appearing substance. This kimono is wrinkled etc. Appears to have been recently washed,"[403] Bemis recorded.

The sash from Marcia's kimono, which was a gift from a friend. Marwayne said she looked like a China doll in it.

Feeling she could force a confession, Rose suggested speaking to Howard without Bemis present or a recording device. After having lunch at Marwayne's, Bemis returned her to Howard's around 5:00 p.m. so they could have dinner and review the session. Howard had requested that Rose return that evening since he was lonely. She convinced Bemis that she would be safe since her husband would accompany. Ultimately, Rose was unsuccessful at getting a confession, leaving Bemis to finish the police report: "It's also interesting to note that Howard Alltounian has advised Rose Gallacher that he does not like this officer, and he is very evasive apparently with me. He has been trying to give me the impression that he is enthralled with my working on this case. And he has told her the complete opposite."[404]

Despite the unsuccessful attempt, Lt. Bemis was riled up and phoned Howard's ex-wife Tina in an attempt to shed more light on the sexual problems and molestation that Rose picked up on. Bemis charged in untactfully, however. An upset Tina phoned Marwayne, relaying that Bemis had blindsided her with intimate questions regarding their sex life, going so far as to suggest that she would be wise to prevent Howard's own daughter Kimberly from visiting him. Residing about forty miles south in North Bend, Tina was unaware of the circumstances surrounding Marcia's disappearance but hoped Marwayne would fill her in.

In what would mark candidly important insight into their failed marriage, Marwayne agreed to meet Tina alone at a restaurant halfway between Lynnwood and North Bend. Tina confided that Howard had always been erratic in moods, was difficult to live with, and frequently berated her in front of the children, often saying "don't pay any attention to your mother; she is full of shit."[405]

She further revealed that their marriage hadn't simply unraveled due to irreconcilable differences, as Marwayne later journaled: "She said that the last two years of the marriage they had had an 'open marriage' at Howard's request. Seems he had fallen in love with an airline stewardess, and wanted freedom to woo her."[406] Tina went along for a while, as their sex life had gone cold anyway, but in the end, she considered it tacky and herself monogamous, leading her to file for divorce.

During their conversation, Tina divulged to Marwayne a glimpse of the resentment: "She said that right after Christmas 1978, right after she had surgery…a hysterectomy…that Howard came up to North Bend where their home is, and his visit ended in a terrible quarrel, more violent than any they had ever had. She said he was sitting on the side of the bed when he suddenly said, 'Do you know what I think of you?' There followed a tirade of abuse in which he called her money-grubbing and other similar names…. She worried about the fact that Howard had guns (a former hunter). She said that she was uneasy about him, and had on occasions feared him. I asked her if he ever struck her, and she replied that he had. She believes that Howard hates women…. She did not think her ex-husband is homosexual, but thought that he possibly has some deep psychological problems as a result of his childhood…. She asked me if I thought she should tell Lt.

Bemis any of this, and I told her I saw no reason to volunteer it, but that if Bemis came up to see her, that she should tell him whatever she could that might be of any help in solving the case."[407]

By all accounts, Tina never came forward, and Lt. Bemis never revisited the subject of Howard's past with her.

NOTEWORTHY DEVELOPMENTS

On Saturday, February 3, Marwayne visited with Liz Jenkins, who wanted to elaborate further on her psychic impressions while in the duplex. "She told me that when Howard and I had been there that she immediately felt he was heavily involved in his wife's disappearance, but that she had not said so of course, knowing that it would only cause great trouble and not solve anything. She said when she first picked up the rather rumbpled, unironed robe, her first feeling was 'fear', and then she picked up that the robe had been washed very recently."[408]

In the midst of their conversation, Liz suddenly fell into a trance. Apparently channeling Marcia, she became nauseous and said, "Oh my God," several times, as tears flowed down her cheeks. Liz perceived that Marcia was near an old vehicle, fairly close to the road, where the road joined the freeway, "and she said Campbell or Campbell Road and Star,"[409] Marwayne noted.

Liz claimed that in a rage Howard struck her violently, knocking her around like a rag doll, causing severe pain to her head and stomach. "Liz said he had killed her this way, and she thought he had dismembered the body, and it was in more than one place. She thought she had something pink on or was 'in' pink,"[410] Marwayne noted. Liz suggested that Howard does not remember the incident because he possibly suffers from split-personality disorder. Marwayne relayed the conversation to Lt. Bemis. For Howard's sake, she hoped Liz was wrong.

The next day John Moore informed Howard that the monthly disbursements from Marcia's two trust funds would be discontinued to prevent anyone from cashing checks on the accounts. It surprised Marwayne that Howard took the news in stride, owing to his newfound idea about how to get by. Vowing to continue Marcia's work, he figured that her book royalties, plus the funds he had the legal authority to withdraw from the Ananta Foundation as president and treasurer, would be sufficient. Ironically, after accusing Mark Douglas of murder, Howard was now working with him about publishing the foundation's *Hypersentience Bulletin*.

During the conversation, Marwayne was stunned by something else Howard revealed about where his future means could come from, reiterating that the typewritten note about Marcia's impending death was written at *his* suggestion. Elaborating, he anecdotally conveyed that shortly before she vanished, he broached the subject of how he would get by if anything ever happened to Marcia. According to Howard, after she joked that he should've married a younger woman with more money, Marcia later seriously revisited the subject, saying, "You know, Howard, you are right. What would you do in the event of my death? I feel that the ketamine research was the main reason for you leaving your job, and I have a responsibility about that." Howard claimed to have said to Marcia in reply, "You know, Marcia, if you are really concerned you could do this: If the tables were turned, and I had a trust fund which my parents had left me, and I were concerned about what would happen to you, I would see to it that that trust fund were turned over to you."[411]

Purportedly Marcia agreed to phone the bank the next day but then realized that a phone call wouldn't be enough. "Then Howard said, you could 'write a letter to John and ask him to handle it.' She agreed that this was the way to handle the matter,"[412] Marwayne journaled. He told Marwayne that this became the troubling note Howard said he found in the typewriter the morning Marcia disappeared.

Although Marwayne tipped off Bemis to this admission, it's unclear whether she shared the precise details of the anecdote, which directly contradicted Howard's statement to police that the morning of Marcia's disappearance was the first time he knew anything about the ominous note.

On Monday, February 5, Howard scheduled a 10:00 a.m. press conference with the local media. The day before, Howard called a physician in Arizona to ask his opinion about amnesia possibly being a long-term side effect of ketamine use.

Uncertain whether amnesia could have resulted from heavy use, he said he'd get back to Howard. "He stated he felt she was in complete control of her faculties and assured her that there was no danger whatsoever from taking Ketamine on a daily basis as it is so rapidly eliminated that there wasn't any residual blood level, knowing full well the amount she was taking,"[413] Howard wrote.

The physician had recently seen Marcia, as she'd spent two evenings with him during a trip to Arizona in November 1978, interested in his developmental research on ketamine for Parke-Davis with another doctor from the University of Michigan. Marcia was quite ill and, according to Marwayne, thought she might even be dying, but the doctor assured Marcia that it was only bronchitis. He prescribed antibiotics, which cleared it up.

During the Monday press conference, several news crews took shots of the shrine Howard made to Marcia in the Sai Baba house as he read from a prepared statement: "From the moment I found my wife missing I have directed one hundred and one percent of my energy in order to find her! After three weeks I am certain she is number one ALIVE, and number two she is somewhere out there suffering from amnesia, a side effect from the anesthetic we were doing research with, Ketamine. I have called this news conference so that you may help me find her! Publicity is what is needed at this point. Let's face it, the only reason Patty Hearst was found was because she was Patty Hearst; I want to let people know who Marcia Moore is!!!"[414]

A reporter from the *Everett Herald* and television crew from KIRO, Channel 7 focused on the ketamine use—whether Marcia was addicted and still using after *Journeys into the Bright World* was published. Additional media personnel followed, including the *Enterprise* and *Police Intelligencer*. Howard maintained that Marcia was still alive, after receiving astrological interpretations from notable astrologers.

Dr. Howard Alltounian: "A metaphysical plum pudding"

The *Everett Herald* and *Western Sun*—
reporting on Marcia's disappearance.

Marwayne became miffed at her inclusion as one of those astrologers, noting that she always thought that Marcia may indeed be dead. "My original thought about Marcia was that (1) she was unhappy, (2) taking ketamine out of both psychological addition and for actual physical pain (3) they quarrelled and after he went out to the movies, she simply walked as far as she could walk in freezing weather (about 2 miles maximum I would judge with that bad hip), sat down in some remote place in the woods or brush and waited for hypothermia to take over."[415] However, Marwayne also conceded that Marcia's friends insisted that she would never have committed suicide because of the karmic ramifications. She knew full well that for those who believe in reincarnation, suicide sets one back several lifetimes with dim prospects for ever attaining Samadhi, the yogic concept of enlightenment similar to the Buddhist concept of nirvana.

Overall, Marwayne thought Howard handled the reporters' questions well, though he stumbled in a few places. Digressing into his past, he recapped how he became interested in astrology as a result of his divorce from Tina, admitting to the press that he hated women and thought he would never remarry. Later, she recapped more in her journal: "He told them no one has taken as much as Marcia (Not true. A man name Lilly, in California I think it is, mentioned in her book, took huge amounts of it, and almost short-circuited his brain).... They asked him when he quit taking it, and he said 'six months ago'. The fact is, I know he took ketamine this past weekend, and the weekend before. I think he had had a small amount Monday morning, this morning when he first called me and asked me to come right over if I could."[416]

That afternoon Marwayne caught up with Howard's son Kevin, who appeared troubled. "Kevin had gone to see his Dad who told him 'The sight of you makes me sick. Run away or join the army.'" However, she gleaned some insight about Marcia from Kevin that sustained her conflicted feelings. He mentioned that she had left for several hours before, forcing Howard to look for her. According to Kevin, Marcia once told him, "You will have to excuse the other day, Kevin. I often go walking, and I got lost in the woods." Marwayne seemed unsure about it, pondering in her journal, "I don't think it is possible to get 'lost' anywhere around here, as none of our woods are either that dense or that extensive, as roads are all over the place, and just traffic noise could be a guide as to how to find the way out again, and if one had any sense of direction at all, one could find one's way out of a trail or road."[417]

That evening Channel 5 News aired a segment covering much of the same comprehensive information, with Howard reiterating his certainty that she was amnesiac. Marwayne recalled a recent conversation between Howard and his ex-wife Tina, where he also detailed why he was certain she was amnesiac, going point by point in a costly long-distance phone call.

After watching the segment, Howard returned home, and Marwayne received a phone call from a psychic who had visited Howard's the day before with her husband. "She said that they 'received terrible vibrations even as they approached the house', and that they were almost sick from the vibrations in the house, particularly downstairs, and most especially as they approached the bedroom where Marcia was last seen by Howard."[418] Howard told Marwayne they left in a hurry and figured they thought he was guilty.

The psychic felt that Marcia may be alive but held by some dark force, leaving Marwayne to wonder about the witches Marcia once mentioned in *Journeys into the Bright World*, and all the other sensational rumors of the occult. "I expect the next will be that Howard will grab onto that the dark forces have Marcia, and there will be publicity about witches, goblins, and things that go bump in the night. I hope not, as astrology does not need this kind of bedfellow, with which it is so often linked."[419]

On Wednesday, Howard hatched a new theory, conceding to Marwayne that he should've listened to her about Marcia's children all along. He was now certain Marcia was with her son Stuart. After all, he speculated, they were scheduled to rendezvous with Stuart in mid-January, before he and his wife were to proceed to India. Perhaps Marcia contacted her son for help and decided to tag along to India rather than go to the Rose Festival in Pasadena. Marwayne thought it was a possibility, always maintaining how odd it was for Stuart to continue with his trip to India knowing his mother was missing.

Despite this, Marwayne challenged Howard about suddenly coming around to this theory. "I asked Howard how he could substantiate this when he had claimed all along that Marcia would not do this to him, us, her parents, her friends, not even her worst enemies. He said, 'well maybe I was mistaken' and at this point I have to say it is the only possibility. I said what about the amnesia theory? He replied 'I never did believe she has amnesia. I only said that to attract the press, get the publicity, and see if that would help locate her.'"[420] It raised an eyebrow with Marwayne that he fabricated the amnesia theory after going on about it at such great length to law enforcement, the press, family, and friends.

That night, Lt. Bemis told Marwayne that he was teeing up Howard for intense questioning the next morning. "He believes Howard is lying, that he has killed his wife, and that he is 'ready to crack,'"[421] Marwayne noted.

Marwayne was nervous for Howard, but by now, Bemis was under intense scrutiny of his own, as Marwayne journaled: "Lt. Bemis is being criticized by superiors for spending so much time on the case when there is no evidence of any kind of foul play."[422]

INTERROGATION

The 9:00 a.m. interrogation on February 8, 1979, was a pivotal point in the case. Earlier that morning, he called Marwayne to report, "'That asshole, Lt Columbo, wants to see me this morning…and so m 'love, I will see you later', and with that he hung up."[423]

Right away Lt. Bemis, accompanied by Detective Seipel, set the tone, attempting to put Howard on his heels by having him read and acknowledge his Miranda rights. Although Bemis had a plan of attack, he allowed Howard to kick off the interview by launching into yet another theory.

Apparently, the twelve-year-old daughter of a real estate agent Marcia worked with in Ojai received a call from a woman who sounded like Marcia the Tuesday or Wednesday after she was reported missing. The call came in at approximately 4:00 p.m. The young girl was certain because she recognized Marcia's Bostonian accent, but the comment would puzzle the Moore family. Marcia didn't carry any sort of working-class Boston affectation or distinctive Kennedy-like nuance.

Nevertheless, Howard speculated that Marcia drove by herself to Ojai on the night of Sunday the 14th for the warm climate of Ojai she preferred, to enjoy a retreat with friends. Although none of their vehicles were missing, the timeline fit, he figured, because the twenty-one-hour drive to Ojai would've meant arrival around Tuesday afternoon.

Howard continued digressing that, while he was finished with the psychics and all their false leads, he now realized that relying on astrology was the way to find Marcia. Rambling at length, he assured Bemis that astrology is science, not myth. "The planets are really there and the [ephemeris] is a daily log of where these planets are chartered and if somebody can set up a chart and properly interpretulate the angles between them, that the aspects, you can come out with a definitive diagnosis just as well as a pathologist can take a slide of tissue and look under a microscope to get a diagnosis."[424]

Lt. Bemis had once again allowed Howard to commandeer the discussion but eventually managed to steer it back to the inconsistencies uncovered in reviewing the case reports. After repeating Howard's version of events on the morning of Sunday the 14th regarding Howard waking up to find Marcia typing what he referred to as the suicide note, Bemis confronted him using Marwayne's tip that he had admitted requesting the note days before Marcia disappeared.

> Lt. Bemis: "Howard, is it not true that you solicited this letter from her on an earlier date?"[425]

Howard repeatedly denied, countering that Sunday was the first time he ever saw her write the note addressed to John Moore. Bemis continued to press, reiterating that he knew Howard solicited the note on an earlier date and was playing games.

> Howard: "I'm not playing games with you. That's the first time I saw that letter and so what I think now, is she may have thought of this and started to do it on the 9th, but when I saw it and she may have typed it out or typed half of it. Now don't forget, that written note was half a note. The type written note was a complete note. Now she may have hand written that on the 9th and maybe started to type it on the 9th and completed it about the same amount that was on the written note and then Sun. decided that

she was going to go thru with it. That's the first time I saw that note. I know there's a discrepancy on the date, but that's the first time I saw it was when I saw her completing it at the typewriter and then signing it. That's the whole truth and nothing but the truth so help me God. I never saw that note before."[426]

Watering down Lt. Bemis' challenge, he failed to get Marwayne's tip as an official statement, preventing him from cornering Howard with the serious lie, nor did he want to compromise Marwayne's risky position of furtively providing future tips. His confrontation on the topic of the note simply petered out.

Instead, Bemis turned his attention to Howard's claim that Marcia had mentioned suicide, but out of nowhere Howard interjected a curious anecdote of a black eye he said Marcia once suffered during a walk.

Lt. Bemis: "You start about this threaten to suicide she had when she went down to Martha Lk in the summer."[427]

Howard: "Yes, yes. That was in Oct., it was just before we were going to Ohi again. There was always a consistency in whenever she had to speak publicly of her you know wanting not to do this and going into a bout of you know depression and threatening suicide. I told you what happened. I got home, it was dark, she wasn't there, I got my flashlight again and ran out and looked for her, I came back in an hour and she just walked in the door and she had fallen down, her eye was bruised, her lip was swollen and I said my God Marcia it's going to look like I beat you or something."[428]

Bemis and Detective Seipel immediately became skeptical about Marcia becoming battered on a walk.

Lt. Bemis: "I just can't really buy the story of a person fall down and get a black eye. I can't buy it, Howard."[429]

Howard: "Well, I don't know why you can't buy it. She told me specifically quote unquote that she had taken a lot of ketamine and was in the woods and she fell down and obviously if you fall down in the woods, your going to hit your face."[430]

Det. Seipel: "Howard, we've [been] in this business a long time and we know how people get body bruises."[431]

Howard: "Well, I'm telling you the truth."[432]

Lt. Bemis: "You don't usually get a black eye from falling down, Howard. Somebody has to pop you in the eye."[433]

Howard: "I've never touched my wife with any finger or any toe as long as we've been married, ever."[434]

Det. Seipel: "Fall down you'd get scratches, abrasions and cuts."[435]

Howard: "Well, I'm telling you she hurt her eye and particularly her lip. Her lip was the thing that was swollen. And she says oh, its alright it'll clear up and it did. It cleared up in a few days."[436]

Bemis pivoted to confronting Howard about lying at certain points in the investigation. He admitted to lying about all of the properties they rented, explaining that he didn't initially mention the Sai Baba house because officers would think he's nuts worshipping a frizzy-haired Indian guru. This was a serious lie if he was suspected of foul play, as it gave him more time to cover up a crime before law enforcement had a chance to inspect the additional property. He also again admitted lying about turning over all the ketamine in his possession, explaining that he kept the one vial in an attempt to contact Marcia psychically.

Howard: "I told you that I used ketamine for the first six months of our marriage which is when the book was written—at that point in time, I just wasn't getting that much out of it and I stopped taking it and I haven't taken it again until you know, until about a couple days later after I kept that one vile and I started thinking about you know, Marcia and myself, the fact that we are soul mates, the fact that we do have sun, mercury conjunctions which means we are telepathic. We were telepathic when she was here and so I figured ok, forget the god damn psychics, their not telling you anything. If anybody could reach her like Rose Gallacher you know. She came down and gave me all this bullshit about she was not only a psychic from four generations, but she was also a medium and she could contact Marcia on the other side and then she says she couldn't reach her. So I says god damn it Marcia and then I found out that if a person, you know, I learned alot thru this. If a person that's psychic such as Marcia does not want to be reached, they can pull in their antennae and they can pull in their own vibrations so that nobody else no matter how psychic they are, can reach them. So I said to myself, ok, you know she's my wife, she's my soulmate, we were naturally telepathic, if anybody's going to reach her, I can reach her. Now I can't reach her in a normal state. There's no way. But I can get out of my body and I can get outside of myself with ketamine. So I did take ketamine for several days. I did reach her. I saw her. I saw her sitting in a lotus position meditating. I told you she looked ravishingly and more beautiful than I've ever seen her. When I came out of it, I was frustrated because I wanted to make love to her. But she didn't speak to me. She didn't say a word and I interpreted that as her possibly

being in a state of amnesia. Now I have stopped taking ket-
amine again, because I realize that it wasn't, you know, I'm
not going to communicate with her. And that's it. That's the
whole truth and nothing but the truth so help me God."[437]

Howard had once again diffused a pointed question using the
occult, leaving Bemis to transition to another falsehood that ketamine
was the only drug he used, but later admitted to smoking pot the day
Marcia vanished.

Lt. Bemis: "You have admitted to numerous people, Howard,
you were high on marijuana the night she disappeared."[438]

Howard: "I did smoke a joint when I left the house after
leaving her when I went up to the movies. When I left the
house, I went up to get some wood, because she wanted me
to stay at the Ci house that night."[439]

Lt. Bemis: "Why?"[440]

Howard: "I don't know."[441]

Lt. Bemis: "You guys had a fight didn't you?"[442]

Howard: "No, we didn't have a fight. We never fought, we
didn't have a fight."[443]

Lt. Bemis: "This isn't the story I'm getting from everybody
that knows you people."[444]

Howard: "Well, I don't think your telling the truth at this
point. I have never argued with my wife."[445]

Lt. Bemis: "I am telling you the truth"[446]

Howard: "Well, I'm telling you the truth"[447]

Lt. Bemis: "I play straight from the shoulder and I expect the people that I deal with, to play straight from the shoulder."[448]

Howard: "Well, I don't think everybody is straight"[449]

Lt. Bemis: "I get very disturbed when people lie to me, Howard."[450]

Howard: "Well, so do I. And I'm telling you the truth."[451]

Lt. Bemis: "I'm getting tired of it."[452]

Howard: "We did not have an arguement."[453]

Lt. Bemis: "If your so worried about your wife getting returned to you, how come you've been an obstructionist thru this entire case?"[454]

Howard: "You've been the obstruction, It's not me."[455]

Lt. Bemis: "I have not."[456]

Howard: "I have tried, I have given, first of all, were all aware of the fact, that most people operate at about 10% of their ability. I'm not saying you've been operating on 10% of your ability, but I am telling you, that you are a policeman, you do have a responsibility, you have to follow police protocol, you are responsible to this organization, if you don't follow thru what their going to tell you to do, your going to loose your fucking job. Now I don't have a job. I'm independent and I don't have to listen to what other people say. I don't have to follow you know, a protocol of a hospital such as the public health hospital, where the protocol just to please the department. Now I have given 100 and 1% of myself to finding my wife. I've done that from the first moment I haven't found her."[457]

Lt. Bemis: "You have done your best to waste our time in this investigation."[458]

Howard: "No, I haven't."[459]

Lt. Bemis: "Dragging us to farms in Snohomish."[460]

Howard: "I've tried to..."[461]

Lt. Bemis: "...cemeteries at Floral Hills."[462]

Howard: "I've tried to coordinate info that I could get from you know, exceptional, outstanding, talented people that you would never have access to in a 1,000 years. I've tried to coordinate that info from these extrodinary people and try to coordinate it with what info you could have, but all that you've done, is keep me at arms length. You have taken the info I have given you. I don't know what the hell you've done it and you've never told me one fuckin thing as to what you've done. Now that is the truth. I have not been an obstruction in this. You have been the obstruction, in terms of keeping me at arms length."[463]

Lt. Bemis: "You have continually lied to me thru this entire case, Howard."[464]

Howard: "That is not true. I'll say that in court."[465]

Lt. Bemis: "I can go thru here and name you..."[466]

Howard: "Ok, anything. I have not lied to you."[467]

Lt. Bemis: "Ok."[468]

Howard: "It's obvious to me, that you don't have a suspect and the only thing you've tried to you, is build a case against me."[469]

Lt. Bemis: "I have a suspect, Howard, you've killed her."[470]

Howard: "That's bullshit. I didn't kill my wife. I love my wife."[471]

The contentious exchange was followed by Bemis pressing Howard about why he was keen on taking over management of Marcia's trusts shortly after they married, insinuating that he called the trust company in Boston in an attempt to get control of her money. Countering that it was Marcia's idea for him to take over managerial responsibilities, Howard denied the accusation, again slipping out of Bemis' grasp.

Howard: "Marcia has wanted me to direct the foundation and to help out as much as I could, because her main concern was only in the writing and not having to be bothered with the mundain things that people are bothered with and that's where I have helped her. And that's it. You know, I don't have any income. It's zero. The only income we had, was from those two trusts, one that we got $1,000 for the large one that her father set up and then the small one that's her own personal trust that she got $400 for. Now we lived on $1,400 a month and out of that $1,400 a month, came all the expenses. The alimony that I paid to my ex-wife $270, the only other thing I have to pay my wife is $400 for child support, but when I retired the public health hospital, I got $20,000. It came right out of my pay check. The government didn't give me one cent of that, they came right off the top of my pay check for 10 years at the public health hospital. I took that $20,000 and I have set that up in the trust funds for my daughter for child support and automatically, every month, $400 goes to my daughter. Now, in terms of the $250 a month that's left, I was paying $400 a month child support and $400 a month alimony. After the first year. This past November, *that $400 was reduced to $250, which we have paid. Now obviously at this point in time, I have no income. Zero. So I called my ex-wife and I told her, I says look Tina, I can't afford to pay anymore alimony. I don't have any money, I don't have any income. Now in the divorce settlement, I got zero, right? She got two thirds of the house, our new car, all the contents, the family and I got $7,000 in bills, the old car and I told you, I spent the summer living out of 7 boxes and I house sat at 7 different places and then I met Marcia and of course, she's put my whole life back together you know. I have a home in a sense, I don't own it, but I have a nice home I'm living in, she bought back all my fishing equipment that I gave away and sold which is foolish when you go thru divorce and you do crazy things. Then I called Tina, I said look, I can't afford to pay any more Tina. I'll give you the house. Now that house is at least worth $60,000, it's probably worth $75,000.... I own a third of it. So I called her up, I says look, what I owe her for alimony, the total amount is $5,500. I owe her $250 a month from now until next November. Then next November that drops down to $150 a month for a year and then it drops down to $100 a month for a year. Now that total amount is $5,500. Now I own one third of the house, that represents $20,000 and I said look, I'll give you the third of the house, let me off the hook. Your going to gain $15,000. She says no. I need the alimony money. I says Tina, I says you've had a free ride from me for 14 months since we've been, you know, for 2 years since we've been divorced. I can't afford to do it any more you know. I have put you thru school, I've given you everything, I can't do it any more."*[472]

Bemis moved on to their ketamine project, predicting that Howard committed professional suicide and no hospital would trust him with anesthesiology in the future.

Bemis: "First of all you've been had twice, because as far as Marcia was concerned, you were her means to getting ketamine and that's it."[473]

Howard: "Well, I was her means of getting ketamine. She couldn't of got it without me. She couldn't have done the work without me. It was impossible. It was impossible."[474]

Lt. Bemis: "Her book is done and I think you feel that she just decided she's going to move on to a new life again and leave you holding the bag."[475]

Howard: "No, I don't think so. I think that my wife has gone thru a personal, mental crisis. I know for a fact, that you don't understand metaphysics as well as I have, because I've been in it longer than you and I've spent more hours studying it. Just as you know a helluva lot more about police science then I do. What is it called when you go to a police major in police science?"[476]

Lt. Bemis: "Police science."[477]

Howard: "Alright. You know much more about that, because it's your field and you've studied it and there's no way that I can possibly know what you know about police work and there's no god damn way you can know what I know about metaphysic because you haven't studied it. Now my wife spent not 90% of her time, she spent 99% of her time out of her body, on the inner planes, involved in you know whatever is going on outside of planet earth."[478]

Lt. Bemis: "That thing didn't cause her any personal crisis, Howard. Ketamine caused her personal crisis."[479]

Howard: "Well, your wrong again there."[480]

Lt. Bemis: "Baloney."[481]

257

Howard: "Ketamine didn't cause her personal crisis. Ketamine was a vehicle."[482]

Lt. Bemis: "If she'd dead right now, Howard, she's dead at your hands, because you supplied her the drugs to her."[483]

Howard: "She's not dead. Your wrong. She's not dead and your wrong. I'm telling you that ketamine was a vehicle. Just like when you get it, just like if you want to get from your home lieutenant Bemis to this office, there's only one god damn way you can do it and that's to get in your car and drive here. There's only one way that Marcia could get out of her body and that's with a vehicle ketamine. It was used as a vehicle, but with that vehicle, she directed most of her attention, most of her life was on the inner planes, she was having a problem with that and what you don't understand..."[484]

Lt. Bemis: "That's contrary to everything she studied."[485]

Howard: "Nope. That's not."[486]

Lt. Bemis: "It most certainly is."[487]

From there Bemis shifted the discussion to the discrepancy regarding the shoes Marcia wore the night she vanished.

Lt. Bemis: "Ok, you described in here these hiking boots she's wearing, right?"[488]

Howard: "I, I, I am supposing, that she is wearing hiking boots, because those are the only shoes that I can find that are missing. All the other shoes are there."[489]

Lt. Bemis: "Right. Their also the shoes you said that their the only shoes she wore when she went out walking."[490]

Howard: "That's correct. She did."[491]

Lt. Bemis: "That is a bunch of malarkey. Nobody in the neighborhood has ever seen her with those shoes on. She wore black shoes when she walked."[492]

Howard: "Alright, why don't you talk to the next door lady, Cline and his wife Bud Miller. I can't think of her. She's got a crazy name—Eberdeen. Claude & Eberdeen Miller are our next door neighbors, their our landlord, ok? You call them up and ask them if she wore hiking boots when she walked."[493]

Lt. Bemis: "I don't have to, Howard."[494]

Howard: "Well, your going to have to, because I'm telling you the truth and whoever else your talking to, is giving you some misinformation. Because she wore those hiking boots every time she went out walking into the woods."[495]

Lt. Bemis: "That's not the way it is. She wore black shoes or medium length of heels."[496]

Howard: "What else would you like to know, Lt. Bemis?"[497]

Bemis dropped the topic and delved into Howard's troublesome childhood. Confirming that he had been sexually abused by his ex-convict stepfather from the age of five, Howard added that he went by his stepfather's last name, Cogo, for the better part of his life, as divorce was more scandalous in those days. He was afraid of his stepfather, who along with his mother prevented him from seeing his biological father for the next twenty-five years of his life. Even co-workers at the hospital knew him as Dr. Paul Cogo. He'd also tried the first name "Haig" for a short period, apparently the Armenian for "Howard," as Marwayne understood it. Only recently had he changed his surname back to Alltounian and reconnected with his biological father.

Lt. Bemis: "You recall and incident when you were, your mother put you, I believe, on a refrigerator?"[498]

Howard: "That's correct. My mother put me up on the refrigerator when I was a young child and she told me to jump, that she would catch me. I did jump, she let me fall to the ground and she says, I want to teach you one thing. She says, never trust anybody, not even your own mother. And of course Marcia knew this and Marcia's point, was to get me to trust her and I did. I trust her explicitly. The biggest time that I had to make the biggest decision in terms of trusting Marcia, was when I left my job at the public health hospital. I was deputy chief, I had 10 years seniority, I was the first one there, I've had the most seniority of anybody in that anesthia department, consequently my job was most secure. I was making $47,000 a year. I had the best possible mal-practice insurance, the best possible Blue Cross, Blue Shield policy when I had my accident and my hospital was $35,000, I got stuck with $1,000. I had a retirement fund, I had ample time off, I had an 8 hr job, I had free times on the weekends, I had time for post-graduate work and I had time for vacations. It was a perfect job. I left that job because Marcia wanted me to, in order to help her you know, write full time. That took all the faith that I could muster in another human being, in order to do that and I did do it, because I do have explicit faith."[499]

Lt. Bemis: "She's now violated your faith by running out on you, isn't that right?"[500]

Howard: "No, she hasn't. She has not violated my faith. I think that if Marcia needed to get away and needed a personal time, you know, for a retreatment and to get her head back together, I would give it to her willingly, if she didn't come back for a year, I wouldn't mind, the only thing that I'm concerned about is the fact that she's alive and in good health. I would wait adinfinitum. In fact what you don't realize, is the fact, I will get Marcia back and it doesn't matter whether she's dead or alive, first of all, I know she's alive. And I'm almost certain, that she will be back by the end of this month. Why do I think so? Your not going to pay any attention to it from the astrology. Ok, so I really...[501]

Lt. Bemis: "*You astrologers have lead me so far astray in this thing, with your whackie ideas all during this case, Howard, that I'm getting sick of it.*"[502]

Howard: "*The astrologers are factual. Now let me tell you something. I'll get Marcia back in the very near future, but if Marcia is not alive and I honestly believe that she is, she will come back again, because reincarnation is just as factual as the fact that your sitting there and because you don't believe in it, doesn't change the facts. Again, you haven't studied it. There's so much proof you know, that any idiot and your obviously not an idiot, can read it and understand that reincarnation is a fact. Ok, so No. 1, if you believe in reincarnation and you know it to be true, Marcia if she's not here, will come back again and I'll meet up with her again in my life time. It may take 20 years, but I'll wait for her. She's my soulmate, we've had many lives together, I can't live with another human soul. There's nobody that has the quality of her soul. Any other woman to me, is like an empty shell. I'll get her back this month, this year or 20 years from now. I'm not worried about it. I'll wait for her. Is there anything else you'd like to know?*"[503]

Lt. Bemis: "*I just want to tell you one thing, Howard, I know in my own mind, that you know where Marcia's at, your covering up something, you've been deceitful in stuff in this entire investigation, you've been obstructing this investigation the entire time I've been working with you.*"[504]

Howard: "No, false. You've only continued to do one thing. You've done it consistently. You have no other suspect, consequently because of your stupid statistics of 95% of the time, it's always the spouse or somebody living in the house, I'm the only possible human being that you know, that you can pin this on and as I've said, I'm innocent, I love my wife, I would never kill her, I couldn't kill anybody and you know, your going to stop building a case against me because I'm not the guy. Your wasting your time. I told you from the beginning, god damn it, don't waste the time with me, go out there and find her. This is precious time. The first week when you played Columbo games, I says, you know you're wasting your time here, go out and find her man."[505]

Howard had begun mockingly refer to Lt. Bemis as "Columbo," named after the long-running and popular detective television series starring charismatic actor Peter Falk, who often feigned absentmindedness, but pestered perpetrators until an abundance of clues resulted in a confession or arrest.

Lt. Bemis: "Howard, you don't even know what the truth is any more. Every time you open your mouth, out comes a lie."[506]

Howard: "Not true."[507]

Lt. Bemis: "I'm frankly getting sick and tired of your games your playing."[508]

Howard: "I'm not playing any games, Lt. Bemis."[509]

Lt. Bemis: "You either know something about this, this is either a publicity stunt for your book, you've done something with her and you know where she's at."[510]

Howard: "In the polygraph test, one of the questions on the polygraph test, was is this you know, a scheme for publicity and I gave the answer, it was correct and it was shown that I didn't lie, this was not a publicity scheme. So you know the answer to that question."[511]

Lt. Bemis: "You and Jim Batchelor sat and talked about how you could beat the polygraph, is that not true?"[512]

Howard: "Jim Batchelor told me that there was a way to beat it, that if you constrict your anal muscles every time they ask you a question, that you could do it. I didn't pay any attention to Jim Batchelor. I think Jim Batchelor is capable of doing something like this and some day your going to be looking for Jim Batchelor, because he is a kook and I'm telling you, he's capable of commiting a ridiculous crime such as this. That's why I suspected him. I would never listen to anything he had to says, because his reputation he's a prophet of doom. I'm not a prophet of doom. I think only positively, I don't think negatively."[513]

Having thrown everything at Howard, Lt. Bemis tried a last provocation by insinuating that he had the characteristics of a mass murderer. In late 1978, Ted Bundy had been identified in Florida and charged with the horrific Chi Omega sorority house murders. By the time of Howard's interrogation, coordinated efforts by federal, state, and local police began tying Bundy back to killings in Colorado, Utah, and eventually Washington, including King County, the adjacent county south of Snohomish. Possibly overshadowing Marcia's disappearance, Bundy's sensational murder trial transfixed the nation.

Lt. Bemis: "Have you ever asked an astrologist how close your chart comes to Ted Bundy's?"[514]

Howard: "No. I'm not a Ted Bundy and you've used that as a part of your technique to play your Columbo games you know, you didn't fool me from the beginning, do I know about Ted Bundy."[515]

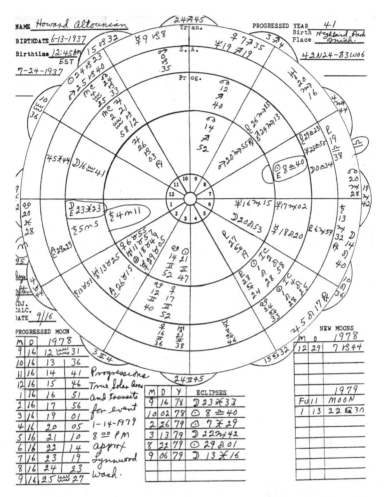

Howard's natal chart—one of many pertinent times and dates analyzed by Marwayne, who consulted numerous psychics and astrologers concerning Marcia's disappearance.

Lt. Bemis: "I've had numerous astrologers that you have talked to, have called me and told me, hey this guy is another Ted Bundy."[516]

Howard: "Well, I'm not a Ted Bundy."[517]

Lt. Bemis: "There's your divine science for you, Mr. Alltounian."[518]

Howard: "Well, it all depends what astrology you know, there are policeman and there are policeman. I'm sure this ass hole cops and there are compident qualified and intelligent policeman like yourself, who get nominated for the FBI academy. Well, there's ass hole ridiculous astrologers out there, who are reading this shit in the paper and just trying to get their you know, some publicity themselves and get involved with a big thing because Marcia Moore is a big thing. She's internationally known. I'm telling you, if you want to talk to some competent qualified astrologers, talk to 3 people. Marwayne [Leipzig], Dorothy B. Hughes & Florence Jones. Now if they tell you that I'm a Bundy, then I'll listen to that. Now if you want to talk to any other astrologer, that's bullshit."[519]

Lt. Bemis: "Well, why don't you go down and ask your astrologers that are doing this work for you, how close your chart compares to Ted Bundy's?"[520]

Howard: "I will. I'll ask Marwayne when I get back."[521]

Lt. Bemis: "Oh, don't ask Marwayne. She's too closer related to you. Ask those people in Seattle you've been on, you know? Don't harass her, she's a neighbor."[522]

Howard: "You know, what, that's ridiculous. This is just part of your Colombo games."[523]

Lt. Bemis: "It's not. The astrologers, all of them that you've been talking to down there in Seattle, call up here and say, he has a very good ability for ..."[524]

Howard: "Alot of people have told me that your an ass-hole, too."[525]

Lt. Bemis: "That's really tough you know."[526]

From there they digressed into Howard's prospects for returning to medicine. Bemis insisted that his career was ruined, that no hospital would trust him in anesthesiology after reading the bizarre content in *Journeys into the Bright World,* and at the very least, he was negligent in Marcia's deteriorating health the last few months. Once again, Howard denied this, reiterating his impeccable fifteen-year record.

Bemis then returned to the topic of the note, again accusing Howard of soliciting the note prior to Marcia's disappearance. Ultimately, an exasperated Bemis had run out of ammunition.

Lt. Bemis: "At this point, Howard, I want to tell you again, you are covering something up in this case, your obstructing something in this case, the investigation, as far as I'm concerned, I've went over board to try to assist you in finding your wife. I'm turning this entire investigation over to Det. Twitchell. Any leads you may get, you want to follow-up, she will be glad to assist you and don't bother to call me until you can tell me the truth."[527]

Howard: "I have told you the truth."[528]

Lt. Bemis: "You have not."[529]

Howard: "I am telling you the truth. I will tell you the truth. I will not call you again to find my wife, because I don't think at this point, you can find her, but I'm certain that in time, I will find her. What I really know for a fact, is that someday, just like Liz Jenkins told me, when I first saw Liz Jenkins the psychic that I know locally, she told me 3 things: No.1 she walked out that night and was picked up in a car and she says it was with a friend and she says she going to walk back thru that door and that's what going to happen. Were not going to find Marcia. Maybe I'll find her thru some friends who are looking for her, but most probably, when she's ready, she'll walk back thru that door and when she does, I'll call you."[530]

Lt. Bemis: "Ok, if she walks thru the door, you can call me, but don't call me with any more of your malarkey tales, your false leads, your false suspects and all the stuff we've gone thru in this entire case. Is that understood?"[531]

Howard: "That's fine."[532]

Lt. Bemis: "Also, I'm not going to buy any story that she was up in a space ship while she was gone either. I'm not going to buy any story that she dematerialized and reappeared."[533]

Howard: "No, you couldn't begin to understand that. That's a possibility, but you couldn't understand that."[534]

Lt. Bemis: "I'll tell you something, if you come up with that story there either one of those, I'm going to shoot you out of the saddle."[535]

Howard: "I won't come up with it, because it's too far fetched for anybody to possibly understand."[536]

Lt. Bemis: "Ok. At this point, we'll end this conversation. The time is now 9:58 am. The date is 8 Feb. 1979."[537]

Bemis had laid all his cards on the table, but Howard hadn't cracked as predicted. In the absence of sworn statements to corner him with lies and inconsistencies, Howard simply wiggled off the hook time and again. Lieutenant Bemis had tried to break Howard Alltounian—and failed.

THE UNRAVELING

B ob Dodge, a gruff sheriff with an uncontrollable temper, had once even come to blows with a fellow officer, breaking his jaw. Although a veteran of the police force since 1951, he was only two years in as sheriff of Snohomish County, when the missing persons case of Marcia Moore began unraveling in the hands of Lt. Bemis.

After three weeks, there was no body, nor forensic evidence to work with. Although the likelihood of finding Marcia alive was now remote had she become disoriented in the woods or sustained an injury, she may have simply skipped town. The possibility remained entirely plausible given her financial means and background as a lecture circuit traveler, not to mention her marital history.

That was just the start. Lt. Bemis was rapidly depleting department resources on the case with Howard's multiple search requests and accusations, use of the helicopter at $285/hour, thousands in long-distance phone charges, and manpower redirected from other cases. Additionally, Bemis landed in Dodge's crosshairs by breaking ranks, personally investigating the case, and going over the sheriff's head in a few important respects. Rather than using the county polygraph examiner, Bemis insisted on bringing in his own, a tactic that backfired after Howard passed.

Additionally, in Dodge's eyes, Bemis had irreparably tainted the investigation, not only by indulging the input from a cornucopia of psychics and astrologers, but by officially soliciting their premonitions and interpretations on the case record. If Lt. Bemis contended that Howard was complicit in Marcia's murder, what district attorney would allow an indictment resting partly on the testimony of psychics?

Finally, although there clearly were inconsistencies, even incriminating lies in Howard's account and statements, Bemis secured little on record to confront him with. Correctly, he challenged Howard about soliciting the note from Marcia prior to her disappearance, but the anecdote relayed from Marwayne was not an official statement.

Bemis also didn't have the whole story in other aspects of the investigation. Although Howard had once used Liz Jenkins' astrological analysis in his favor, Bemis was unaware that Liz privately confided to Marwayne her suspicion of Howard's guilt. Moreover, post interrogation Marwayne was not privy to the transcript, having no knowledge of Howard's repeated denial about soliciting the note or the continued lie about his amnesia theory.

Missing were the sworn statements, affidavits, the corroborated tips necessary to properly paint Howard into a corner. Furthermore, the sheriff's office had become inundated with calls and letters from crackpots across the county, smothering the chances of credible tips shining through. Now the interrogation was over and just as the pressure on Howard was ebbing, it was intensifying on Lieutenant Darrol Bemis.

Meanwhile, Howard returned home the victor, boasting to Marwayne that he had stuck to his guns and that Bemis wound up with egg on his face. "I expected to see him red faced and frothing at the mouth with anger," Marwayne journaled. "He WAS angry, but he seemed to be almost gloating and was very strong in his position.... Howard became more and more excited as he related all this, and finally was waving his arms and cussing about what a stoop Bemis is. He often referred to him as 'that goddammed Bemis'. But he seemed to me to be very strong. He showed no nervousness or fear. He felt powerful and seemed to me to relish that he had countered Bemis effectively and that there wasn't 'a damn thing that goddammed Bemis can do'. Later in the day he told me that 'you know, Marwayne, I will never be afraid of anything again.

You don't know this, but in my youth, I was afraid, and I was fearful and I thought I wasn't as good as others, I had inferior feelings. But that is all gone now. I felt like a giant. I will never be afraid of anything again.'"[538] In a *Hypersentience Bulletin*, Howard wrote: "That evening Dr. Ed Severinhaus picked me up, and we went to the Thursday evening Sai Baba...meeting where I sang my heart out!"[539]

Reflecting on everything that had transpired, he admitted to Marwayne that Marcia wasn't happy, chalking it up to the strain and frustration his son Kevin put on the marriage, and the amount of time he spent with his ex-wife Tina following her hysterectomy. In her journal, Marwayne doubted this and recalled a conversation where Marcia graciously wanted him to look after Tina, as she had done for him following a horrific car accident that left him hospitalized almost a decade prior.

That evening they spoke again by phone. Howard recounted to Marwayne a phone call with Marcia's brother John, who was upset after being told by Bemis that he felt Howard lied about everything during the interrogation, particularly concerning soliciting the note and the sequence of when Howard smoked the pot on Sunday, January 14. Howard again denied soliciting the note but slipped to Marwayne about when he smoked the marijuana.

During the interrogation, Howard stated that he smoked it *after* leaving for the movies. Contradicting this, he had dramatically divulged to Rose Gallacher that, while under the influence of ketamine, he smoked the pot hours *before* he left Marcia, concluding that doing so clouded his judgement. The discrepancy wasn't just a secondhand account as Marwayne suddenly realized that he had previously told her the same. "I said, 'Howard, but you told Rose Gallacher that you smoked it BEFORE, and you cried out and lamented that you had done so, crying that you would never have left her if you had not done that, and blame yourself for so doing.' There was a silence on the phone. Then he said, matter-of-factly, 'Did I? Well I don't know why I said that, because I smoked it AFTER I left her.'"[540]

By now the media coverage had ramped up. A crew from a Vancouver television station arrived at the duplex and spent two hours crafting a ten-minute segment that he considered thorough and sympathetic. Howard was also excited that he was invited to appear on *Seattle Today* on Monday, February 12, a light-hearted morning show similar to *Good Morning America*, starring personable cohost Shirley Hudson. Ironically, Marcia had appeared on the show over a year ago, speaking as a specialist on reincarnation, past-life regression, and the concept of karma. Marwayne informed Lt. Bemis about Howard's scheduled appearance, leaving him hopeful that he could reignite the investigation, "Boy, that is one I don't want to miss. I will be watching that. Good. I can subpoena all that footage if I need it."[541]

Marwayne was increasingly straddling a precarious line. On one hand, she remained a loyal friend to Howard, at times protecting him from intense scrutiny and not divulging incriminating holes in his story. She never told Lt. Bemis about her private conversation with Tina about their abusive marriage. On the other hand, Marwayne had become somewhat of an informant to Bemis and John Moore, providing tips and what she considered inconsistencies, unbeknownst to Howard.

On Sunday, February 11, she and Liz Jenkins, accompanied by Marwayne's eldest daughter, conducted their own search for Marcia, using Liz as somewhat of a psychic bloodhound. They set off in the direction of Floral Hills Cemetery, but Liz sensed nothing, remarking in her characteristically no-nonsense manner, "She ain't here."[542]

Marwayne and the gals returned to their car and made a quick stop to connect with Lt. Bemis, where he was coaching soccer. "Hey Colombo!" she joked as they approached, using the same name Howard used to mock the lieutenant. After connecting with Bemis, they proceeded to find the Campbell road that had come up in multiple psychics' premonitions, and to which Bemis had provided directions. Realizing that they had driven too far, they were making a U-turn when suddenly Liz was struck by a psychic bolt, saying, "Oh my God,"[543] and becoming nauseous in the same manner as the last time she channeled Marcia in Marwayne's presence.

They drove on a bit, approaching an old lover's lane. An overgrown evergreen shrub complemented a long-ago abandoned house. Downhill from the house stood an old, dilapidated barn covered in green moss and mildew. Making their way approximately one hundred yards along a narrow lane, they were flanked by thick overgrowth of brambles and blackberry vines, as Marwayne later journaled: "We went inside the barn and looked all around. Floor boards were rotting and it all smelled musty, but there was no indication that anyone had been there, or torn up any of the floorboards…we agreed that anyone trying to reach the barn from the road above, where we had originally been, would likely be detected as he/she walked down through the field which sloped from that road above down to the barn. There was indeed an old vehicle nearby, but we decided no one would leave a body there for essentially the same reasons…difficulty of access. So, we crawled back through the barbed wire and walked on down toward the car. It was raining hard now, and we were getting soaked. As we walked down, Liz and I saw an old undershirt, body thermo type, caught in blackberry brambles. We pulled it loose, and looked at it. It was quite new. The front of it had many muddy places on it, but also some stains that looked like blood to us. We decided to take it with us and show it, as well as the cap we had found, to Lt. Bemis to see what he thought."[544]

Soaking wet, they drove home tired and a bit punchy. They asked Marwayne about Howard's marijuana use, and she confirmed that he used it recreationally and that she once smoked with him in keeping him company but didn't enjoy it.

Lightening the mood, they proposed Marwayne do it again in an attempt to get Howard to admit killing Marcia. "I replied, 'Oh boy',… and 'I can just see how that would go. I would say, Howard you know goddam well you did 'er in', and then I would laugh and laugh'. We all three burst into laughter. 'I can just see Howard and me, laughing our heads off.' We all agreed that this might not be a good tack, and should abandon the idea of getting 'stoned' with Howard, because then we could see Howard, laughing, saying 'Marwayne, goddamit, you are absolutely right, and now, love, you're next, and 'haw haw haw'. We laughed hilariously at that, and drove on home, three tired, wet, hungry, unsuccessful "sleuths."[545]

Lost in throws of the day, and unbeknownst to the three women, they had stumbled upon a location closely resembling the spot where Marcia's skull would be found in two years' time.

HUNTER & HUNTED

By mid-February, a month had passed since Marcia Moore vanished.

One day Lieutenant Bemis called Marwayne's home. They had become chummy and he wanted to introduce his wife and two children, since they were in the neighborhood. Caught off guard, as Howard happened to be in the room during the call, she nonetheless agreed. After she hung up, Howard emphatically asked Marwayne why Bemis would want to visit, leaving her uneasy that he might suspect her of secretly providing information.

It was an awkward situation when Bemis and family arrived with Howard there, but as day became night, the tenuous rapport between hunter and hunted thawed. "Gradually they warmed up. I think it was good they had this meeting under a social condition, as I think Bemis will be more compassionate to Howard, and I think Howard will have more respect for Bemis."[546]

Caught in between the two men, Marwayne remained as conflicted as ever. "I don't know what to think anymore. Logic tells me she is not alive, but Howard's anguish at times is very real and very believable."[547]

Monday, February 19, Howard left Washington for an interview with Channel 8 in Vancouver. The station brought in a psychic to augment the program, as well as the owner of Mystic Arts bookstore in Surrey, the place where Marcia suspected that malevolent witches were casting psychic attacks against her a couple years prior, marking the origin of her hip pain.

The program was set to air on cable, which Marwayne didn't have, so Howard left his key for her to watch from the duplex. She informed Lt. Bemis, who asked her to snoop around a bit, perhaps locate some of her unpublished manuscripts that might uncover clues. Bemis theorized that if Marcia skipped town, she would've taken them. Unable to locate them, she did remove a few hairs from a shower cap, thinking perhaps it might help detectives.

An eerie feeling overcame Marwayne as she milled around the duplex alone with most of the lights off. "I went downstairs into their bedroom. Their whole house has always had such a pleasant smell about it. Rather a fresh, green smell is the only way I can describe it, and I believe it is from an incense[xii] that Marcia liked. It is distinctive only to her house. I have never smelled it elsewhere. As I came into the house and smelled that certain 'fragrance' I felt almost sick, and my whole body tightened up. I was very nervous."[548]

Marwayne came across a couple of interesting finds. Inside a hanging file folder in Marcia's desk drawer was the ominous typewritten note describing her severe pain, impending death, and desire to have her smaller, personal trust bequeathed to Howard.

Something else grabbed Marwayne's attention. Tucked inside the folded note she found a carefully preserved, two-inch-long receipt for a movie ticket purchased from the Lynn-Twin, dated Sunday, January 14. It was an adding machine type in the amount of $2.50 but did not specify a movie time or title. "I did not think too much about this piece of paper at the time, although I realized it was proof he had paid an admission to the theater. Question is, did he stay all evening at the theater? No one seems to know. Later I thought a lot about that piece of paper."[549]

Marwayne also looked through Marcia's car. There was no indication that Moore had been put in the front or backseat as far as Marwayne

---

[xii] Sandalwood

could detect. Papers in the glove compartment appeared unrelated, and the car was clean.

The cable program rehashed much of what had already been reported, with Howard speaking to the safety of ketamine compared to other drugs. His appearance was rather cut and dried, felt Marwayne. "He made all the same by note statements as before about how ketamine is a safe drug, how his wife is mature, etc." Marcia was not flighty, he said. She would not just run away, and therefore must be suffering from amnesia, possibly a side effect of prolonged ketamine use. "He seemed rather stiff, with little or no expression in his face, and he did not look into the camera,"[550] Marwayne wrote.

The telephone rang a couple of times while Marwayne was watching the program, but she didn't answer, and it fell to the answering machine. "Each time it rang I was startled. Once I thought I heard someone at the front door, but it was just imagination.... It was too strange, sitting there on the bed...watching the program.... Sitting on that warm bed was like sitting on it when someone had just gotten up from it, and I kept thinking of Marcia, lying there, as described by Howard the last time he saw her."[551]

Out into the cold, dark night, she rushed to her car and hastily drove away.

On Tuesday, Howard returned, pleased with his portrayal on the program as Marwayne chronicled in her journal: "He even said, 'Marwayne I am getting so good at this. I don't feel nervous at all, no stage fright, nothing. I eat it up. They have asked me all the questions they can ask, and I have answered them all. I love being on television'. I thought this was strange, in view of the fact the subject matter of his appearances are the disappearance of his wife."[552]

Meanwhile, Lt. Bemis continued to converse with psychic Rose Gallacher, and the next day Howard stormed into Marwayne's home in a rage: "He said, 'That fucking Lt. Bemis told John I injected Marcia with 500 mg of ketamine, and that I told Rose Gallagher this, and she has a witness. Marwayne, i never said anything like that. I never injected her with any 500 mg. That is a lethal dose,'…and 'why is he trying to discredit me with the family?' and 'I am glad I wrote to Robin.'"553

He had indeed written a rather peculiar letter to Marcia's brother Robin the day he left for Vancouver, kicked off by telling him that he was a very sensitive person, and questioning Robin about not returning his calls. From there Howard launched into his advocacy that astrology would ultimately be the method to find Marcia. He stated that she did abuse ketamine but he is certain that she is still alive, and that he will win back her hand by romantically writing her as he had done before they wed.

The letter then digressed into Howard's frustration with law enforcement: "I am tired of being harassed by Lt. Darrol Bemis…. Robin, our God, Marcia's and mine, is Satya Sai Baba, the God of truth and love! I do not lie. I have not lied or been obstructionist in this case. I have only tried to cooperate 100% with Lt. Bemis and the Snohomish County Police Department since this whole catastrophic mess began! On the other hand, he has never to this day told me anything, and has only kept me at arms length, and what's worse is his attempt to discredit me in the eyes of the family! Why he has done this I honestly do not know; but after all he is a cop and is not used to dealing with honest people. I am also tired of John immediately siding with this idiot and also casting disparaging remarks at me."554

The letter concluded by offering to reassure the family that he had nothing to do with Marcia's disappearance. "Robin, it is hard enough without having these intimidations from Lt. Darrol Bemis and his supporters. If you want, I will willingly take a polygraph with the Boston and New York police, if that would satisfy the family. I love Marcia with my whole heart and soul to the extent that no one else can replace her. I will wait however long it takes, whether it is a few months, a few years or a lifetime. I literally must reunite with her soul. When once you have been with your soulmate, there can be no other."555

Howard was now relieved that he had preemptively countered Bemis' assertion to John about injecting Marcia with 500 mg of ketamine. Nevertheless, Bemis continued to work with Rose Gallacher despite the aggravation from Sheriff Dodge. Rose confidently claimed she could pinpoint the location of Marcia's body and planned to return that weekend. Securing a helicopter to assist, Bemis would end up requesting reimbursement from the Moore family. Revealing to Marwayne that the sheriff's office could spend no more money on the disappearance of Marcia Moore, he later asked John to pay the helicopter company directly to avoid detection by Sheriff Dodge. Rose arrived on the rainy weekend of February 24, but the search proved fruitless.

Saturday night, February 24, Lt. Bemis abandoned the pretenses, defying Sheriff Dodge by diving headfirst into the occult. He invited Marwayne to participate in a séance in his own home with Rose and another psychic named Helena Ram, and even brought along a young prosecutor friend. By now there were whispers circulating through the department that the case was bordering on the absurd, as he had previously advised other officers to attend a séance in order to familiarize themselves with the occult.

The business card used by Bemis to schedule a séance, in hopes of discovering answers that might lead to finding Marcia Moore.

Even considering what had already transpired with the investigation, it was a strange evening. Helena Ram explained to the group that while in the trance, she would likely say things that could be shocking, warning them not to gasp, sigh, or touch her. She took some deep breaths, dropped her chin on her shoulder, and sighed a few times. Then she stirred, sat up straight, and in a Chinese accent said, "Good evening. I am Dr Ling. I am so pleased to be here with you,"[556] then fell back into a stupor before supposedly reemerging as Marcia.

Rose asked her to recount what happened on the night of January 14. Crying out in pain and anguish, the psychic uttered, "My head is so mixed up…he is injecting me again. I am so weak, I cannot stop him," Marwayne later journaled. Rose asked how much she was getting, to which she responded, "10 CC…'now someone else has come into the room with him. It is that man. They are taking me out to the car. They are putting me on the back seat. I do not want to go. Why are they doing this to me? I am afraid of them. They are laughing at how weak I am', etc. etc."[557] According to Helena, they laid her on the backseat and drove off. Trying to get outside of her body, she recognized the number 99, street sign 119th, and "Redmond."

However, Rose interjected some made-up names and information to test the psychic, including asking the conjured Marcia whether she missed her cigarettes, as it was well known that Marcia detested smoking. Helena Ram took the bait and played along with Rose's suggestions for a while. Eventually, the spirit of Marcia apparently crossed back into the spirit world and Ram came out of the trance as Dr. Ling, thanking everyone before she reemerged as herself. A tired Marwayne made her goodbyes, but not before chatting with Rose that they largely thought Ram was a fraud.

A couple of days later, Howard phoned Marwayne around midnight, severely distraught and lonely. It seemed to her that he was at a breaking point, so she notified Bemis that she would call Howard's therapist friend, Dr. Ed.

By the time he arrived, Howard had mellowed somewhat, but re-agitated and vehemently refused when Dr. Ed suggested a hospital stay for a few days as a sabbatical. Just after Dr. Ed left, Howard burst into tears alone with Marwayne, sobbing like a child.

Marwayne sympathized with Howard's heartache, but also sensed an opportunity to induce a confession if he truly had something to hide. "I knelt beside him on the couch, put my arms around his shoulders, and said, 'Howard, this is killing you. You are in such terrible torment. What is tormenting you so? Where is Marcia?' He almost yelled, waving his arms 'I DON'T know!' I said, 'You cannot go on this way. It is killing you.' He wept uncontrollably, and I held him and rocked him. Then I said again, 'What is tormenting you so terribly that you cannot tell me. Let it out. You must let it out. It is killing you.' He buried his head in his hands, and wept, sobbing, 'Oh, Marwayne, it is so horrible. It is too horrible'. 'What is so horrible, Howard?' Then, he put on the brakes. He told me that before he married Marcia he told her he didn't love her and didn't think they should get married, but she told him she had made all these plans, changed her arrangements, and thought they should go through with the wedding, that she always wanted 'to marry a nice man like me', and I don't know what all else. I said, 'Well, Howard, that was honest. Good for you. But Howard, that was a year and a half ago. Surely that is not tormenting you to this extent'. He blubbered that he should have been better to her, and she would never have run away, etc."[558]

There would be no confession. Dr. Ed returned and tucked him into the waterbed downstairs. After Marwayne relayed some of Howard's recent odd behavior, Dr. Ed agreed that it was indicative of guilt and told Marwayne he would speak with Lt. Bemis and John about it.

Howard's distraught state and erratic behavior continued. One night he called Marwayne's elderly mother just as she was drifting off to sleep. It was about 8:30 p.m. She staggered to the phone to answer it.

"This is Howard, Grandma,"[559] he said.

"Howard who?"[560] Marwayne's mother replied in surprise. They were not acquainted.

"You know Howard the doctor. Marwayne's friend, and I just want you to listen to me for five minutes. You know Gemini people like to have somebody listen to them, and I don't want to offend you, I love you too much to want to embarrass you. I just want to talk to you a few minutes so just listen to me please."[561]

Marwayne's mother allowed Howard to launch into how he met Marcia.

"I went to her meeting and waited patiently for it to end,"[562] Howard said.

Then he explained how he'd sent letters to her in Vancouver.

"I just want to ask a favor of you Grandma,"[563] he continued.

"I am too old to get involved in any of this!"[564] she replied.

Howard asked how old she was.

"Almost eighty-one,"[565] she said.

"Perfect, you are forty years older than I am and are almost sure to go on before I do, and when you get up there, will you please look up Marcia and tell her how much I love her and ask her to wait for me? Will you do that for me grandma?"[566] Howard asked.

Dumbfounded, Marwayne's mother agreed.

"I've taken an oath of celibacy and swore I would never hold another woman in my arms…"[567] Howard concluded the call. Then he thanked her, and repeated that he hoped he hadn't offended her.

Glad the bizarre call was over, she hung up and returned to bed.

Marwayne's daughter Cris and her grandmother.

CONFRONTATION

As February became March of 1979, Howard put the finishing touches on the Spring Equinox edition of the *Hypersentience Bulletin* he took over in Marcia's absence, even eliminating her name as an author and from the copyright. He imposed on Marwayne much of the typing, editing, folding, and stamping without much regard for her own day-to-day responsibilities, as fatigue began to mount. "Saturday he did thank me, but I must say that he acted like a churlish spoiled little kid most of the day, because he finally realized what a monumental piece of work getting this bulletin out was," Marwayne grumbled. "I had told him Friday night, in a phone call, that I had gone about as far as I could go on the whole thing, that I could not expend any more emotional energy on it, that I could not bring Marcia back nor could I locate her, that I had to get on with my own work, and detach myself from it all."[568]

The bulletin included Howard's exhaustive efforts to find Marcia, as well as disparaging remarks about Lt. Bemis. He also included information about the trust funds, dispelling any motive for money since, as he put it, they immediately reverted back to the Moore family upon her death. However, he omitted any mention of the note whereby Marcia described her impending death and desire to have the smaller trust transferred to him.

Previously, Howard also characterized, "My 'friend', Lieutenant Darrol Bemis of the Snohomish County Police Department notified the FDA and for a period of about one week two inspectors came each and every morning at 8 o'clock sharp and interrogated me for hours and hours and hours."[569] Now Howard had lawyered up as a consequence of "harrassment from Lt. Bemis and his underling."[570] The bulletin concluded with his conviction that Marcia was alive, and to demonstrate his devotion to her readers, reiterated that he had taken a vow of celibacy until her return.

On Monday, March 5, Howard was back at Marwayne's to hot tub. "It makes him feel better," Marwayne noted. "He says it 'gets out the evil spirits.'"[571] He spent most of the evening sharing a new lead that Marcia might be staying with a "hippie-type" woman friend on Lopez Island, about eighty miles northwest of Lynnwood. Although there was little to go on, Howard notified Bemis, as Marwayne journaled: "I can only imagine Bemis' attitude, as there have been so many different 'herrings'. We suspect that he keeps dragging up more and more possibilities to be checked out, stalling for time. Is it so that when the body IS found, it will be so decomposed, or chewed up by animals, that it will be unidentifiable?"[572]

Despite claiming to Lt. Bemis that he was done with the drug, Howard also continued to try to get ketamine. On the evening of March 14, he entered a veterinary clinic wearing a dark-rose velour shirt, presenting credentials indicating that he was a licensed physician and wanted to purchase ketamine for research. An employee placed a bottle on the counter and left the room to ask if it was legal to sell to him. When the worker returned, he found the bottle missing and fifteen dollars in its place. Another vet said Howard came in and requested the same but was refused. He recognized him as Dr. Paul Cogo, and assumed Howard was now using an alias. Lt. Bemis promptly instructed all vets in the area to notify him or the FDA going forward, and a doctor in Kent warned against dispensing ketamine in a veterinary newsletter.

At the end of March, Marcia's former lover Robert Byron notified Howard that he and wife, Carol, would be flying up from California to learn more about Marcia's disappearance. Marwayne asked Howard what Byron hoped to achieve by flying up here and adding to the fray. Howard was unsure but after they arrived, Marwayne instantly took a liking to the couple, now hoping Byron could perhaps shed new light on the situation.

Saturday night, March 31, she met with Byron at a nearby Holiday Inn until 2:00 a.m., encouraged that they might piece everything together. However, Byron confided a suspicion of Howard's involvement from the get-go. They kicked around a few theories, including the possibility that assisting Marcia with suicide led to his emotional breakdown saying, "It is too horrible," but Byron remained unconvinced.

The next day, Marwayne invited Byron, Carol, and Howard for brunch. In a provoking tone as they ate, Byron challenged Howard on several aspects, and his anger visibly mounted. "Howard was caught in a tight place," Marwayne wrote. "He wanted to appear to be tremendously cooperative, especially in front of me, but finally his composure broke, and he got red in the face and started yelling at Byron, 'I don't care what you think. Goddammit, what did you come here for. I am tired of your snooping. Just take the list you want (a list of bookstores throughout U.S. of metaphysical nature), and get the fucking hell out of here', or words to that effect. Everyone's temper rose.... He told several lies to Byron about their relationship, such as 'they had never had a quarrel' and Byron knows Marcia too well to accept that."[573] Marwayne's son Pete piped up and told Howard that he was sick and tired of him using up so much of his mother's time and energy.

After brunch, Byron and Marwayne discussed Howard's outburst and the extent to which he was prone to uncontrollable anger. She recalled an even more intense anecdote with Howard's son Kevin just a week prior in her living room. Kevin had asked his father if he could sleep in the duplex until he found another place. Marwayne had mandated that he stop crashing and leave April 1, since he was staying rent-free. "His dad yelled, 'No, goddammit, NO.... I told you NO,'" Marwayne wrote. "'I told you never to ask me again'...'Can't you get that through your head...NO!!!'...and then, 'If you don't get the hell out of this fucking living room, I am going to GO HOME!' with his voice so loud you could hear him a block away. I was shocked. This was an outburst I had never anticipated, although I had heard about his outburst with Tina right after her surgery."[574]

After the incident, Kevin came moping down the hall to the bathroom shaking and muttering, "Asshole, that asshole," Marwayne recalled. She told Kevin just to keep calm, not to say anymore, and she would talk to him later. In a few minutes, Howard came in rather red-faced, trying to appear composed, as if he'd been quietly reading the whole time. "Well I am going home now,"[575] he calmly said. Reflecting on the incident, it struck Marwayne that his demeanor reverted so quickly as he made a casual goodbye, as if the whole thing hadn't happened.

While in town, Byron questioned everyone available, including Marwayne's daughter Cris, about Howard's ex-wife. "He asked Cris if she knew if Howard had ever hit Tina, and Cris told him that Tina had said that he has…. He asked her if Tina had ever told them anything about their sex life, and Cris replied that she had said that Howard was a selfish lover, thinking only of himself mainly, and that he was inclined to be jealous and possessive." After conferring with John Moore and Lt. Bemis, Byron decided that confronting Howard again about his inconsistencies was appropriate, but Marwayne's son Peter felt it would be futile and unnecessarily put his mom in a precarious situation. Still, Byron wanted to seize the opportunity. "Byron clearly feels that Howard knows what happened, and likely where she is, and he believes she is dead. He thinks Howard either killed her after a violent quarrel, or that he assisted in her suicide."[576]

They considered the possibility that Marcia agreed on suicide with Howard's help beforehand, leaving her enough ketamine to overdose, then staging the movie alibi. "Not wanting to expose the amount of ketamine that had been used in that house (this was the only area Bemis said on which he was shaky on the polygraph- test), he moved her body out into the woods somewhere behind the house. This would account for why he felt so absolutely positive that she was in the woods, and why he 'led' the psychics as he did, saying 'I know she is in the woods, just tell me where to look in the woods', etc."[577] thought Marwayne.

That afternoon, Marwayne and Byron visited Liz Jenkins, who put forth her own theory. "Somehow Howard found out that she was going to leave him, maybe overheard a telephone conversation on the other phone or something like that, confronted her with it, a violent quarrel ensued, in which he struck her on the side of the head, threw her against a wall, she was nauseaus, perhaps vomiting, bleeding, maybe with a cut mouth or hit against mouth. He knocked her unconscious,"[578] Marwayne later wrote of Liz's comments. Jenkins thought it possible that Howard called Jim Batchelor in a panic for help, but Lt. Bemis dismissed the possibility and telephone records showed no calls to Batchelor's residence on or around January 14.

That evening a harrowing incident for Marwayne unfolded. An upset Howard called just as she and Byron sat down for supper, as Marwayne later captured in her journal: "'Oh Marwayne, you know I loved you, how could you do this to me', sob-sob etc. I said 'What are you talking about?' He said, 'How could you discredit me with the family. You know I loved Marcia. John Moore doesn't think I ever loved Marcia.'"[579]

Apparently, John Moore had recently called Howard, confronting him about his admission to Marwayne that he didn't love Marcia when they married, among other disparaging comments. Howard knew that Marwayne was the only person John could've learned it from. Leaving her in a pickle, Marwayne later wrote, "I was flabbergasted. I didn't know what to say. How could John Moore do such a thing? I was furious with him. This had been told to him in complete confidence. I felt that he had 'blown my cover', and there was no way I could possibly be of any further help in the case."[580]

Pleading with Howard that it was a misunderstanding, she invited him to drop by to clear the air. She even offered to call John Moore in front of him, trying to think of some way to regain his trust. After she hung up with Howard, she let Bemis have it. "I called Bemis and told him John Moore had just blown me away, and that I was very angry about it. Byron talked to Bemis, only to have Bemis tell him that he,

Bemis, knew that John had told this to Howard! But Bemis failed to tell us so, only 15 minutes be-fore! Great!"[581]

While Marwayne nervously waited for Howard, John phoned, and Marwayne promptly fumed that what she told him was in strict confidence, undoing her ability to assist on the case. John tried to explain the importance of conveying to Howard where the family stands, that it was time to confront him. "I said, 'Great! You confront him from Connecticut. I am one block away. This man has an arsenal of guns in his basement, and he is on his way to see me, thinking I have betrayed him, thanks to you. Just great!...You guys have me playing Russian Roulette with a madman, and you think YOU should confront him?'"[582] Howard was somewhat of a gun collector. In fact, at one point during the investigation, he insisted Lt. Bemis accept the gift of a Smith & Wesson if he could find Marcia, but naturally Bemis refused due to the conflict of interest.

Meanwhile, Byron, a diminutive man with a severe birth defect in his legs and weak hands, wouldn't be much help if a potentially enraged Howard was on his way over. He suggested they call Marwayne's son Peter for backup before Howard arrived. Marwayne frantically called the tavern he had gone to, but the line was busy. She pleaded with the operator to interrupt the call, but the line was out of order. "Great," thought Marwayne. "Now it was up to Byron, Carrol and Marwayne to face Howard alone, and we didn't know what his state of mind was, whether he would come down furious, revengeful, ranting and raving, or HOW he would be. We were afraid."[583]

Carol offered to pick up Peter from the tavern, while Byron and Marwayne strategized. "We were beginning to act quite paranoid!" Byron asked if there were any tools nearby. "Do you mean a hammer?" Marwayne asked. "That is exactly what I mean," Byron replied. Marwayne got one for him, and he hid it under a sweater on a table in the living room, trying to make it appear as if it were casually laying there; then they tried to calm themselves. "I seated myself at the organ, set the controls and switches, and when the electricity warmed up the motor, began to play loudly, hitting all kinds of klinkers, but I charged on no matter. About that time Howard came in. I acted as if I did not hear him...which is often the case when I am playing. He stood there a part of a minute, when I kept on playing. I turned and said, 'oh, hi, Howard', and went on for a few bars."[584]

Marwayne tried to appease him by thanking him for the tea and cookies he brought earlier. As they made their way to the kitchen, Peter, his girlfriend Margaret, and three more men arrived, much to her relief. "Pete had brought his arsenal. I think one of the guys was Kevin, and I wondered if Kevin would tell his dad that we had sent for Pete. But there was no way to get around that."[585]

Marwayne's mind raced as she searched for an excuse. Eventually she managed to pull Howard aside and explain the reason for relaying the anecdote to John about him not being in love with Marcia at the time of their wedding: Howard was under the influence of ketamine, which Marwayne said acted as a truth serum. She cleverly latched on to Marcia's commentary in *Journeys into the Bright World* that it carried those properties. Hence, although he said he didn't love Marcia, he also claimed that he did not know where Marcia was, and was therefore telling the truth about not being involved in her disappearance. "Howard smiled, wanly," Marwayne observed. "He was very 'down.' And I repeated that that was the reason, that I felt it was an absolute test of your innocence and that I wanted him to know I felt you did not know any more than you had told. He seemed placated."[586] Howard and Byron talked for a while longer, then everyone finally left.

John had requested that Marwayne return his call afterward, but she was still shaken by the incident. "I have not CALLED him back as of the next morning, Tuesday, when I typed this, nor will I do so. I will keep him hanging. He can call me if he wants to and when he does, I will tell him I want no more of the entire case, there is nothing further I can do, that he has blown my cover and I will allways be apprehensive that even if Howard appears to trust me that he does NOT trust me, and that is the truth."[587]

Lt. Bemis phoned after Byron left Tuesday morning. Marwayne insisted that she was out of the investigation and whether Marcia committed suicide, skipped town, or Howard murdered her, so be it. She was at her wit's end. Bemis relented, understanding the difficult position John put her in, thanking her for the cooperation all the same.

She wasn't out of the woods yet. Howard visited a short time later. He asked her to retell the reason why she had told John about how he felt before the wedding, and how Bemis came to know anything about him soliciting the suicide note. She again scrambled to reassure him, later journaling, "This was a distinct key to me that Howard no longer trusts me!"[588]

Months later she would write to John Moore, "Ever since he thinks I told you about the note Marcia wrote dated Jan 9, 1979 and he gave Marcia 500 units (or whatever) of ketamine he has been suspicious, and maybe much more than I know, and of course he practically forced Rose into phoning you and telling you that he did not say that in her presence. As an example of his change in trust, ever since then, he has never asked me to get his mail, or water the plants, or left a key with me, etc. So, caution, please John."[589]

Overall, Marwayne thought it was good that Byron had come. It was a kind of purging. She knew Howard was emotionally exhausted, as was she.

If Marcia had skipped town, committed suicide, or met with foul play, sooner or later they would know it. In the meantime, there was nothing else she could do to help find her. "You have done everything you could, Marwayne," Howard said. "So have you Howard," Marwayne replied. "And now, somehow, you must leave this lay…and not let it consume you further, you have got to go on with your life, and get productive again," she urged. "You don't seem to understand, Marwayne. I can never get over this," Howard replied. "I can't…. It was the biggest failure of my life…. I can't get over that I should have loved her more, and then this would never have happened. I am just going to wait a year, and then I am going to program myself out. Heart condition runs in our family. Or my high blood pressure."[590]

Howard's son Kevin expressed concern about his frame of mind: "He kept asking me if I thought his father was in danger of suicide, that he had talked suicidally to Kevin almost constantly. This worried the boy terribly and I felt that it was a cheap shot on Howard's part to talk this way to his son."[591] Plenty of men have lost whole families in airplane accidents or train disasters, yet picked up and went on to live productive lives, Marwayne stressed. Howard could too, and he mustn't wallow further in obsession about theories like dematerialization, she recommended.

Meanwhile, Marwayne reiterated to Lt. Bemis that she could assist no more. The fallout was immense. Not only was she Howard's closest confidant, and therefore uniquely positioned to provide insight to Bemis, but now the case itself hit stall speed, running short on leads without his primary, albeit conflicted, source of information.

Feeling liberated that she had put an end to the clandestine cooperation with Lt. Bemis and John, nevertheless Marwayne couldn't help but make a few reflective entries in her journal that day:

> "Time will give the answers. I do not know, after all this, whether Howard has any more guilt than that 'he should have loved her more. If I had this would never have happened'. I only know that I feel very sorry for him, wish it had NEVER happened, whatever happened."

> "I recall his telling me that Marcia had said to him, 'I wish I did not have to put you through all that you will go through.'"

> "Then I recall Peter saying that Howard told him, 'There will be a trial. I will be tried for murder. But I won't be convicted, because they will never find her'."

> "Marcia…My God…where are you? Come back, or surface, one way or another, and put an end to this terrible nightmare, this awful charade. I beg of you."

> "Let the truth be known."[592]

WILD THEORIES

Shortly after Byron's departure in April, 1979, Howard traded Marcia's little white car for a used Ambassador station wagon from a dealer in Bellevue. "After her disappearance, Howard drove the jeep most of the time. I always wondered that if he had assisted her in a suicide that they had used her car, and he was uncomfortable about that car,"[593] Marwayne pondered. When Byron learned of the sale, he was upset, having told Howard that he wanted to buy it.

That April, Howard also attended the World Symposium on Humanity, a second conference in California where Marcia was scheduled to speak. In her place, Howard read her speech, sold their works, and implored people to pray. He'd go on to autograph Marcia's books with things like: "This is Marcia's finest book. It is a plum pudding laced with ketamine instead of rum,"[594] or "You always get more from Marcia Moore."[595] He felt that the symposium was a great success. Even back home, things started to settle down.

With Marwayne mostly out of the picture and Lt. Bemis under pressure from superiors, Howard, with the help of the media, mostly filled the void as spring turned to summer. Retelling much of the Ananta Foundation spring bulletin, he wrote a summer solstice bulletin, going to great lengths to emphasize that Marcia loved walking day or night and had no fear of the woods—or anyone. He also introduced a few new astrological angles. One astrologer said Saturn sitting on the third house cusp of Marcia's natal chart will force action and she may return. According to another, there were some negative transits in play, but nothing indicating death or murder.

Howard then regurgitated the dematerialization theory. Back in January, *Seattle Times* journalist Erik Lacitis had spoken with one of the Rainbow Rose Festival organizers in Pasadena, who said, "I guess this sounds kind of far out, but a lot of psychics here think she dematerialized. In the Indian philosophy, you can raise your consciousness, keep developing yourself like Jesus Christ and some of the gurus, that you reach a point where you just zap out."[596] In the following months, Howard would latch onto the idea and was now pushing it.

By the summer of 1979, the *National Enquirer* published their piece, with Howard now also leveraging the Lacitis article, speculating that Marcia may have dematerialized. The article flatteringly portrayed him as the forlorn husband holding vigil until she returned, reiterating his vow of celibacy until their "idyllic" marriage could resume.

"It all points to dematerialization," Howard told the *Enquirer*.

He continued to indulge all the metaphysical angles he could get his hands on to feed the press, Marcia's readers, and law enforcement, although it didn't always work to his advantage. In July, Howard called Liz Jenkins for a psychic reading, but she rebuked him, as Marwayne later journaled: "This time when he called, she told him 'Howard, I am tired of your game and I am not playing it with you. You KNOW what happened to Marcia, and I know what happened to Marcia, and you know that I know, so don't call me any more.' She said he made no response, and she hung up. This conversation occurred July 5, 1979, but to date Howard has never mentioned it to me, nor has he ever talked about Liz again."[597]

Meanwhile, Ann Rule, under her pen name Andy Stack, published a poignant vignette about the case in the August issue of *True Detective* magazine, boosting the national attention to the story. The article included a comprehensive breakdown of the case and brief history of Marcia's life, her marriages, and the happenstance of meeting Howard. A rundown of Marcia's dabbling in the occult, expertise in yoga, and immense meditative/psychic abilities kicked off the piece. Interestingly, it included an anecdote that ex-husband Mark Douglas, under her tutelage, was able to beat a lie detector in a clinic setting through controlled breathing and heart rate.

Spicing up the article, Rule included the interpretation from three prominent psychics—Pam Barrett, Barbara Easton, and Shirley Teabo.

In a tarot reading done the week after Marcia disappeared, and before she knew anything about the case, Barrett sensed that Marcia's body was hidden behind a Tacoma woman's house, amongst blackberry vines and thick woods between the property and a boatyard. She sensed a petite woman with a Cleopatra hairstyle, who wore low-cut shoes. She was adamant that Marcia would be found in the spring.

The more renowned Easton, who did readings with playing cards and promoted an accomplished degree of accuracy, perceived the complicity of a man concerned about a lucrative real estate transaction, a marriage on the rocks in which Marcia was secretly preparing for divorce, a violent death, and an eventual court trial.

Teabo, who according to Rule also had no foreknowledge of the case, correctly foresaw the four-week window of the disappearance between mid-December and January. She picked up a trip over water, perhaps out of state, and like Easton, a troubled marriage and a lucrative real estate deal or money that someone was trying to take away from her. Furthermore, she sensed two women—one friend, the other a violent foe. She sensed an illness possibly resulting in institutionalization but also turned over a card with an image of a coffin, indicating burial.

Ann Rule interviewed Howard for the piece, with his reiteration that he was currently using ketamine to make contact with Marcia on the spirit plane, still maintaining that she was suffering from amnesia.

The ever-expanding media attention resulted in another deluge of letters pouring into the sheriff's office from interested readers with a cornucopia of theories and premonitions offered from astrologers and psychics. One duo implied Howard's guilt by cross-referencing research with an I Ching interpretation. From a lead-chasing standpoint, Lt. Bemis was still spinning like a top.

That August, Marcia's former lover Akeva, who helped manage the Ananta Foundation, visited from Ojai. Unlike Byron, Akeva hit it off with Howard. Marcia and Howard had attended Akeva's wedding in October of 1978, and the newlyweds made their home in the house Marcia paid the rent for on Gridley Road, which served as headquarters of Ananta. Akeva held little interest in the circumstances surrounding Marcia's disappearance, instead making the visit to hammer out the continuation of the foundation headquarters, since it served as Akeva's residence.

Akeva liked to gamble, so Howard and Marwayne went to the track. On the way back, Howard became dejected as he came up empty picking horses. He bet for a fun time out, but the money wasn't trivial at that point. The cost of printing and mailing the spring and summer *Hypersentience Bulletins* exceeded the income from subscribers. He still had the duplex and Sai Baba house rent to pay. He also owed child support, and although he eventually convinced John Moore to pay Marcia's share of their 1978 taxes out of the trusts, Howard became frustrated. "You know, I have half a mind to go after that trust Marcia wanted me to have, when she wrote that suicide note," he vented to Marwayne. She countered that "the family could easily 'break' that, as it was not worded in any way as a will, nor was it witnessed. It was merely a 'request' to her brother to have the trust pay Howard on one of the trusts, the smaller one, a monthly payment (about $400), not a suicide note as such, and certainty not a will.... Howard became rather worked up about it all...."[598] Curiously, Akeva interjected that it was worth a try.

After lamenting John Moore treating him like a leper, Howard became increasingly revved up about being cut off from the trusts and said, "Why, WHY, why...why do they treat me this way?" Marwayne reminded him that "they were not going to give him any money, and not going to take him into the family bosom, for the reason that they think he killed her."[599]

She asked him to imagine how he would feel if such a thing happened to his daughter, and although he acknowledged their point of view, he remained frustrated. "Anyway, as we drove along that day, he became quite vocal about it, and said 'Goddam it, this is a community property state. I married Marcia. She was my wife,'" Marwayne journaled. "I was aghast! I told him that the fact that they were married in a community property state did not make her property before the marriage in any sense 'his' after they were married, and he seemed quite surprised! I said, what was hers <u>before</u> the marriage is still hers, including the trust, inheritance, anything else. Only income which they made jointly after marriage, such as royalties from the last book (a joint effort)...or income she made as a result of work done <u>after</u> the marriage...could be considered joint income. Howard did not say any more. For the first time I wondered if Lt. Bemis was right about murder having been done for money. Here, for the first time, appeared to be a 'motive.'"[600]

In late August, Akeva left Lynnwood. Marwayne considered it a pleasant visit that lifted Howard's spirits a bit. However, she was surprised to learn in conversation with Howard the following week that Akeva tried to get in contact with Wendy, Jim Batchelor's ex-girlfriend. Howard had given Marwayne's number to Batchelor to schedule an astrology session, despite formerly accusing him of abducting or murdering Marcia.

Although he had recently married, apparently Akeva was quite persistent in calling Wendy, and so Marwayne picked Batchelor's brain about it after he arrived for the astrology reading. Batchelor was still lovesick over Wendy and struggling greatly with moving on with his life. "I asked him why Akeva contacted Wendy, and he said he didn't really know, but that 'pardon my expression, Akeva and he (meaning Howard)…are both 'horny studs'…or 'running studs'…or some such expression. I am not quoting it quite correctly, because I do not remember his EXACT expression. I was very surprised at this."[601]

After the reading, they turned to discussing the case: "I asked him where he thought M is, and if he had picked up any psychic impressions about this. He believes she is dead. He believes Howard is a multiple personality, not just two. He believes Howard killed her, but has buried that. He, Howard, simply cannot look at that at all, and consequently lives through another personality, and that personality believes completely everything he is saying. He thinks M has been moved twice since her demise! He thinks she was still alive when she was carried out of the house, knew what was happening, but had no strength or will to resist it. Perhaps was only semi-conscious…. He also said that there is the possibility he is wrong about Howard, and whether or not he is wrong, that he feels enormous compassion for him, and wants to help him…. Jim Bacheler feels that the whole thing will end with Howard's suicide, because 'it is the only thing he can do.' He believes that the personality that conceals the murder of Marcia will surface from time to time, and each time the anguish is worse, and eventually Howard will kill himself as there is no other escape."[602]

Batchelor returned a month later to have Marwayne look at his chart. "He said he 'may' go to the S. Francisco area, and it would be dangerous…. He stated he would like to tell me the nature of the business for this trip, but could not, that it was highly secret. One of the reasons he had trouble with Wendy was that he could not tell her everything about what he was doing. Also, that it was one of the reasons Lt Bemis never considered him a suspect, as he, Bemis, knew what he was doing."[603]

Marwayne never found out what it was, though Bemis told her that Batchelor was in a mental institution after Marcia's disappearance, as the whole episode caused him great trouble. Batchelor said he had tried to block out all events from that period and get on with his life. Marwayne speculated that he might be an undercover narcotics agent, but never learned the truth. "Either that, or the man IS stark, raving insane and this is all one of his fantasies," she wrote. He had a pleasant manner and was easy to converse with. "But it is my opinion that he is quite a disturbed person. His horoscope shows some powerful pressures at the time of Marcia's disappearance (as does Howard's also). So, maybe, just maybe he IS involved in some way in her disappearance although I do not think so."[604]

As the fall of 1979 narrowed to an end, so did Howard's financial means. He was forced to make an arrangement with the landlord to permanently move into the Sai Baba house, now relegated to living space about half the size of the duplex. The landlords had a fit about the condition of the duplex. The walls and ceiling were tarnished and the stove dusty from all the incense they burned.

Even the Sai Baba house had a smoky layer all over the ceiling and curtains, the kitchen dusty with soot. The walls were blackened about two feet up from every heater, in both properties. Howard said they had been doing that since the electrical blackout some weeks earlier. "We had the same blackout at our house for 3 days! Our heaters have not smoked,"[605] thought Marwayne. The ceiling also looked shabby due to a leak. Howard ultimately agreed to help the landlords paint, but they kept the deposit, forcing him to sell off more of Marcia's furniture. Years later, the Sai Baba house became so dilapidated, it was torn down.

A sense of melancholy overcame hard-luck Howard as Marwayne prepared to drive him to the airport to attend a metaphysical conference in Oklahoma, where he would read Marcia's prepared speech about the current state of the reincarnation movement.

Aside from the financial woes, a reputable astrologer in Nutley, New Jersey, working with Marwayne by mail, sent an interpretation that Marcia was murdered and implicated Howard. Beyond their terrible astrological compatibility, the astrologer said, the cosmic alignment on the weekend Marcia disappeared—Jupiter conjunct Mars—meant an explosive fight had taken place. Marcia's astrologer friend Mac McLaughlin had noted the same.

Days before his Oklahoma trip, Howard prepared a concise will in case something happened to him while traveling. Despite the conversation with Marwayne and Akeva about not having a claim on Marcia's trusts since they were established before they wed, Howard tried anyway. The will he gave Marwayne left most of his possessions equally divided between his two children. It was a simple, one-page document, but among the assets, he instructed, "All of Marcia's belongings, jewelry, clothing, silverware and her small trust fund that she willed to me ($400 a month) shall go to Kimberly…as this was Marcia's implicit wish."[606] The "will" from Marcia he referred to was the concise typed note describing her impending death.

Marwayne noticed Howard's will wasn't notarized, but an additional piece of paper certified that he'd appeared before a notary in Everett. Although Marcia had no official will, *his* will now specified that Marcia's will was in a safety deposit at a local bank. "Howard has not given up the idea of trying to force that this moneys be paid to him, and in 'willing' the funds to Kimberly, he mentioned to me that 'that was Marcia's wish,'"[607] noted Marwayne.

HOWARD'S NEW LIFE

As the winter of 1979 approached with far less ferocity than the prior year, the investigation had lost steam as well.

In early November, Lt. Bemis was transferred to a trailer in the nearby town of Bothell that served as a police substation, reassigned from his position as lieutenant in charge of detectives to watch commander. "I don't know exactly what happened, but it looks like a demotion to me,"[608] Marwayne journaled, after Bemis phoned one day to tell her that he was her new neighbor. He still discreetly worked the case so as not to incur Sheriff Dodge's wrath.

The dust was settling, as Marwayne described further distancing herself in a letter to John Moore. "I have been weaning Howard away from us all possible this past month, for his own sake too. I lock my doors now when I leave. (I used to come home and find him sitting in my house). And he has quit asking me, pretty much, where I was, etc., or why somebody or other called me. Actually I do not think he trusts me all that much any more, so I do have to be very careful. I will do ANYTHING I can to help solve the mystery of Marcia's disappearance, and if he is guilty...which I more and more doubt.... I will not feel any concern about helping bring that out. But you must understand that he is clever and IF he is guilty, then he is a madman, and I would be in danger were he to learn that such a journal existed and that I had shared it with you."[609]

Howard turned his attention to rekindling his anesthesiology career, mailing hundreds of letters to attorneys along the Pacific Northwest, offering his services in medical malpractice lawsuits. There would be no takers, leaving Howard to reiterate to Marwayne that he had been blackballed.

Meanwhile, Marcia's children used their allotments of their mother's trust funds to hire a private investigator. A pair of detectives from New York were promptly dispatched out west to shake the bushes in an attempt to jar something loose on the case. Lt. Bemis criticized the PIs for throwing their weight around and boasting they were going to find the big break the investigation so desperately needed.

The mistrust and friction between the private investigators and law enforcement unfortunately left both camps holding their respective casework close to the vest. Although Lt. Bemis and John had possession of a key piece of information that could've dramatically changed the aggressiveness of the interview, the alleged suicide note was never shared with the private investigators before they interviewed Howard on November 29.

The private investigators began the interview by asking if he'd take another polygraph, to which Howard readily agreed, even under Sodium Pentothal. Then they asked about Marcia's state of mind. Despite Howard's acknowledgement that Marcia wouldn't commit suicide because of the karmic ramifications, he maintained that she mentioned it the morning she vanished, but that he talked her out of it. Then he retold the peculiar anecdote about her returning from the woods with facial injuries. "One day I got home from the hospital and I was still working, and it was late, and I came in and she wasn't home yet, and she came in a few minutes later and she had at time a cut lip and bruised eye, and I said Marcia, you know, Marcia, what happened, and she says, well, I went in the woods and I was going to commit suicide, I had taken a lot of ketamine and I fell down and when I woke up I thought how silly it was and…I said, God, Marcia, people are going to think I beat you up or something.…

So, initially, when she did vanish, my first thought, when I got home and she wasn't there, was, God, she walked into the woods, and I'm going to find her under a tree.... So the first week I thought she was dead in the woods."[610]

The PIs inquired further about Marcia's state of mind, and although it was ruled out by Lt. Bemis several months ago, Howard renewed the theory that Mark Douglas may be involved. "I thought she was on the verge of a mental breakdown," Howard told the PIs. "She had taken a lot of ketamine and she took it on a daily basis and, you know, she was in a weakened state, you know, if somebody beat her up at that point, you know, she wasn't obviously as vital as she usually is. So, anyway, he accidentally killed her, he then, you know, if this is true, I don't know if its true, he then immediately got out of here, you know, he parked that motor home somewhere, jumped on a plane and flew back to Boston and admitted himself to a hospital to establish an alibi."[611] Although he tried to revive the accusation, nothing became of it.

Howard then expounded on Marcia's love of walking: "Marcia's favorite pastime was walking. She loved to hike. She had no fear of the woods, she had no fear of anybody, whether it was day or night."[612] This despite the revelation that, prior to moving to Washington in 1977, Marcia had been brutally raped one night in the woods in Ojai, which the PIs confirmed in person when they visited Ojai to look for clues. Howard told them about the rape during the course of the interview, but the PIs didn't think to question how she could still hold no fear of anyone or walking alone at night. He also repeated several times during the course of the interview that he was certain that Marcia must've worn hiking boots the night she allegedly vanished.

Surprisingly, after the cursory questioning about the night Marcia vanished, they spent a considerable remainder of the interview asking for Howard's opinion on reincarnation and astrology. Little new information came of the exercise, although there were some revealing comments.

The PIs asked if Lt. Bemis followed up on any of the suspects or the supernatural leads Howard provided. "No, I don't think he really did much. It was not after...it wasn't too much after they thoroughly interrogated me and, you know, I passed the polygraph test, they just kind of lost interest," Howard replied. "It was, you know, a couple, two or three weeks later maybe a month, I don't know, it's hard to recall, you know, after almost…its ten and a half months. Uh, when I did go back to him, he'd say, well, you know, your wife's a missing person and we've had a number of homicides since then and, you know, its on the back burner. The thing that I found out when dealing with the police is that they're not interested in missing persons. Its got to involve the kind of violence, you know, murder, suicide, or something, or they're not interested."[613]

By the turn of the decade, the case had quieted down. Around the one-year anniversary of Marcia's disappearance, Howard had even begun dating again, setting aside his solemn vow of celibacy to chase a girl in the class adjacent to Marwayne's astrology course, that Marwayne described as a "nice girl, kind of top class hippy look, educated, well mannered. She felt sorry for Howard, and tried to help him."[614] It was short lived and Howard found himself back down in the dumps.

In April 1980, Howard visited his mother and sister who wanted him to come down to Southern California so they could straighten out his burgeoning alcoholism and help land him a job. "Couldn't stand southern Cal," Marwayne journaled. "Their apartment was next to freeway, the noise was bad, his sister and mother both chain smoke, he is vegetarian and they are not, plus he had to share a room with Kevin and you can bet he couldn't take much of that. So, he came back."[615]

When he returned to Washington, he had a new plan. While in California, he'd gone to see Akeva, who encouraged him to go to the Tenri, Nara religious retreat in Japan. Howard's family was vehemently opposed to the idea, Marwayne learned. "They are Armenian, Christian, probably something like Greek orthodox. His mother sewed crosses in all his clothes while he was in California."[616] His selling point was that an austere, monk-like existence would help him purge his drinking problem.

The short overseas sabbatical was facilitated through Akeva, but Howard wrote Marwayne conveying his misery shortly after leaving: "This is day one, and I am already homesick. I do not know if I can stick this out, but if I can, I will return the most disciplined I have ever been in my life. The people are kind. The food is very Japanese. Please write. Love Howard."[617]

Meanwhile, Lt. Bemis turned his attention to new cases, later assisting on the Green River Killer task force, although Marcia never wandered far from his thoughts. Every time an unidentified homicide victim was discovered, he held out hope that dental records would result in a match. The new detectives who inherited Marcia's case provided their contact information to Howard but didn't bring him back in for questioning. Even the psychics and astrologers lost much of their appetite, and consequently the outlandish speculation of readers eventually ran its course.

There was still the occasional newspaper article, and pulp magazines and tabloids kept abreast of the case to include in their portfolio of juicy supernatural and conspiratorial stories. A lengthy piece about the case appeared in the November 1980 issue of *Startling Detective*, a provocative rival of *True Detective* magazine. In typical fashion, it focused on the sensational ketamine angle as well as psychics and other wild theories. It portrayed investigators as continually baffled by the case, having uncovered no motive to abduct or kill Marcia Moore. The growing consensus in the media appeared to be that Howard Alltounian was the innocent victim of a perplexing tragedy.

The Seattle Times carried a follow-up article on Howard's sorry state, in which he was forced to sell off possessions to get by, including his furniture, gun collection, and the fishing boat and gear Marcia replenished after his divorce. He again claimed to have been unfairly blackballed in the medical community as a result of the backlash from *Journeys into the Bright World*.

Eventually an old colleague facilitated a position for Howard in a Detroit hospital where he was able to resurrect his anesthesiology career. He hated to leave Washington, but by late 1980 his prospects for work in the Seattle area were dim. The writing was on the wall, forcing Marwayne to prod the reluctant Howard into making the best of the situation. "I was really vicious with him. I told him he couldn't make enough money to pay his rent, and that he owed his children something more than that.

I told him Kimberly had a mouthful of crooked teeth which needed straightening, and no money to do it. That she had a horse he bought her, and they couldn't afford to take proper care of the horse.... I was really hard on him. I told him to get his behind out of that house and get back to work as fast as he possibly could."[618]

Howard relented and resettled in Detroit where he lived out the remainder of the year far away from police scrutiny, whispering locals, psychics, astrologers, and uninterested employers. Returning for the holidays marked a time of reflection as Howard visited his ex-wife, the kids, and Marwayne. "When he was here at Christmas 1980, he looked good, had lost weight, said he wasn't drinking now, and he thanked me for being so tough on him then. He said he had driven by the Sai house and thanked God he wasn't there anymore, and said, 'Marwayne, if I had stayed there, I would be dead by now.'"[619]

On March 5, 1981, an exhausted but jubilant Howard typed a letter to Kareen Zebroff, Marcia's Canadian author friend and television personality. Having driven cross-country from Detroit in two days' time, catching a few hours of sleep in his car at truck stops along the way, Howard had finally relocated back to "the garden of Eden—Washington State," as he put it. "When I crossed the Washington State line I rolled down the window, lit up a big cigar, & yelled 'HOME AGAIN'."[620]

Howard had turned down more lucrative offers in Oregon and Alaska to resettle in South Bend, Washington. A friend facilitated a position as head of anesthesiology at Willapa Harbor Hospital, although the facility was so small it only required one anesthesiologist. It was merely an afterthought that the salary was less than what could be commanded in larger hospitals and cities. Howard was finally home, glowingly writing Kareen about South Bend's coastal beauty, the nearby rivers teeming with steelhead, salmon, razor clams, and oysters.

Lamenting all he had been through in two years' time, he told of the arduous journey back. "It was so dark & so black, & so bleak for so long, but finally the ray of light has shined through," wrote Howard. "I have now let Marcia go completely. Where ever she is God bless her, I am now going on with my life."[621]

The slings and arrows from law enforcement had ebbed. Lt. Bemis, his dogged pursuer, had long since been reassigned, the resources of the Snohomish County Sheriff's Office marshalled toward more pressing investigations. Howard could now breathe in quiet comfort and start over in the Pacific Northwest. His life was finally coming together, and the man who swore to wait forever in celibacy until Marcia "rematerialized," was now regularly dating again.

Although it seemed that he had finally found closure, his newfound serenity would last just two weeks. Letting go of Marcia *completely* would turn out not to be so easy.

GRIM DISCOVERY

On the afternoon of Friday, March 20, 1981, George and Carroll Walden, residents of Bothell, a small town that borders Lynnwood to the southeast, were clearing brush from their yard. The brothers were readying it for future building projects but had abandoned the property for some time, making it an arduous task.

Although their modest home, near the intersection of 173rd Street Southeast and Bothell Everett Highway, stood only about fifteen yards off the two-lane roadway, the parcel comprised around three acres that sloped moderately down from the rear of the home. An old barn, once badly burned in a fire, was nestled towards the northwest corner of the property where the slope steepened, approximately one hundred yards downhill from the house.

A blend of towering cedars, alders, and firs appeared to stand guard, lining the perpendicular edges of the lot, but in between was a dense mass of overgrown, thorn-laden blackberry vines, brambles, weeds, and marshy terrain. By 1981, the blackberry vines had infiltrated so aggressively that little more than the roof of the small barn was visible. It was of such density that earthmoving equipment was needed to clear the brush. Fortunately, a narrow pathway once cut from the house down to the barn remained intact, allowing enough space for the equipment to come in off the highway and find a toehold for the clearing.

As Carroll Walden walked down the steepening slope toward the northwest corner of the yard, he glimpsed a streak of white and glint of gold through a patch of grass near a triangular-shaped tree cluster, about seventy-five yards downhill from the barn. Curiosity piqued, he pulled away a patch of sod adjacent to a cluster of tall cedars, only to recoil as he uncovered an almost bleached-white skull cap lying face up on a bed of dry leaves, exposing the top half of a human skull with several gold crowns. He immediately called George at work, who told him not to touch it and wait for police.

The hastily dispatched officers found no obvious signs of wounds as they cordoned the area and waited for detectives. Snohomish County Sergeant Zitzer and Detective Allen Zurlo arrived to photograph and do a cursory search. Due to darkness, the search was soon terminated until 9:00 a.m. the following morning with an additional fourteen-member team. The search yielded little else.

Marcia Moore's skull found in swampy conditions behind this dilapidated barn badly damaged in by a fire. Strangely, her skull was found around the incorrect date Howard gave as Marcia's birthday, telling police she'd been born in March, when it was May. Perhaps odd given how big a deal Marcia often made about them both being Gemini. Several astrologers based charts off the wrong birthdate, while numerous outlets reported fifty-one as Marcia's age, when she was fifty. The mistake had to be corrected on her death certificate by her family.

The skull was released to forensic dentist Dr. Keith Leonard for examination and dental identification, then meticulously compared to dental charts and X-rays provided by the Moore family. On March 23, the verdict was in: Marcia Moore had been found. As if back on stage from beyond the grave, she had fittingly resurfaced right on the button of the astrologically significant Spring Equinox.

On March 28, over fifty searchers and a helicopter from Snohomish County Search & Rescue arrived to conduct a more intensive grid search of two hundred by four hundred yards, but the terrain was rough. North Creek, which lies between the edge of the property and nearby North Road, had seeped into the surrounding soil so profusely that some searchers found themselves knee-deep in marsh as they searched for additional remains. Aside from a few other bones, determined to be of animal origin, and a partially decomposed raincoat that did not appear to be related, no other remains were initially found around the skull. Subsequent media reports of a partial jaw bone and a leg bone found, were never confirmed to be Marcia's.

Given the conditions, the search was called off after a few hours. Since the skull was found unattached to any other skeletal remains, the surrounding ground was not excavated. The search team would never return.

On March 31, Dr. Daris Swindler, an anthropologist from the University of Washington who also worked on the Ted Bundy case, provided a report. He was unable to determine if the skull had been buried, but it may have been for a time, then "unearthed and became bleached out while lying on the surface of the ground."[622] He concluded that it would be impossible to determine the cause of death by skull examination. No evidence of foul play was readily observable, just the bite and claw marks of rodents and other foragers.

Twenty-six months of searches, prognostications, conjecture, psychic premonitions, alien and mafia conspiracies, astrological interpretations, and an unfortunate abundance of sensationalism came to an abrupt end. Theories of escape to India, kidnapping by a coven of witches, and of course *dematerialization* vanished just as suddenly as Marcia had that fateful weekend of January 14, 1979.

All that remained was the tragic conclusion of Marcia Moore's final days—and many unanswered questions.

AFTERMATH

Despite the acrimony that resulted from John Moore blowing her cover in April 1979, Marwayne felt obligated to keep the Moore family abreast of the local developments after the skull was discovered, writing John multiple times in the weeks that followed. She also notified Lani, Marcia's friend and protégé, who promptly burst into tears. "I told her, 'Don't cry over the bones honey. Marcia is warm and well and happy where she is, and she wouldn't want you to weep over her remains,'"[623] wrote Marwayne.

A couple days later, Lani called back, feeling compelled to relay something Marcia once confided to her. "She told me something interesting today, namely that Marcia had told her that 'it was over...that she didn't have to do that anymore'...and Lani took this to mean the marriage was in deep trouble."[624] In the moment, however, Lani conceded that she may have simply become disoriented while walking.

The reactions from the Moore family were mixed, all mourning the tragedy in their own way. Eleanor pragmatically resigned herself to the fact that Marcia had been playing with fire for years. She focused on Howard's possible criminal negligence as a physician, if Marcia was in the failing health he claimed, and suicidal to boot.

Robert Moore sorrowed in his characteristically quiet, solemn fashion. He anguished more deeply than the rest as the lifelong philosophical bond formed with his only daughter was now extinguished, leaving him to contemplate for the rest of his days the extent to which he stoked the metaphysical fire that contributed to her fatal path.

Brother John Moore, who spent the most time in Washington and in correspondence from Concord with Lt. Bemis and Marwayne, concentrated on fulfilling his legal and fiduciary duties as trust custodian. Despite the typed note Howard gave him asserting that Marcia was on death's doorstep, with her last wish instructing John to transfer the smaller trust to Howard, he never saw another penny.

Brother Robin Moore, sensationalist as ever, asked the coroner if the head was neatly severed, an obvious tipoff to him that a satanic cult or ritualized killing was involved. The coroner promptly replied that it was impossible to determine since only the upper portion of her skull was found.

Daughter Louisa had been wrestling with feelings of abandonment and what she perceived as her mother's delusions of grandeur finally catching up to her. She reflected on Marcia's vanity, and belief that she would rather perish like a shooting star than slowly watch her beauty erode. Instead, she aligned with Eleanor that if Howard was guilty of anything, it was dereliction of duty as a physician to properly care for her physically suffering and allegedly suicidal mother, while supplying her with dangerous quantities of ketamine.

Marcia's son Christopher considered all the possibilities, including that Marcia may have been picked up by a lunatic, but also that she may have committed suicide. He took Howard's story at face value that she was possibly delusional and manic depressive.

A couple of weeks after the skull was found, a small box containing Marcia's remains was shipped to the Moore family in Concord. In a disgracefully cruel twist, according to Lt. Bemis her gold crowns were removed and subsequently went missing while in the possession of the coroner's office. A private ceremony was held in Sleepy Hollow Cemetery in Concord, where Marcia was laid to rest preceding her parents and brothers.

Ruminating over everything that had happened in two years' time, Marwayne couldn't help but reconsider the possibility that there may indeed be another side to Howard. In addition to Lani's insight into their marital problems, she wrote a couple of letters to John portraying Howard's uncontrollable anger, including the anecdote where two years earlier he flew into a rage at Kevin, then moments later acted as if nothing had happened.

She further wrote John about an interesting visit from Carol Phillips, an old friend of Marcia's who helped introduce Howard to Marcia back in the summer of 1977. Carol stopped by to chat shortly after the skull was found. She said when she last saw Marcia, she looked awful, and remembered a comment that Marcia eventually wanted to live out the remainder of her days in India. However, she also informed Marwayne about her acquaintance with Howard, back when he was romantically interested in Carol, and her strange experiences with him. Marwayne recapped their conversation in her letter to John:

> She said Howard had been chasing her, "hot and heavy"!...Carol told me that Howard attended the lecture where Marcia spoke, (which we knew) and by his own admission sat in the front row. mesmarised by her. I had been told by someone else, some time ago, that Howard crashed a party afterward which was given in Marcia's honor; Carol told me that he pressured her into taking him to the party, and that she gave in and took him although she did not want to. During this party, Howard invited Marcia to go for a walk, (which we already knew,) and they talked, and he kissed her while they were out on this walk. Later he told people, in front of Tina his wife, and Carol, that she, meaning Marcia, "made me so horny I had to go home and screw Tina"! And this during the period where he and Tina were living apart, or at least living separate lives in what he termed "an open marriage" whatever that is. Needless

to say I consider this a very crass, insensitive remark… Carol also told me that she has seen a very rough, perhaps even violent side to Howard, but that fortunately it occurred over the telephone so she was not endangered. It seems that Carol and Marcia and Mac McLaughlin were going to drive from Seattle over to SkyMeadows on a trip which was to be a rest for them all. Sky Meadows is the name of a mountain resort area, where horses are kept, big expanse of meadow and trails, and individual, summer cabins. In the winter it is covered with snow, and there is quite a bit of snowmobiling done. Anyway, Howard wanted to go along, but the three of them had agreed it was to be a trip for rest…and they…principally Carol and Mac…did not want Howard along.

Marcia, I think, would have liked to have him go, but according to Carol said she "would abide by Carol's decision" and agreed the purpose of the trip was for rest, and meditation. So, Carol told Howard he could not go with them. She said there followed an explosion from him (on the telephone) in which he called her "every dirty name in the book!" She was dumbfounded. She did say that in a couple of days he called her up and apologized, but that she had not forgotten how violently and vehemently he had spoken to her…. She agreed with me that it is possible Marcia walked out there by herself, became disoriented, and died of the exposure and cold. But I knew from the way she talked that she really believes Howard has some guilt in Marcia's death, as do I. We agreed, however, that there is so far no absolute evidence, although many small pieces, as a jig-saw puzzle, that are damning.[625]

Meanwhile, Marwayne informed John that by all accounts Howard was now lying low, refusing comment requests by multiple news outlets that hounded him once they discovered he was back in Washington. He even sought Marwayne's counsel about whether to make a statement. "I told him I wouldn't presume to advise him on this matter, but I would think that sooner or later he would have to say SOMETHING. (Why wouldn't a man who has just found out that his missing wife's skull was located NOT want to talk to police or press?????? If my husband were missing, and just located part of him, I would be hounding the police for more information, not holing up or withdrawing.)"[626]

The scrutiny and stress Howard had worked so hard to put behind him reflowered just as spring had sprung. Despite this, the Snohomish County Sheriff's Office was mostly silent. Lt. Bemis wasn't initially contacted even as a courtesy when the skull was found. The forensic evidence gleaned from the pathological examination of the skull was paltry—no bullet holes, no cracks or indentations consistent with blunt force trauma. No clothing identifiable to Marcia was ever found, no hard objects like the glass and metal syringes Marcia preferred, nor the hiking boots Howard insisted she always wore. When detectives regrouped to lay out what they had on the case, the prospects for demonstrating foul play were dim.

Aside from the lack of forensic evidence, no one had made contact with Marcia Moore Sunday, January 14, and not a single eyewitness spotted her walking that night. No forced entry was observed in the duplex, no sign of a struggle, no money missing from her purse, no stolen cars, nor evidence that anyone cleaned the duplex or Sai Baba house to cover up a crime.

There would be few follow-up statements from police, friends, and family. Detectives would never again bring Howard back in for questioning. The missing persons case of Marcia Moore would end with the official decree: cause of death—*unknown.*

THE DECADES HENCE

For the next three decades, that would largely be all. The speculation would continue of course, coming on like a fever once in a while, then ebbing just as fast. Little in the way of fresh evidence would be introduced until Lt. Bemis helped us resurrect the story.

Over the years, Lt. Bemis graciously gave his time, met with me in Everett, Washington, and assisted in securing the case file from the Snohomish County Sheriff's Office. We drove from the duplex by roadway and visited the Waldens, surveying the distance and terrain. They were gracious, told what they remembered, and even handed me a small bone found back then.

Marwayne chipped in as well, turning over her journal, letters, and astrological interpretations and corresponding sporadically with us until she began suffering the effects of acute dementia. Marcia's friends willingly told fond stories and tried to provide any information that could help. Daughter Louisa provided us with a collection of private letters spanning most of her life, dozens of pictures, and of utmost importance, candid, unvarnished insight about the Moore family.

The trove spawned several new contacts and leads. As we lined up the data, connecting scattered fragments of information never cross-referenced before, it became increasingly clear that a different story was materializing before our eyes.

Suddenly we felt a great responsibility. We alone held the jigsaw pieces Marwayne referred to, so we undertook the daunting and painstaking task of properly fitting them together. Scrutinizing the details over and over, we bounced theories off those we interviewed and some contacts in law enforcement, knowing that the case would have to be analyzed through the prism of conventional detective work. Excerpts from these interviews illuminate a more encompassing version of events and candid insight into their marriage, culminating in an alternative theory of what happened to Marcia Moore.

There are certainly a few plausible explanations. Could Marcia Moore have simply gone for a walk and become lost on that fateful second weekend of 1979? Could she have been depressed and desperate, wanting to end it all? Could she have purposely or accidentally taken a sizable dose of ketamine out in the woods and become disoriented or injured, succumbing to hypothermia?

The answer to these possibilities is, of course, yes. In fact, these theories were most readily accepted by some in her family, friends, the press, and fans. Marcia's unconventional path in life, her marriage missteps, and naivety with money did nothing to dissuade the Moore family from accepting these explanations.

Surely the ketamine angle and cornucopia of psychics and astrologers fit a tantalizing narrative for the media and fans. Despite their enduring suspicions of Howard, for law enforcement any one of these theories makes for a conveniently tidy case closed.

But what if these are not the only—or even the most likely—explanations? What if connecting dots in new ways presents a dramatically different outcome? What if Howard Alltounian was far more culpable? In order to properly consider that alternative, it's necessary to ask some fundamental questions and dispel the misinformation that clouded the picture for the Snohomish County Sheriff's Office.

The first place to start is to consider how Marcia Moore's skull ended up behind the Walden house. Had she walked along the roadways, the distance is approximately 2.7 miles, heading north from the duplex on Larch Way, east along 164th Street, then south along Bothell Everett

Highway. Though not impossible, it would have likely been out of her range, factoring in the elements and Marcia's hip ailment at the time. During a visit to the Moore's summer home in Massachusetts as early as September 1978, the family observed her difficulty simply climbing stairs.

Shortly before she vanished, Marwayne noticed that Marcia was experiencing such pain that she could not put full weight on her hip socket and was walking in half-steps. Sometimes she resorted to using a cane even for the mere one-block stroll over to Marwayne's to soak in their pool, which she enjoyed during the summer to soothe the tension in her hip. Moreover, no one traveling along 164th Street or Bothell Everett Highway witnessed a woman walking between the hours of 8:30 p.m. and Howard's return between 1:00 and 2:00 a.m. the night of January 14.

The paralyzing effects of the historic cold system that blanketed much of the United States must also be taken into account. According to Howard, neither her coats nor heavy sweaters were missing from the duplex, while the evening temperatures of that fateful weekend were well below freezing. Marcia's friend Lani recalled questioning Howard on the matter. "And what I didn't understand was, I could remember saying to Howard, well if she went out for a walk, why didn't she take her coat? She had a big huge, um, knitted sweater coat thing that she wore. And you know she only weighed eighty pounds. She was tiny."[627] Additionally, in her book *Hypersentience*, Marcia describes her own innate and "abnormal dislike of the cold." She believed it originated in a past-life brought forth during a regression session. "I endeavored, with middling success, to recollect that dreadful period of suffering from chill and exposure during which I finally died alone on the dungeon floor."[628]

In the group interview on Thursday, January 18 with Lt. Bemis, John Moore, and Cris Leipzig, Howard describes the road conditions as covered with glare ice, a hazardously slick condition extremely difficult to navigate by foot or car. Howard had trouble searching one block north by Martha Lake, let alone a distance of almost three miles by roadway.

Had Marcia avoided the roads and walked due southeast, straight from the back door of the duplex, the trek would've stretched approximately 1.7 miles. On its face, the distance is within range for Marcia, who occasionally enjoyed the two-mile walk with Lani to Floral Hills Cemetery before her hip increasingly became an issue. According to Lani, however, they always stuck to the roads and established footpaths. Although there were fragmented trails in certain parts, the topography coupled with the weather conditions and her hip condition would have made the route to where her skull was discovered considerably more arduous than walking the roadways, if not impassable.

Back in 1979, the expanse stretching between the duplex and the barn behind the Walden residence was predominately a mishmash of small housing tracts, undeveloped forestry, brambles, tall weeds, and thorny vines, with creeks and ponds in between. The densely uneven terrain sloped steeply downward at points, especially the gulley the neighborhood kids referred to as "hidden valley."

Marwayne's daughter Cris recalled that during repeated searches in the woods southeast of the duplex, her horse went to its knees a few times, her legs scraped from the icy terrain. Had Marcia somehow managed the trek and reached the rear edge of the property, the next hundred yards to the barn area were an obstructed mass of thorn-laden vines and brush so dense that it necessitated earthmoving equipment to clear.

Even if foraging animals dragged body parts in different directions to protect their meals, it's unlikely that her skull would've ended up amongst the densest thicket, so far from the duplex. A simpler explanation is that she was driven, dead or unconscious, along the roadways and dumped by the burned-out barn. The pathway cut from the abandoned Walden house down to the barn was narrow, but just wide enough for a small vehicle to pass, as Lt. Bemis theorized when we interviewed him in 2010. "He [Howard] knew all the old roads around there. He liked to explore and stuff like that...had that '56 Jeep station wagon, narrow wheel base and I, I think what he probably did, he probably backed down there and I'll bet that dollars to doughnuts she didn't even have a stitch of clothing on, 'cause no clothing at all was found there, and there should have been."[629]

If she was driven, it could also explain why the bloodhound never picked up a scent trail while searching for hours around the duplex the morning after Marcia disappeared.

Down by the barn, foraging animals would have only had to drag her a short distance to the spot where the skull was ultimately found. If the jeep didn't fit on the pathway, the abandoned house and an unattached garage are situated along the frontal edge of the property, parallel to the road, providing cover for her body to be carried downhill to the barn area out of sight of motorists.

It is also important to determine if there is any validity to Howard's contention that "Marcia had no fear of the woods or being alone[630]... whether it was day or night."[631] When I visited Marwayne, she denied Howard's statement, as she remembered Marcia walking no more than the short distance to her house at nighttime. More importantly Lani, the friend who accompanied Marcia on walks at least once a month for a year, emphatically denied the claim and was shocked all these years later to hear that Howard insisted as much. "No! Oh my God no," Lani recalled. "I don't remember her ever walking at night."[632] In reviewing all of the materials and interviews surrounding this case, there is nothing to substantiate Howard's claim. Tabloid reports of her moonlit escapades to Floral Hills Cemetery to worship the fountain were based on Howard's account, uncorroborated, and salaciously embellished to juice the story.

Fountain in the cemetery where Marcia was said to
have liked to walk, as seen on a clear day.

If anything could be supported, it would be that Marcia avoided walks alone at night stemming from the brutal rape a couple years prior in Ojai. In the November 1979 interview with private investigators, Howard himself describes the rape as told to him by Marcia. "In that particular instance she dropped her car off and she went for a, she used to walk in the foothills of Ojai. Some nut picked her up, and I guess, you know, he was in his early 20's, or whatever, ah, she ended up spending the night with him in the woo…you know, in the woods, he raped her, he beat her up, ah, she was able to get away from him though, she out-walked him. And she walked back to the police in Ojai, California and they went and arrested the guy and he was booked and charged."[633]

Lani reiterated that they stuck primarily to the light footpaths and established trails due south of the duplex toward Floral Hills Cemetery, away from the eastern direction of Bothell Everett Highway. Surrounded by tall, closely knitted trees that offered insulation from traffic noise, Floral Hills Cemetery was their favorite place precisely because of its serenity. They were peaceful walks for quiet contemplation and medita-tion. "We never did any striking out on our own in, into the woods like, no. She would never have done that."[634]

320

Nonetheless, Howard maintained that Marcia was capable of making that journey because of the Vibram-soled hiking boots he claimed she wore the night of her disappearance. However, there is no corroboration that she owned such hiking boots, and the subject of her footwear remains an unresolved discrepancy. Following Howard's very first call to the police, the all-points bulletin on January 15 stated: "SUBJ. ON FOOT WITH LIGHT CLOTHING, POSS NO SHOES OR COAT."[635] Hours later the following commentary from Howard appears in Sergeant John Taylor's search and rescue report: "He indicated that she was possibly wearing a green turtle next sweater, bulky type, green cord pants and some type of low shoes, black in color with a short heel on them."[636]

Yet by the group police interview on Thursday the 18th, Howard's account completely changes. "When I got back at 1:00 o'clock, she was gone. And the first thing I did was to look to see if she had her coat. And all her coats were here. All her shoes were here, except her hiking boots. And I thought okay, and I thought for sure she had gone out to commit suicide. Was going to walk right out in those woods somewhere and so do herself in."[637] If Howard's first instinct in the four-hour span before calling police was to catalog her coat and shoes, why was there any confusion or conflicting accounts regarding the type of shoes, or if she was wearing shoes at all?

Howard potentially made the first of a few key material misrepresentations in his first call to police. Had he dumped her body by the barn with little clothing and no footwear, it would explain death by hypothermia, but later he may have realized that the distance was too far, the terrain too rough, and the weather too severe to traverse without shoes. The black, low-cut shoes Marcia routinely walked in were found in plain sight beside the bed, leaving him forced to assert that she was wearing something else—something more rugged.

Negotiating such uneven and undeveloped ground, thick with forestry and prickly vines, in subfreezing temperature, wearing light clothing and suffering from a debilitating hip condition would have been extremely difficult in her walking shoes. But Lani never knew her to own a pair of hiking boots and stated that she never wore such boots in her presence, only the dark-colored loafers. Routinely accompanying Marcia on walks for over a year, she often slept over Friday and Saturday nights inside the duplex but never saw the elusive hiking boots Howard insisted she always wore during the fourteen months of their relationship. During the February 8 interrogation, Lt. Bemis briefly challenged Howard on the discrepancy, but it never amounted to a proven misstatement.

In addition, the direction in which Marcia's skull was found in relation to the duplex was curiously spoon-fed to search and rescue by Howard. In the initial missing person report, just hours after Marcia disappeared, the responding officer noted after speaking with Howard that the subject would, on previous walks, head *southeast* of the residence. A couple of days later in Thursday's group police interview, Howard pushed the southeasterly direction even further toward the highway: "And Chris told me that, you know, the search and rescue only went to the north road. But where that gas line comes out, she says there is a whole stretch of woods that comes out at the end of 183rd street which is off the Bothell-Everett Highway."[638] Shortly after Marcia's skull was found, Marwayne wrote John Moore, mentioning that her daughter Cris and Howard walked beyond Bellflower Road during the search Howard directed and may have been very close to where the skull was found.

If Howard killed Marcia, why would he purposely steer search and rescue in the general direction of Marcia's remains? Obviously if he was too precise, it would've been tremendously incriminating, but there's a simple answer. A body must be found in order for Howard to collect on the proceeds of the smaller trust he claimed was bequeathed to him in the typed note. It's also possible that he wanted the body found within enough time to determine the cause of death was ketamine related.

Having closed the case shortly after the skull was found, no one from law enforcement revisited the peculiar way in which Howard continually directed search and rescue, or bothered to substantiate whether Marcia ever walked in the direction of Bothell Everett Highway.

STATE OF MIND

nother important question to answer is: What was Marcia's state of mind that fateful weekend? It remains a crucial facet of the case, as Howard made it the focal point of the very first contact with police. In the initial police bulletin, the responding officer records the following stated by Howard regarding Marcia's frame of mind: "SUBJECT IS DISTRAUGHT, & THREATENED SUICIDE THIS DATE. SUBJ. POSS. MAINIC DEPRESSANTE, HAS THREATENED SUICIDE IN THE PAST, AND HAS LEFT RESIDENCE ONLY TO RETURN SEVERAL HOURS LATER.[639]…SUBJ. MAY BE SUFFERING FROM AMNESIA OR OTHER MENTAL DISORDER FROM USE OF KETAMINE."[640] Quite a troubling list of afflictions Howard set the tone of the investigation with.

The amnesia theory can be disregarded since Howard admitted to Marwayne in February 1979 that he perpetuated and later sustained that lie for two years, simply to draw attention to the search for Marcia. The remaining question is whether she was manic depressive and suicidal. To answer, it is necessary to examine where the claim originated. Howard alleged these emotional/mental troubles primarily for three reasons.

The first was that Marcia became suicidal because of her inability to convince her ex-husband, Mark Douglas, to republish *Astrology the Divine Science* and *Astrology in Action* into paperback. According to

Lani, and Marcia's daughter Louisa, she was sometimes frustrated with Mark, but they readily dismissed the notion that republishing two books brought about depression. Both books were published back in the 1960s, so the royalties were no longer a meaningful portion of her income. The vast majority came from her trusts and speaking engagements. In the almost weekly correspondence to her parents and friends, there is hardly a mention of this purported melodrama regarding republishing the books. Marcia was working on multiple new books and enthusiastic about an upcoming joint venture of launching a magazine devoted to reincarnation with peers in Ojai. Republishing the older books in paperback may have slightly augmented her income or upped the breadth of circulation by penetrating new markets, but there is no indication that it was a matter of life and death.

Secondly, Howard offered that Marcia was suicidal owing to physical pain, as he claimed in the first interview with Lt. Bemis on Thursday, January 18. But he contradicted his own statements by asserting that she had soothed the pain through yoga and was fine by the weekend of her disappearance, perhaps in an attempt to explain how she could've physically managed a couple-mile walk in the hazardous conditions that night. In the police interrogation with Lt. Bemis on February 8, Howard states: "She did have a sore hip. She did limp, but the last week that we were together, she wasn't limping and I didn't notice that her hip was bothering her. Now Marwayne says that she didn't think she could walk over 2 miles. Maybe that's true, but as far as I can dicerne you know, it wasn't true. She was walking 3 hrs a day all summer, all spring."[641]

There is a critical inconsistency here. His portrayal directly contradicts the mysterious "severe pain" described in the note allegedly typed on the day she vanished. Investigators never challenged Howard to explain how she could simultaneously be so close to death, as described in the note, yet healthy enough to walk several miles during the worst winter in decades.

The third suicidal suggestion is Howard's contention in the February 8 interrogation that "there was always a consistency in whenever she had to speak publicly of her you know wanting not to do this and going into a bout of you know depression and threatening suicide."[642] Of all the explanations put forth for Marcia's alleged suicidal tendencies, anxiety from public speaking is preposterous, the notion completely rejected by all of Marcia's friends, family, fans, and peers. An exceptional public speaker, Marcia felt most comfortable in her own skin lecturing, artfully using intriguing mystical prose to illuminate and promote metaphysics. She instinctively knew how to captivate audiences with an arsenal of ethereal adjectives that attracted laypeople and was known as an ebullient speaker that emanated charm and magnetism. Lt. Bemis verified that Marcia never cancelled with the Rainbow Rose Festival's organizers and spoke enthusiastically with them for an hour the week prior.

When asked if Marcia ever displayed an anxious or depressive state in advance of public speaking, Lani replied, "No way, she flourished. She loved it. That's why she wrote the books, really. She told me she never made any money writing books. It was the lecturing and the traveling that gave her the inspiration to continue with her work…. I don't believe that at all. Not at all."[643] This sentiment is echoed by all of the contacts we interviewed, including her daughter Louisa.

Lani conceded that Marcia was only saddened in the weeks leading up to her disappearance because she felt that Pelu, her spirit guide since she was a young girl, had abandoned her. She remembered consoling Marcia as she explained that it was a matter of animosity between Pelu and Sai Baba. However, Lani perceived it as a further indication that Marcia's relationship with Howard was ill-fated, since his spirit guide was at odds with her own. "Her feelings about it were beginning to change. She lost contact with her guide. She was extremely upset…. That's why she got that out of her house, the whole Sai Baba thing."[644]

Having stayed in the Pasadena area for the entire convention between January 20 and 27, Lani was completely unaware of what Howard told police about Marcia's troubled state of mind just before she vanished. "No, she was not manic, that's just plain evil of Howard to imply that," Lani said. "She never expressed any suicidal thoughts, no, no, no, no, I would have gone straight to her…. No, I would have come unglued, we would have taken her out of there…. She was very disturbed about losing contact with her guide, but she was excited for the festival. In fact, she was looking forward to it."[645]

Marcia did speak about death, with great perspective. In a speech prepared for the April 1979 symposium in Los Angeles, she introduced a concept called "thanasecendance," which essentially defined the proper art of dying. The context was about rethinking our cultural fear and disparagement of relinquishing when physically near death, or involuntarily using medical technology to prolong death until the bitter end. The point was to broaden our understanding of reincarnation, rebuking the notion of death's finality and the tendency for society to view it in a negative, sorrowful light.

In that same speech, however, Marcia staunchly criticized suicide as the conscious extinguishment of life before one's time, stating that it severely repressed the karmic advancement of the soul. She professed that we are to learn from the *entirety* of each lifetime in preparation for the next. The speech included an account of what she believed to be her own past incarnation as a southern belle named Miss Miranda, who slowly drank herself to death with rum. Marcia believed that purposefully ruining this previous life tainted her existing life experiences, fated to lovers and husbands afflicted with acute alcoholism and other destructive habits like smoking. It was an obvious shot at ex-husbands Simons and Mark Douglas, but also reflects an important rejection of suicide.

The combination of these factors casts serious doubt on Howard's claims. Even Howard characterized as much in the private investigator interview, but he hedged to leave the possibility open: "If you believe in reincarnation, which Marcia obviously did, she has written books on the subject, the worse thing you can possibly do is to commit suicide, because what happens is you come back in a body, you know, wanting desperately to live, but not able to, such as, say a woman with young children having a terminal disease, and that's what happens; if you commit suicide, you come back in a diseased body, wanting desperately to live. It would be the last thing she could do...could ever conceive of, but none the less she did talk about suicide...."[646]

Despite all three versions of Howard's claim that Marcia was suicidal and about to die, the timeline presents another crucial contradiction. The concise note that Howard alleged Marcia typed on the morning of January 14 included the line "I am in severe pain and do not know how much longer I have to live."[647] But this typewritten note is dated January 9, with Howard theorizing that it was a continuation of a partial hand-written note also dated the 9th.

Phone records show that Marcia spoke by phone with Lani at 6:21 p.m. on January 8, and Lani spent most of the day with Marcia on Wednesday, January 10. It would have to be believed that Marcia, pur-portedly suicidal, amnesiac, manic depressive, suffering from a mental disorder, and in physical pain of such severity that she was on death's doorstep, didn't divulge or exhibit even a hint of this when Lani spoke with her by phone less than twenty-four hours prior, nor when she visited for most of the day less than twenty-four hours after. Even Marwayne conceded that Lani was Marcia's closest friend in Washington, but Lani remains adamant that she was in good spirits those days in anticipa-tion of the trip and made no mention of pain, nor expressed any sui-cidal thoughts.

Furthermore, on Saturday morning, January 13, in addition to a pleasant call Marcia had with her brother's wife, Lani says she spoke by phone with Marcia in making final plans. They enthusiastically discussed the Rainbow Rose Festival itinerary and the sizable group of friends and peers in Southern California she was excited to introduce to Lani. Yet Marcia allegedly typed the complete note the next morning. Once again, no mention was made of pain, or a suicidal, manic depressive state; no hint of this was detected by Lani that Saturday. Lani distinctly remem-bered that during their conversation, Marcia wished they could make it a girls' trip and leave the husbands behind.

If suicide is improbable, accidental overdose is even more unlikely. As even Howard admitted, it would've been nearly impossible to do so self-injecting ketamine intramuscularly, even several orders of magnitude more than her regular doses. She habitually injected less than seventy-five milligrams, nowhere near enough to cause death intramuscularly, as ketamine is considered a safer alternative to traditional anesthetics.

In Howard's own words, and in clinical research, this is precisely why it is still used on infants and animals. Larger doses of ketamine also rapidly immobilize patients. Consequently, unless Marcia took a sizable quantity with her, the chances of walking even a short distance after injecting a massive dose at the duplex is remote. There also wasn't a sufficiently fatal dose missing from the duplex that she might've taken with her. This is supported by the following exchange between Lt. Bemis and Howard three days after Marcia was reported missing:

> Lt. Bemis: *"Was there, when she came up missing, was there any ketamine missing? that you know of?"*
>
> Howard: *"No. No. I don't think she had any when she went out into the woods. I think she had taken some before she left. And that's why I'm certain…"*
>
> Lt. Bemis: *"But there is no supply missing with her?"*
>
> Howard: *"No."*
>
> Lt. Bemis: *"You're absolutely sure?"*
>
> Howard: *"No. It's all there. And that's why I thought, first of all I didn't think she would get very far."*[648]

Marcia repeatedly espoused responsible use of ketamine, chronicling her experimentation in *Journeys into the Bright World*, where she initially upped the dosage but then backed off until ultimately calibrating less than seventy-five milligrams. In his own words, Howard explains, "We were using in the research, a total dose of 50 miligrams, 25 and 25. And for anesthesia you would generally use one milligram per pound, which is used for induction. Now if you are 175 pounds, you would be given 175 milligram intravenously, or twice that amount intramuscularly as an initial dose, and then it is repeated every half an hour or 45 minutes, and as much as 1,000 miligrams is used, and this is common now, in a three-hour period. So when you start talking about 1,000 miligrams intravenously and 25 or 50 miligrams intramuscularly, you know, it is like two drops in a glass of water as compared to the ocean."[649]

Given that no paraphernalia was ever found, the scenario that could fit Howard's explanation, however unlikely, is that Marcia took a massive unaccounted-for dose near the duplex and within minutes fell unconscious or died. Then foraging animals tore her apart with such ferocity that her remains were scattered miles apart, completely out of detection of searchers and residents in the two years she was missing. Curiously, none of the sturdier parts of her corpse such as the thorax, hip bones or spine were ever found during the grid searches right after she vanished.

It's also noteworthy that as 1978 came to an end, both Lani and Marwayne observed that Marcia was discontinuing her ketamine use after *Journeys into the Bright World* was published, since it failed to generate the buzz they had hoped for. Despite his claims that Marcia continued daily use right up to her disappearance, not one single written or taped ketamine session after publication was provided by Howard or turned over to police. The ketamine use drew criticism from her family, certain friends, the FDA, and clinicians. In fact, some of Marcia's peers openly derided her for taking a chemical shortcut in lieu of a disciplined, purely meditative/hypnotic approach to past-life regression. A few months after Marcia disappeared, a Dr. Swami Gitananda wrote Howard a letter from India warning, "I have noted also your statement that 'you have risked everything to learn the secrets of the bright world.' Perhaps you did not know the cost of that statement alone, at least Karmically speaking."[650]

While it certainly cannot be ruled out that Marcia committed suicide or accidentally overdosed, it's also true that Howard had free rein to perpetuate any story regarding Marcia's state of mind and any version of her demise, despite the fact that letters to her parents and friends leading right up to her disappearance reflect lucidity, enthusiasm, and plans for the future.

MEANS, MOTIVE &
OPPORTUNITY

The foundational elements for establishing foul play in a criminal investigation are conventionally known as means, motive, and opportunity. They remain a hallmark of the criminal prosecutorial process. If Howard purposely killed Marcia, these three pillars justifying an indictment were potentially there for the taking, had the investigation taken a different course.

Little time is required to demonstrate two of the three elements, starting with opportunity. With Marwayne on vacation in Hawaii and the landlord away at their home on San Juan Island, Howard had ample, undisturbed opportunity that fateful weekend of January 14, 1979.

To reiterate, the last time anyone other than Howard saw or heard from Marcia Moore was on Saturday, January 13 at approximately 2:30 p.m., when she brought her houseplants over to the landlord, before they left town for the weekend.

It is actually plausible that Marcia died Saturday evening because of two odd encounters that escaped investigators. The first was Saturday night when Marwayne's son Peter, accompanied by his new girlfriend, Margaret, ran into Howard by himself at the nearby Lynn-Twin theater, where all three saw *Superman*. It bothered the young couple for decades that Howard again bought a ticket to the theater the very next day. After Marcia's disappearance, Peter overheard Howard tell detectives that he saw *Superman* again on Sunday because he never finished the film Saturday night. Peter and Margaret knew this was a lie. They saw Howard throughout and briefly chatted with him about the film afterwards. Peter later spoke with police and told them that Howard stayed for the whole film Saturday night. Shortly thereafter, Howard changed his story, claiming he saw a double feature of *Pink Panther* films the next night. No one in law enforcement confronted him with the discrepancy.

Even decades later, the change stuck with Peter and his girlfriend because it came on the heels of a peculiar comment they distinctly remembered Howard saying when he showed them the renovations he completed on the Sai Baba house in the winter of '78, commenting that if "anything happens to Marcia," he would still have the smaller place to live. Howard told Marwayne the same: "Then he said 'And if anything happens to Marcia, I have this little house, and I can live in this little house'. I thought it was a rather strange remark. Later I learned he had said the same thing to my children."[651]

Margaret and Peter, who used to refer to Howard as "How-weird," long believed that their encounter Saturday night somehow interfered with Howard's actions or alibi, forcing him to buy a ticket the next night to reestablish an alibi.

The discrepancy about the change in movie title is corroborated by other sources. Robin Moore spoke with Howard by phone on Tuesday, January 16 about his version of events the night Marcia disappeared. John Moore typed a recap of their conversation at the time, which included the following: "Robin asked Howard what movie he had seen, and after a pause Howard said Superman."[652]

In fact, an article published in the *News World* on January 20 included a direct quote from Lt. Bemis that Alltounian had stated seeing *Superman* alone on *Sunday* night. This represents sufficient evidence that Howard changed and lied about the title of the movie he saw the night he reported Marcia missing.

Howard himself potentially slipped about which night Marcia disappeared in the November 1979 interview with private investigators: "Well, Marcia disappeared—I left her *Saturday* night about 8:30—and went to the movies and I got back at one o'clock in the morning, and she had vanished. Only she was gone, nothing else in the house was disturbed, I have an excellent memory and everything was just the way it was."[653] The private investigators didn't catch the discrepancy or challenge him about it.

The movie title was potentially another mistake by Howard, who may have realized that viewing the same film on back-to-back nights would draw suspicion. A double feature also provided more time to account for the 8:30 p.m. to 1:00 a.m. window when he allegedly left Marcia resting in bed and returned to find her missing.

The second odd encounter happened Sunday morning. According to Lani, Howard called to tell her that he couldn't find Marcia. Lani swore it was Sunday when Howard called, not Monday. He claimed Marcia had taken off walking, and that she'd been missing since he'd returned home from the movie at 2:00 a.m. the night before.

Howard hadn't planned on it, but Lani insisted on coming over to help. Lani arrived around 10:00 a.m., but Marcia still hadn't turned up, so she made herself useful washing dishes. She knew Marcia liked to keep things tidy, especially before a trip.

As Lani stood at the sink washing dishes, she sensed tremendous tension, that a big fight had occurred the night before. "They had a fight, a big one Saturday. I don't know how I know that. I was in the house alone and Howard was out trying to find her walking and I knew they had a huge fight I could just feel it, I mean a huge fight...I was so upset that her big huge sweater was there...I just didn't understand. There was a lot that happened right in there that didn't make any sense to me. It didn't make any sense to me at all."[654]

Lani pointedly asked, "You guys had a great big fight didn't you?"[655] The accusation seemed to stun Howard. He gave no answer, tied his shoes, and said he had to get ready for his walking party. He had a stethoscope around his neck, perhaps to show that Marcia may still be alive and he might need to check her vitals if she was found injured. At that moment, Lani glimpsed a couple of people walking by the window but couldn't make them out. Lani then told Howard she likely would not be there when he returned, since she had to catch the ferry back to Vashon Island.

It was Sunday, Lani said, because there was no commotion. There were no police, bloodhounds, helicopter or search teams. It had to be Sunday, thought Lani, because she was scheduled to drive to California for the Rose Festival early Monday morning and never changed her plans.

Perhaps Howard was planning to call police that Sunday morning, but Lani's direct accusation about the fight threw him off. Could that be why Howard decided to go to the movies again Sunday, and why he waited until 4:38 Monday morning to call police? He knew full well Lani was leaving for Ojai at dawn. With Lani on the road for a twenty-hour trip, followed by a week away in California, there'd be no one to challenge his story. Not forcing Howard to account for his whereabouts since 2:30 p.m. Saturday when Marcia was last seen by her landlady gave Howard ample opportunity to get his story straight.

Beyond opportunity, means can also be easily established. Standing six feet tall, Howard towered over the diminutive five-foot-three, 90-pound Marcia. A couple of hard blows could've knocked her unconscious, if not killed her. Furthermore, Howard had a sizable collection of firearms and, post departure from his job at the Seattle Public Health Hospital, retained a medical bag with a potent assortment of chemical sedatives that included valium and ether, to say nothing of the twenty-six vials of ketamine Lt. Bemis eventually confiscated from the duplex. In fact, an empty bottle of ether was found on the floor when officers first inspected the duplex. Of the three elements, means is practically a foregone conclusion.

With means and opportunity established, the key to the investigation and this entire mystery is to demonstrate the extent to which motive was culminating in the weeks leading up to her disappearance. It remains a confounding blunder that neither detectives, nor private investigators, failed to establish sufficient motive to justify an indictment.

In late 1980, an article quoted an unnamed investigator saying, "Where the hell do you start?...There is no motive and nobody has anything to gain from her death or disappearance."[656] But if the investigation hadn't become bogged down by psychics, astrologers, Howard's misdirection, and had the case information, particularly the ominous note, been shared, a more incriminating conclusion should have been reached. Motive was hiding in plain sight.

To establish motive, it's important to reexamine Howard's circumstances shortly before he knew anything about Marcia Moore. Early in 1977, Howard seemingly had it all. As a long-tenured anesthesiologist at the Seattle Public Health Service Hospital, he enjoyed a splendid salary, unblemished record, and ample time off. Along with his ex-wife and kids, he resided in a fine home in North Bend, glowingly describing it in the February 8 interrogation. "It's on two lots, there's a half acre, it's a beautiful place. It's a beautiful country home. I don't think you've been out there, but its lovely. Mt. Si is in the back, there's a creek in the front, it's got a two car garage, a wood shed, a sauna, it's got everything."[657]

Unfortunately for Howard, it wasn't enough. Bored with his love life according to Tina, he pushed his ex-wife for open marriage so he could chase an airline stewardess. Tina went along initially, but by the summer of 1977, she had her fill of the situation and Howard's antics, filing for their second divorce.

Unexpectedly, his cozy life began unraveling. After failing to show for the divorce hearing, an onerous settlement was decreed against him. Howard lost the house, his beloved Saab EMS, and his fishing equipment and was saddled with $7,000 in bills, not to mention $270 per month in alimony and $400 per month in child support.

Making matters worse, there is evidence suggesting that Howard was on increasingly tenuous footing in his position as deputy chief of anesthesiology, well before he quit in June of '78, purportedly to work on *Journeys into the Bright World*. Following the divorce in May 1977, he hoped to divine some answers by turning to astrology and began espousing it at work. He went so far as to complete a presentation on astrology and holistic medicine to fellow co-workers, referencing a book published in 1975 titled *Occult Medicine Can Save Your Life*. As Marwayne described in her journal, this "set the teeth" of his conservative Baptist boss, recently promoted above Howard. "I was deputy chief in the anesthesia department for the last ten years."[658] Howard said. "And the fellow who was a black man. It was politics. I should have been made chief at one point in time, but I wasn't, and this other fellow was. And there has always been a problem, you know, with he as my supervisor because when he first came I was his supervisor. Then they took him out of a subordinate position and make him my supervisor."[659]

Having already gotten off on the wrong foot with his new boss, he exacerbated the situation by getting caught smoking marijuana on hospital grounds and griping to staff members about being passed over. While trying to help Howard restart his anesthesiology career, a year after Marcia disappeared, Marwayne recapped the situation in a letter to John Moore: "A nurse anaesthesist that he worked with, Rita, has called me a couple of times inquiring for him, and she told me that he could never get back on at the Public Health Hospital, not only because of the ketamine research project and lack of FDA approval during the time of the research, but because he had grown sour on the hospital and had badmouthed it while he was there. His superior, a black Baptist, took a very dim view of his talking astrology, regression, etc., so he was on very thin ice."[660]

As was her tendency in keeping up appearances, Marcia spun the situation back then in letters to her parents. "To spend 15 years in an operating room amidst all that pathological mess of blood and gore is enough for a person as sensitive as Howard.... Also, he was in a 55% income bracket working at a job he hated, with most of what did come to him going out for alimony and child support. We knew there had to be a better way to go, and are finding it via our 'samadhi therapy' which should lead to research grants, donations to the foundation, or some sort of income less vulnerable to punitive taxation.[661]... It is sheer joy to see him getting rested after so many years of fatigue and strain."[662]

It is of utmost importance to demonstrate just how quickly his fortunes had turned in the latter half of 1977. In mere months, Howard went from having almost everything he coveted to packing up all of his belongings into seven boxes, rotating from one housesitting arrangement to the next to get by, all at the age of forty. In typical fashion, Howard blamed others. He blamed his ex-wife Tina for loafing through the fruitless college courses he paid for. He blamed her for not reminding him of the divorce hearing, and later for straining his marriage to Marcia with alimony and child support. He blamed his irresponsible son Kevin for additional strain. He blamed his new boss for marginalizing him and the hospital for blackballing him. In Howard's first interview with Lt. Bemis on January 18, he conveyed telling insight into his hard-luck feelings: "I had my divorce and I was trying to find some reasons as to why, everytime I seemed to get my act completely together, the bottom falls out."[663] Enter Marcia Moore.

After first seeing Marcia on television, then on a book jacket, then attending her lecture, a mesmerized Howard found a way out of his mounting misery. As Carol, president of the local astrological society, disclosed to Marwayne after the skull was found, the "chance" encounter between Marcia and Howard at the party in her honor was nothing of the sort. He imposingly insisted that Carol take him as her guest and facilitate an introduction.

It is essential to note Marcia's vulnerability at that particular moment. She was only a few months removed from the collapse of an abusive marriage with ex-husband Mark Douglas and the tumultuous fallout of an unfavorable divorce settlement of her own. Mark usurped several of her assets including stock certificates and properties in Maine, among other real estate holdings. Marcia's parents cast evermore derisive remarks Marcia's way for being so thoroughly used by Mark, then once again leaving her children behind and her parents to clean up the mess.

Marcia fled clear across the country to the place she felt most at home, the sunny and mellow atmosphere of the Ojai Valley. Sadly, even this thriving oasis of the New Age movement couldn't completely provide solace. She tried to make inroads at Meditation Mount, but despite the Moore family being a generous benefactor, she was rebuked from the facility for meddling in their affairs and openly discussing ketamine use.

In a revealing insight into the lifelong frictional relationship between Marcia and her mother, Eleanor wrote the Mount curator, strongly suggesting they prevent Marcia's access and affiliation. After her children caught wind of the ketamine use, they became increasingly critical as well.

Marcia eventually managed to carve out a niche in Ojai, establishing the Ananta Foundation. She became serious with Byron for a while, but tragedy soon followed. Rival self-proclaimed witches she encountered in Vancouver scorned and harassed her; there were a few hangers-on she had a habit of supporting with her trust funds. She was then viciously raped and beaten by a stranger. Eventually, even her relationship with Byron fizzled, and she was left aimlessly bouncing from town to town on lecture circuits.

A few quotes from *Journeys into the Bright World* encapsulate her loneliness:

> Everyone is a potential companion upon the way we all must travel together. And yet, when the moment came to pack books and clothes and continue on, I always seemed to be alone. Generally I remained in one place no more than three days. Often, there would be a bed for the night or a spot beside the road where my sleeping bag could be laid out under a tree. Many times I curled up and slept behind the steering wheel of my mini-station wagon, regretting having purchased a model with the brake jutting up between the two front seats. Indeed, so bonded did I become to my car that gradually I came to regard myself as some sort of mythic creature—half woman and half station wagon.... Always, there were couples sitting on benches or strolling by the water. "Why," I wondered, looking up at the stars, "when all the world goes in pairs, is there no one for me?"[664]

Another quote demonstrates the impact of meeting Howard at that time in her life:

It had been five years since I had spent more than three months in one place. More often it was just a matter of days or weeks before the necessity arose to move on. Was I finally permitted to rest? Howard's welcome was such as to make me feel that at last I had come home.[665]

Well before she met Howard, a lonely Marcia was essentially a ship without port. These quotes reflect a weary Marcia naively misinterpreting her serendipitous introduction to Howard as predestined, unbeknownst to her that he had schemed the entire encounter. Compounding the sentiment, she was in the midst of planning the ketamine research and was now seeing an anesthesiologist with easy and virtually unlimited access. For a woman who built her life around the belief in synchronicity and predestiny, it is no wonder that Marcia Moore impetuously relented to Howard's over-the-top courtship.

Marcia desperately wanted to make a name for herself in esoteric circles, believing that using ketamine psychotherapeutically and to enhance past-life regression was the ticket to set herself apart. Howard gave her unlimited access to ketamine, plus she could boast to her parents that she was being wooed by an accomplished doctor. As she did several times throughout her life, she opened the door to someone she didn't fully understand.

On Howard's end, he might even attain his own degree of fame in occult circles by riding Marcia's coattails, which Marwayne's daughter Cris and others believed. He was fed up with being overpassed and the office politics at the hospital. More importantly, he could replenish everything lost in the divorce and then some.

Shortly after they wed in late November 1977, Howard called Old Colony Trust Company in Boston, inquiring about the management status and control of the trust funds; then an interesting development occurred. In 1977 the stock market dropped over 10 percent. Prodded by Howard, in June 1978 Marcia wrote a pointed complaint to her father Robert and brother John about the losses, requesting more control over the trust, since Howard was now interested and was reading a few books on the subject. "The trust has lost enough money in one year alone to have bought us a house!" Marcia wrote. "Howard has called the bank three times to ask for an explanation."[666] She included an insinuation that angered Robert and John, namely that John undeservedly benefitted from his compensation as trust custodian following a year of such poor performance.

Robert Moore penned a stinging reply, defending John and admonishing his daughter for speaking on matters she knew little about, by cherry-picking one poor year despite the successful long-term performance. He included a clear gibe at Howard recently leaving his job because he couldn't take it anymore, and his curiously sudden interest in money management.

However, while the larger trust was irrevocable, the absolute key to motive in this case is that Robert yielded regarding the possibility of having the smaller trust, a balance of approximately $80,000, turned over to her and Howard's control. Washing his hands of the matter, Robert instructed them to initiate the transfer with John, since only he could relinquish the funds as custodian.

Marcia sheepishly replied, apologizing for the misunderstanding and in typical fashion keeping up appearances by covering for Howard, stating that she made him leave his job to work on the book. Despite the newfound tension with Robert and John, their marriage was still on relatively solid footing. Wanting to focus on her new writing projects, Marcia was agreeable to Howard's desire to handle their money. Although she hadn't officially set up his check-signing authority with her bank, in July of '78 she made the fateful decision of appointing him president and treasurer of the Ananta Foundation, which granted Howard legal co-control over the foundation coffers, a crucial aspect and point in time of the case.

During the next couple of months, Howard and Marcia learned that they could apply for tax-exempt status of the Ananta Foundation as a religious nonprofit organization, so Marcia instructed her personal lawyer to assist in the filing. By October, the tax-exempt status of the Ananta Foundation was in hand, while they were still working with John to have the smaller trust transferred to their control, primarily so they could buy a home in Washington's scenic Olympic Peninsula "where Howard could fish to his heart's content,"[667] Marcia described in her final book.

Consequently, John recommended transferring the $80,000 balance of the smaller trust *into the foundation,* to avoid the steep capital gains tax in place in the 1970s, as John informed Bemis in their private interview four days after Marcia vanished. "So I said if you really wanted to use these funds, let me know. I told her that maybe one way to do would be to get the actual stock back from the smaller trust, and maybe you could make a tax free contribution to the new tax except foundation you have just set up, and wouldn't have to pay capital gains tax non the stock. This stock was all no-cost stock, and she would have had to pay 30 cents on the dollor, every dollar of proceeds. So I mentioned this as a possibility. She wrote me a letter back saying that she was going to turn over all her financial affairs to Howard, and Howard would be in touch with me about this matter, about liquidating the smaller trust."[668]

As fall became winter, the wheels were set in motion for Howard to have control over a considerable sum of money. The $80,000 balance of the smaller trust more than matched the current value of his beloved North Bend home he lost in the divorce, and in today's dollars would be well north of $250,000.

By September 1978 he was already dreaming of restoring some of the luxuries he used to have. He wrote a hokey letter to automobile manufacturer Saab, proposing an advertising campaign with the catchphrase "Look into your Saab-conscious mind."[669] All he asked for in return was a new car to replace the EMS he lost in the divorce.

Unsurprisingly, there was no response from Saab. However, the letter revealed some interesting insight into his desire for material goods, in contrast to the modest, Bohemian existence he touted among the metaphysical community and Marcia's parents. "The other day I happened by the Saab dealers and saw a new silver Saab Turbo with interior tailored in Bordeaux Red, and drooled all over the showroom floor,"[670] he wrote Saab. Conversely, Marcia spun to her father: "We work now with music, flowers, and beautiful settings with people who are honestly trying to help themselves. Howard himself is not in the least money oriented. The very last thing he wants is for us to move from our small comfortable place or in any way increase our (most adequate) standard of living."[671]

Additionally, the proposed home in the Olympic Peninsula became a fixation for Howard, essentially to restore what he lost in the divorce. Throughout the course of 1978, Howard pushed for it on several occasions, even during one of his absurd ketamine sessions documented in *Journeys into the Bright World*:

> Howard. This is the universal trip. Wow. Merry Christmas. The Sun and the Moon. I hate to sound omnipotent. What a beautiful puzzle! Gentle…soft… pillow…fluffy…wow. (Slowly) Who am I? Why am I?… Time and hypertime. It's all love, happiness. Happiness has to have sadness…(Authoritatively) When I set foot on Ashram North…. It will be, it will be. True Ashram North will be in Olympic Peninsula. And they'll come from all over the globe.[672]

Another quote from the book reflects Howard's eagerness to influence their future expenditures: "Howard started out by questioning our intention to purchase an expensive van for our travels, and suddenly switched to the idea that the same money could be applied toward a down payment on a larger house farther out in the country."[673]

Sometime between August and October, however, their relationship profoundly deteriorated. A few issues became more than just sources of frustration, namely the work involved in completing *Journeys into the Bright World*, and of course, money. Marcia awoke daily at dawn to diligently write, type, and battle the FDA about retaining their permission to use ketamine for research.

Despite the fact that Howard was unemployed in the second half of 1978, he contributed little more than initially injecting Marcia and participating in a few sessions. As the book went to print in September, the FDA ordered them to halt their ketamine experimentation, adding more stress to the marriage. Future book royalties would undoubt-edly be curtailed since the book's premise of FDA-sanctioned ketamine research for therapeutic use was being revoked. Lani remembered that during this time Howard rarely contributed, mostly out fishing while Marcia toiled away finishing the book.

Characteristically, Marcia concealed their marital strife behind a blissful facade, as she had done so many times throughout her life, and this understandably muddied the waters for law enforcement. The case file includes a response letter from Marcia to a fan dated August 17, 1978, with the following: "I spent 3 years anticipating my own death, tying up loose ends, preparing to set sail for nowhere. Instead a marvel-ous man—my own true soulmate—miraculously appeared and carried me off to an enchanted land far beyond and better than my most roman-tic dreams."[674]

The letter was forwarded to Lt. Bemis' attention in an attempt to help with the case, obscuring their deteriorating marriage in the weeks leading up to her disappearance. As late as January 3, 1979, Marcia wrote the following about Howard in a letter to her father: "He cer-tainly rescued me at a time when I was nowhere, but I have done the same for him and his family.... There are very few men in the world as kind and intelligent and understanding of everyone as he is."[675]

Marcia was raised in an era when it was culturally imperative to avoid airing the dirty laundry of a marriage, no matter how abusive or estranged it may be. Although she had no reticence asserting herself as an independent woman who wouldn't follow the aspirations of her parents, she simultaneously succumbed to a lifelong need to continually seek their approval. Letters spanning over thirty years of her life are chock-full of developments and achievements that she hoped would impress Robert and Eleanor, largely to no avail. After she met Howard, she played up his qualifications as a doctor and established career in anesthesiology, as well as the great lengths he went to woo her.

Despite the inertia of working on the trust fund transfer into October of '78, by then small fissures in their marriage were widening into serious hemorrhages. Marcia alone visited the family at the Moore summer home on Cuttyhunk Island in September. Considering Howard was unemployed, it's peculiar that Howard did not accompany her to meet the family for the first time. A haunting and telling poem Marcia scribbled on a notepad during the Cuttyhunk visit potentially reflects her inner turmoil:

> Apple Fairy. We're making this fruit look good but its hard. Got to keep up the appearances no matter what even though it's <u>just so hard</u>. Well, I'm going to put this tinge of crimson on my apple skin no matter what but <u>my gosh it's just so hard</u>. Yes, I'm going to stick with it, the show must go on. <u>Even though it's so hard</u>. People don't realize that behind that rich red skin I'm really all white and at the core look quite dark, cause I work so hard to <u>make it</u> all look <u>just perfect</u>.[676]

Happier times—teenage Marcia on the dock in New Bedford, MA, waiting for the ferry to Cuttyhunk.

Right up to the end, Marcia was still writing her parents about Howard in glowing terms, despite ample evidence that yet another marriage was falling apart. Her close friend Lani revealed crucial insight that as fall became winter, Marcia was exasperated by Howard and his former family. Her lifelong restlessness began rearing its head again as she griped about the mundane chores of a housewife, as well as the dullness of rural north Washington, longing to be back where the metaphysical action was in Ojai. A family member once remarked that Marcia "detested the thought of being ordinary or living an ordinary life. She wanted to do exotic things…exciting things, things people would talk about."[677]

As with most investigations involving possible foul play, money also became a serious issue. After Howard quit his job in June of '78, the financial burden of the duplex rent, the Sai Baba house rent, their living and travel expenses, Howard's alimony, child support, fishing trips, and additional costs like the stabling and upkeep of Kimberly's horse were shouldered by Marcia, primarily via her trust funds. Marcia bought Howard a jeep and new fishing boat. "Marcia was generous with everyone and everything, but there had to be a limit. I think she had reached that limit,"[678] wrote Marwayne.

Lani remembered a telling phrase that Marcia would mockingly say after forking over evermore money for Howard's ex-wife and the children, referring to the payments as supporting "the establishment in North Bend."[679]

Moreover, invoices from Henry Schein, Inc., a New York–based pharmaceutical company, reveal that Marcia spent upwards of $300 a month on ketamine orders in the months leading up to her disappearance. She paid by check via mail order, using Howard's medical license number. It's possible Marcia was stockpiling ketamine in the event that she and Howard separated, which only added fuel to the fire of their strained finances. But Lani revealed a different explanation, that in the weeks leading up to her disappearance she wasn't taking ketamine after the book was published. Instead, Marcia told her that Howard was the one using it "all the time with his buddies.… She told me that they were getting stoned at night, and falling around the apartment, because the stuff made you immobile and off, and she never did that!.… They were partyin' and driving her crazy in their apartment at night, and during the day.… There's is no way a woman can write the kind of writing that she did and be stoned on drugs like that all the time.… He didn't have the money to buy it anyway. He had to buy it in her name."[680] Marwayne also noted in a letter to John Moore that "since Marcia's disappearance, I think Howard has taken 100 mg quite frequently."[681]

By mid-October they were spending considerably more time apart. They traveled together to Ojai to hold a board of directors meeting at the Ananta Foundation headquarters, but he returned to Washington for a Halloween party, while Marcia continued on to Arizona and Mexico, returning to Lynnwood in mid-November. The board minutes addressing financial business include the statement: "It was agreed that Howard S. Alltounian and Marcia Moore would be the two directors authorized to sign the Ananta checking and savings accounts."[682]

All of a sudden, the full weight of granting co-control of her foundation to Howard, just as John was proposing transferring the $80,000 trust there, was sinking in at a time when their relationship was experiencing a sea change.

Understandably, Marcia may have gotten cold feet, having been burned so many times by the men in her life. Aside from the board meeting, they were in town to attend Akeva's wedding. At the reception, Marcia cryptically confided to her close friend Maria Comfort that she would return to Southern California for the Rainbow Rose Festival in mid-January to stay with her alone for a sabbatical.

Another overlooked development occurred when Moore extended her stay into mid-November, in part to work out a new real estate transaction that likely stunned Howard when she returned. Being back in Ojai, surrounded by dear friends, made her long for the place she felt most at home. While Howard was back in Washington, she rekindled working relationships with two notable authors in the field of reincarnation. One was Helen Wambach, Ph.D., who published two books, *Reliving Past Lives* and *Life Before Life*.

The other friend, LaVedi Lafferty, was known locally as an instructor at Ojai's World University in 1977, and had recently published *The Past Life Memory Program*. The three ladies discussed future projects and the idea sprang forth to launch a new magazine from Ojai focused on reincarnation and the past-life regression movement.

Unfortunately, LaVedi was suffering from multiple sclerosis and having trouble making ends meet. Partly to help a friend in need and partly to reestablish a home base in Ojai, Marcia impulsively invested $19,000 as a co-owner of LaVedi's hot springs property.

When she returned to Washington in mid-November to break the news to Howard, it exacerbated the conflict of future control of their dwindling funds. After months of trying to coax her into buying a new home in the Olympic Peninsula, in the blink of an eye Marcia committed $19,000 to a house in Ojai at a time when their expenses consumed all of the monthly disbursements from the trusts and then some, as she wrote her father just before she vanished: "I poured a lot of our foundation funds (indeed just about everything) into helping La Vedi get her place in the canyon—which we will all use...."[683] Clearly the $19,000 would have to be recouped from the liquidated smaller trust once the transfer to Ananta Foundation was finalized.

This was a watershed moment for an aggravated Howard, who must've realized that not only was he not going to be in total control of a trust fund that abruptly took a haircut, but Marcia had reestablished permanent residence in Ojai, where her foundation was also headquartered.

Suddenly the prospect of Howard's dream home in Washington was waning as the prospect of Marcia relocating back to Ojai emerged, just as their marriage was increasingly on shaky ground. "I know that she was totally bored with that whole scene, that scene of, you know, the um, the ex-wife and the kids and all. She was bored to death with it,"[684] Lani reflected. Back then she overheard Howard derisively say to Marcia, "You just can't wait to go out and get in that car and go to Ojai, can you?"[685] For Howard Alltounian, the bottom was quite possibly about to fall out yet again.

Another critically overlooked development occurred, whereby Marcia permanently moved Howard into the Sai Baba house. Lani recalled an anecdote that reflected the crumbling state of their marriage. "I remember the first day she took me over there. Howard was, Howard was never around when I was there. He'd go fishing or be off doing something else. And um, she took me over and she said 'This is the Sai Baba house and, and, I've rented it for Howard.' So I look at her with big eyes and she just, just you know, gave me that look like she was just more than fed up."[686] Moreover, Marwayne noted that Howard lied about staying there: "He told me he had slept in the Sai house (previously he said they had slept together in the bedroom on Saturday night)...."[687]

It is an astounding aspect of the investigation that detectives failed to discover that Howard did not just sleep separately from Marcia the night she disappeared, as he admitted during the February 8 interrogation. Howard had been sleeping in the Sai Baba house—*for weeks.*

At the end of November 1978, Marwayne offered to throw them a one-year anniversary party but Marcia declined, leaving Marwayne to reflect that in the last few months Howard and Marcia appeared quite distant.

In her journal, Marwayne then remembered utter disaffection while hosting them on Christmas Eve. Howard showed up alone that evening, and only after being prodded by Marwayne, invited Marcia over. They sat on opposite sides of the room, barely acknowledging each other. "Christmas 1978: Marcia made no preparation for Christmas at all, that I could see. Quite a difference from the Christmas of 1977, when she gave an open house party, decorated the house and the door, cooked Christmas foods, hung cards, dressed up for her party, etc.[688]... She came to the door in an all silver, woven, top and pants, looking for all the world like a feminine Prince Valiant. It was very attractive.[689] ... I thought it a very strange Christmas between Howard and Marcia, the Christmas of 1978, just three weeks approximately before her disappearance,"[690] Marwayne wrote. Howard stayed until 2:00 a.m., while Marcia left hours earlier.

The extent to which Marcia kept up appearances to the bitter end was never more evident than in a letter to her parents dated December 26. In the letter, she embellished the Christmas Eve festivities at Marwayne's, then portrayed a joyous Christmas day with Howard, his ex-wife, and their kids in North Bend. Sadly, it seemed all a lie. Aside from the estrangement Marwayne observed on Christmas Eve, the truth is that only Howard spent Christmas Day in North Bend, while Marcia spent the day alone in the duplex. Lani remembered casually asking Marcia how her Christmas was, only to be shocked that she spent it alone while Howard enjoyed a festive day with his ex-wife and children.

Just after Christmas, his ex-wife had a hysterectomy, and Howard spent extensive time caring for her in North Bend, though it was not without tumult. The stresses and strains of the marriage had reached critical mass. While at his ex-wife's, Howard launched into an expletive-laden, abusive tirade, calling her money-grubbing and blaming her for ruining his new marriage. It fueled his resentment, if not rage, that he now found himself relegated to an unheated tiny house, quite possibly in another marriage on the brink, with the prospect of having to start all over again with alimony and child support obligations at the age of forty-one.

By the week of Marcia's disappearance, all of Howard's frustration, resentment, and anger was quite possibly boiling over, and something happened that prompted Marcia to dramatically write John on January 9: "Dear John, This is a sad letter to have to write, so...."[691] This unwrinkled, handwritten note was found in a wastepaper basket. No one can know for sure what Marcia intended to fully write or why she stopped or was interrupted. Given the tenuous and impersonal relationship with her brother, she was almost certainly writing about the trust. As her daughter Louisa confirmed, Marcia never confided in John about personal matters. They did not enjoy an affectionate sibling relationship; it would have been about business.

Howard claimed that the finished *typewritten* note, whereby Marcia requested transfer of her trust to him upon her death, was a continuation of that unfinished, handwritten note. But there may be another possibility detectives failed to consider. If she intended to leave Howard and return to Ojai, the partial note may have been an instruction to John to *suspend* the liquidation and transfer of the smaller trust until she and Howard sorted out a separation settlement.

Howard may very well have seen the writing on the wall. The distinct possibility was materializing that he would be taken to the cleaners once more, back to readying all of his possessions into a few boxes, with child support due and this time unemployed, with a tarnished reputation from the ketamine project severely limiting his employment prospects. Painted into a corner, consciously or subconsciously, he may have felt there was only one way out of being left holding the bag again.

Unfortunately, the investigation became bogged down with psychics and astrologers as well as Howard's clever misdirection of pointing the finger at numerous suspects. Had detectives uncovered key contacts like Lani, the ominous forces tearing apart their marriage, the fact that they were sleeping in separate quarters for weeks, and the importance of the trust about to slip through Howard's fingers—this could very well have constituted motive.

Knowing full well that means and opportunity were easily established, Howard was desperate to do everything in his power to eliminate the all-important motive element for building an indictment. He did so cleverly and effectively with misdirection and obfuscation. He conjured wild theories of dematerialization, psychic accounts, and astrological predictions. Pointing the finger at numerous suspects, he exhausted police resources and flat out lied in certain instances, whether it was perpetuating the theory that Marcia was amnesiac, which movie he saw, whether he solicited the note, withholding ketamine, or lying about the state of their marriage. He skillfully diffused incriminating lines of questioning, particularly why he was sleeping in the Sai Baba house, the discrepancies of when he smoked the pot and whether Marcia owned hiking boots, always digressing into the occult to distract an overwhelmed Snohomish County Sheriff's Office.

Making an indictment more of an uphill climb, one month before Marcia vanished, a labor dispute caused significant disruption and delays within the Snohomish County prosecutor's office. "The result is a huge backlog of more than 800 cases," a local paper reported. "Deputy prosecutors blame the backlog on the recent change of administration which saw several experienced deputies resign…. Four of the office's most experienced deputies began leaving the office in mid-December for other jobs."[692]

Something went horribly awry between Marcia and Howard the weekend Marcia vanished. Marwayne, Lani, and Cris all commented that an explosive argument took place. Cris claims that Howard directly told her as much just hours after he reported Marcia missing on Monday the 15th. He made the admission while Cris was on horseback preparing to search. She distinctly remembered it because her beloved horse became agitated by Howard's unnerving energy. "Well, when he found out they weren't going to California…he had a shit fit, just had a fit…. They were scheduled to go to California to a big deal meeting of esoteric society people…and he was, in my opinion and in a lot of other people's opinions, very much riding on her coattails…because he knew actually very little astrology. It was…his first scheduled speech…it was a very big deal. They had an argument the night she disappeared, and he went to the movies. He says…that he asked her to go to the movies. That's not right. That is absolutely a lie."[693]

Even though Howard repeatedly claimed that they never even argued, there may be a simple reason why Howard initially admitted the fight. There are indications that it became violent, possibly that he struck Marcia in the face, leaving her with a black eye. Had Marcia's body been found in the days following her disappearance, he may have preemptively tried to explain the bruises. But he was perhaps conflicted, reasoning that it would be too incriminating to inform law enforcement that his dead wife sustained a black eye resulting from a fight. By the time of the February 8 interrogation, Howard changed his tune, denying that he ever fought with Marcia in the fourteen months of their relationship. That still left Howard with a problem of how to rationalize any facial injuries if Marcia was suddenly found.

He oddly pushed for an explanation as early as January 18, in the group interview. "Well, as I said, in late October when I got home one evening, she wasn't here, and so I went out, and I knew the trails that she went on, and so I would often catch her on the way back. I looked all over and I couldn't find her. And when I got home, she got home five or ten minutes after I came home, it was dark. She came in and her lip

350

was swollen, and her eye was bruised. And I asked her, you know, what happened? It looks like somebody beat you up."[694]

Then again during the interrogation, Howard awkwardly segued to the dubious anecdote of Marcia allegedly walking out in the woods the previous summer to commit suicide, only to return several hours later with a black eye and cut lip after falling down. Lani, who walked with her frequently throughout that summer, never observed or was told by Marcia about the alleged October incident. Although Lt. Bemis and Detective Seipel challenged the believability of his account, he wiggled off the hook again, since Marcia's body wasn't found soon enough to discover any bruises.

Had Howard stated that they fought no more than the average couple, the topic may have gone unnoticed. But Howard adamantly maintained to law enforcement that beyond never laying a finger on Marcia, they never once had an argument throughout what he characterized as their "idyllic" marriage. This is a blatant lie that contradicts multiple accounts, including Lani's firsthand observations. "That is nonsense. They fought all the time," she insisted. "I knew what was going on between she and Howard was real serious, I knew they were fighting all the time but I didn't know what the subject was...I think the issue was the money...I know she was totally supporting him. He didn't work, she was supporting everything. It was frustrating for her. He wasn't contributing to the writing process. He was going fishing and she was paying his alimony and child support."[695]

Marwayne's daughter Cris held her own assessment: "During that fourteen months, their relationship got more uptight, and more uptight, and more uptight, as every month went by."

Furthermore, a financial astrologer and author from Southern California named John Bradford told Marwayne in November 1979 that "in a conversation with Howard, Howard admitted that he and Marcia had had a serious quarel."[696]

Taken together with other material misrepresentations, this should have been seriously incriminating. Unfortunately for the investigation, detectives lost the upper hand by not securing statements from Cris or

Marwayne about the fight, or ever tracking down Lani. "Nobody told me about a violent argument," Lt. Bemis remembered. "I thought it was a lovey-dovey little couple and she disappeared."[697]

If Howard Alltounian was culpable in Marcia's death, the most plausible scenario, after scrutinizing all of the case materials, is that Marcia broke the news to Howard, or he figured out that she either didn't want him to accompany her to Ojai, or she was planning to stay there indefinitely, and that the marriage was doomed. Lani believes that leading up to the trip, it was all but over: "If we'd all gone down there for the convention, I don't think she would ever have come back. And I think she would have walked away from everything and we would've had to send her sterling to her. She was done with him. She moved him into that Sai house…. She basically got rid of him."[698]

Marcia breaking the news to Howard, or Howard secretly figuring it out on his own, could very well have sent him into an uncontrollable rage that he had exhibited before, ending with a blow to her face. Once this happened, he may have felt there was no turning back and he'd be left with nothing. From that moment, he would have ample time and means to inject her full of ketamine, which was the perfect cover, dispose of her body, then establish an alibi at the movie theater.

That left one more order of business: ensuring the transfer of the trust fund to the Ananta Foundation went through, where he would remain the appointed president and treasurer with exclusive access to withdraw funds. Marcia's death and discovered remains alone wouldn't suffice because the transfer was in limbo—hence the need for a signed note instructing Marcia's brother John to complete the transfer.

THE INFAMOUS NOTE

O f all the data points, facts, statements, clues, and scraps of information, the completed note allegedly typed by Marcia Moore stands head and shoulders above the rest as the most suspicious. Although incriminating elements of the interviews, journals, letters, and case file certainly aroused enough suspicion to contest the publicly held explanations for Marcia's disappearance, the note impelled the push to dig much deeper.

Howard stated to Lt. Bemis that on Sunday morning, January 14, shortly after he awoke and walked over to the duplex from the Sai Baba house, he encountered Marcia finishing the brief note. In the police interrogation, he insists that it was the first time he knew anything about it. It's important to underscore that despite this statement, Marwayne explicitly writes in her journal that Howard admitted to previously asking Marcia to write the note, an incriminating lie. According to what Howard told Bemis, that morning she pulled it from the typewriter and signed only her first name above the typed name, with her purple-ink pen. It reads:

9 January 1979

Dear John,

This is a sad letter to have to write so I'll try to make it brief. I am in severe pain and do not know how much longer I have to live. When I go I am most anxious to have the funds in my own personal trust account go to Howard who has been so good to me and seen me through so many difficult times.

Please do this for me,

Marcia[699]

It is a glaring contradiction for Howard to contend that Marcia was in pain of such severity that death was imminent as described in the note, yet claim that Marcia was capable of walking multiple miles with a bad hip during a brutal cold front because she had miraculously snapped out of it during the day.

Additionally, if this story provides any insight into the essence of Marcia Moore, it illustrates her lifelong aspiration to write poignantly. Marcia was nothing if not verbose. Yet the last letter she would ever write is a seventy-five-word paragraph, the thrust of which is a wooden, express wish to bequeath her smaller trust fund to her fourth husband known for a total of fourteen months—who was not even sleeping under the same roof?

A woman who could conjure at will insightful, esoteric, and dramatic prose included no long goodbyes, no heartfelt message to her parents, children, friends, peers, and fans? Marcia Moore spent a lifetime contemplating the profound mysteries of the universe, yet refrained from a single philosophical remark in deference to the metaphysical community she yearned to leave an indelible mark upon? Linguistically the note does not fit. Certain fragments like "when I go" reflect plain speak uncharacteristic of the entire body of Marcia's writings, putting aside the fact that there is no reason why she would feel compelled to "try to make it brief" if this was to be her final goodbye.

Moreover, upon death the lingering loose end she was most anxious to resolve, out of all the relationships and causes she cared deeply about, is ensuring that Howard receives her smaller trust fund? There are no instructions to bequeath her book rights/royalties, nor a single personal memento, nor wishes for the larger trust containing a balance three times the size of the smaller trust.

Finally, having known each other just over a year, without much of what could be considered traumatic experiences, there is little to substantiate the phrase "seen me through so many difficult times." In reality, the argument can be made that Howard contributed more than his share of strain on the marriage financially, scantily participating toward writing *Journeys into the Bright World*, even though he was unemployed.

Despite the glaring suspicion surrounding the authenticity of the note, the theory detectives and Marwayne deduced was that Howard persuaded Marcia to type it as a continuation of the handwritten partial note. As inconceivable as it sounds, it appears that detectives failed to consider another distinctly incriminating possibility: *Howard Alltounian typed the note after Marcia died and forged her first name.*

Handwritten and typed notes provided to John Moore and police.

Howard potentially had a full day and a half window to contemplate the content of the note, type it, and practice signing her first name with plentiful examples inside the duplex as reference. Marwayne detected a couple of "careful erasures" on the note when she first had a chance to inspect it. Howard may have simply taken the handwritten note fragment, which ironically might have even been an instruction to John to forego the liquidation of the trust, and created the typewritten note to suit his benefit.

Furthermore, given that the note clearly described Marcia Moore's imminent death, why did Howard only give it to John Moore, before John notified Lt. Bemis? Howard gave multiple public statements, held press conferences, appeared on television, and gave interviews to private investigators as well as Ann Rule. Why didn't Howard disclose the note, which would've answered many lingering questions as to what happened? Why leave a cloud of suspicion if the note clearly indicated impending death or suicide? It's possible that Howard didn't want anyone but John, who had the power to transfer the trust, to see the note in order to avoid incriminating questions surrounding its authenticity.

Handwriting analysis was never performed on the signed first name because detectives took Howard's story about waking up to find Marcia typing the note at face value, though it would've been challenging given the small sample of only six letters. However, there are points of letter formation inconsistent with past signatures. A handwriting expert consulted for this book affirmed that based primarily on the linguistic incompatibility and, to a lesser extent, inconsistences in the letter formation, the veracity of the note could be challenged in court with a high degree of confidence.

It's also noteworthy that the finished note is typewritten in contrast to the partial handwritten note Marcia started on January 9. Why change such a concise note five days later if you are attempting to validate it by handwriting? If she truly wanted to authenticate and make it legally binding, why didn't Marcia sign her last name? It is indicative that Howard attempted the bare minimum to authenticate it, which was to type the note and handwrite her first name, simple enough since Marcia often signed in a semi-cursive fashion, easily forgeable.

Unfortunately, because there was friction between detectives, the press, and private investigators from the outset, the note does not appear to have been shared with anyone outside the confines of the Snohomish

County Sheriff's Office. Quotes from a story that ran in the November 1980 issue of *Startling Detective* magazine reflect this: "Two private eyes with an excellent reputation were hired in New York. They readily admitted that they took on the assignment with the preconceived notion that Dr. Alltounian had murdered his wife. But there was one big flaw in the theory. They couldn't come up with a motive for the act. Dr. Alltounian, under conditions of the trust fund, would not receive one cent in the event of his wife's death."[700] Had the note been shared with the private investigators and the press, however, they may have considered the typewritten note an effort to break through the conditions of the trust or complete the liquidation that was in limbo. Suddenly this could've put motive on the table and cast suspicion, and perhaps intense media pressure, on Howard.

Howard clearly shielded the note from outside scrutiny, as evidenced by news reports at the time.

"Dr. Alltounian returned to the house at one o'clock in the morning. Marcia wasn't there. She hadn't left a note telling him where she might be,"[701] one report stated.

"There was no note. Outside, the ground was frozen, so there were no footprints or tire marks,"[702] another article declared.

From another: "Suicide? How? And where? A woman whose whole life had been involved with writing about her conclusions on life and those areas beyond life would certainly have left a note explaining what she was about to do."[703]

Understandably, key pieces of evidence were not initially divulged in order for law enforcement to validate credible tips or admissions, but after a certain point when Howard was suspected of foul play, sharing information was vital to putting additional scrutiny on Howard from the press and private investigators. Due to Bemis' reassignment, the sheriff's office's increasing desire to close the case once Howard passed the polygraph, and the lack of much forensic evidence, the investigation completely lost steam, and the note was never revealed. At a bare minimum, given that Lt. Bemis questioned the note, the typewriter and the note could have been tested for fingerprints to see if Howard's were present, or if the keys had been wiped clean.

Having little reason to believe otherwise, the private investigators and press instead portrayed Howard as a sympathetic figure, as Howard was quoted in the *Startling Detective* piece: "The tragedy of this whole thing is what's happened to me. I am just hanging in by the skin of my teeth. I am destitute. I just spent a whole year of my life devoting all my energy [to] trying to find my wife. Now I'm trying to pick up the pieces of my life. I am 42, and I have another 42 years ahead of me. And I can't get a job. I have been blackballed."[704]

In the end, the note was never legitimately challenged, the truth of their crumbling marriage never exposed, witness statements contradicting his version of events never became part of the official record, and no one came forward to testify.

If nothing else, Howard Alltounian was exceptional at dancing between the raindrops throughout the entirety of the investigation.

"I HAVE TO GET AWAY"

O ne of those raindrops was an ominous exchange between Marcia and her good friend Maria Comfort.

In October 1978, Marcia and Howard attended the marriage ceremony of her former boyfriend Akeva. That trip was the last time her friends from Ojai would ever see her.

At the wedding, friends sensed something off in Marcia's body language, suspecting that she may have wanted to come alone. "When we were at the wedding, he was there at the wedding, and she was not happy about that. She didn't want him to be with her at the wedding," Maria said. It seemed as though she wanted the freedom to talk, but Howard was joined at her hip throughout the ceremony and reception. "Howard did not leave us alone for more than one minute."[705] When he broke away to use the restroom, Marcia hastily seized the moment to talk to her close friend Maria in private.

Maria Comfort had met Marcia Moore in 1972, while attending the First International Astrological Symposium in Montreal. After reviewing one of Marcia's books on reincarnation, Maria invited Marcia to her home to give what would be Marcia's first workshop on regression.

Eventually, she became Marcia's personal astrologer. "Marcia was the sweetest Cancer rising, with big round eyes, and teeny, tiny, petite,"

Maria remembered. "She spoke very, very, well…an intelligent woman, so charismatic. Mercury, a real ability to communicate."[706]

Now sneaking a moment to confide at the wedding, Marcia needed her friend's help. Could she come down to Maria's house to detox? Marcia asked. As long as she was with Howard, she'd continue taking ketamine, she explained, but didn't want to. "I have to get away, I must get away," she told Maria.[707]

Maria knew that Marcia was taking ketamine for research, but she and Howard also got pleasure from it. In a period of one year, Marcia was now walking with a cane, her hip problem possibly exacerbated by ketamine. She had become wan and, although always quite petite, even lighter than her usual hundred pounds. For a master yogi on an eternal quest to reach a higher consciousness, it was a sad change to witness.

Maria assured Marcia that she was welcome to stay and detox. "I knew she was unhappy, and I told her I could see she was unhappy." Cryptically, Marcia replied that she had to get away from Howard, "that the ketamine was killing her, and could kill her, and she had to get off the drug…. She gave me the impression that, as long as she was with Howard, she was going to continue to take those drugs, and that she didn't want to continue to take those drugs, but Howard was insistent that they continue to take those drugs."[708]

At first Marcia was quite excited about Howard, Maria recalled, because she thought that he was someone she could bring home to her family, since he was a doctor. But ultimately, it was a disappointment. Although Howard was an accomplished anesthesiologist, he was classless, friends would say. "He may have been a doctor, but I'm sure fundamentally…he liked to fish, he liked to watch TV…I don't think he was probably very intellectually stimulating or the most exciting person to be with…. She put the man on a pedestal somewhat too,"[709] a family member described.

Some of Marcia's friends suspected he had a narcissistic personality disorder.

"I knew Howard, and I thought he was weird...weird.... He had a very strange energy,"[710] Maria remembered. "Howard had an aura about him that was so bad. Howard was an obvious opportunist."[711]

While confiding in Maria, Moore alluded to money problems but was brief. She would divulge more when she arrived at her place in California, Marcia said. "She just needed to get away from Howard. She wasn't explicit. She was going to tell me everything when she came down and stayed with me.... She told me she wanted to live, and that this was killing her.[712] ... She said, 'I know I have to leave him.'"[713]

After chatting at the wedding, Moore followed up with a lovely letter confirming her plans for mid-January 1979. Marcia would drive part of the way, spend the night in San Francisco, then drive the rest of the way...and she'd be coming *alone*. Marcia told her that Howard wanted to come with her to the convention, then said, "'But he won't.' And she was pretty certain that he wouldn't."[714]

Maria should keep an eye out and expect to see her as early as Sunday, January 14, Marcia said. Instead, she was reportedly last seen by Howard that Sunday. Maria received the shocking news of her disappearance when Lt. Bemis called to see if Maria had heard from her. Detectives discovered Maria's number when they searched the duplex and dialed every number they found.

Could Marcia have broken the news to Howard that she was planning on staying in California indefinitely, and possibly that the marriage was over? Maria wondered. Perhaps a clue lay in the letter to her parents on December 26. "Afterward we will spend some time in Ojai. Probably I'll put Howard on the plane and stay longer myself,"[715] Marcia wrote.

There may have been another undiscovered clue. In the months preceding her disappearance, Marcia rearranged all of the administrative positions and monetary allotments from the Ananta Foundation. The meeting minutes stated the monthly disbursements to Akeva were now discontinued, and instead $400 per month would be disbursed to cover the northern branch of the foundation—the Sai Baba house Howard was living in. Additionally, the minutes stated that Howard would be entitled to receive renumeration for his services. Why would Marcia need to officially detail such future disbursements if they were married and living together? Could Marcia have been setting him up with just enough to live on after separating, with the justification to her parents that he would continue running their new "Sai center" in Washington?

In keeping with her lifelong pattern, perhaps Marcia Moore would let things simply fade with Howard while keeping him afloat, the distance of living in different states between them. Maybe she'd eventually break it off, when things became serious with a future companion, or when enough time had passed to drop the appearances to her parents again—like she had done so many times with men before.

When Lt. Bemis called Maria in the days following Marcia's disappearance, she promptly told him of a vision she'd had, in hopes that it wasn't too late to find Marcia. Maria perceived her being driven in the back of a vehicle. She felt sure she was still alive around the time she disappeared, but just barely.

One thing was certain, according to Maria. Marcia was not suicidal. "The reason she wanted to get away from him was because she wanted to heal...and she couldn't heal with him. She did not want to enter into the ultimate Samadhi. She wanted to live. She wanted to survive all of this,"[716] Maria insisted.

LIVES CHANGED

More than a decade has passed since we began the journey of investigating Marcia's disappearance. Over those years, we learned a tremendous amount about who she really was, hidden behind the material available in her books and online. We sadly learned that Marcia Moore did not lead the charmed life of a beautiful heiress, nor as a renowned priestess of the New Age, as some have portrayed. As we pushed through every roadblock or dead end to discover the truth, we wondered—where were the people willing to do the same back in 1979?

In retrospect though, it isn't difficult to see the indignation that cast a dark cloud over the circumstances surrounding Marcia's demise, limiting the prospects that family and friends would fight to prove foul play to the bitter end. To some degree, she had made a mess of her life and, in a sense, dug her own grave. A zealous pursuit of the occult and an unquenchable desire to stamp her name in metaphysical circles left disaffection and soured relationships in her wake.

The parents she never stopped trying to appease had written off what they considered a life of foolhardiness, especially the ketamine research they didn't properly understand. Although her children loved her and understood her metaphysical quest, estrangement sprouted in place of close-knit maternal bonds with them. A few times, Marcia made the comment that she'd paid off her "kiddie karma," oblivious to the hurt such a flippant remark sometimes caused.

In the August 1981 issue of *Chic* magazine, a lengthy article comprehensively recapped the case. It included, of course, juicy details of ketamine use and the embellished, macabre moonlit walks to the cemetery to channel the dead and pray to the fountain she believed emanated supernatural vibrations.

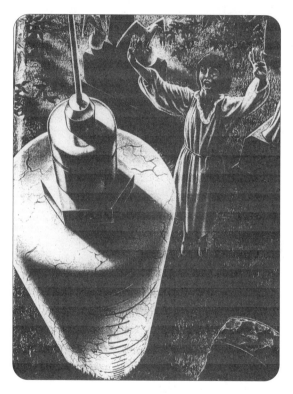

A grotesque caricature of Marcia from a magazine, worshiping a hypodermic needle at the cemetery.

Innocuously mixed among these salacious details, however, were quotes revealing important insight into the conflicted feelings about Marcia from would-be supporters, friends, and family. Incredibly and unknowingly, they provided tremendous cover for Howard Alltounian.

Just a few days after Marcia vanished, during a crucial time for setting the tone of the investigation, Lt. Bemis privately asked brother John Moore for his personal feeling about what happened. In his condescending and dismissive reply, he said about his own sister, "My feeling would be that I would be very pessimistic, that she probably was out of her little mind. She probably took another dose of ketamine, and just walked and headed for the hills or something, and kept walking away. I don't really, I don't rule anything out, or rule anything in…. She probably just walked out of the house. There are many bizarre things but she led a bizarre life. I don't know if anyone will really know what happened. She certainly more and more I think unbalanced in the last few months, and certainly in the last year. And that's why her children I think became more and more unhappy."[717]

After her skull was found, Robin Moore, sensationalizing as ever, maintained that her death was not a suicide, nor accidental, and likely involved a cult. "She was a sort of high priestess," he was quoted in *Chic* magazine. "And the fact that her head was totally separated [from her body] might possibly indicate that the head was severed. I don't know. I do know there are cults in which they behead animals as part of the ceremony…. I don't for one instant suspect that Howard Alltounian murdered my sister. I believe in his sincerity, and I'm not one to be taken in." Incredibly, he deferentially proclaimed that Howard was "if anything, as much a victim as my sister."[718]

Daughter Louisa, who studied astral travel, tried to reach Marcia telepathically in the months following her disappearance. "My gut feeling was that she had passed over and that I would only be able to find her by my own psychic and spiritual means,"[719] Louisa wrote. Understandably resentful about the cumulative effect of her mother's missteps, in one publication she offered, "It may turn out we have been terribly unfair to Alltounian. On the other hand, he is a doctor, and he had a responsibility to hospitalize my mother. He had the professional and personal responsibility to hospitalize my mother. He should have seen that she was a drug addict. He had the professional and personal responsibility not to let her, in effect, destroy herself."[720] Despite the difficult relationship with Marcia, she spearheaded hiring the private investigators using funds from the inherited trusts. After multiple conversations with us and learning about the case information she was not privy to from 1979 to 1981, Louisa began to reconsider the cause of her mother's death.

Christopher Roof, the youngest son Marcia lovingly referred to as "Chrishna," was the most sensitive and closest to his mother. Perhaps partly as a lingering result of the tragedy, Christopher himself disappeared. Stubbornly refusing help, he gave away all possessions and deliberately cut ties with friends and family. Last seen in August 2010, he is presumed dead.

In the following decades, there remained a peculiar familial ambivalence as the Moore family prominence and Sheraton Hotel fortune experienced generational half-life. At family gatherings, there was little in the way of remembrances, lamentations, and trips down memory lane for Marcia. While there was always an odd stoicism with the Moore family, this was something more, a concerted effort to forget the blight on the family reputation. Always the pariah, Marcia's memory was essentially stored away in the family attic, collecting dust in the dingy recesses of the family consciousness.

If her own family felt this way, those surrounding her in Washington weren't much better. Marwayne Leipzig remained as conflicted as ever and in 2010 turned over her journal in the hopes that we would eventually solve the mystery. Still, our conversations and correspondence over the years reflected both her suspicion of Howard, yet the possibility that Marcia wanted to do herself in or became lost in the woods. When I visited her, she repeatedly shook her head in describing how foolish it was that Howard insisted that Marcia frequently walked alone at night. She was also clearly haunted by the memory of how crisp and carefully preserved the movie ticket receipt was that she found while snooping around the duplex. The inner conflict appeared to have frozen in place in 1979, unchanged for over three decades. When she handed me the thick folder containing her journal, letters, astrological charts, and *Hypersentience Bulletins*, there was something about the way she held my gaze. It was as if she wanted to finally unburden herself from the secrets she knew lay inside.

Almost as a way to reconcile the tragedy, and perhaps some guilt, she often concluded by stating what she believed to be the bottom line: "They used each other." Suffering from dementia that steadily accelerated, Marwayne Leipzig died in 2017 in a Seattle area hospice at age ninety-nine.

Sadly, that same year Meditation Mount, Robert Moore's beloved philanthropic endeavor, burned down in the Thomas Fire that ravaged Ojai. It marked the second-largest fire in California's history at the time, and remains under reconstruction.

Marcia's friend Lani grieved perhaps more than anyone in the last forty years. Lani would often think of her. There were times she'd hear whistling wind, or find a feather or shell; once, a hummingbird flew up to her window and looked in, flew away, then returned, as if a confirmation. Lani took them as signs she was near. Marcia believed in that sort of thing. Since no one ever tracked her down, Lani was completely unaware of the case details and developments. When presented with materials in recent years, the full gamut of emotions she tried to reconcile decades ago routinely overcame her. When remembering fond anecdotes and cherished memories, she laughed joyously. But mostly she was stunned, incredulous, and incensed that Howard portrayed her dear and brilliant friend as a suicidal, bipolar ketamine junkie, adamantly denying the mischaracterization to this day.

Lt. Bemis never lost enthusiasm for solving the case until serious health problems began surfacing in 2014. Over the years he graciously made himself available, calling on occasion with a new avenue of research or a new contact to talk to. He took the unsolved case personally, as if he had let Marcia down. Ultimately, he came to grips with mistakes made during the investigation, admitting that Howard's misdirection and the consultation with astrologers and psychics obscured the truth and possibly derailed the investigation. It was a painful acknowledgement that he sincerely hoped to someday make right.

In his defense, it's easy to ridicule such use of psychics and astrologers in the present day. At the time, the Victoria, British Columbia, police recommended psychic Rose Gallacher and claimed she had assisted them in catching a killer. Back in the 1970s, it was not only more prevalent but common after psychics had reportedly helped solve a number of murders and pinpoint the locations of victims. It became a pop culture fascination that even permeated Hollywood. In August of the year Marcia vanished, Stephen King published *The Dead Zone*, which became a bestseller adapted to film starring Christopher Walken. A subplot is how the protagonist used psychic powers to aid the local sheriff in catching a serial killer.

As the years passed, Lt. Bemis' voice became regressively fainter when we spoke, as multiple surgeries took their toll. Yet he never lost hope that someday justice could be had for Marcia and the Moore family. In 2015, he passed away peacefully in the Seattle suburbs he had faithfully served in law enforcement for three decades.

Ketamine's legacy is…complicated. It hasn't shaken the stigma of abuse in the club scene and has unfortunately acquired the stigma of abuse as a date rape drug. Yet it's also becoming popular therapeutically. There's an unavoidable irony that despite Howard's claims that ketamine made Marcia suicidal, it's gaining momentum as a gentler alternative to powerful antidepressant SSRI prescriptions like Zoloft, for treatment-resistant depressive patients.

Howard Alltounian moved to Henderson, Nevada in the second half of the 1980s, far away from the lingering whispers about the story. He continued to practice as an anesthesiologist until he died of heart failure in 2006 at the age of sixty-nine. Mainly he was left alone, except for a book published in 2001 titled *Ketamine: Dreams and Realities*. In 1998, author Karl Jansen, M.D., Ph.D. interviewed Howard in consultation for the book. Two decades after Marcia's death, in his excerpts Howard still claimed that Marcia was suicidal and killed herself in the woods high on ketamine. Unbelievably, he still maintained publicly that she didn't leave a note.

As of 2006, until now, Howard still had the last word.

FINAL RESTING PLACE

Marcia Moore was no saint, her life littered with failed marriages, estranged children, disaffected parents, burned bridges, and squandered money. In her formative years she was at times spoiled, in adulthood reckless, in her later years foolish and neglectful. In lieu of profound wisdom, she took shortcuts, notably ketamine, in a futile attempt to carve out a name for herself in the occult world. She sacrificed everything upon the altar of someday becoming a famous metaphysical writer.

In a cruel twist of fate, Marcia was laid to rest preceding her parents and brothers at famed Sleepy Hollow Cemetery in Concord, Massachusetts, overshadowed by the graves of the literary titans she yearned to someday match like Nathaniel Hawthorne, Louisa May Alcott, Henry David Thoreau, and Ralph Waldo Emerson. At Authors' Ridge to this day, fans leave them gifts of pencils, notebooks, rocks with messages, and other heartfelt mementos. In another part of the cemetery, Marcia's grave goes largely unnoticed.

Final Resting Place—Concord, Massachusetts.

In true Gemini fashion, however, there was another side to Marcia Moore, a noble side that touched many lives. To those who knew her best she was gentle and kind, frequently offering advice, mentorship, and astrological guidance. During her time in Ojai, she routinely regressed people for free and mailed *Hypersentience Bulletins* to those who couldn't afford them. In the cherished time they enjoyed, Marcia helped Lani through a crumbling marriage, teaching her to empower herself no matter what happened. Lani credits her with instilling the fortitude to put her daughters through college post-divorce. Indeed, all of her close friends wept bitterly over her death and carry fond memories to this day. Two years after Marcia's remains were discovered, LaVedi Lafferty published *The Eternal Dance*, which was dedicated to her memory, and the perpetuation of her work in the fields of astrology and reincarnation.

Marcia courageously bucked the imposing establishment she was pressured to conform to, and the affluent life delivered on a silver platter. She was often misunderstood and far ahead of her time in fearlessly exploring metaphysics with new, sometimes controversial ideas.

It's also easy to overlook now, but Marcia was a pioneer of bringing yoga to the Northeast in the 1960s, and instrumental in shaping its prevalence across America today. She would've undoubtedly smiled and taken great pride in watching Lululemon stores pop up across the United

States, or that some high schools now offer yoga in place of physical education, an idea Marcia promoted during a reunion with her Radcliffe alums some fifty years earlier.

She was a daring and hardworking woman, who tirelessly toured the country on lecture circuits to proselytize metaphysics. A freethinker, an imaginative and disciplined writer, she helped many readers overcome challenges and fears through meditation, hypersensing, diet, and holistic medicine. A truly remarkable woman who lived a colorful life, her path was perhaps predestined, given her God-given talent as a writer and insatiable passion for the supernatural.

In some respects, it's symbolic that she perished at the end of the 1970s. Although the study of astrology, yoga, and reincarnation is still alive and well, Marcia died at the crescendo of the New Age movement of the 1970s, a decade of intrigue and exploration. The New Age movement had reached critical mass, honing the spirit and energy of the '60s counterculture, but with more rigorous esoteric study and more disciplined consciousness experimentation. It was a magnificent time for those who believe in more than our earthbound existence. In those circles, people of all metaphysical sects and from diverse backgrounds formed a close-knit collegiate family rarely seen since in American society.

But like all movements and generations, there is sometimes an unconscious saturation and a snap-back from a profound shift in thinking. As the 1970s ushered in the 1980s, the collective cultural rebalancing shifted in the direction of consumerism and the pursuit of wealth. Greed suddenly became good, Madonna proclaimed that we are living in a material world, and *Little House on the Prairie* gave way to *Lifestyles of the Rich and Famous*.

In some ways, Marcia Moore's passing in 1979 symbolized the death knell of a once pervasive engagement in metaphysics across the world. Sadly, her legacy fell far short of the impact she dreamed of achieving since she was a little girl. She became notable for the wrong reasons, for a mysterious disappearance, a grisly death, and as a cautionary tale for those experimenting with psychotropic substances. For someone who spent a lifetime championing spiritualism and reincarnation, one can't help but imagine Marcia cringing in the afterlife, observing the salacious gossip surrounding her death, the tall tales about the "ketamine junkie" told in the four decades since.

Most tragic of all, Marcia was perchance less than twenty-four hours away from moving on from her troubles with Howard, giving up seeking approval from her parents, and resettling in the place she felt most at home, a location she truly loved, surrounded by dear friends and kindred spirits. She may have finally had an opportunity for introspection, and perhaps even to mend the relationships with her parents and children as she entered her twilight years. Unfortunately, she was quite possibly robbed of that opportunity.

Her tragic fate and untimely death were not inescapable. It was potentially the culmination of forces and circumstances favorable to Howard Alltounian, a man she naively underestimated, as she had so many men in her life. Nevertheless, she deserved her day in court and deserved an advocate in law enforcement with laser focus on only direct and circumstantial evidence, who could cut through the misdirection, untainted by psychic premonitions and astrological interpretations.

This story is neither about lampooning or supporting the occult. Some psychic accounts and astrological interpretations ring true and hit eerily close to the mark. However, it must be acknowledged that the supernatural elements as they pertain to the investigation were heavily sensationalized, and clouded the judgment of Marcia's friends, family, fans, even law enforcement. They served Howard well as an immense distraction from a conventional missing persons case, potentially fore-stalling a criminal indictment.

Howard Alltounian may be innocent, or may never have been con-victed of a crime. Marcia's missing remains for a period of over two years presented a daunting task for any detective or district attorney, to say nothing of the complications surrounding the ketamine use and cer-tain aspects where the case was mishandled. But it's important to note that indictments for second and even first degree murder, though rare, are granted even without a corpse, as recently as the infamous Casey Anthony trial. In those cases, the indictments rested squarely on the inconsistencies, obstruction, contradicting statements, weak alibis, and proven lies told to detectives. By that standard, had the full extent of Howard's lies and the suspicion surrounding the note been exposed, an indictment was quite possibly warranted in this case. At the very least, not reigniting the investigation or rigorously re-interrogating Howard after Marcia's remains were found was an injustice to Marcia Moore.

We believe there are people still alive who can shed more light on this mystery. The question is, will they ever come forward? Marcia Moore died four decades ago, but we believe the truth is still shrouded. Her story fades with each passing year, and every drive by a Sheraton hotel is a reminder of how few people know the unusual, hidden story of Marcia and the Moore family.

Yet as long as her memory is kept alive by friends, fans, and family, hope remains that the truth will come to light. After all, Marcia Moore was a steadfast believer in the mystical cycle of death and rebirth. The poem on her epitaph symbolizes as much:

> *There is no death! The leaves may fall, the flowers may fade and pass away. They only wait through wintery hours, the coming of the May.*

Rest in peace, Marcia.

EPILOGUE: MARCIA REINCARNATE

What you come to learn in investigating a mystery is that you inevitably hit some dead ends. You also get a few lucky breaks. When we spoke with Lt. Bemis a decade ago, he would occasionally mention the name Shelley. "Howard's girlfriend," he said. "You should try to find her." He said Shelley lived with Howard for quite a while after he returned from Detroit in 1981 and found a job, but back then we didn't even know the name of the hospital. After three decades, Bemis didn't remember her last name or if she even still lived in Washington. Since she dated Howard after the case was closed, the name Shelley did not appear in any of our materials. The lead went cold, and we moved on.

In the meantime, we corresponded sporadically with Kareen Zebroff, famous Canadian author, television host, and an old friend of Marcia's. One afternoon in 2012, Kareen provided us with the letter Howard wrote her when he jubilantly returned to Washington in March 1981, two weeks before Marcia's skull was found. Kareen had a dream the night before, which was abruptly interrupted when a clear, female voice cried out, "Howard!" in her mind. She went back to sleep and didn't know what to make of it, but it prompted Kareen to look through some old papers in the morning. Howard Alltounian was the only Howard that came to mind. That's when she found the letter and sent it our way. When we received it, we caught one of those lucky breaks—Howard wrote it on paper with the letterhead "Willapa Harbor Hospital."

We suddenly had the name of the hospital where a friend named Dr. Roger Morton[xiii] helped Howard resurrect his anesthesiology career in South Bend. After researching the hospital and contacting some former staffers, we were eventually put in touch with a woman from Raymond who knew him during his time at the hospital. That woman was willing to speak with us.

During our initial conversation about Howard, she gave us an important new lead. She was acquainted with Howard's ex-girlfriend— the name was Shelley Stark. "Shelley's gonna be a whopper for ya,"[721] the woman said. She cautioned us, however. Shelley was very guarded about her time with Howard and had a history of substance abuse. During a dark period after her relationship with Howard, she dated some very shady characters. Given that Lt. Bemis had implored us to find her, we had to try, but it would lead to a tale as strange as Marcia Moore's.

* * *

In the months following Marcia's disappearance, Howard issued her next foundation bulletin. "Shortly after you left, I took a vow of celibacy and plan to wait until you come back, whether it be now or 20 years from now, reincarnated in a new body,"[722] he shared with her subscribers two months after she vanished. "If she has crossed over to the other side (which I do not believe), she will reincarnate this May-June, as she must be a Gemini to be my heavenly twin, and we will meet in 18 or 20 years. In the meantime, I will remain celibate, keep up with our work and wait for her. Once you have experienced the quality of Marcia's soul, all other women, to me, despite their beauty, would be as empty shells. Essentially Romeo will remain of sound body and mind, waiting for Juliet to return. There can be no other ending but a happy one."[723]

[xiii] Pseudonym

Just as he prepared her readers, it seemed as if the reincarnation prediction was coming to pass, although Howard needn't wait the two decades. His solemn vow of celibacy could now be nullified. About a year after she vanished, he began dating again. Then one day a girl walked into his life that reminded him of Marcia.

A year and a half after Marcia's skull was found, Howard began a relationship with a young woman named Shelley. Those who knew Shelley wondered about her choice of new beau. She was only in her twenties, while Howard his mid-forties. Some thought Howard may have chosen someone he could control. They considered her sort of naïve, "not real together," especially along the lines of drugs. "A guy could totally take advantage,"[724] an acquaintance said.

Since the age of eleven, Shelley had been prescribed the now-banned painkiller Darvon. Prone to health issues like headaches and swollen neck syndrome, she also suffered post-traumatic stress resulting from a brother passing away, a difficult relationship with her mother, and a loving father with serious heart problems. Her family continually searched for a cure. Over the years they tried everything, from various pills to hiring a masseuse, even hypnosis. Darvon offered a powerful alternative. Her mother assured her it was safe and non-addictive, but few at the time knew about its serious withdrawal symptoms and danger of acting as a gateway drug.

When Howard entered the picture, he quickly won over her parents and convinced them that ketamine would help ween her off the other prescriptions. "I'm a doctor, you have to move her over to my place," he said—and so they did. It was all presented very professionally. The ketamine had to be administered in two-week intervals. Shelley wasn't to eat anything the night before, just as if she were going into surgery. "I'm a doctor, don't worry, nothing's gonna happen,"[725] he promised, according to Shelley. He'd also make her what he called "ketamine shakes," mixing the anesthetic with fresh roots and vitamins. She drank them every day, but he never allowed her to see all the ingredients, hiding them in the ceiling.

Eerily, Howard began giving Shelley Marcia's possessions, including the blue-and-white Alfred Shaheen wedding dress she'd worn the day they married in Marwayne's home. Although Marcia was shorter, Shelley was a size zero, so it fit. Additionally, he lavished Shelley with two rare lavender star sapphires and a ring that belonged to Marcia, which Howard said bestowed "wisdom." They were given to Marcia by a monk from Nepal who adored her. Reminiscent of the opal talisman he had given Marcia, when he put it on Shelley's finger, he told her, "Don't ever take it off." Then one day he presented her with a gift enclosed in a leather pouch. "Oh, this is a pre-engagement gift,"[726] he said. It was Marcia's opal. All of Marcia's jewelry, even her wedding band, was curiously in the duplex when Marcia vanished.

Howard even took Shelley to meet Marwayne, donned in Marcia's lavender hat. Marwayne read her chart and professed to have never read a more beautiful one. "Howard please be good to her, please, you know what I mean,"[727] she said in front of Shelley.

In addition to receiving her clothes and possessions, after Shelley eventually moved in with Howard, she became tasked with processing the incoming mail in response to Marcia's final published book, *Journeys into the Bright World*. There were doctors and researchers from all over the world she responded to on his behalf, informing them that sadly, Marcia was dead.

One day, when some of Marcia's belongings arrived at Howard's house, Shelley unpacked a painting. "Now when did Howard have that done of you?" her mother asked. Shelley set her mother straight. The picture was not of her. "Fire Lady," she'd once heard it called. "Did you notice the picture on the mantle that's painted blue, that's Marcia on the inner plane,"[728] Howard once told her.

The picture was a favorite that Marcia hung on her bedroom wall in the duplex. Shelley figured Marcia must have commissioned an artist to draw her, perhaps in Ojai. Actually, the picture was not of Marcia. It was drawn by a German artist long before Marcia was born. An idealized, ethereal rendering of a young woman's face, in which many might see their own, with long, whimsical hair of intertwined colors. For

Marcia, it evoked her own likeness, "a nature spirit, sketched in gold and surrounded by wavy emanations,"[729] she wrote in *Journeys into the Bright World*.

"This portrait had accompanied me from Massachusetts to Maine to California to Washington,"[730] Marcia once explained, sitting mesmerized by the picture during a ketamine session. Now the picture hung in Howard's new beach house, and given that he thought the image resembled his new girlfriend, it was even more proof to him that Shelley was Marcia reincarnate.

Marcia wasn't the only thing to come back to him. He now owned some of the sports cars he longed for, lost in the divorce from his first wife. Shelley owned an expensive Saab she took meticulous care of, and somehow Howard had acquired an SM Maserati and four vintage Austin-Healeys, among other exotic cars.

That's how they met. Shelley brought the Saab to the same mechanic who serviced cars at the beach house Howard had recently bought from his friend Dr. Morton. Shelley's car needed repairs, so Dr. Morton suggested she bring it there. Howard was there when he received a call from the hospital that he'd be needed in surgery. He peeked his head into the kitchen where Shelley was waiting and told the attractive young woman she'd have to move her Saab. She must've made an impression because when Howard next saw her, he made his move. "The next thing I know he's telling me about these Austin-Healeys, and he goes 'jump in…. Hey, come with me…I want to give you a ride to show you this car.'"[731] He drove like a maniac, she remembered, and she couldn't wait until the ride was over.

The second time they went out made a strange impression on Shelley. Howard took her to a nearby artesian well, filled a gallon of water, and said, "I only want you to drink this water because it's so pure." "Fairy water," he called it. Afterward they returned to his impressive house, with a long stretch of beachfront property, remarkable fireplace, and grand kitchen. After showing her around, Howard sat on the edge of his bed and asked if she'd join him. All of a sudden he broke down crying, so she asked what was wrong. "Oh, it's been so long since I've been with a woman," he lamented. Despite feeling sorry for him, she replied, "Well um, we're not together and I'm not sleeping with you."[732]

There was something sweet and intriguing about him though. On the drive back to her home, he said, "The way you sit and everything you do, and the way you move, you're just like Marcia." The locals still whispered about Marcia's mysterious death...and Howard's possible involvement. Shelley was familiar too, and even thought she might get the true story by getting close to him. Initially it was "a cat and mouse thing,"[733] she reflected, but unexpectedly she fell in love.

From that point on, Howard took control and started coming by more frequently. Shelley would often awake to Howard sitting in the kitchen, enjoying coffee with her mother, the whole day already planned out.

Shelley was dearly close to her father, and Howard ingratiated himself by going steelhead fishing with the family. Her father's health began failing, but the trips kept his spirits up. They'd sometimes all go together with her brothers and return to the beach house where Shelley would clean and cook the delicious, fresh fish. They enjoyed many fishing trips, and it deepened their love. Howard helped Shelley emotionally prepare herself for her father's death and was by her side as his health deteriorated. He also assisted where he could financially.

From what his new girlfriend came to understand, Howard somehow inherited a lot of money, and there were people who helped manage it for him. On one occasion, some bank reps put her in a nice room with champagne, while Howard worked out some business. It was peculiar but exciting. People would call the house wanting money, and he'd always say he had none. And for whatever reason, Howard buried valuables underground like cash, gold, and jewelry. He also distributed money in various banks. Once, he showed Shelley a bank deposit book with some woman's name on it, before going inside to make a transaction. She never understood who it belonged to.

Howard bought the beach house and many expensive pieces of vintage art, plus inventory from a pharmacy that Dr. Morton owned. Dr. Morton had helped financially turn his life around. He made at least

$5,000 a month just for being on call at Willapa Harbor Hospital, plus lucrative fees for every surgery for which he supervised anesthesia. He even sold off Marcia's extensive book collection to an eager buyer. "I have the most complete metaphysical library in the world,"[734] Shelley heard him boast to the man.

Treating her wonderfully at first, there was never a dull moment. Once, on their way back from Canada, they were pulled over and Shelley's Saab was taken apart piece by piece. He was traveling to veterinarians in Canada for ketamine and other drugs, she guessed, since she herself was stealing ketamine and other drugs for him from the hospital where she worked, like the extremely potent analgesic Sublimaze. He was administering them to her.

Slowly, however, their relationship became turbulent. Howard took Shelley to Los Angeles the first Christmas after they met, but his son Kevin and others warned her about crazy "Mean Jean," the nickname for Howard's mother. They were standing in the kitchen when his mother became agitated. Shelley was eating holiday cookies when suddenly his mother grabbed the cookie, smashed it on the floor, lunged, and began choking her. She was a sturdy woman, plus Shelley couldn't fight back against Howard's own mother. She looked to Kevin for help, but he just stood there with a smug look. Howard entered just as Shelley began to lose consciousness and took her out of there, but she never forgave Kevin's refusal to help.

Shelley never found out what set Mean Jean off, but felt it related to the entire family's focus on money. After Howard's mother remarried, she inherited a great sum from a successful brewery on the East Coast when her husband died. Shelley speculated that his mother may have thought she was trying to make inroads. It was one of the first signs of trouble.

By then, her concerns were mounting anyway. She decided to pay a visit to Lt. Bemis in Lynnwood to talk about Howard. "I wanted to find out what he knew that I didn't or vice versa, and oh god, some of the things he told me were so creepy." Bemis told her that the detectives all thought he killed Marcia, but they could never prove it. He also told her the bizarre anecdote about shortly after Marcia's disappearance when Howard ended up sniffing the panties found on a roadside in trying to find Marcia. Then he told her something more alarming. "He goes 'well these two women he raped, they won't come forward, give any information out, nothing.'"[735]

As time went by, Howard became more erratic and possessive. "Even if I went somewhere, it was either Howard or Kevin had to be with me, no matter where I went,"[736] Shelley remembered. He watched every move, listened in on phone calls, and the more Shelley began distancing herself, the more he turned the screws.

One day, law enforcement summoned Shelley to the sheriff's office, conveniently located just down the hill from the hospital where she worked, where some hospital higher-ups and officers were waiting. Shelley was escorted by the sheriff into a room with one-way glass. He briefed her that they knew about the drugs she was taking from the hospital, but they were only concerned if it was on Howard's behalf—followed by more ominous comments. Howard had killed and would kill again, the sheriff warned, trying to scare her into opening up. They had profilers, and she would be his next target. He was a serial rapist, they cautioned, carrying the same information Bemis warned her about. They knew of at least two women locally and more in Canada, but none of them would go public out of fear and the disruption it would cause loved ones. "We don't want to scare you, but you should be scared,"[737] they warned.

They asked if he was administering her ketamine and other drugs, but she wouldn't budge. Shelley always prided herself on loyalty and privacy for those in her inner circle, no matter what they did. Increasingly worried but still in love, she covered for him, telling them she alone took the drugs. Afterward she tipped off Howard that they were still watching him. She knew Howard wanted the police out of his life. They had followed him forever, he complained. "Thank you for covering for me, you know I love you so much. This just makes me love you more. I trust you more than I trust anything,"[738] Howard praised.

It wouldn't be the last Shelley would hear about possible rapes. While she'd never go public, there was another woman named Vivian[xiv] with a sordid story, who worked with Howard at Willapa Harbor Hospital as an X-ray technician. Occasionally she worked a side job at a seafood restaurant with a cocktail bar near the hospital, owned by some friends.

One night, Howard came in with a man she didn't know, and they invited Vivian to Howard's place after her shift. While she never considered Howard bad looking, she wasn't attracted to him and, like other locals, had always been wary of the circumstances surrounding Marcia's disappearance. But it being a small, kind of dull little town, she thought it might be interesting to meet his friend.

Although she wouldn't plan on staying long, Vivian agreed to drive over to Howard's place after work. Besides, she had somewhere to be the next day with a long drive in front of her. After arriving, they stood around laughing and making chit chat. Someone suggested they smoke marijuana.

That was her last memory. One minute she was socializing in the kitchen, the next she was in a completely different part of the house, with no idea how she got there.

When Vivian came to in the morning, she was stunned to find herself sitting on the floor leaning over Howard, her arm draped over his leg as he sat in a chair. Immediately she was fully alert, looking up at him with total surprise. Compounding the shock, Howard looked her square in the eyes, pointed toward the door, and forcefully told her to get out and never come back. Looking back, it seemed her reaction at finding herself in that awkward position was what set him off.

Howard went to open the front door. His friend was sitting there as she walked across the front room, utterly embarrassed. There was a vague perception that somebody else might have been there. She wasn't sure, but it felt like there were more than just the three of them. "Get out of here, I never want to see you again!" Howard shouted, as he

---

[xiv] Pseudonym

stood at the door while she started her car. It was around 7:00 a.m. She frantically drove away, now late for the three-hour drive in front of her.

The incident would haunt her for decades. Replaying it in her mind over and over, she wondered if she'd been hurt or violated. Her body didn't feel any different. There were no marks or bruises she could discern, and she was fully clothed. From then on, she awkwardly tried to avoid Howard at work.

Shelley eventually heard about Vivian's story, and although she would come to believe that Howard tried to rape Vivian, she didn't believe that particular anecdote. "He would never give a nurse at that hospital a drink with anything,"[739] she maintained. He was too careful for that.

Shelley, however, would go on to have a similar experience.

As seasons passed, her life with Howard became more chaotic and frightening. She suspected that Howard may have a split personality. "I'm either mean Dr. Howard, or sweet, sweet Sunny. I just want you to know that,"[740] he'd remind her. As Shelley would soon learn traumatically, you didn't want to encounter mean Dr. Howard.

She also thought he was taking steroids. Once, Kevin told her he'd walked in on his dad in the bathroom, where Howard was shooting something into his upper leg. For a time, Kevin lived with Howard and Shelley at the beach house. Together, she and Kevin snooped around the bathroom, looking for evidence. They found some needles. Shelley wondered if Howard's outbursts could have been "roid rage." When something seemed to affect him, "his personality would just flip,"[741] Shelley said. He'd fly off the handle one minute, and be completely calm the next.

Pot restored the calmness, she observed. It appears Howard kept in contact with Akeva long after Marcia's skull was found. Akeva was routinely sending him really "good bud" from Hawaii in the mail and, for whatever reason, money. Howard would go out to the stables and smoke weed, then come back acting weird, barefoot and goofy, a completely different person. "I'd just go to bed, couldn't handle it,"[742] Shelley recalled.

Steroids may have explained Howard's muscular physique. He'd jog and tell her, "Gosh, you're so lucky, you have the perfect body. You don't know what it's like to have to work at it." He loved showing her off, but it bothered her. "I was like a hood ornament on one of his fancy cars, and I couldn't stand it anymore,"[743] she said. It was another reason she considered breaking it off with him and leaving town.

One day, Dr. Morton visited while Howard was out, to speak with Shelley alone. "You belong here Shelley," Morton said, trying to persuade her to stay. But Dr. Morton wasn't really one to give advice. He added to the chaos. "It must be hard being you, every guy in town is chasing you. I got caught up in it too,"[744] Morton once told her.

Actually, he'd done more than get "caught up in it." According to Shelley, he assaulted her during an office visit. "I know you're frigid Shelley,"[745] he told her while making an advance. She wasn't frigid, just appalled, especially since she was fond of his wife and their kids, and wouldn't break up a family. There was something really wrong with Dr. Morton, she thought. He was shaking as he ripped off her thin cloth medical gown. Forcibly trying to kiss her and caress her breasts, he maneuvered her hand around to his hard crotch. Jolted by the advance, she froze, freaked out by him. When he saw her reaction, he threw her thick medical folder up in the air. It seemed like slow motion as the papers drifted to the floor, while she scrambled to dress and bolted for the front office. According to Shelley, years later Dr. Morton's wife hung herself. It seemed that every place she turned in her life became tumultuous.

Shelley made up her mind—she had to break free of the toxic situation. A sort of love triangle had also developed between her, Howard, and Kevin. Howard's son was much closer in age to her than Howard. Although he had a difficult relationship with his son, Shelley found Kevin sweet and attentive, somewhat odd and slow but protective of her. She felt sorry for his kids. All Howard would buy them were cheap things like Velveeta cheese and bread, "but he'd take me out to fancy dinners,"[746] she said. Shelley would try to hide leftovers for Kevin. Even Howard's "fairy water" was off limits to the kids, which Shelley thought strange since he promoted its great health benefits.

Kevin became her secret ally. On one occasion, he motioned her over to show her something. After pulling down the attic stairs, he lifted some boards to reveal several astrological charts Marwayne had done on other girls for Howard. One of the charts was of Dr. Morton's granddaughter. "He tried getting a hold of her, but she was way too young. He tried to get involved with her but it was forbidden. Dr. Morton's sister did not approve,"[747] Shelley learned.

Shelley asked Kevin if he thought his father had anything to do with Marcia's disappearance, but she thought him afraid to answer. Kevin wouldn't say for certain, "He was still so afraid."[748] He warned that they had to tread carefully just speaking about it.

Meanwhile, Kevin developed an infatuation with Shelley. Once while getting undressed, she caught him looking at her through the windows, standing there on the big deck gazing in. Shelley half-laughed to break the awkwardness and said, "Hey, would you get out of here," but he just stood there. On another occasion, Kevin sat next to her on the couch and said, "Gosh you're so pretty."[749] Shelley looked to Howard to say something, but he never did.

Eventually, Howard did confront his son. "I know you love her, just say it."[750]

"Yes I do,"[751] Kevin answered.

A physical altercation ensued, quite dangerous for Howard since he had to be extremely careful with his chest. A rib right over his heart had been removed as a consequence of a serious car accident a decade earlier. "In January of 1970 I had hit a truck with a VW, head on, and spent a year in the hospital, nine months in bed and two months in a wheelchair, two more months on crutches and three months on a cane. When I had open heart surgery and had a teflon graph sewed on my ruptured aorta, I got an air embolus to my brain while on the By-pass machine and was paralyzed for two months. I couldn't move a finger or toe on my left side,"[752] Howard once described.

Now they were fighting over Shelley. Howard eventually pushed his son out the front door and locked it, but Kevin didn't want to leave her alone with his enraged father. He banged on the window. "I don't care if you're in your nightgown, I'll carry you to the car. Come on, I'll take you to your mom and dad's. Get out of that house!"[753] Shelley recalled. She didn't move and went into a sort of shock, hiding under a table.

The next thing she knew, a needle plunged into her arm. Howard had injected Sublimaze, and later Sodium Pentothal, aiming to capitalize on its truth serum properties. When Shelley came out of it, he said, "I had to know, so I asked if you loved me, and you said yes."[754]

Purportedly, he also confessed, "I did a bad thing. When you put somebody under, you're never supposed to mess with their psyche," but admitted he did. "You'll never love anybody in this lifetime the way you love me,"[755] Howard repeated over and over, trying to program her.

The conditioning apparently worked to some degree. It reached a point where Shelley went to his house every day even though she tried to fight the impulse. A friend took her to a hypnotist in Aberdeen who tried to deprogram her. It helped a bit, but in a moment of weakness she told Howard that she'd been there. "He had a hold on me,"[756] she said.

Feeling hopelessly trapped by all the crazy dynamics, and with her own mother always taking Howard's side, Shelley became suicidal. She tried to tell her mom about Howard's dark side, but she thought Shelley was making it up. Her closest friends knew the truth and were concerned she'd end up dead, but they feared Howard and ultimately backed away.

She forged a prescription for a powerful sedative and planned her own death. "I was so, I was just had such enough of it, I couldn't get out of it, and so I thought well, suicide…and I had the place all picked out and everything, up in the hills where nobody'd know."[757]

One day while washing her Saab, her mother yelled that she had a phone call. It was the police department. They needed to see her urgently. Shelley drove to the station where she was greeted with, "I hate to do this to you Shelley, but you have the right to remain silent."[758] The prescriptions she forged had caught up with her. Still fearful of Howard, she made up a story that she was suicidal because of family issues, covering for him again. They gave her a break and, without charging her, made her admit herself into drug rehabilitation. That was perfectly fine with Shelley, who needed to get away from the chaos.

The detox center in Tacoma was a scary place, so a week later Howard moved her to a nicer facility in Quilcene, but by then their relationship had soured. He'd call Shelley at the center. "Your doctor is on the line," the staff would inform her. "Look, this guy is not my doctor," she'd tell the psychologist. "I'm trying to break it off with him."[759]

Even before the police called her in, Shelley wanted to finally break from Howard. She mentally prepared for the three-month stint in rehab, knowing it would make her unavailable. Shelley informed the staff and residents that she refused calls from him. From then on, they'd tell Howard they couldn't interrupt a class she was in, or some such excuse. Dr. Morton even tried to call. The decision wasn't without consequence, as Shelley knew Howard didn't take rejection well. "I don't think too many people said no to him." The minute people said no to him, he became aggressive and his ego couldn't handle it, she observed, "but he could act real meek and mild."[760]

After the three-month stint in rehab, Shelley went back to living with her mother. One day Howard waited for her mother to leave, then made a beeline to see Shelley. She had just come out of the shower and walked into the living room, surprised to see Howard sitting with her brother-in-law. Clad only in a kimono, she quickly exited to change into some clothes.

Shelley had been trying to keep him away, "and the more I pulled away, oh boy, the angrier he'd get at me." When she didn't call him after her release from treatment, he angrily said, "Why didn't you call me? I've heard from other people you've been home for a while. Why in the hell, you've been home and you didn't get a hold of me?"[761]

Shelley didn't want to be alone with Howard in the house, but her brother-in-law was about to leave for work. She privately begged him not to go, but he had to. Her father had passed away a month before, and her gut told her that something awful was about to happen, as if she'd no longer be protected. "Hey, Howard loves you. He's not going to hurt you," her brother-in-law assured. Howard had made it a point to build trust with her relatives, and it was now paying off. "I couldn't get anybody to believe me. He had manipulated and won over my family,"[762] she remembered.

When she returned to the living room, there Howard was, sitting and smiling, twiddling his thumbs, with a gleam in his eyes. She knew she was in for it, and her intuition was right. As soon as her brother-in-law left, she claims Howard threw her down like a ragdoll, and although there were big windows in the front room, brutally raped her right there. It was so painful that she couldn't even get up.

Afterward he carried her to her bedroom. "Well, you've been such a good little girl," he told her, then stuck a long needle right through her clothes, undoing her three-month rehab. "S.O.B. just relapsed me,"[763] she believed.

That was the last thing she remembered. She woke up to a knock at her bedroom door. It was her mother telling her that Howard was on the phone. It was now evening. "I'm really angry at you and your mother," Howard said to a groggy and bewildered Shelley. "Well, now that we're back together, you and your mom didn't even bother to invite me to dinner,"[764] he said. She couldn't even speak, still reeling from whatever he gave her, and what he had the nerve to just say.

At one point, Shelley summoned the courage to go back to the police, offering to testify in court against him for rape. "He didn't think I'd do it, but I did," she said. She would testify if the other women would likewise come forward, but in the end, they were too afraid. "And I said, well I'm not gonna to be the only one. I'll never make it to the court-house steps. I'll be dead before then."[765]

Knowing that Howard was never going to stop harassing her, Shelley made the difficult decision to leave town. It broke her heart to abandon everyone she dearly loved, which included Howard's children. She couldn't bring herself to shatter their perception of their father. She took a job through a friend in Olympia. Shelley wouldn't even give her mother the new telephone number or address, because every time she called home, her mother persisted, "Oh, Howard loves you so much, he misses you. He's always coming over here."[766]

When she originally got together with Howard, it was partly because she felt sorry for him that Marcia had disappeared, she'd say. But like many of the locals, she couldn't resist the unsolved mystery and became uniquely positioned to discover the truth, or at least Howard's version of it. Treading carefully, she'd take advantage of calm or lighthearted moments to broach the subject of Marcia's death.

Over time, and despite the price she paid, Shelley says she finally got the story. "I know what happened to Marcia. I mean, he told me," she revealed. "He was very angry, to the point of violence at the end…I know they had a lot of fights at the end."[767] He said he wanted Marcia to stop the ketamine abuse, particularly all the money it was costing them.

Howard explained that they would sometimes go to a nearby lake or river, and he would administer an IV ketamine drip to Marcia and then fish while they floated along in a McKenzie riverboat. She couldn't be sure if they did that on the night Marcia vanished, but that wouldn't have made sense. Nearby bodies of water were frozen by the unusual cold front that fateful weekend, and Howard never mentioned going out on a boat in his accounts. Howard also told Bemis that Marcia never took the drug intravenously, and Lani doesn't believe she ever went with him on a boat to take ketamine. Regardless, the one thing Shelley was certain of was that Howard admitted to pumping Marcia full of ketamine. "She was going out, and I kept popping it up," he told her about the dosage. He injected more and more until he killed her, he purportedly admitted. Then he took her body to a nearby field, "some kind of farmland thing." There he dumped her in a shallow grave, "and I knew the animals would eat her up,"[768] he said.

Money was a main factor in the lead-up. "I could take care of everything with just a little bit of money," Howard said. "Take care of what?" Shelley asked, "and he wouldn't answer me." He was trying to get the Ananta Foundation, Shelley learned. "She had money, and figured if she died, he should get the ashram." Howard apparently also called Marcia's ex-husband Mark Douglas, trying to get money out of him, "to keep the ashram going."[769] He was always calling people to get money, Shelley observed.

But Howard's admissions weren't always consistent. On one hand, he told the story as if he killed Marcia at her behest. "She was older than me, and I had to do everything she said...she wanted to go to the other side." On the other hand, he made reference to her dying "my way,"[286] mentioning that he'd already begun looking for a way out. He figured out that Marcia only married him for access to ketamine. "I know she was just using me because I'm an anesthesiologist," he told Shelley. "He couldn't handle it anymore," Shelley remembered. "And she wanted to die anyway. So, I had to put her out of her misery and go back to my life," Howard allegedly said.[770]

The way he said it resonated with other anecdotes. Howard once told Shelley about critically ill patients he came in contact with at the Seattle Public Health Service Hospital: "These poor old people. They just wanted to die, so I helped them out."[771] He said there weren't rules about that back then, and he knew how to put them to sleep without leaving a trace, as if they died naturally the night before. Shelley didn't know if it was true. Maybe he told her in some strange attempt to sound compassionate, she considered. But if it was true, she didn't know how many patients there may have been.

Shelley never learned all the gruesome details of Howard dumping Marcia in the woods, whether or not she was barely alive or if he dismembered her corpse. She didn't want to know, and it scared her. She knew Marcia's tiny frame provided little margin of safety when it came to withstanding the subfreezing temperature. The cold wave suppressed temperatures into the twenties that fateful weekend.

There were other peculiar remarks Shelley learned. "When she died, she wanted her head cut off.... So the spirit would leave the body...that if her head was cut off, that would release the spirit quicker,"[772] Howard morbidly told her. She couldn't summon the courage to ask if that's why only her skull was found, but he reiterated that the animals must've gotten to the corpse and ripped her apart.

Howard told Shelley that when the skull was discovered, he was glad it was finally over. "Very just matter of fact," she remembered. "He had no empathy at all about it."[773]

At the time, the hospital administrator advised Howard to make some kind of statement, which ended up picked up in local papers. "So I read this article, and I talked to him about it," she said about when they began dating. "He was laughing. 'Well the article in the paper, I wrote it,'" he said. "Verbatim, everything on that article was what I had to say.... The idiot reporter wrote everything I said," Howard told Shelley. "And he was proud of that, that he had framed the story himself," she remembered. "I got really weirded out when he told me that." "Well I wanted to sound right,"[774] he explained.

Later he told her he had traveled to Canada and Seattle for interviews, "and how he loved going on TV, narcissistic as could be,"[775] she thought.

One day in the beach house, she came across a stunning find—a shoebox jam-packed with clippings from all over the world about Marcia's case. "Like a memento, as if he was proud of them," she recalled. "He was bragging how he fooled everybody. 'The police were a bunch of idiots up there in Lynnwood,'" he told her. "I fooled them. I know how to get past the polygraph." He thought anybody could do it; "you could do it too Shelley," he said. Looking back, Shelley thought it rang true. "You have to keep your heart rate and everything stable; and you have to believe what you're saying at the time, and he could do that.... He didn't have a problem with that. He was a sociopath.... No doubt in my mind."[776]

After everything she had been through, Shelley understood how someone like Marcia could have tragically underestimated Howard. "He just had everything planned," she remembered. "That's how he was. He was diabolical."[777]

Howard told her that he wasn't worried about the police reopening the investigation when the skull was found. He had all bases covered. "He was at the movies, conveniently, even had the ticket stub to prove it, which was so corny.... I even said 'you could've come up with something better than that.'... He just laughed."[778]

As Shelley understood it, Howard had tried to point police in the right direction, but for whatever reason they just couldn't find Marcia's body. "They just couldn't, I don't know." They "had helicopters over the whole area and I mean people canvassing the area, and nothing."[779]

Reflecting on it all, Shelley felt that "the night Marcia came to Seattle and made love to Howard, she was alone and lost and he used her. She had kind of a sad life.... Marcia was a Radcliffe graduate and sister of Robin Moore, she was pretty well known, and Howard wanted to get in good with her, gain her trust, humor her. Then it got annoying. It wasn't anything about their love, because he said that didn't last.... 'You know, I was kind of stuck with her, and she was older than I was,'" he confided to Shelley, who carried his admissions with her for decades. "I've kept my mouth shut the whole time.... I feel like the truth needs to be out there,"[780] she reflected.

Years after the turmoil of breaking up with Howard and hiding out in another town, Shelley heard that Howard finally moved away from Washington. "Nevada, why would you want to go there?" a co-worker asked in hearing he was moving. "Well, I'll just tell you this, be careful what you wish for, you might get it,"[781] Howard cryptically replied.

Shelley didn't know all the details, but he became involved in some sort of pyramid scheme called Eureka. Once, she was at the hospital with him when he let out "that evil sort of laugh," and ran down the hall screaming "Eureka!" All the people just looked at him, "I mean dead silence. I had to get out of there, just crazy."[782]

She suspected that Howard may have been running some type of illegal gambling scheme. After she left town, she found out that he started gambling heavily. He acquired a roulette wheel, "and people would come over and gamble all the time. He was obsessed with money and the gambling,"[783] she said.

Ultimately, a relieved Shelley was finally out of Howard's reach. Ann Rule once contacted her for a story, but Shelley didn't want anything to do with it. After learning that Howard moved to Nevada, she even called the clinic to make sure that he was really there, far, far away, as she was still afraid of him. Shelley felt that she would have been dead continuing that lifestyle if she hadn't escaped.

Those sentiments sounded similar to something Marcia Moore confided to her friend Maria just before she vanished—"I have to get away."

ACKNOWLEDGMENTS

This book would not have been possible without the tremendous effort of those willing to collaborate, and the inspiring bravery of those who came forward.

We would like to thank the following content contributors: Shelley—for your incredible courage. Lani—Marcia is smiling upon you. Lieutenant Darrol Bemis—for demonstrating how personally detectives take the one that got away. Astrologer Maria Comfort—for the support and hospitality. Marwayne Leipzig—for choosing us. Cris Leipzig and Lynn Christensen—for your warmth and generosity. Louisa Roof—for the treasure and candid glimpse into the Moore family. Liz Moore—for your faith. Kareen and Peter Zebroff—for the well wishes. Mac McLaughlin—for the astrological insight. John Moore, Margaret Delaney, Dana Dodge, Bob Bevis, and author Louis Acker.

In addition to the entire Post Hill Press team, we would like to thank the following professionals: Post Hill Press Managing Editor Heather King, Consulting Editor Debra Englander, and Managing Editor Madeline Sturgeon. Editor Christine DiSomma—for the painstaking work and unwavering encouragement. Kevin O'Connor—our literary agent, who was there every step of the way. Amie Chessmore—a most patient and gifted graphic designer. Jonas M. Grant—entertainment lawyer extraordinaire. Producer Elisabeth Bentley—for believing. Author

Stella Sands—for the wisdom. *Dannemora* author Charles A. Gardner—for the shared experience. Editors John H. Meyer and Melissa A. Wuske. Snohomish County Sheriff's Office Detectives Jim Scharf and Bruce Whitman. The Snohomish County Sheriff's Office Public Disclosure Unit: Christina Braden, Sergeant Shawn Stitch, and Jessica Payne. The Concord Free Public Library Special Collections staff—Anke Voss, Jessica Steytler, Leslie Wilson, Constance Manoli-Skocay. The Freedom of Information Act—for allowing light to shine in dark corners.

We would like to thank the following people in our lives who personally made this journey possible: Our friends and family—for two lifetimes of love and support. Joseph DiSomma Sr.—for instilling perseverance. Rev. Diana Wint—for the otherworldly affirmation. Astrologer Susie Cox—for the cosmic guidance. Dianna Carter, BethAnne Dittenber, Diane Ferguson, Susan B., Vivian, The Leaf Lady, Timothy Moore, and Stacey Burgess. Jon & Kathy Armstrong, Moises Vasquez, Alicia Macias and the entire DIA family. Special thanks to Ralph Chater. Muses Ann Rule and Frank Miller. Anton Shahsovar, Eugene Smelyansky, Joe Miscione, Max Shifrin, Christopher Weakley, and Caleb Coppola—for the invaluable time away.

ENDNOTES

1. Kathleen Jenks, "A Report on Past Life Regressions with Marcia Moore," September 7, 1974, 35.
2. Ann Rule (Andy Stack), "Mysterious Disappearance of the Psychic Heiress," *True Detective*, August 1979, 60.
3. Marwayne Leipzig, *Untitled Private Journal*, 1979, 44.
4. Marcia Moore to Robert and Eleanor Moore, July 28, 1978.
5. Marcia Moore and Howard Sunny Alltounian, M.D., *Journeys into the Bright World* (Rockport, MA: Para Research, Inc., 1978), 35.
6. Moore and Alltounian, *Journeys into the Bright World*, 112.
7. Moore and Alltounian, *Journeys into the Bright World*, 97.
8. Moore and Alltounian, *Journeys into the Bright World*, 169.
9. Leipzig, *Untitled Private Journal*, 5.
10. Leipzig, *Untitled Private Journal*, 32.
11. Marcia Moore to Robert Moore, January 3, 1979, 2.
12. Howard Alltounian, interview by Paul Sasso and John Cutaneo, Washington, November 29, 1979, 33.
13. Howard Alltounian, interview by Lieutenant Darrol Bemis, January 18, 1979, 17 (Snohomish County Sheriff's Office case file, S079-01101B, 33).
14. Marcia Moore to Robert Moore, June 27, 1978.
15. Marcia Moore to Robert Moore, January 3, 1979, 1-2.
16. Lani Morris, interview by authors, multiple dates.
17. Morris, interview by authors, multiple dates.
18. Alltounian, interview by Bemis, January 18, 1979, 6-7 (S079-01101D, 11-12).
19. Leipzig, *Untitled Private Journal*, 78.

20 Alltounian, interview by Sasso and Cutaneo, 26.
21 Alltounian, interview by Sasso and Cutaneo, 27.
22 Leipzig, *Untitled Private Journal*, 25.
23 Howard Alltounian, interview by Lieutenant Darrol Bemis and Detective Don Seipel, February 8, 1979, 13 (Snohomish County Sheriff's Office case file, S079-01101D, 51).
24 Alltounian, interview by Bemis, January 18, 1979, 3 (S079-01101D, 8).
25 Alltounian, interview by Sasso and Cutaneo, 25.
26 Alltounian, interview by Sasso and Cutaneo, 18.
27 Alltounian, interview by Bemis, January 18, 1979, 3-4 (S079-01101D, 8-9).
28 Leipzig, *Untitled Private Journal*, 78.
29 Leipzig, *Untitled Private Journal*, 78.
30 Leipzig, *Untitled Private Journal*, 78.
31 Leipzig, *Untitled Private Journal*, 79.
32 Leipzig, *Untitled Private Journal*, 20.
33 Alltounian, interview by Bemis, January 18, 1979, 7 (S079-01101D, 12).
34 Alltounian, interview by Bemis, January 18, 1979, 27-28 (S079-01101D, 31-32).
35 Alltounian, interview by Bemis, January 18, 1979, 25 (S079-01101A, 82).
36 Alltounian, interview by Bemis, January 18, 1979, 27 (S079-01101D, 31).
37 Leipzig, *Untitled Private Journal*, 8.
38 Leipzig, *Untitled Private Journal*, 8.
39 Leipzig, *Untitled Private Journal*, 8.
40 Leipzig, *Untitled Private Journal*, 8.
41 Leipzig, *Untitled Private Journal*, 8.
42 Leipzig, *Untitled Private Journal*, 9.
43 Leipzig, *Untitled Private Journal*, 9.
44 Leipzig, *Untitled Private Journal*, 8.
45 Alltounian, interview by Bemis, January 18, 1979, 7 (S079-01101D, 12).
46 R.A. Quay, "Snohomish County Sheriff's Office Runaway/Missing Person Report and Information Sheet," January 15, 1979 (Snohomish County Sheriff's Office case file, S079-01101A, 10).
47 Leipzig, *Untitled Private Journal*, 6.
48 Moore and Alltounian, *Journeys into the Bright World*, 95-96.
49 Louisa Roof, email message to authors, June 1, 2013.
50 Louisa Roof, email message to authors, November 12, 2010.
51 Alltounian, interview by Bemis, January 18, 1979, 8 (S079-01101D, 13).
52 Alltounian, interview by Bemis, January 18, 1979, 8 (S079-01101D, 13).
53 Alltounian, interview by Bemis, January 18, 1979, 7 (S079-01101D, 12).
54 Howard Alltounian, *The Hypersentience Bulletin-Spring Equinox, Vol. 5*, no. 1 (March 1979): 1.

55 Alltounian, *The Hypersentience Bulletin-Spring Equinox,* 1.
56 Alltounian, interview by Bemis, January 18, 1979, 9 (S079-01101D, 14).
57 Alltounian, *The Hypersentience Bulletin-Spring Equinox,* 2.
58 Alltounian, interview by Bemis, January 18, 1979, 9 (S079-01101D, 14).
59 Alltounian, interview by Bemis, January 18, 1979, 9 (S079-01101D, 14).
60 Sergeant John Taylor, "Follow-up/Supplemental Report," January 22, 1979, 2 (Snohomish County Sheriff's Office case file, S079-01101A, 87).
61 Taylor, "Follow-up/Supplemental Report," January 22, 1979, 2 (S079-01101A, 87).
62 Morris, interview by authors, multiple dates.
63 Taylor, "Follow-up/Supplemental Report," January 22, 1979, 1 (S079-01101A, 88).
64 Leipzig, *Untitled Private Journal,* 3.
65 Alltounian, interview by Bemis, January 18, 1979, 11 (S079-01101D, 16).
66 Alltounian, interview by Bemis, January 18, 1979, 11 (S079-01101D, 16).
67 Alltounian, interview by Bemis, January 18, 1979, 11 (S079-01101D, 16).
68 Alltounian, interview by Bemis, January 18, 1979, 12 (S079-01101D, 17).
69 Alltounian, interview by Bemis, January 18, 1979, 11 (S079-01101D, 16).
70 Alltounian, interview by Bemis, January 18, 1979, 12 (S079-01101D, 17).
71 Cris Leipzig, interview by authors, multiple dates.
72 Cris Leipzig, interview by authors, multiple dates.
73 Leipzig, *Untitled Private Journal,* 1.
74 Leipzig, *Untitled Private Journal,* 2.
75 Leipzig, *Untitled Private Journal,* 1.
76 Harry J. Stathos, "Robin Moore's sister missing; kidnap feared," *The News World,* January 20, 1979, 1A.
77 Marcia Moore to Robert and Eleanor Moore, October 5, 1977, 2.
78 Marcia Moore to Robert and Eleanor Moore, September 24, 1977, 1.
79 Mary Olga, "Mary Olga's Notes of Her Conversation with Marcia Moore on Saturday, January 13, 1979," 1.
80 Olga, 1-2.
81 Olga, 2.
82 Erik Lacitis, "Did drug 'kidnap' missing psychic?" *Seattle Times,* February 5, 1979, 77.
83 Olga, 2.
84 John Moore, "Events Concerning Marcia's Disappearance as Compiled by John Moore," 3.
85 David Suffia, "Drug Cultist's Mysterious Disappearance," *Chic Magazine,* August 1981, 80.
86 Unknown author, "Witches blamed for death of an heiress," *Weekly World News,* April 28, 1981.

87 Erik Lacitis, "Marcia Moore: Mysterious disappearance baffles police," *Seattle Times*, January 29, 1979.
88 Alltounian, *The Hypersentience Bulletin-Spring Equinox*, 3.
89 Alltounian, interview by Bemis, January 18, 1979, 13 (S079-01101D, 18).
90 Alltounian, interview by Bemis, January 18, 1979, 13 (S079-01101D, 18).
91 Alltounian, interview by Bemis, January 18, 1979, 13 (S079-01101D, 18).
92 Lt. Darrol Bemis and Cris Leipzig, interview by authors, Everett WA, July 2010.
93 Alltounian, interview by Bemis, January 18, 1979, 14 (S079-01101D, 19).
94 Bemis and Leipzig, interview by authors, July 2010.
95 Alltounian, interview by Bemis, January 18, 1979, 14 (S079-01101D, 19).
96 Alltounian, interview by Bemis, January 18, 1979, 9 (S079-01101D, 14).
97 Detective Don Seipel, "Follow-up/Supplemental Report," January 18, 1979, 1-3 (Snohomish County Sheriff's Office case file, S079-01101D, 2-4).
98 Moore and Alltounian, *Journeys into the Bright World*, 9.
99 Seipel, "Follow-up/Supplemental Report," 2 (S079-01101D, 3).
100 Seipel, "Follow-up/Supplemental Report," 3 (S079-01101D, 4).
101 Seipel, "Follow-up/Supplemental Report," 3-4 (S079-01101D, 4-5).
102 Bemis and Leipzig, interview by authors, July 2010.
103 Taylor, "Follow-up/Supplemental Report," January 22, 1979, 3 (S079-01101A, 89).
104 Alltounian, *The Hypersentience Bulletin-Spring Equinox*, 4.
105 Leipzig, *Untitled Private Journal*, 1.
106 Alltounian, interview by Bemis, January 18, 1979, 1 (S079-01101D, 6).
107 Alltounian, interview by Bemis, January 18, 1979, 1 (S079-01101D, 6).
108 Alltounian, interview by Bemis, January 18, 1979, 1 (S079-01101D, 6).
109 Alltounian, interview by Bemis, January 18, 1979, 1 (S079-01101D, 6).
110 Alltounian, interview by Bemis, January 18, 1979, 1 (S079-01101D, 6).
111 Alltounian, interview by Bemis, January 18, 1979, 1 (S079-01101D, 6).
112 Alltounian, interview by Bemis, January 18, 1979, 1 (S079-01101D, 6).
113 Alltounian, interview by Bemis, January 18, 1979, 1 (S079-01101D, 6).
114 Alltounian, interview by Bemis, January 18, 1979, 1 (S079-01101D, 6).
115 Alltounian, interview by Bemis, January 18, 1979, 1 (S079-01101D, 6).
116 John Moore, interview by Lieutenant Darrol Bemis, January 19, 1979, 1 (Snohomish County Sheriff's Office case file, S079-01101E, 35).
117 Moore, interview by Bemis, January 19, 1979, 1 (S079-01101E, 35).
118 John Moore, "Events Concerning Marcia's Disappearance as Compiled by John Moore," 4.
119 Moore, interview by Bemis, January 19, 1979, 1 (S079-01101E, 35).
120 Robert Moore to Marcia Moore, July 9, 1978, 3.
121 Robert Moore to Marcia Moore, July 9, 1978, 4.

122 Robert Moore to Marcia Moore, July 9, 1978, 4-5.
123 Robert Moore to Marcia Moore, July 9, 1978, 5.
124 Moore, interview by Bemis, January 19, 1979, 2 (S079-01101E, 36).
125 Moore, interview by Bemis, January 19, 1979, 2 (S079-01101E, 36).
126 Marcia Moore to John Moore, October 28, 1978, 1.
127 Leipzig, *Untitled Private Journal*, 1.
128 John Moore, statement and interview by Lieutenant Darrol Bemis, January 19, 1979, 1 (Snohomish County Sheriff's Office case file, S079-01101E, 31).
129 Jess Stearn, *Yoga, Youth, and Reincarnation* (New York, NY: Bantam Books Inc., 1965), 24.
130 Moore and Alltounian, *Journeys into the Bright World*, 79.
131 Jack Heise, "A Case That Will Boggle Your Mind: One of America's Psychics Is Missing!" *Startling Detective*, November, 1980, 13.
132 Bemis and Leipzig, interview by authors, July 2010.
133 Heise, 13.
134 Marcia Moore, *Hypersentience* (New York, NY: Crown Publishers, Inc., 1976), 198.
135 Ernest Henderson, *The World of "Mr. Sheraton"* (New York, NY: Popular Library and David McKay Company, Inc., 1960), 9.
136 Henderson, 68.
137 Louisa Roof, email message to authors, April 30, 2013.
138 Alice A. Bailey, *The Unfinished Autobiography* (New York, NY: Lucis Publishing Company, 1951), 4-5.
139 Bailey, *The Unfinished Autobiography*, 12-13.
140 Alice Bailey to Marcia Moore, November 10, 1949, 2.
141 Bailey, *The Unfinished Autobiography*, 38.
142 Louisa Roof, email message to authors, July 27, 2013.
143 Louisa Roof, email message to authors, May 18, 2012.
144 Marcia Moore to Robert and Eleanor Moore, August 12, 1956, 1.
145 Marcia Moore to Robert and Eleanor Moore, August 2, 1974, 1.
146 Simons Roof, *A Psychosynthesis Autobiography* (unpublished, 1972), 2.
147 Roof, *A Psychosynthesis Autobiography*, 21.
148 Simons Roof to Robert and Eleanor Moore, June 8, 1955, 2.
149 Marcia Moore to Robert and Eleanor Moore, June 17, 1955.
150 Marcia Moore to Katharine and Wilmon Brewer, June 25, 1955, 1.
151 Marcia Moore to Katharine and Wilmon Brewer, June 25, 1955, 1.
152 Marcia Moore to Robert and Eleanor Moore, July 1, 1955.
153 Marcia Moore to Robert and Eleanor Moore, July 1, 1955.
154 Marcia Moore to Robert and Eleanor Moore, July 1, 1955.
155 Marcia Moore to Robert and Eleanor Moore, July 25, 1955, 2.
156 Marcia Moore to Robert and Eleanor Moore, August 2, 1955, 1.

157 Marcia Moore to Robert and Eleanor Moore, September 18, 1955, 1.
158 Simons Roof to Robert and Eleanor Moore, June 8, 1955, 2.
159 Marcia Moore, "India A Land of Contrasts," *Concord Journal*, October 20, 1955, 8.
160 Moore, "India A Land of Contrasts," 8.
161 Edward L. Bernays to Robert Moore, October 21, 1955, 1.
162 Marcia Moore to Robert and Eleanor Moore, October 23, 1955, 1.
163 Marcia Moore to Robert Moore, December 28, 1955, 1-2.
164 Moore, "India A Land of Contrasts," 8.
165 Marcia Moore to Robert and Eleanor Moore, November 7, 1955, 1.
166 Marcia Moore to Robert and Eleanor Moore, November 27, 1955, 1-2.
167 Robert Moore to Marcia Moore, January 1962, 1.
168 Marcia Moore to Robert Moore, November 29, 1955, 1.
169 Marcia Moore to Robert Moore, November 29, 1955, 1-2.
170 Marcia Moore to Robert and Eleanor Moore, April 6, 1956, 1.
171 Marcia Moore to Robert and Eleanor Moore, April 1, 1956, 1.
172 Marcia Moore to Robert and Eleanor Moore, April 1, 1956, 1.
173 Marcia Moore to Robert and Eleanor Moore, November 7, 1955, 1.
174 Marcia Moore to Robert and Eleanor Moore, September 25, 1955, 1.
175 Marcia Moore to Robert and Eleanor Moore, August 12, 1956, 1.
176 Marcia Moore to Robert and Eleanor Moore, August 8, 1956, 1.
177 Marcia Moore to Robert and Eleanor Moore, November 15, 1956, 1.
178 Marcia Moore to Robert and Eleanor Moore, January 28, 1957, 1.
179 Marcia Moore to Robert and Eleanor Moore, January 16, 1956, 1.
180 Marcia Moore to Robert Moore, December 28, 1955, 2.
181 Marcia Moore to Robert and Eleanor Moore, May 6, 1956, 1.
182 Marcia Moore to Robert and Eleanor Moore, May 6, 1956, 1.
183 Marcia Moore to Katharine & Wilmon Brewer, December 14, 1956, 1.
184 Marcia Moore to Robert and Eleanor Moore, November 17, 1956, 1.
185 Marcia Moore to Robert and Eleanor Moore, December 6, 1956, 1-2.
186 Simons Roof to Robert and Eleanor Moore, November 18, 1956, 1.
187 Marcia Moore to Katharine and Wilmon Brewer, June 12, 1956, 1.
188 Marcia Moore to Robert and Eleanor Moore, July 1, 1956, 1.
189 Marcia Moore to Robert and Eleanor Moore, July 18, 1956, 1.
190 Marcia Moore to Robert and Eleanor Moore, July 26, 1956, 1.
191 Marcia Moore to Robert and Eleanor Moore, August 19, 1957, 2.
192 Marcia Moore to Robert and Eleanor Moore,, January 16, 1956, 1.
193 Marcia Moore to Robert and Eleanor Moore, August 27. 1956, 1.
194 Marcia Moore to Robert and Eleanor Moore, February 16, 1957, 1.
195 Marcia Moore to Robert and Eleanor Moore, May 4, 1957, 1.
196 Marcia Moore Katharine & Wilmon Brewer, June 9, 1957, 1.

197 Marcia Moore to Robert and Eleanor Moore, September 18, 1957, 2.
198 Marcia Moore to Robert and Eleanor Moore, August 12, 1956, 1.
199 Marcia Moore to Robert and Eleanor Moore, August 16, 1956, 1.
200 Astro-Dynamics Research founding documents, September 26, 1960, Boston, MA.
201 Marcia Moore to Katharine & Wilmon Brewer, May 22, 1961, 1.
202 Robert Moore to Marcia Moore, January 1962, 1.
203 Marcia Moore to Robert and Eleanor Moore, 1.
204 Marcia Moore to Robert and Eleanor Moore, 1.
205 Marcia Moore to Robert and Eleanor Moore, 1.
206 Marcia Moore to Robert and Eleanor Moore, 1.
207 Roof, *A Psychosynthesis Autobiography*, 14.
208 Louisa Roof, background information, multiple dates.
209 Louisa Roof, background information, multiple dates.
210 Stearn, 21.
211 Louisa Roof, background information, multiple dates.
212 Louisa Roof, background information, multiple dates.
213 Marcia Moore to Robert and Eleanor Moore, February 15, 1973, 1.
214 Marcia Moore to Robert and Eleanor Moore, February 15, 1973, 2.
215 Marcia Moore to Robert and Eleanor Moore, December 1965, 1-2.
216 Louisa Roof, interview by authors, September 2012.
217 Louisa Roof, email message to authors, November 5, 2013.
218 Louisa Roof, background information, multiple dates.
219 John Moore to Marcia Moore, January 20, 1966, 1.
220 "ITT Sheraton Corporation History," accessed March 7, 2021, www.fundinguniverse.com/company-histories/itt-sheraton-corporation-history/.
221 Steve Miletich, "Writer Moore Says Witches May Have Slain His Sister," *Seattle Post Intelligencer*, March 26, 1981.
222 Marcia Moore to Robert and Eleanor Moore, August 23, 1966, 1-2.
223 Robert Moore to Marcia Moore, August 30, 1966, 1.
224 Louisa Roof, background information, multiple dates.
225 Pearl Higley to Robert Moore, June 27, 1972, 1.
226 Robert Moore to Pearl Higley, July 3, 1972, 1.
227 Marcia Moore to Robert and Eleanor Moore, May 27, 1968, 1.
228 Marcia Moore to Robert and Eleanor Moore, May 27, 1968, 1-2.
229 Marcia Moore to Robert and Eleanor Moore, May 27, 1968, 2.
230 Louisa Roof, email message to authors, June 19, 2013.
231 Leipzig, *Untitled Private Journal*, 75.
232 Marcia Moore to Robert and Eleanor Moore, February 15, 1973, 1.
233 Marcia Moore to Robert and Eleanor Moore, November 24, 1956, 1.
234 Robert Moore to Marcia Moore, April 15, 1956, 1.

[235] Marcia Moore to Robert and Eleanor Moore, January 24, 1973, 2.
[236] Louisa Roof, email message to authors, May 29, 2012.
[237] Marcia Moore to Robert and Eleanor Moore, January 8, 1972, 1.
[238] Marcia Moore to Robert and Eleanor Moore, April 27, 1973, 1.
[239] Marcia Moore to Robert and Eleanor Moore, January 24, 1973, 1.
[240] Marcia Moore to Robert and Eleanor Moore, April 27, 1973, 1-2.
[241] Marcia Moore to Robert and Eleanor Moore, 1973, 2.
[242] Marcia Moore to Robert and Eleanor Moore, October 18, 1976, 1.
[243] Marcia Moore to Robert and Eleanor Moore, May 3, 1973, 1-2.
[244] Marcia Moore to Robert and Eleanor Moore, June 30, 1973, 1.
[245] Robert Moore to Marcia Moore, March 9, 1976, 1.
[246] Robert Moore to Florence, February 12, 1973, 1-2.
[247] Marcia Moore to Robert and Eleanor Moore, February 15, 1973, 2.
[248] Louisa Roof, email message to authors, July 14, 2013.
[249] Marcia Moore to Robert and Eleanor Moore, January 8, 1972, 3.
[250] Marcia Moore to Robert Moore, January 3, 1979, 1.
[251] Marcia Moore to Robert and Eleanor Moore, December 12, 1976, 1.
[252] Marcia Moore to Robert and Eleanor Moore, May 3, 1973, 2.
[253] Marcia Moore to Robert and Eleanor Moore, July 13, 1973, 2.
[254] Marcia Moore to Robert and Eleanor Moore, February 9, 1974, 1.
[255] Moore and Alltounian, *Journeys into the Bright World*, 43.
[256] Marcia Moore to Robert and Eleanor Moore, 1973, 1-2.
[257] Marcia Moore to Robert and Eleanor Moore, June 30, 1973, 1.
[258] Marcia Moore to Robert and Eleanor Moore, July 8, 1973, 1.
[259] Marcia Moore to Robert and Eleanor Moore, November 29, 1976, 1.
[260] Eleanor Moore, memo, August 1973.
[261] Marcia Moore to Robert and Eleanor Moore, 1.
[262] Louisa Roof, email message to authors, August 8, 2010.
[263] Marcia Moore to Robert and Eleanor Moore, December 25, 1974, 1.
[264] Marcia Moore to Robert and Eleanor Moore, February 25, 1974, 1.
[265] Marcia Moore, *Hypersentience* (New York, NY: Crown Publishers, Inc., 1976), 2.
[266] Marcia Moore, *Hypersentience* (New York, NY: Crown Publishers, Inc., 1976), 12.
[267] Marcia Moore to Robert and Eleanor Moore, June 21, 1974, 1.
[268] Marcia Moore to Robert and Eleanor Moore, December 2, 1975, 1.
[269] Marcia Moore to Robert and Eleanor Moore, December 12, 1976, 1.
[270] Marcia Moore to Robert and Eleanor Moore, December 18, 1976, 1.
[271] Howard Alltounian, *The Hypersentience Bulletin-Summer Solstice, Vol. 5*, no. 2 (June 1979): 19.
[272] Alltounian, interview by Sasso and Cutaneo, 25.
[273] Marwayne Leipzig to John Moore, March 28, 1981, 1.
[274] Alltounian, interview by Sasso and Cutaneo, 24.

275 Marcia Moore to Robert and Eleanor Moore, September 24, 1977, 1.

276 Alltounian, *The Hypersentience Bulletin-Summer Solstice,* 10.

277 Leipzig, *Untitled Private Journal,* prologue.

278 Alltounian, *The Hypersentience Bulletin-Summer Solstice,* 11.

279 Alltounian, *The Hypersentience Bulletin-Summer Solstice,* 11.

280 Ideala Foster, notes regarding conversation with Howard Alltounian, February 21, 1979.

281 Moore and Alltounian, *Journeys into the Bright World,* 23.

282 Moore and Alltounian, *Journeys into the Bright World,* 22.

283 Marcia Moore to Robert and Eleanor Moore, August 11, 1977, 1.

284 Alltounian, *The Hypersentience Bulletin-Spring Equinox,* 19.

285 Moore and Alltounian, *Journeys into the Bright World,* 35.

286 Marcia Moore to Robert and Eleanor Moore, September 24, 1977, 1.

287 Moore and Alltounian, *Journeys into the Bright World,* 24.

288 Moore and Alltounian, *Journeys into the Bright World,* 25-26.

289 Rose Gallacher and Howard Alltounian, interview by Lieutenant Darrol Bemis, January 28, 1979, 10 (Snohomish County Sheriff's Office case file, S079-01101A, 62).

290 Marcia Moore to Robert and Eleanor Moore, September 7, 1977, 1.

291 Marcia Moore to Mac McLaughlin, October 5, 1977, 1.

292 Marcia Moore to Robert and Eleanor Moore, September 24, 1977, 1.

293 Marcia Moore to Robert and Eleanor Moore, October 16, 1977, 1.

294 Marcia Moore to Robert and Eleanor Moore, November 12, 1977, 1.

295 Marcia Moore to Robert and Eleanor Moore, September 24, 1977, 1.

296 Marcia Moore to Robert and Eleanor Moore, October 5, 1977, 1.

297 Marcia Moore to Robert and Eleanor Moore, September 24, 1977, 1-2.

298 Marcia Moore to Robert and Eleanor Moore, October 8, 1977, 1.

299 Marcia Moore to Robert and Eleanor Moore, October 16, 1977, 1.

300 Marcia Moore to Robert and Eleanor Moore, November 17, 1977, 1.

301 Marwayne Leipzig to John Moore, November 23, 1979, 1.

302 Karen to Marwayne Leipzig, 1977, 1.

303 Unknown astrologer to Marwayne Leipzig, 1977, 1-3.

304 Unknown astrologer to Leipzig, 1-2.

305 Unknown astrologer to Leipzig, 1.

306 Unknown astrologer to Leipzig, 2.

307 Unknown astrologer to Leipzig, 2.

308 Moore and Alltounian, *Journeys into the Bright World,* dedication page.

309 Marcia Moore to Robert and Eleanor Moore, October 5, 1977, 1-3.

310 Marcia Moore to Robert and Eleanor Moore, November 12, 1977, 2.

311 Marcia Moore to Robert and Eleanor Moore, February 21, 1978, 1.

312 Moore and Alltounian, *Journeys into the Bright World,* 10.

313 Morris, interview by authors, multiple dates.

314 Moore and Alltounian, *Journeys into the Bright World*, 100.

315 Moore and Alltounian, *Journeys into the Bright World*, 13.

316 Moore and Alltounian, *Journeys into the Bright World*, 14.

317 Moore and Alltounian, *Journeys into the Bright World*, 15.

318 Moore and Alltounian, *Journeys into the Bright World*, 15.

319 Moore and Alltounian, *Journeys into the Bright World*, 16.

320 Moore and Alltounian, *Journeys into the Bright World*, 41.

321 Moore and Alltounian, *Journeys into the Bright World*, 99.

322 Moore and Alltounian, *Journeys into the Bright World*, 91.

323 Moore and Alltounian, *Journeys into the Bright World*, 90.

324 Moore and Alltounian, *Journeys into the Bright World*, 73.

325 Moore and Alltounian, *Journeys into the Bright World*, 48.

326 Moore and Alltounian, *Journeys into the Bright World*, 77.

327 Moore and Alltounian, *Journeys into the Bright World*, 102.

328 Moore and Alltounian, *Journeys into the Bright World*, 111.

329 Moore and Alltounian, *Journeys into the Bright World*, 107.

330 Howard Alltounian, *The Hypersentience Bulletin-Fall Equinox, Vol. 4*, no. 2 (September 1978): 2.

331 Maria Comfort, interview by authors, November 12, 2010.

332 Leipzig, *Untitled Private Journal*, 22.

333 Marcia Moore, *The Hypersentience Bulletin-Spring Equinox, Vol.3*, no. 4 (March 1978): 3.

334 Frances Adams Moore to Robert and Eleanor Moore, July 27, 1978.

335 Eleanor Moore to Frances, 1978, 1-2.

336 Robert Moore to Frances, July 31, 1978, 1.

337 Marcia Moore to Robert Moore, January 3, 1979, 2.

338 Marcia Moore to Robert Moore, January 3, 1979, 1.

339 Alltounian, interview by Bemis, January 18, 1979, 2 (S079-01101D, 7).

340 Moore, interview by Bemis, January 19, 1979, 4 (S079-01101E, 38).

341 John Moore, "Events Concerning Marcia's Disappearance as Compiled by John Moore," 18.

342 Moore, interview by Bemis, January 19, 1979, 6-7 (S079-01101E, 40-41).

343 Moore, interview by Bemis, January 19, 1979, 6 (S079-01101E, 40).

344 Jim Batchelor, statement and interview by Lieutenant Darrol Bemis, February 6, 1979, 2 (Snohomish County Sheriff's Office case file, S079-01101E, 45).

345 Moore, interview by Bemis, January 19, 1979, 7 (S079-01101E, 41).

346 Moore, interview by Bemis, January 19, 1979, 7 (S079-01101E, 41).

347 Leipzig, *Untitled Private Journal*, 72.

348 Moore, interview by Bemis, January 19, 1979, 7 (S079-01101E, 41).

349 Leipzig, *Untitled Private Journal*, 70.

350 Batchelor, statement and interview by Bemis, 3 (S079-01101E, 46).
351 Leipzig, *Untitled Private Journal*, 70.
352 Wendy Crothers, statement to Lieutenant Darrol Bemis, January 21, 1979, 2-3, (Snohomish County Sheriff's Office case file, S079-01101E, 28-29).
353 Batchelor, statement and interview by Bemis, 4 (S079-01101E, 47).
354 Crothers, statement to Bemis, 3, (S079-01101E, 29).
355 Crothers, statement to Bemis, 3, (S079-01101E, 29).
356 Batchelor, statement and interview by Bemis, 4 (S079-01101E, 47).
357 Bemis and Leipzig, interview by authors, July 2010.
358 Alltounian, *The Hypersentience Bulletin-Spring Equinox,* 4.
359 Leipzig, *Untitled Private Journal*, 13.
360 Leipzig, *Untitled Private Journal*, 13.
361 Leipzig, *Untitled Private Journal*, 13.
362 Lacitis, "Marcia Moore: Mysterious disappearance baffles police."
363 John Moore to Lieutenant Darrol Bemis, January 31, 1979, 2.
364 Alltounian, *The Hypersentience Bulletin-Spring Equinox,* 10.
365 Leipzig, *Untitled Private Journal*, 21.
366 Bemis and Leipzig, interview by authors, July 2010.
367 Alltounian, *The Hypersentience Bulletin-Spring Equinox,* 10.
368 Leipzig, *Untitled Private Journal*, 21.
369 Leipzig, *Untitled Private Journal*, 4.
370 Taylor, "Follow-up/Supplemental Report," January 22, 1979, 1 (S079-01101A, 88).
371 Leipzig, *Untitled Private Journal*, 4.
372 Leipzig, *Untitled Private Journal*, 5.
373 Marcia Moore, "Spirit Guides," (Snohomish County Sheriff's Office case file, S079-01101E, 6).
374 Alltounian, interview by Bemis, January 18, 1979, 9 (S079-01101D, 14).
375 Leipzig, *Untitled Private Journal*, 9.
376 Leipzig, *Untitled Private Journal*, 10.
377 Leipzig, *Untitled Private Journal*, 11.
378 Howard Alltounian, *The Hypersentience Bulletin-Fall Equinox, Vol. 5*, no. 3 (September 1979): 19.
379 Ron Caylor, "Missing Psychic has Become Invisible & 'Is Somewhere Out in the Cosmos," *National Enquirer,* August 1979, 28-29.
380 Caylor, 29.
381 Leipzig, *Untitled Private Journal*, 11.
382 Leipzig, *Untitled Private Journal*, 11-12.
383 Leipzig, *Untitled Private Journal*, 12.
384 Heise, 13.
385 Stathos, 1A.

386 Alltounian, *The Hypersentience Bulletin-Spring Equinox,* 7.
387 Alltounian, *The Hypersentience Bulletin-Spring Equinox,* 7.
388 Regis O'Donnell to Lieutenant Darrol Bemis, August 6, 1979 (Snohomish County Sheriff's Office case file, S079-01101E, 9).
389 Annie E. Abernathy to Snohomish County Sheriff's Office, April 17, 1980 (Snohomish County Sheriff's Office case file, S079-01101A, 107).
390 Melinda to Lieutenant Darrol Bemis (Snohomish County Sheriff's Office case file, S079-01101C, 50).
391 Lacitis, "Marcia Moore: Mysterious disappearance baffles police."
392 Ann Rule, *The Stranger Beside Me* (New York: Gallery Books; Reprint edition, 2018), 223.
393 Leipzig, *Untitled Private Journal,* 2.
394 Leipzig, *Untitled Private Journal,* 20-22.
395 Morris, interview by authors, multiple dates.
396 Chief Constable J.F. Gregory, City of Victoria, British Columbia Police Department to Lieutenant Darrol Bemis, January 26, 1979 (Snohomish County Sheriff's Office case file, S079-01101A, 52).
397 Gallacher and Alltounian, interview by Bemis, 6 (S079-01101A, 58).
398 Gallacher and Alltounian, interview by Bemis, 7 (S079-01101A, 59).
399 Gallacher and Alltounian, interview by Bemis, 8 (S079-01101A, 60).
400 Gallacher and Alltounian, interview by Bemis, 9 (S079-01101A, 61).
401 Gallacher and Alltounian, interview by Bemis, 11 (S079-01101A, 97).
402 Gallacher and Alltounian, interview by Bemis, 14 (S079-01101A, 100).
403 Gallacher and Alltounian, interview by Bemis, 14 (S079-01101A, 100).
404 Gallacher and Alltounian, interview by Bemis, 16 (S079-01101A, 102).
405 Leipzig, *Untitled Private Journal,* 14.
406 Leipzig, *Untitled Private Journal,* 14.
407 Leipzig, *Untitled Private Journal,* 14.
408 Leipzig, *Untitled Private Journal,* 16.
409 Leipzig, *Untitled Private Journal,* 16.
410 Leipzig, *Untitled Private Journal,* 16.
411 Leipzig, *Untitled Private Journal,* 17.
412 Leipzig, *Untitled Private Journal,* 17.
413 Alltounian, *The Hypersentience Bulletin-Spring Equinox,* 11.
414 Alltounian, *The Hypersentience Bulletin-Spring Equinox,* 12.
415 Leipzig, *Untitled Private Journal,* 18.
416 Leipzig, *Untitled Private Journal,* 19.
417 Leipzig, *Untitled Private Journal,* 19-20.
418 Leipzig, *Untitled Private Journal,* 23.
419 Leipzig, *Untitled Private Journal,* 24.
420 Leipzig, *Untitled Private Journal,* 29.

[421] Leipzig, *Untitled Private Journal*, 29.
[422] Leipzig, *Untitled Private Journal*, 27.
[423] Leipzig, *Untitled Private Journal*, 30.
[424] Alltounian, interview by Bemis and Seipel, 3-4 (S079-01101B, 19-20).
[425] Alltounian, interview by Bemis and Seipel, 5 (S079-01101B, 21).
[426] Alltounian, interview by Bemis and Seipel, 5-6 (S079-01101B, 21-22).
[427] Alltounian, interview by Bemis and Seipel, 6 (S079-01101B, 22).
[428] Alltounian, interview by Bemis and Seipel, 6 (S079-01101B, 22).
[429] Alltounian, interview by Bemis and Seipel, 6 (S079-01101B, 22).
[430] Alltounian, interview by Bemis and Seipel, 6 (S079-01101B, 22).
[431] Alltounian, interview by Bemis and Seipel, 6 (S079-01101B, 22).
[432] Alltounian, interview by Bemis and Seipel, 6 (S079-01101B, 22).
[433] Alltounian, interview by Bemis and Seipel, 6 (S079-01101B, 22).
[434] Alltounian, interview by Bemis and Seipel, 6 (S079-01101B, 22).
[435] Alltounian, interview by Bemis and Seipel, 6 (S079-01101B, 22).
[436] Alltounian, interview by Bemis and Seipel, 6 (S079-01101B, 22).
[437] Alltounian, interview by Bemis and Seipel, 8 (S079-01101B, 24).
[438] Alltounian, interview by Bemis and Seipel, 8 (S079-01101B, 24).
[439] Alltounian, interview by Bemis and Seipel, 8-9 (S079-01101B, 24-25).
[440] Alltounian, interview by Bemis and Seipel, 9 (S079-01101B, 25).
[441] Alltounian, interview by Bemis and Seipel, 9 (S079-01101B, 25).
[442] Alltounian, interview by Bemis and Seipel, 9 (S079-01101B, 25).
[443] Alltounian, interview by Bemis and Seipel, 9 (S079-01101B, 25).
[444] Alltounian, interview by Bemis and Seipel, 9 (S079-01101B, 25).
[445] Alltounian, interview by Bemis and Seipel, 9 (S079-01101B, 25).
[446] Alltounian, interview by Bemis and Seipel, 9 (S079-01101B, 25).
[447] Alltounian, interview by Bemis and Seipel, 9 (S079-01101B, 25).
[448] Alltounian, interview by Bemis and Seipel, 9 (S079-01101B, 25).
[449] Alltounian, interview by Bemis and Seipel, 9 (S079-01101B, 25).
[450] Alltounian, interview by Bemis and Seipel, 9 (S079-01101B, 25).
[451] Alltounian, interview by Bemis and Seipel, 9 (S079-01101B, 25).
[452] Alltounian, interview by Bemis and Seipel, 9 (S079-01101B, 25).
[453] Alltounian, interview by Bemis and Seipel, 9 (S079-01101B, 25).
[454] Alltounian, interview by Bemis and Seipel, 9 (S079-01101B, 25).
[455] Alltounian, interview by Bemis and Seipel, 9 (S079-01101B, 25).
[456] Alltounian, interview by Bemis and Seipel, 9 (S079-01101B, 25).
[457] Alltounian, interview by Bemis and Seipel, 9 (S079-01101B, 25).
[458] Alltounian, interview by Bemis and Seipel, 9 (S079-01101B, 25).
[459] Alltounian, interview by Bemis and Seipel, 10 (S079-01101B, 26).
[460] Alltounian, interview by Bemis and Seipel, 10 (S079-01101B, 26).
[461] Alltounian, interview by Bemis and Seipel, 10 (S079-01101B, 26).

462 Alltounian, interview by Bemis and Seipel, 10 (S079-01101B, 26).

463 Alltounian, interview by Bemis and Seipel, 10 (S079-01101B, 26).

464 Alltounian, interview by Bemis and Seipel, 10 (S079-01101B, 26).

465 Alltounian, interview by Bemis and Seipel, 10 (S079-01101B, 26).

466 Alltounian, interview by Bemis and Seipel, 10 (S079-01101B, 26).

467 Alltounian, interview by Bemis and Seipel, 10 (S079-01101B, 26).

468 Alltounian, interview by Bemis and Seipel, 10 (S079-01101B, 26).

469 Alltounian, interview by Bemis and Seipel, 10 (S079-01101B, 26).

470 Alltounian, interview by Bemis and Seipel, 10 (S079-01101B, 26).

471 Alltounian, interview by Bemis and Seipel, 10 (S079-01101B, 26).

472 Alltounian, interview by Bemis and Seipel, 11 (S079-01101B, 27).

473 Alltounian, interview by Bemis and Seipel, 14 (S079-01101B, 30).

474 Alltounian, interview by Bemis and Seipel, 14 (S079-01101B, 30).

475 Alltounian, interview by Bemis and Seipel, 14 (S079-01101B, 30).

476 Alltounian, interview by Bemis and Seipel, 14 (S079-01101B, 30).

477 Alltounian, interview by Bemis and Seipel, 14 (S079-01101B, 30).

478 Alltounian, interview by Bemis and Seipel, 14 (S079-01101B, 30).

479 Alltounian, interview by Bemis and Seipel, 14 (S079-01101B, 30).

480 Alltounian, interview by Bemis and Seipel, 14 (S079-01101B, 30).

481 Alltounian, interview by Bemis and Seipel, 14 (S079-01101B, 30).

482 Alltounian, interview by Bemis and Seipel, 14 (S079-01101B, 30).

483 Alltounian, interview by Bemis and Seipel, 15 (S079-01101B, 31).

484 Alltounian, interview by Bemis and Seipel, 15 (S079-01101B, 31).

485 Alltounian, interview by Bemis and Seipel, 15 (S079-01101B, 31).

486 Alltounian, interview by Bemis and Seipel, 15 (S079-01101B, 31).

487 Alltounian, interview by Bemis and Seipel, 15 (S079-01101B, 31).

488 Alltounian, interview by Bemis and Seipel, 15 (S079-01101B, 31).

489 Alltounian, interview by Bemis and Seipel, 15 (S079-01101B, 31).

490 Alltounian, interview by Bemis and Seipel, 15 (S079-01101B, 31).

491 Alltounian, interview by Bemis and Seipel, 16 (S079-01101B, 32).

492 Alltounian, interview by Bemis and Seipel, 16 (S079-01101B, 32).

493 Alltounian, interview by Bemis and Seipel, 16 (S079-01101B, 32).

494 Alltounian, interview by Bemis and Seipel, 16 (S079-01101B, 32).

495 Alltounian, interview by Bemis and Seipel, 16 (S079-01101B, 32).

496 Alltounian, interview by Bemis and Seipel, 16 (S079-01101B, 32).

497 Alltounian, interview by Bemis and Seipel, 16 (S079-01101B, 32).

498 Alltounian, interview by Bemis and Seipel, 17 (S079-01101B, 33).

499 Alltounian, interview by Bemis and Seipel, 17 (S079-01101B, 33).

500 Alltounian, interview by Bemis and Seipel, 17 (S079-01101B, 33).

501 Alltounian, interview by Bemis and Seipel, 17 (S079-01101B, 33).

502 Alltounian, interview by Bemis and Seipel, 17 (S079-01101B, 33).

503 Alltounian, interview by Bemis and Seipel, 17-18 (S079-01101B, 33-34).
504 Alltounian, interview by Bemis and Seipel, 18 (S079-01101B, 34).
505 Alltounian, interview by Bemis and Seipel, 18 (S079-01101B, 34).
506 Alltounian, interview by Bemis and Seipel, 18 (S079-01101B, 34).
507 Alltounian, interview by Bemis and Seipel, 18 (S079-01101B, 34).
508 Alltounian, interview by Bemis and Seipel, 18 (S079-01101B, 34).
509 Alltounian, interview by Bemis and Seipel, 18 (S079-01101B, 34).
510 Alltounian, interview by Bemis and Seipel, 18 (S079-01101B, 34).
511 Alltounian, interview by Bemis and Seipel, 18 (S079-01101B, 34).
512 Alltounian, interview by Bemis and Seipel, 18 (S079-01101B, 34).
513 Alltounian, interview by Bemis and Seipel, 18 (S079-01101B, 34).
514 Alltounian, interview by Bemis and Scipel, 18 (S079-01101B, 34).
515 Alltounian, interview by Bemis and Seipel, 19 (S079-01101B, 35).
516 Alltounian, interview by Bemis and Seipel, 19 (S079-01101B, 35).
517 Alltounian, interview by Bemis and Seipel, 19 (S079-01101B, 35).
518 Alltounian, interview by Bemis and Seipel, 19 (S079-01101B, 35).
519 Alltounian, interview by Bemis and Seipel, 19 (S079-01101B, 35).
520 Alltounian, interview by Bemis and Seipel, 19 (S079-01101B, 35).
521 Alltounian, interview by Bemis and Seipel, 19 (S079-01101B, 35).
522 Alltounian, interview by Bemis and Seipel, 19 (S079-01101B, 35).
523 Alltounian, interview by Bemis and Seipel, 19 (S079-01101B, 35).
524 Alltounian, interview by Bemis and Seipel, 19 (S079-01101B, 35).
525 Alltounian, interview by Bemis and Seipel, 19 (S079-01101B, 35).
526 Alltounian, interview by Bemis and Seipel, 19 (S079-01101B, 35).
527 Alltounian, interview by Bemis and Seipel, 22 (S079-01101B, 38).
528 Alltounian, interview by Bemis and Seipel, 22 (S079-01101B, 38).
529 Alltounian, interview by Bemis and Seipel, 22 (S079-01101B, 38).
530 Alltounian, interview by Bemis and Seipel, 22-23 (S079-01101B, 38-39).
531 Alltounian, interview by Bemis and Seipel, 23 (S079-01101B, 39).
532 Alltounian, interview by Bemis and Seipel, 23 (S079-01101B, 39).
533 Alltounian, interview by Bemis and Seipel, 23 (S079-01101B, 39).
534 Alltounian, interview by Bemis and Seipel, 23 (S079-01101B, 39).
535 Alltounian, interview by Bemis and Seipel, 23 (S079-01101B, 39).
536 Alltounian, interview by Bemis and Seipel, 23 (S079-01101B, 39).
537 Alltounian, interview by Bemis and Seipel, 23 (S079-01101B, 39).
538 Leipzig, *Untitled Private Journal*, 30-31.
539 Alltounian, *The Hypersentience Bulletin-Spring Equinox*, 15.
540 Leipzig, *Untitled Private Journal*, 33.
541 Leipzig, *Untitled Private Journal*, 35.
542 Leipzig, *Untitled Private Journal*, 38.
543 Leipzig, *Untitled Private Journal*, 39.

[544] Leipzig, *Untitled Private Journal*, 39.

[545] Leipzig, *Untitled Private Journal*, 40.

[546] Leipzig, *Untitled Private Journal*, 42.

[547] Leipzig, *Untitled Private Journal*, 42.

[548] Leipzig, *Untitled Private Journal*, 42.

[549] Leipzig, *Untitled Private Journal*, 43.

[550] Leipzig, *Untitled Private Journal*, 44.

[551] Leipzig, *Untitled Private Journal*, 44.

[552] Leipzig, *Untitled Private Journal*, 44.

[553] Leipzig, *Untitled Private Journal*, 46.

[554] Howard Alltounian to Robin Moore, February 19, 1979, 1-2.

[555] Howard Alltounian to Robin Moore, February 19, 1979, 1-2.

[556] Leipzig, *Untitled Private Journal*, 47.

[557] Leipzig, *Untitled Private Journal*, 47-48.

[558] Leipzig, *Untitled Private Journal*, 50.

[559] Foster, February 21, 1979.

[560] Foster, February 21, 1979.

[561] Foster, February 21, 1979.

[562] Foster, February 21, 1979.

[563] Foster, February 21, 1979.

[564] Foster, February 21, 1979.

[565] Foster, February 21, 1979.

[566] Foster, February 21, 1979.

[567] Foster, February 21, 1979.

[568] Leipzig, *Untitled Private Journal*, 51.

[569] Alltounian, *The Hypersentience Bulletin-Summer Solstice,* 22

[570] Alltounian, *The Hypersentience Bulletin-Spring Equinox,* 15.

[571] Leipzig, *Untitled Private Journal*, 41.

[572] Leipzig, *Untitled Private Journal*, 51.

[573] Leipzig, *Untitled Private Journal*, 55.

[574] Leipzig, *Untitled Private Journal*, 55.

[575] Leipzig, *Untitled Private Journal*, 55.

[576] Leipzig, *Untitled Private Journal*, 56.

[577] Leipzig, *Untitled Private Journal*, 57.

[578] Leipzig, *Untitled Private Journal*, 57.

[579] Leipzig, *Untitled Private Journal*, 58.

[580] Leipzig, *Untitled Private Journal*, 58.

[581] Leipzig, *Untitled Private Journal*, 58-59.

[582] Leipzig, *Untitled Private Journal*, 60.

[583] Leipzig, *Untitled Private Journal*, 59.

[584] Leipzig, *Untitled Private Journal*, 59.

585 Leipzig, *Untitled Private Journal*, 59.
586 Leipzig, *Untitled Private Journal*, 61.
587 Leipzig, *Untitled Private Journal*, 60.
588 Leipzig, *Untitled Private Journal*, 62.
589 Marwayne Leipzig to John Moore, April 20, 1980, 4.
590 Leipzig, *Untitled Private Journal*, 63.
591 Leipzig, *Untitled Private Journal*, 79.
592 Leipzig, *Untitled Private Journal*, 63.
593 Leipzig, *Untitled Private Journal*, 80.
594 Leipzig, *Untitled Private Journal*, 81.
595 Alltounian, *The Hypersentience Bulletin-Summer Solstice,* 29.
596 Lacitis, "Marcia Moore: Mysterious disappearance baffles police."
597 Leipzig, *Untitled Private Journal*, 66.
598 Leipzig, *Untitled Private Journal*, 65.
599 Leipzig, *Untitled Private Journal*, 65.
600 Leipzig, *Untitled Private Journal*, 65.
601 Leipzig, *Untitled Private Journal*, 68.
602 Leipzig, *Untitled Private Journal*, 71-72.
603 Leipzig, *Untitled Private Journal*, 72.
604 Leipzig, *Untitled Private Journal*, 72.
605 Leipzig, *Untitled Private Journal*, 53.
606 Leipzig, *Untitled Private Journal*, 74.
607 Leipzig, *Untitled Private Journal*, 73.
608 Leipzig, *Untitled Private Journal*, 77.
609 Leipzig to John Moore, November 23, 1979, 1.
610 Alltounian, interview by Sasso and Cutaneo, 6-7.
611 Alltounian, interview by Sasso and Cutaneo, 12.
612 Alltounian, interview by Sasso and Cutaneo, 15.
613 Alltounian, interview by Sasso and Cutaneo, 38.
614 Leipzig to John Moore, March 28, 1981, 1.
615 Leipzig to John Moore, April 20, 1980, 2.
616 Leipzig to John Moore, April 20, 1980, 2.
617 Leipzig to John Moore, April 20, 1980, 4.
618 Leipzig to John Moore, March 28, 1981, 3.
619 Leipzig to John Moore, March 28, 1981, 4.
620 Howard Alltounian to Kareen & Peter Zebroff, March 5, 1981, 1.
621 Alltounian to Kareen & Peter Zebroff, 3.
622 "Follow-up/Supplemental Report," April 1, 1981 (Snohomish County Sheriff's Office case file, S079-01101A, 115).
623 Marwayne Leipzig to John Moore, March 26, 1981, 2.
624 Leipzig to John Moore, March 26, 1981, 2.

625 Leipzig to John Moore, March 28, 1981, 1-2.

626 Marwayne Leipzig to John Moore, April 2, 1981, 1.

627 Morris, interview by authors, multiple dates.

628 Marcia Moore, *Hypersentience* (New York, NY: Crown Publishers, Inc., 1976), 78.

629 Bemis and Leipzig, interview by authors, July 2010.

630 Alltounian, *The Hypersentience Bulletin-Summer Solstice,* 1.

631 Alltounian, *The Hypersentience Bulletin-Spring Equinox,* 1.

632 Morris, interview by authors, multiple dates.

633 Alltounian, interview by Sasso and Cutaneo, 15-16.

634 Morris, interview by authors, multiple dates.

635 "Attempt to Locate," January 15, 1979 (Snohomish County Sheriff's Office case file, S079-01101C, 13).

636 Taylor, "Follow-up/Supplemental Report," January 22, 1979, 2 (S079-01101A, 87).

637 Alltounian, interview by Bemis, January 18, 1979, 6 (S079-01101D, 11).

638 Alltounian, interview by Bemis, January 18, 1979, 13 (S079-01101D, 18).

639 "Attempt to Locate," January 15, 1979 (Snohomish County Sheriff's Office case file, S079-01101C, 13).

640 Quay, "Snohomish County Sheriff's Office Runaway/Missing Person Report and Information Sheet," (S079-01101A, 10).

641 Alltounian, interview by Bemis and Seipel, 21 (S079-01101B, 37).

642 Alltounian, interview by Bemis and Seipel, 6 (S079-01101B, 22).

643 Morris, interview by authors, multiple dates.

644 Morris, interview by authors, multiple dates.

645 Morris, interview by authors, multiple dates.

646 Alltounian, interview by Sasso and Cutaneo, 6.

647 Unverified author to John Moore, January 1979 (Snohomish County Sheriff's Office case file, S079-01101A, 108).

648 Alltounian, interview by Bemis, January 18, 1979, 23 (S079-01101D, 28).

649 Alltounian, interview by Bemis, January 18, 1979, 21-22 (S079-01101D, 26-27).

650 Alltounian, *The Hypersentience Bulletin-Summer Solstice,* 7.

651 Leipzig, *Untitled Private Journal,* 7.

652 John Moore, "Events Concerning Marcia's Disappearance as Compiled by John Moore," 3.

653 Alltounian, interview by Sasso and Cutaneo, 2.

654 Morris, interview by authors, multiple dates.

655 Morris, interview by authors, multiple dates.

656 Heise, 10-11.

657 Alltounian, interview by Bemis and Seipel, 11 (S079-01101B, 27).

658 Gallacher and Alltounian, interview by Bemis, 10 (S079-01101A, 62).

659 Gallacher and Alltounian, interview by Bemis, 11 (S079-01101A, 97).

660 Leipzig to John Moore, April 20, 1980, 1.

661 Marcia Moore to Robert and Eleanor Moore, July 17, 1978, 1.

662 Marcia Moore to Robert and Eleanor Moore, July 28, 1978 1.

663 Alltounian, interview by Bemis, January 18, 1979, 3 (S079-01101D, 8).

664 Moore and Alltounian, *Journeys into the Bright World*, 17.

665 Moore and Alltounian, *Journeys into the Bright World*, 35.

666 Marcia Moore to Robert and Eleanor Moore, June 30, 1978, 1.

667 Moore and Alltounian, *Journeys into the Bright World*, 114.

668 Moore, interview by Bemis, January 19, 1979, 2 (S079-01101E, 36).

669 Howard Alltounian to Saab, August 5, 1978, 1.

670 Alltounian to Saab, 1.

671 Marcia Moore to Robert and Eleanor Moore, July 17, 1978, 1.

672 Moore and Alltounian, *Journeys into the Bright World*, 92.

673 Moore and Alltounian, *Journeys into the Bright World*, 103.

674 Marcia Moore to Barbara Gee, August 7, 1978, 1.

675 Marcia Moore to Robert Moore, January 3, 1979, 1.

676 Marcia Moore, September 1978, Cuttyhunk, MA.

677 Louisa Roof, interview by authors, December 9, 2011.

678 Leipzig, *Untitled Private Journal*, 16.

679 Morris, interview by authors, multiple dates.

680 Morris, interview by authors, multiple dates.

681 Marwayne Leipzig to John Moore, March 27, 1979, 5.

682 "Minutes of the Second Meeting of the Board of Directors of Ananta Foundation," October 17, 1978, 5.

683 Marcia Moore to Robert Moore, January 3, 1979, 1.

684 Morris, interview by authors, multiple dates.

685 Leipzig, *Untitled Private Journal*, 20.

686 Morris, interview by authors, multiple dates.

687 Marwayne Leipzig to astrologer Eugene Moore, 1979.

688 Leipzig, *Untitled Private Journal*, prologue.

689 Leipzig, *Untitled Private Journal*, 10.

690 Leipzig, *Untitled Private Journal*, prologue.

691 Marcia Moore to John Moore, January 9, 1979 (Snohomish County Sheriff's Office case file, S079-01101E, 70).

692 Jim Haley, "Cases pile up as prosecutor looks for help," *Everett Herald*, January 8, 1979.

693 Bemis and Leipzig, interview by authors, July 2010.

694 Alltounian, interview by Bemis, January 18, 1979, 4 (S079-01101D, 9).

695 Morris, interview by authors, multiple dates.

696 Leipzig, *Untitled Private Journal*, 87.

697 Bemis and Leipzig, interview by authors, July 2010.

698 Morris, interview by authors, multiple dates.

699 Unverified author to John Moore, January 1979 (S079-01101A, 108).

700 Heise, 60.

701 Heise, 13.

702 Lacitis, "Marcia Moore: Mysterious disappearance baffles police."

703 Rule, "Mysterious Disappearance of the Psychic Heiress," 56.

704 Suffia, 80.

705 Comfort, interview by authors, November 12, 2010.

706 Comfort, interview by authors, November 12, 2010.

707 Comfort, interview by authors, November 12, 2010.

708 Comfort, interview by authors, November 12, 2010.

709 Louisa Roof, interview by authors, September 12, 2012.

710 Comfort, interview by authors, November 12, 2010.

711 Comfort, interview by authors, June 30, 2019.

712 Comfort, interview by authors, November 12, 2010.

713 Comfort, interview by authors, June 30, 2019.

714 Comfort, interview by authors, March 12, 2021.

715 Marcia Moore to Robert and Eleanor Moore, December 26, 1978, 1.

716 Comfort, interview by authors, November 12, 2010.

717 Moore, interview by Bemis, January 19, 1979, 3-4 (S079-01101E, 37-38).

718 Suffia, 80.

719 Louisa Roof, "Communications from Marcia Moore," March 11, 1979, 3.

720 Suffia, 80.

721 Susan B., interview by authors, November 23, 2012.

722 Alltounian, *The Hypersentience Bulletin-Summer Solstice,* 34.

723 Alltounian, *The Hypersentience Bulletin-Spring Equinox,* 17

724 Susan B., interview by authors, November 21, 2012.

725 Shelley Stark, interview by authors, multiple dates.

726 Stark, interview by authors, multiple dates.

727 Stark, interview by authors, multiple dates.

728 Stark, interview by authors, multiple dates.

729 Moore and Alltounian, *Journeys into the Bright World*, 101.

730 Moore and Alltounian, *Journeys into the Bright World*, 101.

731 Stark, interview by authors, multiple dates.

732 Stark, interview by authors, multiple dates.

733 Stark, interview by authors, multiple dates.

734 Stark, interview by authors, multiple dates.

735 Stark, interview by authors, multiple dates.

736 Stark, interview by authors, multiple dates.

737 Stark, interview by authors, multiple dates.
738 Stark, interview by authors, multiple dates.
739 Stark, interview by authors, multiple dates.
740 Stark, interview by authors, multiple dates.
741 Stark, interview by authors, multiple dates.
742 Stark, interview by authors, multiple dates.
743 Stark, interview by authors, multiple dates.
744 Stark, interview by authors, multiple dates.
745 Stark, interview by authors, multiple dates.
746 Stark, interview by authors, multiple dates.
747 Stark, interview by authors, multiple dates.
748 Stark, interview by authors, multiple dates.
749 Stark, interview by authors, multiple dates.
750 Stark, interview by authors, multiple dates.
751 Stark, interview by authors, multiple dates.
752 Alltounian, *The Hypersentience Bulletin-Spring Equinox,* 9.
753 Stark, interview by authors, multiple dates.
754 Stark, interview by authors, multiple dates.
755 Stark, interview by authors, multiple dates.
756 Stark, interview by authors, multiple dates.
757 Stark, interview by authors, multiple dates.
758 Stark, interview by authors, multiple dates.
759 Stark, interview by authors, multiple dates.
760 Stark, interview by authors, multiple dates.
761 Stark, interview by authors, multiple dates.
762 Stark, interview by authors, multiple dates.
763 Stark, interview by authors, multiple dates.
764 Stark, interview by authors, multiple dates.
765 Stark, interview by authors, multiple dates.
766 Stark, interview by authors, multiple dates.
767 Stark, interview by authors, multiple dates.
768 Stark, interview by authors, multiple dates.
769 Stark, interview by authors, multiple dates.
770 Stark, interview by authors, multiple dates.
771 Stark, interview by authors, multiple dates.
772 Stark, interview by authors, multiple dates.
773 Stark, interview by authors, multiple dates.
774 Stark, interview by authors, multiple dates.
775 Stark, interview by authors, multiple dates.
776 Stark, interview by authors, multiple dates.
777 Stark, interview by authors, multiple dates.

[778] Stark, interview by authors, multiple dates.

[779] Stark, interview by authors, multiple dates.

[780] Stark, interview by authors, multiple dates.

[781] Stark, interview by authors, multiple dates.

[782] Stark, interview by authors, multiple dates.

[783] Stark, interview by authors, multiple dates.